Conflict Resolution in the Twenty-first Century

Conflict Resolution in the Twenty-first Century

Principles, Methods, and Approaches

Jacob Bercovitch and

Richard Jackson

THE UNIVERSITY OF MICHIGAN PRESS

ANN ARBOR

Copyright © by the University of Michigan 2009
All rights reserved
Published in the United States of America by
The University of Michigan Press
Manufactured in the United States of America
∞ Printed on acid-free paper

2012   2011   2010   2009   4   3   2   1

A CIP catalog record for this book is available from the British
Library.

Library of Congress Cataloging-in-Publication Data

Bercovitch, Jacob.
    Conflict resolution in the twenty-first century : principles,
methods, and approaches / Jacob Bercovitch and Richard Jackson.
        p.   cm.
    Includes bibliographical references and index.
    ISBN-13: 978-0-472-07062-6 (cloth : alk. paper)
    ISBN-10: 0-472-07062-2 (cloth : alk. paper)
    ISBN-13: 978-0-472-05062-8 (pbk. : alk. paper)
    ISBN-10: 0-472-05062-1 (pbk. : alk. paper)
    1. Conflict management.   2. Conflict management—International
cooperation.   3. Pacific settlement of international disputes.
I. Jackson, Richard, 1966–   II. Title.

JZ6368.B43   2009
327.1'72—dc22   2009014541

ISBN: 978-0-472-02218-2 (e-book)

To Gillian and Michelle. Again, of course!

Acknowledgments

This project has been with us for a long time indeed. We have both experienced many personal and professional changes in the course of writing this book but have remained throughout it all good friends and as committed as ever to making the subject of conflict resolution more palatable to a wider audience. We have worked together on a previous book, we have both been teaching courses on various aspects of conflict resolution at different universities for many years, we know each other's publications and research record pretty well, and despite some intellectual and methodological differences we are both truly committed to the principles of constructive and peaceful conflict resolution, and the need to understand how to deal with the myriad new conflicts we face in the world today. This has been our overriding objective in approaching this project, and we hope we may have gone some way toward meeting it. We hope that our readers will think we tried our best to meet our goals.

In a project of this magnitude, where the two authors are far away from each other, and when each is competing with the other as to who has more commitments, we have inevitably accumulated many debts. It is a pleasure to be able to acknowledge these here.

The project was originally commissioned by Jim Reische from the University of Michigan Press. Jim has been a stalwart supporter of the project. He believed in this project. He encouraged us to keep at it; he offered support, counsel, and wise words. He kept us in check, and the project on track, and he did so with a sense of humor and self-effacement that we both found irresistible. Jim left the

Press and was replaced by Melody Herr. In the short time that we worked with Melody we have become more than impressed with her professionalism, her support, her understanding, and her loyalty to the project. If anyone could have taken over from Jim and made us feel even more welcome at Michigan, it had to be Melody. The editorial team at Michigan just knows how to pick winners, and we are the beneficiaries of their wise choices.

Our graduate students, at Aberystwyth, Manchester, Castellon, Canterbury, Georgetown, and other places we taught at were exposed to many of the ideas contained in the book. They consistently challenged us but also offered tremendous insights on how to sharpen the presentation, focus our analysis, and make the whole book more readable. We have tried to take much of this on board.

We received feedback, criticism, and many useful comments from many good colleagues. Three anonymous reviewers provided very helpful comments in the initial phase of the project. We tried to respond to all their points. People such as Raymond Cohen, Eileen Babbit, Yaakov Bar Siman Tov, Lise Howard, Peter Wallensteen, Dean Pruitt, Dan Druckman, Fen Hampson, Ayse Kadyifici, John Vasquez, William Zartman, Scott Gartner, Zeev Maoz, Valerie Rosoux, and many other colleagues made us rethink many of our ideas and forced us to present them more coherently. None of them should be held responsible for anything written here; we take full responsibility for that!

We are grateful for the assistance, both research and administrative, given to us by Terry Genet, Jill Dolby,

Jean Bailey, Claire Newcombe, Alice Mortlock, and Julia Johnstone.

Parts of this project were supported by generous grants from the University of Canterbury in New Zealand and Manchester University in the United Kingdom. We are also grateful to the Marsden Fund of the Royal Society of New Zealand for their encouragement and financial support.

The book is dedicated to the two persons who have barely interfered in the writing of this book but gave us unstinting support, total commitment, absolute devotion, and the usual wise guidance and counsel.

Contents

CHAPTER ONE
International Conflict and Its Resolution: Moving from the Twentieth to the Twenty-first Century
1

International Conflict Environment 2
New War, Postmodern War, Beyond War 5
The Cold War Era 6
New-Generation Approaches to Conflict
    Management and Resolution 8
New Actors 11
Perspectives for a Post-Westphalian World 14
Conclusion 16

PART ONE   Principles and Traditional Approaches

CHAPTER TWO
International Negotiation
19

On Conflict and Conflict Resolution 19
Conceptual Framework for Bargaining
    and Negotiation 20
Characteristics of Bargaining and Negotiation 21
Elements of Bargaining and Negotiation 21
Approaches to the Study of Bargaining
    and Negotiation 23
Factors Influencing the Bargaining and
    Negotiation Process 25
Bargaining and Negotiation Strategies 29
Conclusion 30

CHAPTER THREE
Mediation and International Conflict Resolution
32

A Conceptual Framework for Mediation 33
Definition of Mediation 33
Approaches to Mediation 36
Factors Influencing Mediation 37
Strategies of Mediation 43
Evaluating Mediation 45
Conclusion 46

CHAPTER FOUR
Arbitration, Adjudication, and International Law
47

Conceptualizing Legal Methods of
  Conflict Resolution 48
Law-based Methods of Conflict Resolution 49
Evaluating Legal Methods of Conflict Resolution 57
Conclusion 59

CHAPTER FIVE
International Organization: The United Nations
60

International Organization and the Resolution
  of Conflict 61
UN Methods of Conflict Resolution 63
Evaluating UN Conflict Resolution 68
Conclusion 74

CHAPTER SIX
Peacekeeping
75

Traditional Peacekeeping 76
An Overview of Traditional Peacekeeping,
  1956–88 78
Evaluating Traditional Peacekeeping 80
Conclusion 83

PART TWO Twenty-first-Century Methods and Approaches

CHAPTER SEVEN
Preventive Diplomacy
87

Conceptual Framework for Preventive Diplomacy 88
Components of an Effective Conflict
  Prevention Regime 90
Preventive Diplomacy: Actions 94
Factors Influencing the Success of
  Conflict Prevention 95
Obstacles to Preventive Diplomacy 98
Conclusion 99

CHAPTER EIGHT
Humanitarian Intervention
101

Conceptualizing Humanitarian Intervention 102
An Overview of Humanitarian Intervention
  since 1989 105
Assessing Humanitarian Intervention 108
Conclusion 117

CHAPTER NINE
Regional Task-Sharing
119

Conceptualizing Regional Task-Sharing 120
An Overview of Task-Sharing 125
Evaluating Regionalism and Task-Sharing 129
Conclusion 135

CHAPTER TEN
Nonofficial Diplomacy
137

Nonofficial Diplomats and International
  Conflict Resolution 138
Conceptualizing Nonofficial Diplomacy 140
An Overview of Nonofficial Diplomacy 141
Evaluating Nonofficial Diplomacy 143
Conclusion 149

CHAPTER ELEVEN
Reconciliation and Justice
151

The Internationalization of Justice   *152*
Conceptualizing Reconciliation and
    Justice Approaches   *152*
Modalities for Dealing with Past Abuses   *155*
Evaluating Reconciliation and Justice Approaches   *157*
Conclusion   *166*

CHAPTER TWELVE
Peacebuilding
168

The Origins of Peacebuilding   *169*
Conceptualizing Peacebuilding   *171*
An Overview of Peacebuilding in Practice   *176*
Evaluating Peacebuilding   *178*
Conclusion   *182*

Conclusion
184

References
191

Index
207

CHAPTER ONE

International Conflict and Its Resolution

Moving from the Twentieth to the Twenty-first Century

In this book we hope to offer a truly comprehensive survey and analysis of the major methods of conflict resolution. We do this because we believe that conflict resolution is an important activity that concerns us all, and because we can see that there has been a fundamental shift in the approach, understanding, and evolution of conflicts. As conflicts change, so do the approaches required to deal with them. We want to trace in this book the so-called traditional approaches to resolving or managing conflicts, and the newer methods that have evolved in recent years. We argue that these newer methods are more comprehensive, more all-embracing, and more focused on the basic issues and structures of a conflict, than the earlier methods that were designed primarily to achieve a cessation of violence or reduction in hostilities. These new approaches, more typical of the twenty-first century, are all about resolving the basic and underlying issues, not just managing conflicts. We want to explore this major paradigm and practice shift.

To start with, we wish to explain what we mean by *conflict resolution*. The term is often used so bewilderingly as to defy any attempt at analysis. Conflict resolution is not about suppressing, eliminating, or controlling conflicts. Nor is it about avoiding a conflict, and it is certainly not about using superior force to conquer your adversary. These activities do take place in conflict, but they have little to do with its resolution. By *conflict resolution* we mean a range of formal or informal activities undertaken by parties to a conflict, or outsiders, designed to limit and reduce the level of violence in conflict, and to achieve some understanding on the key issues in conflict,

a political agreement, or a jointly acceptable decision on future interactions and distribution of resources. Conflict resolution is about accepting a conflict, recognizing that there are ways out of it, and engaging in some tacit or explicit coordination, without which none of these goals can be achieved. There are of course many ways to achieve these goals, and we will explore the most significant ones later.

The international arena has undergone a major transformation in the aftermath of the Cold War. With the end of the bipolar conceptualization of the world, a new wave of democratization and the globalization of information and economic power inspired unprecedented hope for a more just, democratic, and interconnected world. The unpredicted collapse of the Soviet Union and the resulting end to the Cold War proved a watershed in the dynamics of international conflict. We have begun to witness more frequent efforts at international coordination of security policies, a decrease in the frequency of and death toll related to interstate wars, and a redefinition of state sovereignty to encompass a state's responsibilities to its citizens and the international community more generally.

However, the grand hopes held by many for a more peaceful world order were soon shattered, as violent conflict underwent a structural and conceptual metamorphosis. While a superpower-driven Third World War was no longer feared, internal conflicts assumed new significance and have become recognized as a major threat to international peace and security. The sheer intensity and resulting casualties of these conflicts have been so high that the

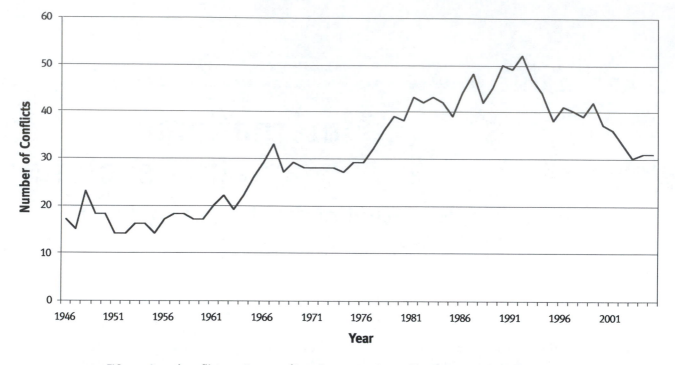

FIG. 1.   Armed conflict, 1946–2005. (Data from Uppsala Conflict Data Program [UCDP] 2006.)

first post–Cold War decade came to be known as the bloodiest since the advent of nuclear weapons. Figure 1 shows the changing levels of conflict from 1946 to 2005; there were 231 armed conflicts, just over half (51.5 percent) of which occurred in the immediate aftermath of the Cold War, from 1989 to 2005.

In the course of its evolution, the theory and practice of conflict resolution has witnessed different approaches and conceptualizations. The first approach, which has dominated the field since the emergence of international relations as an academic discipline, is the realist, state-centric one based on the Westphalian system that pays great attention to the notion of state sovereignty. This approach framed activities in the international system within power politics and excluded other actors and issues that were not strictly the concern of states. The changing nature of international conflict has led to the development of new approaches and has necessitated a paradigm shift from conflict management to conflict transformation and conflict resolution. More recently, we have witnessed the emergence of new actors who attempt to yet again redefine what is a conflict and how best to resolve it. We are thinking here of conflicts with terrorist groups that call for yet another change or evolution in the way we deal with conflicts.

International Conflict Environment

The End of the Cold War

The demise of the Soviet Union caused many analysts to believe that the international system would experience a sustained period of peace and stability, freed from the distortions of ideological struggles. While the end of the Cold War signified to many the triumph of liberal capitalism, proclamations such as Fukuyama's (1992) "end of history" thesis were unduly hasty. The end of the Cold War made a significant contribution toward ending some enduring conflicts, such as proxy wars fought by client states in places like Afghanistan, and peace processes were initiated in Lebanon, South Yemen, Namibia, Angola, Ethiopia and Eritrea, and Cambodia. Perhaps most significant, Germany was reunified. However, while historically conflict-prone regions such as Latin America experienced a decrease in conflict in the past decade, other conflicts contained during the Cold War exploded into full-fledged wars. This trend was particularly marked in Africa, a region that, in the eyes of Western countries, generally lost its geostrategic significance with the end of

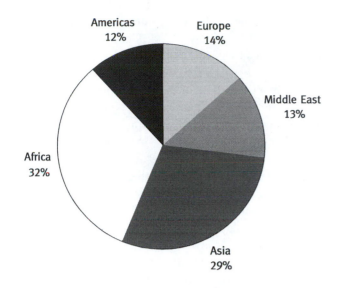

FIG. 2. Regional distribution of conflict, 1946–2005. (Data from UCDP 2006.)

with the Middle East, Southeast Asia, and the Pacific, are now the most conflict-prone regions of the world. Figure 2 presents the distribution of conflict regionally as a percentage of global conflict.

In recent decades, the major shift in the nature of conflict has been away from interstate conflict, leaving internal conflict and the proliferation of ethnic, religious, cultural, and resource-driven conflicts as the major threats to international peace and security. The Peace Research Institute of Oslo has documented all conflicts since World War II with a death toll of over 25 (www.prio.no) and concludes that since 1945, there have been 1,776 conflicts, and that 1,540 of these, or 86.7 percent, are internal conflicts. In addition, as figure 3 shows, an overwhelming majority (89.3 percent) of all conflicts since 1989 consist of intrastate conflicts.

These conflicts stem from poverty, deepening social inequalities, weak or corrupt governance, the proliferation of factions, and blurred distinctions between the warring parties and international crime. Self-determination, ethnic and religious divisions, resources, private armies, and warlords all characterize these conflicts. The complex web of social, economic, cultural, political, and religious factors involved in these violent conflicts make them seem intractable. As John Paul Lederach (1997) points out, most

the Cold War. The situation in states such as Angola, Mozambique, Ethiopia, Zaire (Democratic Republic of Congo), Somalia, and Liberia, countries significantly dependent on superpower patronage during the Cold War years, has deteriorated rapidly. Sub-Saharan Africa, along

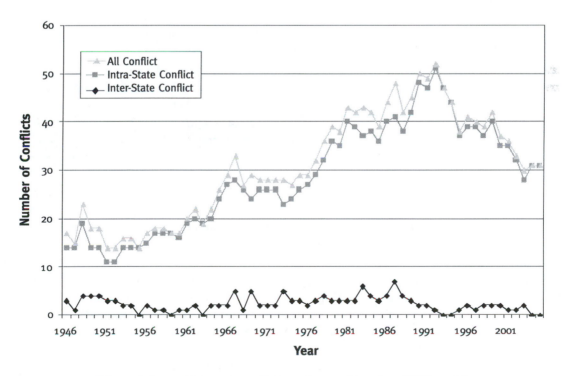

FIG. 3. Intra- and interstate conflict, 1946–2005. (Data from UCDP 2006.)

current wars are deep-rooted intrastate affairs. This development has led to a redefinition of *international conflict* to include both interstate and internal conflicts. In addition to these new types of conflicts, we are also witnessing the persistence of armed interstate conflicts in regions such as Southwest Asia, between India and Pakistan, and the Middle East, where the Arab-Israeli conflict continues unabated. In addition, a number of enduring and protracted conflicts continue to be ignored by the media in many parts of the world, Myanmar being a prime example.

Although they do not take place between states, many intrastate conflicts are viewed as threats to international peace and security, and therefore resolving them becomes important for the international community in general. This is particularly true for those international conflicts where there are violations of universally accepted norms such as self-determination and human rights, as well as those conflicts that have a potential to spill over into other countries in their region (Collier et al. 2003).

Many intrastate conflicts become internationalized, through the involvement of diaspora communities (Collier 2001: 155), or regionalized through a spillover effect into neighboring countries (Collier et al. 2003: 2–3). Such developments tend to further complicate and exacerbate an already complex conflict situation. Civil wars have significant consequences for the neighboring countries, especially in terms of the potentially destabilizing effect of refugee flows. This has occurred in many parts of Africa, particularly Sierra Leone, and it also heightens ethnic tensions by creating new minority groups. Across Africa many conflicts have led to an increase in refugees, together with the spread of diseases, malnutrition, starvation, social deterioration, and economic decline. These factors in turn aggravate and intensify conflicts in the region.

The last decade of the twentieth century witnessed several particularly severe conflicts, including cases of genocide, where internal conflicts have rapidly escalated into serious crises, humanitarian disasters, and state collapse. A salient example of this type of escalation is the horrific genocide that occurred in Rwanda in 1994, perhaps the worst case of genocide since World War II. The recent tragic developments in places like Rwanda, Bosnia, and East Timor have contributed to a redefinition of international conflict that is able to take into account these new dimensions. These real-world developments and conceptual re-evaluations have prompted policymakers and scholars of conflict resolution to consider new ways of understanding and managing contemporary conflicts.

While the number of violent conflicts reached an all-time high in the early 1990s, it is not the end of the Cold War that is responsible for the emergence of these violent internal conflicts; internal conflicts have consistently formed the majority of conflicts ever since the era of decolonization began after 1945 (Sadowski 1998: 12). Hence while the ending of the Cold War has certainly influenced the nature of recent conflicts, many other causal processes are at work. Important among these is the legacy of colonialism. The arbitrary boundaries created by the colonial powers had divided territories and put different identity groups under the same "national" governance. Controlling these new state entities depended highly on artificial and problematic authority structures. In Africa the struggles for independence were often dominated by the mixed urban populations who experienced various intertribal differences (Blanton, Manson, and Athow 2001). As the colonial power ebbed away, competition for central state power among rival tribes intensified. During the Cold War much of this conflict was forced to remain latent as the territories concerned were considered strategically significant spheres of influence for both the United States and the Soviet Union. Both superpowers supported corrupt and authoritarian governments in an effort to maintain their influence in these strategic regions, forcing discontented populations to remain subject to client and puppet regimes.

Following the collapse of the Cold War, support for these authoritarian regimes ceased, and state economies and central governments were subsequently weakened. Substate allegiances reemerged with devastating consequences, triggering various identity groups to battle for political power, state dominance, and control over resources. Angola, Democratic Republic of Congo, Sierra Leone, and Liberia are but a few examples of states that have disintegrated into ethnic and religious conflicts as a result of this development. Those regions possessing significant natural resources such as diamonds and gold have been the setting for some of the most intense violent conflicts, with competition for these resources producing major friction and the revenues from their sale being used to fund and prolong conflicts (Humphreys 2005).

In addition to these ethnic conflicts, we are also witnessing conflicts that are based on religious identities. Conflicts in places like Algeria and Indonesia, and between India and Pakistan, among others, have been colored by religious extremism and the rise of violent fundamentalist movements. In many cases (e.g., Kashmir and Bosnia) religious and ethnic identities tend to overlap.

Ethnic and religious conflicts involve intangible issues of identity. Since identity is not a scarce resource, conflicts over identity defy the materially driven conception of conflict as inherently zero-sum—that is, one's gain means the other's loss. In most cases, recognition of one party's identity does not come at the expense of another, assuming that critical psychological barriers to mutual understanding can be overcome. Therefore, these conflicts can be defined as "positive-sum," where one side's gain need not result in the other's loss. For this reason, policymakers and scholars should rethink traditional approaches to conflict and its resolution.

One crucial aspect of identity conflict is that it incorporates psychological, physical, and social dimensions, since identity is an intrinsic element of the self. A perceived threat to self, or a sense of insecurity based on a distinctive identity, will usually override rational thought and reason; therefore a wider social recognition of identity and effective participation in social, economic, and political processes are recognized today as basic needs of all humanity (Azar 1986). Denial of identity can lead to feelings of victimization that may lead to conflict, and conflicts that are based on identity are inherently more complicated and harder to resolve than those over resources. Moreover, since ethnic conflict will usually take place within a community, and often in a community with a history of hostility, the situation is further complicated. Hence, words such as *intractable* and *protracted* have been employed to describe these new types of conflicts. Although not all intractable conflicts are ethnic conflicts, ethnic conflicts have a greater tendency to become intractable.

The political exploitation of ethnic differences is common to intrastate conflict, resulting in severe levels of violence aimed at particular ethnic groups and, in extreme cases such as Burundi and Rwanda, in genocide. Ethnicity is not the root cause of conflict; rather, collective myths and fears shared by ethnic groups often lead to mass- or elite-driven mobilization that spurs ethnic conflict (Kaufman 2001). If conflicts are to be dealt with effectively, we need to look beyond ethnicity and consider other primary causes, such as the increasing poverty and marginalization of the poor in many regions. The unequal access to power and resources that results from this situation allows elites to mobilize otherwise latent or harmless ethnic differences or grievances as a way of maintaining power and sustaining conflict (Sambanis 2001: 263).

In addition to identity conflicts, the post–Cold War era has also witnessed a plethora of conflicts stemming from poverty. Although poverty alone does not necessarily lead to violence, awareness of relative poverty and expectations of a better life have been potent ingredients for conflicts. According to Gurr's theory of relative deprivation, violence may well be the result of perceived expectations and actual capabilities (Gurr 1970). When an individual or group has significantly less of a scarce resource than anticipated, they experience frustration, which can result in a violent response. Other scholars have argued that when states lose strength and lack the resources necessary to provide security, groups will prepare for and invest in violence, a situation that often leads to violent conflict (Lake and Rothchild 1996; Rose 2001).

The effects of globalization (in terms of the dispersion of economic, political, and informational resources) have led to increased awareness of the global inequality of wealth and resources. The unequal distribution of wealth and resources within states has not gone unnoticed either, especially when the distribution of wealth and resources coincides with ethnic and/or religious divisions. Economic factors, combined with resentment toward colonial authorities, the weakening of authoritarian governments, and the increased dissemination of ideas such as democracy, have all contributed significantly to the rise of conflict within states.

Over the past decade, there has also been a change in the form of warfare. Belligerents have used nontraditional and horrific forms of warfare, including mass rape, torture, ritualistic violence, and mutilation of the civilian population as well as of armed combatants. Violent armed conflicts by definition imply human suffering, but the degree of human suffering increases when the civilian population is either not distinguished from combatants or becomes the target of armed conflict. The twentieth century has witnessed a trend of progressively higher levels of destruction visited upon civilians in conflict. This pattern increased after World War II and again at the end of the Cold War. During World War I, over 80 percent of deaths were combatants, while in the 1990s over 90 percent were noncombatant civilians (Cairns 1997), a figure that starkly demonstrates the precarious condition of ordinary people in times of internal warfare. The integration of civilians into warfare as both combatants and targets pose a serious challenge to the international system on a number of levels. It also makes the practice of conflict resolution that much more complicated.

New War, Postmodern War, Beyond War

Transnational organizations such as NGOs, multinational corporations, criminal organizations, and the media vie for space in the international system, along with government agencies and international and regional organizations, lending weight to the argument that the international community is evolving into a post-Westphalian system. The new wars, increasingly characteristic of the conflict environment, can be described as post-Westphalian or postmodern, as they are increasingly ambiguous in their nature. These conflicts are transnational, dislocated, and decentralized; they defy borders and the boundaries between states and nonstate actors. In such circumstances, crime and violence are often indistinguishable from each other. Indicative of this increasing ambiguity of war is terrorism, which defies existing international norms, laws, and values. Terrorism is not a new phenomenon, but what distinguishes contemporary terrorism from its previous forms is the decline in state-sponsored terrorism. It is increasingly apparent that in an age of instant communications and illicit financing, groups like al Qaeda are able to carry out their operations despite the loss of their home base in Afghanistan. Not only are there other failed states where rent is cheap, but advanced technology allows terrorist groups to function as multinationals would during periodic disruptions. As Jessica Stern (2003: 27) recently argued, "al Qaeda's already decentralized organization has become more decentralized still," making it potentially more unpredictable and dangerous than ever before. The forces of globalization have opened borders and linked societies, and access to information technology has allowed local conflicts to turn into worldwide movements. In keeping with other industries in a globalized world economy, terrorism too has gone global.

In comparison to interstate wars, which were fought between opposing armies in distinct territories, terrorism in its current form operates in a "beyond war" location, which Richmond (2003: 296) describes as "a symbolic space in which symbols of power and control are targeted because civil insecurity is seen to be more effective and attainable through the spread of terror than via the stylized character, and trappings, of inter-state [conflict]." How do we approach such conflicts where spatial and organizational considerations are so different from the traditional notions of well-defined states in conflict?

The Cold War Era

Traditional Approaches to Conflict

Characteristic of the Cold War Westphalian international system is what we term *traditional conflict resolution.*

Approaches to international relations and conflict resolution in this era were informed by the experiences of World Wars I and II, nuclear threats, the primacy of power, and the bipolar conceptualization of the international system. The main goal of this approach was to resolve conflicts so as to protect order and security and by reinforcing the ability of states to pursue their own interests. Based on this state-centric Westphalian system, traditional tools of conflict management revolved around legal methods, peacekeeping, mediation, and negotiation frameworks, and incorporated actors defined in terms of either states or insurgents (Brownlie 1990). Within this system, the mainstream international relations theories and conflict resolution approaches deemed power, authority, and legitimacy to emanate from states, through the decision-making process (Richmond 2002). Thus conflicts in Latin America, Asia, Africa, and the Middle East were characterized as "state-centric," revolving around the interests of existing states.

This first cluster of conflict management approaches was based, to some extent, on maintaining the status quo and state security, rather than on justice and human security. The mechanisms associated with this approach were derived from the traditions, norms, and culture of Western diplomacy, as it evolved since the Treaty of Westphalia, favoring stylized and formal communication between sovereign representatives, militaries, and diplomats. In such an environment, states have favored a "power politics" approach to addressing conflicts, where state sovereignty, noninterference into domestic politics of a state, and the primacy of national interests form the fundamental principles. It was assumed that state behavior was dictated by state interests; therefore, conflict between states was intrinsically a conflict of interests and thus defined as zero-sum. Coming from this perspective, states, alone or by entering into alliances, sought to prevent or mitigate violence by using threats of armed force in the form of deterrence, coercive diplomacy, and/or defensive alliances, such as the North Atlantic Treaty Organization (NATO). In addition to these coercive military measures, states also utilized traditional diplomatic channels such as mediation and negotiation, as well as economic means of influence, such as economic boycotts and the withdrawal of financial aid.

International organizations such as the League of Nations and its successor body the United Nations (UN) were established to function as a procedural means to manage international disputes and increase the effectiveness of diplomacy. These organizations were bound by the framework of international law, within a system where civil conflict and political violence were to be re-

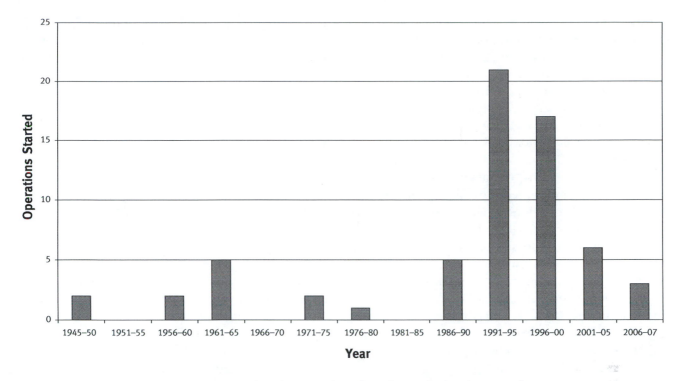

FIG. 4.   UN peacekeeping operations. (Data from United Nations 2008.)

solved by local, democratic, and constitutional processes, regarded as the responsibility of the states and not subject to international supervision and intervention. In accordance with this perspective, military personnel were used in peacekeeping, observation, policing, and humanitarian roles to provide a stable environment for negotiation and mediation, and consent of the disputants was regarded as a critical requirement (Richmond 2002: 41).

Since the end of the Cold War, the UN has taken a much more active role in conflict management. Figure 4 shows the dramatic increase in the number of UN peacekeeping missions that have taken place since the late 1980s. UN peacekeeping has evolved to include tasks such as disarmament, demobilization, resettlement of refugees, police training and supervision, election monitoring, and transitional administration of war-torn societies, thus linking peacekeeping and peacebuilding. The UN, mainly at a procedural level, provides good offices, a forum for meetings, a potential chairman, and conveyance of messages, and often involves informal contacts and suggestions on behalf of the secretary-general. Occasionally, the secretary-general will act directly as a mediator, giving suggestions and offering ideas and recommendations to the Security Council that may lead to Security Council resolutions.

During the Cold War these procedures usually resulted in weak resolutions, and the UN mainly served as a face-saving device. Moreover, the UN is often seen as a last-resort mediator, one that "lacks physical resources to guarantee a settlement. It is dependent upon the moral consensus it represents, the forum it provides and diplomatic skills of Secretary-General and the supporting role of peacekeeping force" (Richmond 2002: 50).

Within the state-centric system of the Cold War era, the UN did not intervene in ethnic conflicts unless they became significantly internationalized, due to the principles of self-rule and territorial integrity that underlined the Westphalian system. As noted earlier, this system favored negotiations between two disputing states to settle the conflict and to maintain the status quo. Ethnic conflicts, which usually involve nonstate actors, were considered as a threat to the status quo in a system that privileged the state above all else, especially because on most occasions the conflict involved issues of self-determination, autonomy, secession, and/or recognition of a particular ethnic identity.

The nuclear threat during the Cold War caused states to be more sensitive to the balance of power in the international system. In the face of an ever-present nuclear threat, states sought security alliances and established security regimes to establish norms reducing the risks of nuclear escalation. In this process, negotiation, based on balancing or trading competing interests, was one of the major tools to prevent the use of nuclear weapons. The search for a common ground to prevent escalation of conflict was crucial when escalation potentially involved the use of nuclear weapons.

Negotiation as the major conflict settlement tool in this system was inherently constrained, since the negotiators had the choice of agreeing, refusing to agree, or continuing to talk to improve the terms of the agreement (Assefa 1990: 181). Negotiation is essentially an approach to conflict that is symmetric, equal, and voluntary. This means that parties in negotiation may use stalling techniques to produce deadlocks and disillusionment, often requiring the addition of a third party as a mediator to assist the parties to get out of an impasse.

Mediation, as a form of conflict resolution, is derived from the tradition of diplomacy. The dominant view holds that mediation entails a mixture of carrots and sticks, where control of the process and procedure depends on the mediator's own objectives and resources, level of skill in controlling the process of interchange, and the flexibility of the disputants.

In practice, however, mediation, based on the state-centric Westphalian system, has offered little effective resolution. This may be the result of disputant perceptions of international norms such as territorial integrity, non-intervention, and self-determination in the context of human rights and democratization (Richmond 2002: 62). These norms reproduce the status quo based on the balance of power system and tend to compromise normative justice at the local level. The mediator's role is seen as facilitating a return to order through a trilateral bargaining process to find a balance between negotiators' positions through the use of carrots and sticks, and the resource capacity of the mediator is crucial for success. From this perspective, mediation does not aim at addressing the root causes of conflict. As such, this method is limited in its ability to address intangible issues such as those that often play a central role in ethnic conflicts.

The realist and Western-centric nature of this system of negotiation and mediation between official and sovereign representatives is stylized and formal. Unofficial actors are denied legitimacy in this system and are therefore marginalized from the process. Power-based mediation during the Cold War focused on the short-term settlement of disputes and was inherently incapable of addressing issues of identity, state failure, and economic underdevelopment that form the basis of many modern conflicts. We contend

that approaches to conflict resolution during the Cold War era were thus predicated on formality, conventional norms of state behavior, short-term goals, and absence of concerns with deep-rooted issues in conflict.

New-Generation Approaches to Conflict Management and Resolution

A Changing Paradigm from Conflict Management to Conflict Resolution

The shift in the nature of conflicts raises questions regarding the way we should deal with conflicts in the new millennium. With the end of the Cold War, the demise of the accompanying bipolar system, and the prevalence of religious and ethnic wars based on identity issues rather than territorial ones, the "traditional" approaches to conflict resolution have been rendered largely ineffective. As a result of these developments, scholars of conflict have come to an understanding that these new types of conflict require different approaches than those employed for traditional interstate conflict. The establishment of just and democratic political orders, the resuscitation of failing or collapsed states, the promotion of human rights, the creation of emancipatory political structures, reconciliation and truth commissions, international tribunals, and preventive diplomacy and early-warning systems are all goals and tools that will aid the international community to address these new conflicts. Scholars have recently focused on various approaches previously neglected, such as Track II diplomacy (Aggestam 2002), problem-solving workshops (Kelman 1992; Burton 1972), peacebuilding and conflict prevention measures (Sambanis and Doyle 2000; Hartzell, Hoddie, and Rothchild 2001). It is increasingly recognized that the combination of conflict resolution efforts at both official and unofficial levels is important, as is the potential for combining new approaches with traditional mechanisms where appropriate. Furthermore, some of these old tools such as negotiation and mediation are becoming more important than ever and are being applied in innovative ways to these new types of conflicts.

These new approaches to conflict resolution are built on the shortcomings of the traditional methods presented earlier. Their focus is more emphatically on resolving deep-seated and structural issues, and they involve as many nonofficial actors as official ones. This group of approaches examines the root causes of conflict based on human nature, human behavior, and social structures. It adopts a more intersubjective view of conflict, including politics, particularly with respect to representation and identity. Thus, it offers a new perspective on human security, and on the role of states and individuals in world politics. Individuals matter, as do states, and human security is as sacrosanct as state sovereignty.

It has been suggested that this new set of approaches to conflict resolution has emerged partly as a reaction to the "balance of power" conflict management techniques associated with positivist, realist approaches that dominated the Cold War era (Richmond 2002). For example, Galtung argued, in a critique of traditional methods, that conflict is much more than simple physical violence but also violence at structural and cultural levels. He argued conflict is "a dynamic process in which structure, attitudes, and behaviour are shifting constantly in the context of each other, in which disputants' interests come into conflict, and their relationship becomes oppressive, they develop conflictual behaviour, leading to escalation which may also draw in other parties" (Galtung 1996, cited in Richmond 2002: 79).

Richmond differentiates explicitly between the two approaches, noting that "the distinction between the first set and second set rests on two different views [. . .] of what constitutes peace: negative peace is characterized by the absence of direct violence and preventing war, while positive peace encompasses the broader issues relating to human security" (2002: 79). The new current approaches to conflict resolution have as their goal not just the cessation of violent behavior, but the establishment of new forms of interactions that can reflect the basic tenets of justice, human needs, legitimacy, and equality. This is, we must say at the outset, a very tall order indeed.

For instance, Burton (1987, 1990) argues that conflicts should be understood from the perspective that universal human needs are inexhaustible and often are not allocated correctly. Since these needs are distinct from interests and hence nonnegotiable, their suppression can lead to conflict because their pursuit is an ontological drive common to every human being (Azar 1986: 29). Thus this perspective, propounded by Burton, holds that conflict should be approached as a sociobiological problem. Only when human needs are met, can a conflict be said to be truly resolved, Burton argues.

Scholars such as Kelman (in Crocker et al. 1996), Saunders (1999), Azar and Burton (1986), Burton (1990), and Doob (1970) have developed "Problem-Solving Workshops" and introduced the idea of "Conflict Trans-

formation." This approach adopts facilitated meetings at which parties in conflict explore each other's perspective and worldviews, in order to alter the disputants' negative stereotypes of each other. The ultimate goal is to transfer the insights and ideas gained from these interactions into applied debate and decision making between the conflicting communities (Kelman 1998: 190). The 1993 Declaration of Principles signed in Washington, DC, by Israel and the PLO has been regarded as a crucial success for problem-solving workshops (Kelman 1998) and Track II diplomacy (Aggestam 2002).

Problem-solving workshops have inherent limitations, however. To have any substantial impact they must be included in the wider political process. Moreover, the central challenge to the problem-solving workshop approach is that of transfer—that is, how the positive changes achieved in the workshop are subsequently disseminated into the host societies to foster substantial constituencies for peaceful conflict management (Fisher 2001). In order to be successful, they must be run in conjunction with official diplomatic processes. Richmond (2002) notes other results of the workshops.

Much of the analysis has been conducted on how problem-solving workshops can be run and can aid disputants in understanding their conflicts, but little has been said of the indirect results of the workshops other than in terms of success and failure at the citizen level and in the realms of diplomacy . . . The indirect effects of the alternative understandings of conflict fostered by conflict resolution approaches lie in the participants' perceived understanding of their role and the role of facilitators, but also in the changing relationship between participants and their own community in wider understanding of identity and human security as opposed to state security. (127)

Track II diplomacy is based on coordinated efforts of unofficial actors to form unofficial channels for communication and influence in relations between disputing parties. It creates opportunities for exploring options for confidence-building measures and deescalation of conflict as well as a way to empower citizens to participate in important decision-making processes, similar to how problem-solving workshops do. Joseph Montville defines Track II diplomacy as "unofficial, informal interaction between members of adversary groups or nations which aims to develop strategies, influence public opinion, and organize human and material resources in ways that might help resolve their conflict" (1987: 7). An important contribution of this approach is its focus on affecting social constituencies and changing public opinion.

Another new approach, articulated by John Paul Lederach, advances the notion of sustainable peace, which is defined not only as the initiation of "a movement from confrontation to negotiation to dynamic, peaceful relationships," but also as the creation of "a proactive process that is capable of regenerating itself over time" (1997: 75). This approach attempts to transform the conflictual relationship into a peaceful one through reconciliation efforts that are sensitive to social-psychological dimensions of the conflict by integrating peace initiatives at different levels of society. His model also suggests that, depending on the nature of the conflict and the identity of the parties, an insider-partial mediator (one that has a level of involvement in the conflict) may have a greater chance of succeeding in building trust between communities and establishing sustainable peace.

Multidimensional Approaches

Traditional approaches are best described as both monodimensional and narrowly defined. The new more recent approaches to conflict resolution are becoming increasingly multidimensional including UN peace operations, intergovernmental organizations, regional organizations, and global, regional, and local nongovernmental organizations (NGOs). Thus the new approaches to conflict resolution have evolved at the global, regional, and local levels, and are designed to produce inclusive structures and long-term settlements of conflicts.

The objective of modern conflict resolution is to rebuild societies (not just states) via both top-down high-level and bottom-up grassroots methods. Multidimensional efforts are characterized by the inclusion and/or establishment of state administrations incorporating human security in a broader context than the limited state-centric approaches (Richmond 2002). These approaches aim at creating multidimensional processes that include diverse actors, issues, norms, and frameworks for understanding and organization, not just in systemic and strategic terms, but also at a normative level.

> This ad hoc or coordinated framework for peacemaking, through economic, political, and social concurrence on common norms (part of the growing interdependence of political communities) might be viewed as a significant departure from previous approaches to making peace, which sought to fit the conflict to the processes and the outcome within the state-system. (Richmond 2002: 141)

A multidimensional approach to conflict resolution necessarily operates on an extemporized basis as the mechanisms for resolution must be specifically appropriate for the conditions of each conflict. This approach presupposes a universally agreed normative and cultural basis for peace and the order that approaches to ending conflict replicate, and it assumes that interventionist practices will be properly supported by all actors with the requisite resources (Richmond 2002: 141). Despite this assumption, multidimensional approaches are better equipped to generate a contextually relevant resolution to conflict, especially in the case of internal conflicts, than the traditional approaches.

As the global arena changed dramatically during the 1990s, "world politics became far less exclusionary with legitimacy and authority beginning to flow from multiple actors in a greater diversity of directions" (Richmond 2002: 142). While the state remains the dominant actor, this shift created a space for other actors to become involved in peacemaking and peacebuilding processes. Increasingly, alternative and more fluid types of forces and issues from both above and below now impact the ability of the state to perform peacebuilding functions. In this context, scholars such as Burton, Azar, Galtung, and others, although their work is essentially positivist in nature, have developed frameworks that include "human needs" and "structural sources of violence." These frameworks broaden the spheres in which conflict analysis and resolution operate and enable retrieval of the individual and the intersubjective in conflict. These frameworks and mechanisms illustrate an attempt to provide a bottom-up influence on state behaviors, and indicate the need for structural reforms for the resolution of conflict (Richmond 2002: 184).

Fundamental changes in the nature of the international system, as already mentioned, have ushered in a new thinking with respect to traditional approaches to conflict resolution, which sought to preserve the status quo. Consequently, multidimensional approaches involve both practical and normative dimensions. In terms of practical dimensions, these approaches attempt to bring diverse actors at different levels together to address the root causes of conflict, including subjective issues. These developments are reflected in the evolution of peacekeeping forces, which have increasingly become directly and indirectly involved in civil affairs, administration, democratization, and human rights. Parallel developments have occurred at regional and local levels, often sponsored by intergovernmental organizations that include both official and unofficial actors. Responding to developments such as these, former UN secretary-general Boutros-Ghali pointed out in his *Agenda for Peace* that the tension between sovereignty and self-determination must be resolved in the context of democratization at all levels in order to deal with the underlying sources of conflict (cited in Richmond 2002: 171). Furthermore, the *Agenda for Peace* suggests a coordinated strategy including preventive diplomacy, peacemaking, peacekeeping/enforcement, and postconflict peacebuilding as part of a general commitment to a broader notion of peace and security.

A similar philosophy has been adopted by Kofi Annan, Boutros-Ghali's successor as UN secretary-general. Annan continued to concentrate on developing UN peace operations and has argued for a "multidisciplinary approach based on a combination of 'coercive inducement' and 'induced' consent, requiring more resources, clearer international commitment, and the ability for the UN to take decisive enforcement action." The notion of a broader and more holistic conception of peace and security is summarized in the Brahimi Report, which outlines how peacekeepers and peacebuilders are inseparable partners in the quest to foster sustainable peace. The report also calls for broad and integrated approaches to achieving rapid responses, based on consent and impartiality of parties concerned, but with the potential for enforcement if necessary (United Nations 2000).

New Actors

A crucial development in the post–Cold War era is the expansion of political and nonpolitical actors who deal with conflict and its resolution. In recent years the impact of international organizations (e.g., UN, NATO), regional organizations (e.g., the Organization of American States [OAS], the European Union [EU], and the Pacific Islands Forum), nongovernmental organizations (e.g., Amnesty International, International Crisis Group, The Carter Center, The Centre for Humanitarian Dialogue in Switzerland), individuals, and others have all become increasingly involved in various aspects of conflict resolution. There is also a new tendency in favor of multilateral approaches to conflicts, especially with the potential for spillover effects. In this new era, political organizations are also increasingly being used in new ways (e.g., the Organization of American States has undertaken demining operations in Latin America).

The international community is becoming more and more sensitive to the destructive consequences of conflicts, and although peacekeeping missions are still used to separate disputing parties, they are increasingly part of a wider mandate to provide critical services, such as humanitarian relief, refugee resettlement, and infrastructure development.

Together with traditional actors in the international community, we are witnessing the increasing role that nongovernmental organizations and transnational corporations play in conflict resolution and conflict prevention efforts. Because NGOs are not directly dependent on power politics, they are in a unique position to contribute to conflict management by deploying the emerging tools of conflict resolution, such as organizing grassroots activities and coordinating citizen diplomacy (Aall 2005: 368). In recent years, NGOs have promoted conflict transformation by sponsoring interactive conflict resolution tools. Table 1 shows non-UN interventions and peacekeeping missions between 1990 and 2005.

In an examination of post–Cold War diplomacy, Chester Crocker (cited in Aall 1996) highlights the new role NGOs may play, by recognizing that intervention may "be physical, spiritual, bilateral, or multilateral,

TABLE 1. Non-UN Peacekeeping and Interventions, 1990–2005

Single State and Coalition Interventions	
State	Location of Interventions
Great Britain	Sierra Leone
France	Central African Republic, Ivory Coast, Lesotho
South Africa	Burundi
French-led Coalition	Democratic Republic of the Congo
Italy	Albania
U.S.-led Coalition	Haiti
Australian-led Coalition	East Timor, Solomon Islands

Regional Organization Peacekeeping	
	Location of Peacekeeping Operations
Africa	
Economic Community of West African States	Liberia (twice), Sierra Leone, Guinea-Bissau, Ivory Coast
Southern African Development Community	Democratic Republic of the Congo, Lesotho
Economic and Monetary Community of Central African States	Central African Republic
African Union	Burundi, Sudan
Europe	
Commonwealth of Independent States	Moldova, Georgia, Tajikistan
European Union	Bosnia, Macedonia
Americas	
North Atlantic Treaty Organization	Kosovo, Afghanistan

Source: Data from Bellamy and Williams 2005.

involving direct action, skills transfer, or institution build-ing." Accordingly, many now recognize NGOs as signifi-cant actors in the expanded menu of new conflict man-agers (Aall 1996: 434). While it is imperative that NGOs continue their traditional activities, they have the poten-tial to play key roles in the conflict resolution process and accordingly must adopt a long-term perspective on their activities (Aall 1996). NGOs may play an informal third-party role in conflict resolution as either facilitators or mediators, as they often have local expertise. They also have the advantage of being in conflict-prone zones before violence occurs and may therefore have critical knowledge of societies and cooperative relationships with local ac-tors. A relationship of trust established over time cannot easily be created by external parties who intervene only when violence has broken out (Lederach 1997; Carl 2000). As John Paul Lederach and Paul Wehr discovered in South America, conflict parties look for *confianza* (trust), which local NGOs as insider partials can offer. Lederach and Wehr (1991) promote the training of local people with skills in conflict resolution that may be com-bined with indigenous traditions.

The negotiation and resolution of humanitarian issues can build bridges in war-torn societies, decrease tension, and resolve ill-feeling. Conversely, failure to do so can hinder further negotiations and negatively impact rela-tions between adversaries. The experiences of the Centre for Humanitarian Dialogue (HD Centre) in the Indonesia-Aceh conflict illustrate a mandate of humanitarianism being used to move beyond conventional concerns such as minimizing civilian casualties or resettling refugees, toward a goal of a negotiated political settlement of the root causes of the conflict. Framing the dialogue in hu-manitarian terms provides a face-saving opportunity for concessions by both parties, making compromise appear as purely motivated, a noble act rather than a strategic loss. HD Centre founder Martin Griffiths calls it "The New Humanitarianism"—identifying common humani-tarian interests between warring factions as a tool to move beyond the immediate results of violence, such as civilian deaths and refugee crises, toward the more ambi-tious goal of resolving the root sources of the conflict (Kay 2003). The raison d'être of humanitarian mediation, ac-cording to the HD Centre, is to bring the conflict parties together in order to reach agreements that reduce the human cost of the conflict, increase human security, and ultimately contribute to the resolution of the conflict itself (HD Centre 2002). Humanitarian mediation is an evolu-tion of traditional humanitarian negotiation/mediation, where the purpose is to alleviate humanitarian suffering,

often based on a mandate of strict neutrality, and is a nec-essary response to increasingly inhuman wars.

Within the post–Cold War system the UN has played a more prominent role in implementing measures of world security and conflict prevention. In the aftermath of the Soviet Union's collapse, the unified effort in the Gulf War led observers to believe that perhaps the Security Coun-cil, freed from the superpower rivalry of the Cold War, would have the power to pass and implement UN resolu-tions and conventions on the management and resolution of conflict. However, the Gulf War was fought between sovereign states, and military, strategic, and material in-terests provided a powerful incentive for the intervention of the hegemonic powers.

For the UN to intervene in the internal affairs of a state is more difficult. The Charter declares that the UN should work to achieve international cooperation in solv-ing international problems of economic, social, cultural, or humanitarian character; to promote and encourage re-spect for human rights; and to promote fundamental freedoms for all without discrimination as to race, sex, language, or religion (UN Charter Article I). Article II of the Charter, however, specifically states that the organiza-tion does not have the right to interfere with matters that fall under the domestic jurisdiction of any member state. Hence, the UN Charter provides no provisions for auto-matic intervention in internal conflict, as many of these conflicts involve only domestic issues.

Within the framework of his *Agenda for Peace,* which acknowledges the increasing ethnic, religious, social, and cultural tensions within state boundaries, former UN secretary-general Boutros-Ghali called for a refocusing of the UN's principal aims through the practice of preven-tive diplomacy. Despite this new initiative, the UN is still fundamentally constrained by the principle of absolute state sovereignty (Bertram 1995), which often prevents adequate and timely intervention in internal conflict. Within the UN framework, a state must give its consent and invite UN intervention, or the UN must acknowl-edge that there is a wider threat to international peace and security.

Currently a dilemma exists as to what circumstances justify armed military intervention in support of humani-tarian ends. The "right" of intervention challenges the hitherto revered principle of state sovereignty. "The impli-cations of human rights abuses and refugee flows for inter-national peace and security are forcing us to take a fresh look at sovereignty as a matter of responsibility, not just power" (Annan 1998). Richmond notes that this dilemma occurs in "the context of post-Westphalian norms based on the dominance of human security and needs over sovereignty, global, and regional intervention over isolationism" (2000: 8).

Although the UN has taken significant steps in the realm of conflict resolution, its limitations require the involvement of various nongovernmental organizations and civil society groups to support the peacemaking processes. Increasingly, more international organizations, community-based action groups, single-issue pressure groups, academics, and policy advisers are taking interest in conflict management efforts. Nongovernmental volunteer organizations in rich and strong countries are supporting their counterparts in poorer states. Organizations such as Human Rights Watch and Amnesty International and religious institutions such as Catholic Relief Services are providing invaluable services in the direction of human rights and conflict management.

The increasing impact of these organizations has enhanced their power; for example, NGOs have the potential to influence the behavior of states by threatening prospects for international assistance with a bad human rights report or by leaving a country because humanitarian efforts are being thwarted (Stern and Druckman 2000b). Increasingly, there is communication and cooperation between diverse groups, cutting across the traditional boundaries of their official, state-based counterparts, and more coordinated efforts of communication and action are being taken by governments, institutions, communities, and individuals at international, regional, and local levels.

Given that norms of human rights, democracy, and self-determination are increasingly dispersed, they challenge the principle of noninterference in internal affairs of sovereign states, which has previously been guarded jealously. The Helsinki Final Act of 1975 gives the UN permission to oversee the human rights conditions in the territories of each of the thirty-five signatories. Another example of this trend is that the UN Charter and other related international documents are increasingly becoming embodied in transnational institutions that can exert influence on states.

The international tribunals for Rwanda and the former Yugoslavia, in addition to developing independent state judiciaries, have generated an important campaign for the creation of a permanent international criminal court. NGOs such as Amnesty International and Earthaction, among others, have called for an end to the ad hoc creation of these tribunals and argued that the existing systems are both expensive and inefficient. In that line of thought, they called for the establishment of the international criminal court. Efforts to establish the International Criminal Court (ICC) were a result of similar concerns shared by a majority of the world community. After the ratification of the ICC by the sixty-fifth signatory in April 2002, the court is now in effect. While the ICC's effectiveness in bringing peace, security, and justice to the world is yet to be proved, and while it is not supported by the United States, its establishment reflects international actors' changed attitudes toward crimes against humanity and an increased willingness to take responsibility. Nonetheless, it is important to note that these developments are not merely a result of altruistic considerations. Conflicts are increasingly costly, and instability and violence in a given state usually impacts its neighbors and even the international community. Furthermore, the economic costs of rebuilding societies after conflict are often prohibitively high. Because communities and countries are becoming inextricably interconnected, attempts to manage, resolve, and prevent conflict constitute an inescapable feature of our contemporary world.

In addition to NGOs, international financial institutions have also begun to incorporate conflict resolution and postconflict reconstruction departments in their bodies, most importantly the World Bank's Post-Conflict Reconstruction Unit. This shift is, in part, the result of a more holistic understanding of peace and conflict resolution that has led various scholars and practitioners to link conflict with development issues. Recognition that fifteen of the twenty poorest countries in the world have had a major conflict in the past fifteen years, that these conflicts have spilled across borders, affecting their neighbors, and that nearly every low-income country is adjacent to a country that has experienced breakdown and war, has led the World Bank and other development agencies to develop a better understanding of the nature of violent conflict and of the accompanying social and economic disintegration (Holtzman, Elwan, and Scott 1998). The Bank defines its objectives as facilitating the transition to sustainable peace after hostilities have ceased and support of economic development to reconstruct the enabling conditions for a functioning peacetime society (Holtzman, Elwan, and Scott 1998). Primarily founded on an economic understanding of the sources of conflict, the Bank suggests that for peace to be maintained, the world community must continue to be engaged in projects and efforts even after the conflict is resolved. Although many conflicts have a base in ethnic or religious competition, "the underlying factors beneath these manifestations are more complex and impinge upon economic, social, and political relationships" (World Bank

1998: 3). Any conflict resolution or reconciliation efforts must include a long-term postconflict agenda in order to be successful. Therefore, "what is needed is the reconstruction of the *enabling conditions* for a functioning peacetime society" (World Bank 1998: 4). Coordinated reconstruction efforts to normalize society in the postconflict period are required, through capacity building, economic restructuring and recovery, civil society building, demining, demobilization, and reintegration of ex-combatants and refugees into society.

Perspectives for a Post-Westphalian World

Conflict is a universal and inevitable aspect of social life (Dixon 1996: 655). That being said, conflict "must be channelled within a set of agreed norms that foster discussion of difference, proscribe violence as a means of settling disputes, and establish rules for the limited kinds of violence that are condoned" (Stern and Druckman 2000b: 2). The traditional state-centric paradigm fails to provide the necessary explanations for and answers to the pressing challenges of the present era, namely, internal conflicts and asymmetric warfare. As the international system moves into a post-Westphalian era, where human security, identity, poverty, and representation issues are included within hegemonic discourses in international relations and conflict studies, innovative and dynamic approaches to peacemaking are becoming increasingly relevant. We can quite convincingly argue that conflicts cannot properly be resolved unless a more complete or even radical approach to deal with its root causes are undertaken. Guided by a Western, realist/positivist, hegemonic discourse, traditional methods have not so much resolved conflict as perpetuated it by maintaining the territorial integrity of the status quo, and they have enabled a binary understanding of the parties to conflict, which perceives belligerents through Western stereotypes. To achieve durable peace, a culturally sensitive peacemaking and peacebuilding is required at the local, regional, and global levels, one that does not perceive insiders as the problem and outsiders as the solution. For sustainable peace to be achieved, the peace process must be anchored in a long-term framework that addresses the multiple sources of the conflict, including broader structural change, and must include previously marginalized groups and actors. An increasingly globalizing world should encourage policymakers and scholars to redefine sovereignty, community, and citizenship. Moreover, the future of conflict resolution de-

pends on the use of new forms of addressing conflict and sustaining peace that have not been traditionally associated with conflict resolution. An inclusive definition of conflict resolution allows for a wider variety of actors to be involved, which, in the traditional conflict management approach, would have been neglected.

Studies of conflict analysis and conflict resolution have until recently also failed to address the issue of gender. To a large extent, this can be attributed to the dominance of the Westphalian discourse in international relations, which is a state-centric, male-dominated diplomatic world, and focused exclusively on the official sphere of politics, which largely excludes women, especially in those countries most affected by conflict in recent years. The increased recognition of local peacemaking initiatives, in which women often play an integral role, demonstrates an increasingly inclusive space, enabling the participation of traditionally marginalized segments of society. "When women are excluded from contributing to peace negotiations, the realities of a conflict in terms of its impact on communities may not be fully comprehended" (Miall et al. 1999: 61). The inclusion of all parties affected by conflict, including women, is imperative if a true understanding of the roots of conflict is to be achieved, if obstacles to the peace process are to be removed and insights into alternative methods of peacemaking are to be gained. Women and men experience war differently, they die different deaths, and they are tortured and abused in different ways, sometimes for biological, social, or psychological reasons. While more men are killed in combat, among other things women experience slavery, rape, forced pregnancy, and the deliberate infection of HIV/AIDS as a weapon of war (Morris 1996). The inclusion of all sectors of the society in the peacemaking and peacebuilding process furthers the development of innovative, viable solutions and the establishment of sustainable peace.

An important factor in post–Cold War conflict is the accessibility and pervasive presence of the global media. The global media comprises technologies, peoples, and practices that bring the reality of conflict to every citizen almost instantaneously. The question arises whether the global media can play a role in conflict prevention, resolution, and peacebuilding. The media is both a vehicle for positive social change and one that can perpetuate and intensify violent conflict. By sensationalizing conflict, perpetuating stereotypes, reinforcing or reflecting elite and status quo views, the media can be a force for stagnation and violence, rather than peace and stability. The use of "hate radio" in Rwanda illustrates this phenomenon.

However, the media also has the ability to change the dynamics of the conflict and enhance the public's understanding of it by avoiding simplistic and sensationalist reporting, reducing suspicion by showing the human side of each party, deobjectifying the protagonists, and identifying the underlying interests of the parties. The media can also be used as a legitimate outlet for expressing grievances and emotions, and, consequently, conflict can be expressed and resolved through the media rather than fought with physical violence. During the mediation or negotiation process the media can be used by the parties to address their constituencies and keep them informed, which can help build support for peace initiatives and proposals. Despite the ever-growing accessibility of the media, it is important to note that media influence is unevenly distributed globally, and there remains a large digital divide.

It is necessary for conflict resolution studies to recognize the importance of changes made in the Internet and the impact these new communications and information technologies may have on conflict and its resolution. The Internet has made possible easier and faster exchanges of information and communication, and these exchanges transcend geophysical boundaries. For this reason they have affected the way most peace, humanitarian, and conflict resolution organizations operate, be they professional, academic, or voluntary. Developments in information and communications technology (ICT) have had an important impact on conflict transformation, especially through education, in part because the Internet provides a medium to publish and disseminate information at a relatively low cost. Sanjana Hattotuwa argues that "the peaceful and just resolution of conflict can at best be engendered and nurtured by ICT" (2002: 1). The Internet is a tool for gathering up-to-the-minute information, and e-mail and instant messaging allow for instant global communication. Local NGOs can connect with global organizations, and different agencies with different and perhaps complementary skill sets may be linked. ICT can be used as a means of protest, where "networked international communications can empower people to act against government authority" (1).

While the pervasiveness of cyberspace and the continual development of ICT can be beneficial for conflict resolution and transformation, it may also be utilized for a negative purpose, much like the traditional media. The concept of netwar is indicative of changes in the conflict environment and the involvement of new actors, in a post-Westphalian era. In netwar, the attackers are not combatants in the conventional sense, but the information revolution has allowed a new generation of combatants, both at home and abroad, to pursue their interests in innovative ways. Arquilla and Ronfeldt argue that netwar combatants "are organizing into loose, transnational networks that allow for increased coordination and cooperation among dispersed groups and individuals who are able to stay securely separated in case anyone is caught and incriminated" (1993). As access to technology in the information age disperses and deepens, new methods of conflict develop using these technologies. A pertinent example is known as cyberwar; the method of "conducting, and preparing to conduct, military operations according to information-related principles" (144). Cyberwar aims to disrupt, if not completely destroy, information and communications systems, including those of the military, affecting the ability of an organization "to know itself: who it is, where it is, what it can do and when, why it is fighting, which threats to counter first, and so forth" (Arquilla and Ronfeldt 1997: 30). Significantly and perhaps most interestingly, cyberwar has fundamental parallels with the German World War II technique of Blitzkrieg in its potential to affect the information adversaries rely on to successfully make war, and scholars have noted that "as an innovation of warfare, we anticipate that cyberwar may be to the 21st century what Blitzkrieg was to the 20th" (31).

While cyberwar is concerned with traditional military aspects like command, control, communications, and intelligence, and so-called smart weapons systems, netwar represents the civilian side to technological warfare. *Netwar* refers to "information related conflict between societies, a largely psychological exercise of trying to affect what a target population knows or thinks about itself and the world" (Strobel 1997, 288). Netwar techniques may focus on public or elite opinion, or both; they may involve public diplomacy measures, propaganda and psychological campaigns, political and cultural subversion, deception of or interference with local media, infiltration of computer networks and databases, and efforts to promote dissident or opposition movements across computer networks. An early example of netwar occurred in the former Yugoslavia in the early 1990s, when Serb hackers defaced NATO Web sites with pro-Belgrade messages (Denning 2001: 239). They also forced the network temporarily offline through a technique known as *flood net* (Hess 2002: 56–57).

In a world where the power and scope of transnational corporations (TNCs) is gaining ground at the expense of traditional state power, their potential for positive involvement in conflict management, resolution, human rights protection, and postconflict reconstruction in turn increases. The sheer scale and reach of TNCs is illustrated by the fact that fifty-one of the world's one hundred largest economic entities in 2005 were TNCs such as Wal-Mart and Exxon Mobil generating revenues larger than the gross domestic product (GDP) of countries such as Denmark and Indonesia (Downey and Lucena 2005). TNCs and foreign investment are often associated with areas affected by conflict, usually in a negative light. TNCs are concerned with protecting their own interests, and in the past have done so by supporting repressive regimes, often in relation to the arms industry or extractive resource industries such as oil or diamonds. In 2003, Shell Oil admitted that its extraction operations in Nigeria "sometimes feed conflict by the way we award contracts, gain access to land, and deal with community representatives" (BBC News 2004).

In much the same way that NGOs possess a local advantage when engaged in a country prior to conflict, TNCs can become involved in the peacemaking process. They may also have an indirect effect on conflict by increasing economic development in the country, thereby reducing the economic sources of the conflict and increasing employment. While the private sector has a potentially significant role in conflict resolution, it should not act alone in its efforts but should work in cooperation with other parties and more traditional methods. Haufler (2001: 672) notes that "direct action by the private sector to prevent or resolve violent conflict can be looked upon as a risky but potentially fruitful alternative therapy."

A shift in the understanding of war has led to the lines between terrorism and warfare becoming increasingly blurred (Laqueur 2003). In contrast to the traditional conception of war as armed hostility between the armies of states, in modern conflicts the methods used to compel one's enemy have become increasingly blurred and are no longer limited to traditional military techniques. While the field of conflict resolution struggles to deal with new wars, terrorism appears to be an even greater challenge. Terrorists' newfound power to assert themselves globally demands a more sophisticated understanding of terrorism itself. An intersubjective approach to terrorism, which marries the approaches of conflict resolution and terrorism studies, is essential, as is an attempt to prevent violent conflict or terrorism by creating obstacles to the employment of such strategies and preempting the conditions that create these types of conflicts in the first place. The conditions that allow political entrepreneurs to recruit followers are embedded within the gross inequalities that exist in the international system and that continue to marginalize and deny legitimacy to groups who then see no alternative but to resort to acts of violence, including terrorism (Ehrlich and Liu 2002).

Conclusion

The potential promise that emerged at the end of the Cold War for a world of peace never eventuated. Instead, a world of increasingly violent internal conflict has emerged, where the majority of deaths are civilian, where failed states become havens for terrorist networks, where identity conflicts dominate and poverty is a common theme. Because these new conflicts defy the traditional image of conflict, previous tools of conflict resolution now need to be supplemented, some would say supplanted, by newer approaches to conflict.

Traditional conflict resolution techniques were operated from a state-centric perspective, where preservation of the status quo was the ultimate goal. Second-generation techniques contributed the notion of human security as opposed to state security, allowed for the inclusion of social movements, and attempted to address the root causes of conflict, thereby complementing traditional methods of conflict resolution. While second-generation techniques focused on the notion of conflict transformation as opposed to resolution, the field remained one-dimensional in its approach to violent internal conflict and appeared to operate within the Westphalian context. The nature of modern conflict dictates a paradigm shift toward a post-Westphalian, multidimensional lens for international relations in general and conflict resolution in particular.

In recent years, nontraditional conflict resolution techniques have evolved in order to achieve greater contextual specificity. Including both practical and normative aspects to conflict resolution, modern conflict management recognizes the importance and potential of local actors, the different ways war is experienced by men and women, and the need for both official and unofficial channels of communication. Applying a relevant conflict resolution approach is especially significant due to the difficulty of UN intervention implied by the principle of state sovereignty. Recent developments in the approach to conflict resolution signal the beginning of a paradigm shift in the international community, a shift that holds greater potential for addressing the violent internal conflicts that are likely to prevail in the twenty-first century. It is this shift that we wish to explore, chart, and study in some detail in the chapters that follow.

PART ONE

Principles and Traditional Approaches

CHAPTER TWO

International Negotiation

The aim of this chapter is twofold: first, to highlight the main features of bargaining and negotiation as an important approach to conflict resolution, and second, to highlight the social-psychological framework in the study of bargaining and negotiation. Negotiation has become something of a growth industry offering the prospect of resolving every dilemma; as a result, a sense of order and a measure of realism are long overdue. We do not aim to formulate a general theory of negotiation but rather to evaluate the current state of knowledge and present a framework that may explain the effectiveness and performance of negotiations in international relations.

Negotiation is the most frequently employed of all methods of international conflict resolution, not only "because it is always the first to be tried and successful, but also because states may believe its advantages to be so great as to rule out the use of other methods, even in situations where the chances of a negotiated settlement are slight" (Merrills 1998: 2). States are exhorted, under Article 33(1) of the UN Charter, to seek recourse to negotiations first in any dispute between them. The practice of negotiation predates the modern international system by thousands of years; diplomatic envoys have been used by different groups and societies to resolve their disputes throughout history. Negotiations today are embedded in the modern diplomatic structure of communication between states.

We think of negotiation as a mechanism designed, through some joint decisions, to regulate conflict and to limit or prevent the escalation of its attitudinal or behavioral components, and, when possible, reach a political agreement that may set the stage for better interactions in the future. Although various issues can be raised regarding the negotiation and bargaining process (e.g., what kinds of conflicts are most amenable to negotiations, how should concessions be offered?), the particular question we wish to address is, why do some negotiation efforts fail, while others succeed, and when is negotiation an appropriate response to a conflict? This question will be considered under the following headings: (1) What are the characteristics of bargaining and negotiation as a conflict resolution technique? (2) How can the important elements of bargaining and negotiation be best defined? (3) What are the major approaches to the study of bargaining and negotiation? (4) What are the major factors that influence the process and impede success? (5) How can it best be structured and analyzed?

On Conflict and Conflict Resolution

Few subjects seem more central to the social sciences than the concept of conflict, yet few have created more confusion or been studied less systematically. The proliferation of internal conflicts, poverty and economic inequality, refugees and terrorists, and the enduring political disagreements between nations have all combined to produce an unprecedented amount of interest and scholarship focused on issues of conflict and conflict resolution (Dedring 1976; Mitchell 1981).

As our approach throughout is both interdisciplinary

and eclectic, we define conflict as a perception of incompatibility between two or more actors and the range of behavior associated with such perceptions (Mack and Snyder 1957; Fink et al. 1968; Schmidt and Kochan 1972; Bercovitch 1980). This broad definition makes it quite clear that conflicts can occur in any system of interaction, ranging from the interpersonal to the international, and that we can study something about its causes by looking at conflicts at any level. We also argue that conflicts must be managed or resolved, because their non-resolution can, at the very least, be dysfunctional for the system within which it occurs (Deutsch 1973). This notion of conflict resolution suggests that a conflict can be dealt with, by the adversaries or outsiders, in such a way as to experience more values and benefits and to decrease the costs associated with conflict. This is what we hope to achieve with any approach to conflict resolution.

Generally speaking, conflicts are said to be resolved when (1) a discernible outcome has been reached; (2) conflict behavior terminates; and (3) a satisfactory distribution of values and resources has been agreed on. The processes by which conflict resolution is achieved are both varied and complex. Approaches can be classified in terms of the participants in the process (i.e., unilateral, bilateral, or multilateral conflict resolution), or in terms of the modalities utilized (i.e., violent or nonviolent). Conflict resolution is therefore a process that, if successful, may help parties in conflict achieve a new and better modus vivendi.

With regard to conflict outcomes, three types of outcomes may be distinguished: avoidance or withdrawal; conquest, domination, or imposition; and a compromise agreement (Boulding 1982). These outcomes may be effected by one or both parties, and they may be brought about, wholly or partly, by parties outside the conflict system (this corresponds to the distinction between endogenous vs. exogenous conflict resolution). In this chapter we propose to examine the connection between negotiation and a mutually satisfactory outcome.

Conceptual Framework for Bargaining and Negotiation

Defining Bargaining and Negotiation

Before discussing the specific variables that influence negotiation, it is first necessary to establish a clear definition of the phenomenon. Negotiation and bargaining are con-

flict resolution strategies that aim to stop violence and reach an agreement through a joint decision-making process involving all parties to a conflict. It is a process where an exchange of concessions is regarded as common, even when the parties' preferences have not been completely satisfied. As a conflict resolution mechanism with a wide range of applications at various levels of behavior, bargaining and negotiation can be defined in a variety of ways, which emphasize different aspects of the process. The diversity that exists between these definitions is a reflection of the difficulty of adopting a formal definition of such a wide-ranging, abstract concept. The process of bargaining and negotiation includes a succession of experiences and the occurrence of many borderline experiences with blurred boundaries (e.g., adjudication, debate, conciliation). This does not mean that we should not draw any lines; rather, it means that the lines we draw are arbitrary and drawn for some specific heuristic purpose.

The simplest definition of negotiation is provided by Sir Harold Nicolson from the *Oxford English Dictionary,* defining it as the "method by which these relations are adjusted and managed by ambassadors and envoys, the business of the diplomat" (Nicolson 1950: 7). McGrath draws attention to the *representative* nature of bargaining and negotiation, defining it as "an occasion where one or more representatives of two or more parties interact in an explicit attempt to reach a jointly acceptable position" (1966: 121). Conversely, Fred Ikle (1964) and Arthur Lall (1966) emphasize the objective of reaching an agreement and realizing common interests where bargaining and negotiation become a process of moving toward a common agreement. Some authors define it as a situation of interdependence involving a power relationship (Schelling 1960; Walton and McKersie 1965). Most writers on the subject focus on the transition of the conflict system from a state of conflict toward some form of an outcome such as the process of exchanging information proposals (Coddington 1968; Cross 1969; Nicholson 1970; Siegel and Fouraker 1960).

Of the many definitions, both narrow and wide, the most satisfactory definition, and the one that accounts for the openness of scientific terms at the same time as reflecting the manner, context, and objectives of bargaining and negotiation, is the one offered by Stephenson and Morley (1977). They refer to negotiation as "any form of verbal (or non-verbal) communication, direct or indirect, whereby parties to a conflict of interest discuss, without resort to arbitration or other judicial processes, the form of any joint action which they might take to manage a dispute between them" (Morley and Stephenson 1977: 7). This definition will form the conceptual basis of our approach to international negotiations.

─────────────────────────────────────

Characteristics of Bargaining and Negotiation

The growing interest in conflict and conflict resolution has brought together scholars from diverse fields and has produced an astonishing proliferation of centers, associations, conferences, and publications. This academic enthusiasm has led to a bewildering multiplicity of studies on bargaining and negotiation (Rubin and Brown 1975; Druckman 1977). The absence of rigid criteria as to the precise boundaries of conflict resolution and the interdisciplinary nature of its practitioners has brought together concepts from economics, sociology, social-psychology and politics, and has given impetus to the study of bargaining and negotiation; an impetus which emphasizes the centrality of this approach to conflict. From this avalanche of theoretical and empirical studies, the following list covers the essential characteristics of bargaining and negotiation.

1. The bargaining and negotiation process is a conflict resolution mechanism embedded in all social systems (because it contributes to their continued existence) and involving at least two analytically distinct parties in a conflict over resources or values.

2. These parties come together in a voluntary process designed to manage their conflict. The voluntary nature of the process implies that the actors may choose whether to: (i) enter into such a process to manage their conflict; and (ii) whether to accept or reject any potential solution that may emerge from the process. Bargaining and negotiation is a *joint* decision-making exercise.

3. Parties are brought together in a social relationship in which they have both conflicting and common interests (if their interests are totally opposed, there is no basis for conflict management; if their interests are totally convergent, there is no point in it). Such a relationship is referred to as a mixed-motive relationship.

4. The bargaining and negotiation process is a conflict resolution mechanism anchored in the perception of those involved. Therefore, a negotiation relationship involves attempts to influence each other's perception and evaluation of the situation by using a wide variety of nonviolent informational strategies (e.g., making demands, threats, concessions, and promises).

5. Bargaining and negotiation is a conflict resolution mechanism that operates within two somewhat conflicting

parameters: (i) expanding cooperation in the interests of the system or environment; and (ii) maximizing each actor's objectives and interests.

6. The pattern of a relationship in bargaining and negotiation is sequential rather than simultaneous (as it might be in an unstructured exchange or argument). It consists of repeated exchanges of information, evaluation, and decisions until (in theory) a relevant and acceptable outcome emerges.

International negotiation has been used mostly in low-intensity conflicts over tangible issues (Bercovitch and Jackson 2001). It is a useful way of resolving conflicts between two roughly equal states, where violence remains pretty low, and the issues are essentially about territory or economic resources. As a method of conflict resolution, negotiation has several key advantages. First, it can provide a useful and agreed-upon outcome for the parties. Second, it is efficient, in that parties enter the process voluntarily, explore any possible agreement they may like, and are free to accept or reject any outcome. Third, it provides a basis for better interactions between the parties by encouraging them to explore emotional and interpersonal dimensions of a conflict. Last, it provides legitimate standards (e.g., objective criteria) for evaluating and accepting any option, without either party appearing to be unduly compromising (Funken 2006). International negotiation is well suited to an international environment of states, all of whom are legally (but only legally) equal, and all of whom guard their sovereignty with equal passions. Given its features, it is no wonder that empirical studies (Bercovitch and Jackson 2001) find that negotiation has been used, either directly or in an assisted form, in more than 90 percent of all international conflicts since 1945.

The one major limitation of negotiation is that it is not a panacea, and it is not well suited to every kind of conflict. High conflict intensity, power disparity between combatants, intractable conflicts, and conflicts fought over intangible issues such as ethnicity and religion are all factors that may make a conflict unsuited to bargaining and negotiation (Bercovitch and Jackson 2001). Parties in such conflicts may well seek other forms of resolution.

─────────────────────────────────────

Elements of Bargaining and Negotiation

Every process of negotiation has three core elements. These include (1) the parties, (2) the issues, and (3) the context. Each has an effect on how negotiation is conducted and on the range of options it may achieve. These elements will be illustrated drawing examples from the interstate conflict between Mali and Burkina Faso that took place between 1985 and 1986. This was a relatively low-intensity territorial conflict resulting from competing claims to the Agacher strip that lies in the border region between the two countries.

The Parties

Parties in a negotiation process consist of primary, directly affected parties and, on many occasions, other interested and potential third parties. Parties in conflict may refer to individuals, groups, organizations, nations, or other systems that are represented in the process. However, determining who the parties are, what their historical relationship is, and who should be represented at the negotiating table is not always an easy task. This is particularly the case in international negotiation where states may face internal difficulties, a serious lack of legitimacy, or unclear lines of internal decision making.

Parties in conflict may themselves contain subsystems or be subsystems of a larger actor. Parties in conflict may experience intraparty friction, or a stronger or wealthier party may manipulate them, or they may not enjoy the support of their constituents. Some conflict parties come to the negotiation table as autonomous, independent units, others can not do so. Some parties have similar structural attributes (e.g., both are democratic states), others are very different. Some parties have a shared commitment to a regional grouping and a set of values and norms, others represent very different groupings. All these issues pertaining to party identity and attributes will have a major impact on whether negotiation takes place and whether it is successful.

Another important element influencing the parties involved in negotiation is the power relationship that exists between the disputants. Zartman and Rubin (2000: 15–19) have considered how this relationship affects negotiation success and have revealed some key insights. They argue that negotiations between parties with relatively equal levels of power are more likely to yield a successful outcome, and that the lower the level of power disparity, the higher the chances of negotiation success. Power disparity may well prompt the stronger power to reject negotiation and seek to press home their coercive advantage.

In the case of the Mali–Burkina Faso conflict, the competing parties were relatively well defined with the two respective governments both seeking control of the contested territory. Negotiation in this case was also aided by

the fact that a rough power symmetry existed between the two disputants with both disputants sharing similar military power. Furthermore, the total power within the system was relatively low as both Mali and Burkina Faso were among the poorest and least developed nations in the world (Pondi 2000: 205).

The Mali–Burkina Faso conflict attracted a broad range of negotiators including leaders of African states and a number of regional organizations. The president of Algeria and the Libyan foreign minister both made early yet unsuccessful efforts to negotiate an agreement between the two parties. Subsequently, the president of the Ivory Coast began working with the OAU (the Organization for African Unity), and shortly after, the Pan-African organization became involved in the negotiations. While these efforts were also unsuccessful, they paved the way for negotiations by Nigeria and Libya that led to the signing of a cease-fire agreement on 30 December 1985 (Pondi 2000: 214).

The Issues

Another crucial element in any negotiation process involves the nature of the issues in conflict. Conflicts are essentially situations in which parties hold divergent or incompatible goals (e.g., toward scarce goods) that can motivate their behavior. These incompatible goals define the issues and the extent of the gulf between the parties in conflict. Issues tell us what the conflict is about, and how close or far removed the parties' positions from each other are; but they are not fixed or immutable, and they can be negotiated singly, sequentially, or linked together in a package of some sort.

Issues in conflict define the logical structure of any conflict situation. If parties in conflict differ widely in terms of their values, beliefs, and goals, it is safe to presume that they will also differ with respect to their perceptions of the issues in conflict. In fact, conflict parties often disagree on the issues in a conflict, or even the fundamental cause of the conflict. One party may see the issues in a conflict as pertaining to the right of self-determination, while the other may see them as pertaining to its security and survival. Achieving agreement between the two parties on the source of the conflict, or getting them to think in terms of similar issues, may go a long way toward successful conflict resolution.

Parties in conflict go through a complicated series of steps where they assign meaning to their experience, conceptualize it in terms of issues, and choose a particular behavior that relates to how they see their issues. This sequence of steps is influenced by factors such as values, needs, historical experience, competence, and context. As these dimensions may differ widely between parties, we can perhaps appreciate why there are so many different interpretations of conflict situations or interpretations of the issues in conflict.

Given the variety of factors that affect the perceptions and definitions of issues in conflict, how can we classify conflict issues? Various categories may be used (e.g., affective vs. substantive, realistic vs. nonrealistic), but a more satisfactory way is to define issues in conflict in terms of: (1) the parties' evaluation; (2) the rewards associated with various issues; and (3) their content.

The issues of the conflict have a direct impact on the negotiation and bargaining process. Empirical data indicate that intractable conflicts that involve issues related to identity, value systems, and beliefs are harder to resolve than conflicts that involve issues over resources (Licklider 1995). In these situations, complementing Track I negotiations with Track II negotiation strategies might prove to be the most useful strategy.

When considering the Mali–Burkina Faso conflict, negotiations were aided by the fact that identity issues were not a key component to the dispute and there was little or no confusion as to what issues lay at the heart of the conflict. Essentially, the conflict was purely territorial as a result of competing claims to the Agacher strip in the border region between the two countries, which was thought to contain substantial natural resources. More specifically, the dispute arose as a result of differing perceptions regarding the frontier that existed at the moment the two countries gained independence from France in 1959 (Pondi 2000: 6).

The Context

Every negotiation takes place within a social context, or a specific political environment. The parameters of this context may significantly affect the nature of the process. Contextual parameters may be described in terms of their complexity, coercive structures, independence of negotiators and their affiliates, and the presence (or absence) of other interested actors. The context of bargaining and negotiation both reflects the nature of the parties' prior relationship and affects their current conflict resolution efforts (Pugh et al. 1969; Inkson et al. 1970; Walton and McKersie 1965; Nicolson 1950). Different contexts characterize different processes and outcomes.

The context in which bargaining and negotiation takes place both affects and is affected by the process. In essence, *context* refers to the environment in which the conflict and the subsequent negotiation and bargaining process take place. Context is shaped by factors such as the history of the conflict, the previous interactions of the parties, and the international environment. The environment within which the parties to a conflict exist plays a major role in shaping their perceptions of the conflict, their options, responses and possible outcomes. Hence, an awareness of the context of a negotiation is indispensable to developing an integrated approach to the study of negotiation.

The context of the Mali–Burkina Faso conflict reveals some interesting dynamics, the understanding of which would be crucial to the success of any negotiation effort. First, the conflict was a result of an ongoing disagreement regarding ownership of the Agacher strip that had first emerged twenty years earlier in 1964, shortly after the two countries had achieved independence. Armed skirmishes between the two countries had already broken out on one occasion in 1974 (Bercovitch and Fretter 2004: 77–78). Second, this conflict, like many others in Africa, must be considered in the context of the region's colonial history. State boundaries were arbitrarily drawn up by colonial powers with little consideration for the tribal and ethnic groups they encompassed (Blanton, Manson, and Athow 2001). Mali claimed that the disputed territory was both ethnically and geographically part of Mali while Burkina Faso argued that French colonial authorities had included it in Burkinabe territory (Bercovitch and Fretter 2004: 92–93). Third, the international environment was another important contextual element of this conflict. When considering the major allies of the two countries, Burkina Faso was on shaky ground with only Libya as its major international ally compared with Mali who had retained stronger ties with the former colonial power France, as well as other influential countries in Africa (Pondi 2000: 211).

Approaches to the Study of Bargaining and Negotiation

The diversity and complexity of international negotiation as a specific form of conflict resolution should by now be pretty clear to any observer. This diversity is matched by the broad variety of theoretical approaches that have been developed to study bargaining and negotiation.

These approaches include historical, material, psychological, cognitive and learning, game-theoretic, and social-psychological approaches. Rather than attempting to cover all of these approaches, the following section will focus on a review and summary of the social-psychological approach. This approach is the most promising in the study of international conflict resolution. The approach considers the structure and contents of a conflict relationship across three time spans (past, present, and future), and is most helpful in generating explanations about the nature and effectiveness of negotiation and the development of an acceptable outcome. This approach also offers, we believe, the best answer to the question of bargaining effectiveness, that is, how to achieve successful conflict resolution, thereby laying the foundation for a closer analysis of the strengths and weaknesses of any form of negotiations (Shea 1980).

Before considering the social-psychological approach, it should be noted that all of the aforementioned approaches concern themselves with: (1) the question of effectiveness in negotiations; and (2) the elements that are regarded as the most important in negotiation behavior, namely, two-party interaction, conflict, adaptive and sequential behavior, mutual cooperation, and joint determination of value distributions. These approaches, however, vary considerably in terms of their reliance on independent variables, internal consistency, and logical completeness. With respect to their assumptions and propositions, these approaches can be classified on a spectrum ranging from the descriptive, through the analytic, to the predictive. While they all have their place and value in the study of international negotiation, we are convinced of the centrality and relevance of the social-psychological approach.

The Social-Psychological Approach

The social-psychological is the only technique that treats bargaining outcomes as products of personal, role, situational, interactional, and impeding factors. This approach provides us with a framework that allows for theoretical and empirical exploration of the process and an integration of the findings. Moreover, this approach takes a systematic look at all aspects of bargaining and brings us closer to the goal of answering the question of bargaining effectiveness. Very importantly, the social-psychological lens to bargaining and negotiation aims to bridge the gap between both conception and relevance, and theory and reality.

The social-psychological approach grew out of the pi-

oneering model developed by Sawyer and Guetzkow (1965) and subsequently elaborated by Druckman (1973). The work of these scholars has a significant influence on the present analysis. The conceptual structure that characterizes the social-psychological approach takes account of different variables as well as their interactive effect at different stages of the conflict management process. The approach calls attention to this complex relationship by suggesting that the general structure of conflict management takes place in three time dimensions: antecedent, concurrent, and consequent (or past, present, and future) (Jackson 2000: 328). The antecedent dimension refers to all those inputs and variables that exist prior to engaging in bargaining and negotiation; the concurrent dimension describes a comprehensive range of factors that characterize the conditions and process of a particular negotiating situation; and the consequent dimension draws attention to the nature of the outcome and the parties' perception of it (Jackson 2000). This approach has made us aware of problems in interpersonal and international negotiation. It suggests variables and patterns of interaction that tend to be associated with successful outcomes, and allows us to examine the effects of various input variables (e.g., secrecy of negotiations) on negotiation outcomes.

Five broad clusters of factors can be distinguished within the social-psychological approach to negotiation: personal/role, situational, interactional, impeding, and goals. Each cluster of factors contains several features that may be examined jointly or individually, and the whole process can be examined from a dynamic, rather than a static or prescriptive, perspective. Negotiation outcomes are thus understood to reflect the specific character of the personalities involved, the setting, and other contingent issues. Only such an analysis, which takes into account the diverse sources of influence on international negotiation, can contribute to a thorough understanding of the phenomenon.

The touchstone of the social-psychological approach is the proposition that outcomes are determined by the interaction of some antecedent factors, and these are mediated through the structure and actual situation of international negotiation. This contributes to our understanding of conflict management by highlighting, for instance, factors that tend to be associated with, or facilitators of, successful outcomes (Bercovitch 1984). It also permits cumulative findings from experimental and real-life studies of bargaining and negotiation, and it tells us the effect on outcomes of the various factors (e.g., while cognitive similarity may be conducive to a successful outcome, situational complexity produces an opposite effect; secrecy of proceedings may help negotiators, publicity hinders them).

The social-psychological approach allows us to blend empirical evidence (e.g., the Camp David negotiations) with theoretical interpretations (e.g., rewarding strategies are more successful than coercive strategies) and to study patterns of bargaining that are characteristic of successful outcomes. We can also isolate the inputs that are predictive of successful processes of conflict management (e.g., absence of audiences, secrecy, and no time pressure). From a practical point of view, this approach is both closer and more relevant to the reality of bargaining and negotiation, and it is fitting that it produces key insights, the adoption of which may help to produce a more desired outcome. Some of these insights can be presented as norms for increasing the likelihood of successful conflict management (the dysfunctional effects of tension and complexity, the importance of various mediation mechanisms, the necessity of decomposing and aggregating relevant conflict issues, and so on).

Given the importance and complexity of bargaining and negotiation it would seem useful to have a conceptual framework that can incorporate the findings of experimentation, simulation, and research in situ and document their effects on bargaining outcomes. The framework developed here lends coherence to these findings and consists of descriptive generalizations, propositions, and explanatory hypotheses at different levels of behavior, all of which bear directly on the central question animating the study of conflict management: how can we manage conflict between individuals and other actors more effectively? An understanding of international negotiation depends on a proper analysis; the social-psychological approach provides just such an analysis.

Factors Influencing the Bargaining and Negotiation Process

The scientific usefulness of bargaining and negotiation may be enriched by connecting it more directly with the experience and the reality of bargaining and negotiation, and distinguishing between various types of this process. In general, we find that the bargaining and negotiation process is influenced by the following factors: personal factors, role factors, situational factors, substance- and process-related interests, and interactional factors.

Personal and Role Factors

Various factors influence the behavior and attitudes of the participants during the process of bargaining and negotiating. If the parties to the process are individuals involved in a conflictual relationship, we refer to this process as *interpersonal bargaining*. If the parties are representatives of groups, nations, or other collectivities, we refer to this as *collective bargaining*. These two categories relate to the level of analysis, and influence which characteristics, pressures, traits, and structural characteristics should be included in the analysis. Moreover, it should not be assumed that the process is uniform irrespective of the level at which it is conducted.

International negotiations at the international level are usually bilateral or multilateral. Typically, senior officials from different ministries represent each party. The negotiations usually take place on an ad hoc basis only (that is to say negotiations are invoked to deal with specific issues only), and they begin once both states are convinced that they can achieve more through negotiation than through fighting. If negotiations drag on and prove unproductive, the level of representation may be upped to include heads of state engaging in summit diplomacy (Merrills 1998). Summit diplomacy is one form of negotiation where the perceived risks of failure are so high (through publicity, loss of face and prestige) that many political leaders would look for any way out of an impasse, rather than face short-term public opprobrium.

In international negotiations the participants represent those who are not present. These participants might be representing senior decision makers, their constituencies, or their country. Negotiators in such complex situations have a challenging task. On the one hand, they have to convince the other party that the concessions made by those they represent are very important and very painful; on the other hand, they have to convince their constituencies that these concessions are not so significant. Furthermore, they have to deal constructively with internal problems, building internal consensus and organizing internal coalitions (Watkins and Rosegrant 2001: 274). Negotiators need to be perceptive and flexible, yet at the same time very persuasive and determined. Thus, although negotiation skills are largely learned, personal/role qualities of the negotiators are also important.

Personal Factors

Personal factors influencing bargaining and negotiation include all the individual characteristics, needs, attitudes, expectations, and other enduring dispositions that the actors bring with them to the conflict management process. These factors exist prior to the conflict management process. They shape an individual's personality and perception of his or her environment and cause people to behave in a characteristically unique way (e.g., John Foster Dulles's pathological dislike of communism was clearly a factor in his aggressive bargaining posture vis-à-vis the Soviet Union). In the negotiation process, the role of personality traits such as charisma, cognitive complexity, or persuasiveness is important, but the idea that "great negotiators are born not made" is incorrect. As Watkins and Rosegrant (2001: xi, xii) state, most negotiating skills such as assessing complex situations, drafting agreements, making concessions, and constructing strategies are learned rather than innate.

Personal factors serve as inputs to the motivational orientation of the parties in conflict. Personal factors help to determine the nature of negotiation and contribute to its resolution. They constitute an important independent variable in any discussion of negotiating behavior, effectiveness, or outcome. Thus, to understand bargaining interactions we must know something about the personality traits of the actors involved in conflict management. Personality traits are expressed in two microcategories: (1) individual characteristics (age, religion, intelligence, and so on); and (2) individual motives and attitudes (trusting, cooperative, authoritarian, and so on) (Greenstein 1967, 1969; Hermann 1980; Hermann and Kogan 1977).

Role Factors

Role factors, on the other hand, refer to a set of influences that stem from a negotiator's reference group, or from expectations attached to his or her position. The juxtaposition of these factors simultaneously prescribes the options available to a negotiator and creates pressures. Role factors—and the degree to which a negotiator is oblivious of or responsive to them—play an important part in shaping negotiating behavior. Role factors transform a dyadic process of interpersonal bargaining to a process of collective bargaining in which the negotiators are concerned with accountability, loyalty and commitment, and the need to maintain public face and receive positive evaluation. In short, role factors determine a negotiator's decision-latitude.

Role factors produce a field of pressures in which each actor in a bargaining relationship has to be responsive to the needs and expectations of his or her own group, to the needs and expectations of the other group, and to the general need to move together toward some acceptable outcome. Role factors affect the posture, expectations, strategy, and behavior of each actor. In this way, they exercise a potent and pronounced influence on the form and process of conflict management (Benton and Druckman 1974; Frey and Adams 1972).

Situational Factors

Situational factors affecting negotiation refer to all the social and physical conditions under which this process takes place.

1. Physical components (e.g., location of bargaining and negotiation, neutrality of site, physical arrangements for conflict management)
2. Social components (e.g., number of parties involved in the process, presence of third parties)
3. Issue components (e.g., tangible or intangible conflict issues, their number and prominence)
4. Components relating to interpersonal orientation (e.g., the nature and use of communication channels, openness or secrecy of the process, and tensions experienced by the parties).

Situational factors impinge upon the process of conflict management and exert a powerful influence on its nature and quality (Druckman 1971, 1977; Rubin and Brown 1975). A particular form of conflict resolution emerges from a set of relevant and contemporaneous conditions. Any analysis of this mechanism is incomplete unless the framework within which it is conducted can be specified. Situational factors serve to remind us of the relevance of this framework.

The main channel of negotiation is diplomatic missions. This channel is typically used when the parties to the dispute believe that the absence of negotiations will harm their interests, whereas the use of negotiations will bring benefits. "Negotiations between states are usually conducted through 'normal diplomatic channels,' that is by the respective foreign offices, or by diplomatic representatives, who in the case of complex negotiations may lead delegations including representatives of several interested departments of the governments concerned" (Merrills 1998: 8).

Situational factors influence the articulation of positions and determine the interests of the parties. The interests of the parties are categorized into two groups: substance-related interests and process-related interests (Watkins and Rosegrant 2001: 23).

Substance-Related Interests

Parties may have conflicting interests, shared interests, or complementary interests. In negotiation situations, parties typically have a mixture of all these interests. An example of this is the 1994 negotiations between the United States and North Korea on North Korea's nuclear armament. Here the conflicting interest between the two parties was North Korea's acquisition of nuclear weapons. The shared interest was manifested by both parties' desire to avoid war. The complementary interest was the trade of the North Korean nuclear program in return for recognition and economic support (Watkins and Rosegrant 2001: 23).

Process-Related Interests

Watkins and Rosegrant (2001) note that process-related interests refer to interests such as how the process unfolds and how the parties appear to others and to themselves. In this regard, the process-related interests include enhancing relationships, preserving reputations, demonstrating competence, remaining consistent, minimizing transaction costs, achieving side effects (such as improving relationships with powerful third parties), and gaining access to new resources.

Process-related interests and substance-related interests interlink with each other in various ways. It may be that a party's interests are such that in an agreement, one side is bound to gain at the other's expense.

A possible way of providing compensation in such a situation is to give the less-favored party control of details such as the time and place of negotiations. The latter in particular, can assume considerable symbolic importance and this constitutes an element that may be used to good effect. A more radical solution is to link two disputes together so that a negotiated settlement can balance gains and losses overall and be capable of acceptance by both sides. (Merrills 1998: 14–15)

Interactional Factors

Interactional factors make us aware of the importance of the parties' prior relationship and the nature of their interdependence, which can be dichotomized as either cooperative or competitive. The response of the negotiators to these factors will influence their attempts to manage their conflict. Interactional factors can affect the nature and strength of the fabric that binds the actors together and thereby the relevance and validity of any form of conflict management.

Two basic types of interactions, each with its own system of activities and internal logic, may characterize the behavior of the parties in conflict. Such interactions may be defined as distributive and integrative (Walton and McKersie 1965; Ikle 1966; Morley and Stephenson 1977). Distributive interactions are characterized by competitive behavior, commitments, misperceptions, and other processes that may intensify a conflict. Communication between the actors is controlled or distorted, and any outcomes that are attained are based upon disassociative policies (e.g., increasing spatial distance) or institutionalization. Distributive interactions tend to be most common in single-issue, zero-sum negotiations, as was the case in the example of the negotiations over nuclear weapons between the United States and North Korea.

Integrative interactions, on the other hand, call for openness, a willingness to countenance new possibilities, and behavior that is exploratory and problem-solving rather than selective and ritualistic. When parties have shared interests or opportunities for mutual gain, and when the negotiations contain multiple issues, negotiations can be integrative instead of distributive (Watkins and Rosegrant 2001: 31). Integrative interactions can lead to associative outcomes that enlarge the common interests of both parties. Integrative interactions are manifestly dissimilar to distributive interactions; consequently, each party must decide whether to engage in the one or other form of bargaining and negotiation. In order to channel the negotiations toward integrative outcomes, negotiators must be able to deal with sets of issues and put together attractive packages that are responsive to the needs of the conflict parties.

The literature on negotiations suggests that for negotiation to be successful there is a need to move from "distributive bargaining" to "integrative bargaining" approaches (Jeong 2000: 170). Distributive bargaining refers to a bargaining structure of zero-sum, where a gain for one side results in a loss for the other. It is hard to reach a favorable outcome when the conflict is perceived as a zero-sum game, since this implies that there are no common interests that can form the basis of any agreement. The best outcome will be achieved only if the parties are convinced that their conflict is not an inevitably zero-sum situation and that a win-win solution is attainable through integrative bargaining. Pruitt and Carnevale (1993) suggest that in order to achieve joint gains through integrative bargaining, several potential points of agreement must exist where one side's gain does not adversely affect the other's interest. This can be achieved by constructing multiple options that contain different combinations of reciprocal concessions. They also suggest seeking outside resources to expand the possibilities of a beneficial outcome to the negotiation. In this sense, joint gains can be found through trade-offs in different priorities, because most conflicts, instead of being strictly zero-sum, entail differentially valued interests.

International factors refer to a multitude of variables that affect the conflict interactions between the parties. The most prominent of these are:

1. The parties' motivation and attitudes toward each other (e.g., cooperative or competitive, symmetric or asymmetric);
2. The distribution of power (e.g., equal or unequal);
3. The process of communication (e.g., open and trusting or misleading and controlled);
4. The utilization of various social influence strategies (e.g., rewarding or coercive strategies).

There is clearly a strong relationship between these variables and bargaining effectiveness (Deutsch 1973; Rubin and Brown 1975).

The institutionalization of bargaining and negotiation as an effective conflict management mechanism is dependent on, and is rooted in, these four classes of factors. Any approach to bargaining and negotiation that does not consider these factors commits itself to the realm of myths and beliefs and to the very periphery of our understanding of conflict management.

Obstacles to Successful Negotiation

Although negotiation is the most frequently preferred conflict resolution method in international relations, it often fails to produce a negotiated solution or a political agreement. Various factors impede the attainment of a negotiated solution. In order to develop a better understanding of the bargaining and negotiation process and to devise better strategies, it is necessary to identify the barriers to effective negotiation and to advance negotiations by overcoming them. The factors that hinder reaching an agreement can be categorized in the following manner.

Structural Barriers

The structure of the negotiations can prove to be a barrier in reaching an agreement. Structural barriers refer to the parties, issues, interests, linkages, and so on. An ex-

ample of a structural barrier may relate to parties refusing to recognize one another (e.g., it is very difficult to get negotiations going in any situation where one party refuses to recognize the validity or legitimacy of the other), refusal to deal with the core issues to a conflict, refusal to communicate honestly, and a basic lack of faith in negotiation. All these will of course lead to continued conflict rather than resolution.

Strategic Barriers

One of the most significant issues that negotiators have to deal with is uncertainty. In circumstances where there is a high level of uncertainty about intentions and the parties feel vulnerable, strategic barriers may rise. This means that negotiators make rational strategic choices that may lead to impasse or suboptimal agreements (Watkins and Rosegrant 2001: 60). In order to overcome strategic barriers and to develop trust, parties have a number of options. They can arrange to observe each other's actions as a way of reducing mutual uncertainty, or they can make credible mutual commitments to devastating retaliation in the event of noncompliance. They may choose to proceed in a series of small and mutually verifiable steps, making future gains contingent on meeting current obligations and embedding current negotiations in a larger context to avoid end-game effects. Another possible option is to involve external guarantors of the agreement who will ensure the parties comply with their predetermined obligations.

Psychological Barriers

One of the crucial obstacles to overcome in negotiations concerns the psychological barriers. Common psychological barriers include rigid mental models, overconfidence, loss aversion, partisan perception, and groupthink. Within this grouping, mental models link observation to interpretation and allow people to make sense of their experience. These mental models reflect the beliefs regarding cause-and-effect relationships, intentions of others, and the way in which history is understood. Overconfidence rests on the desire to feel competent and secure, resulting in negotiators' belief that future uncertainties will be resolved in their favor.

Loss aversion refers to the observation that people tend to be more sensitive to potential losses than equivalent gains. Settlement of a conflict may require parties to accept painful short-term losses in return for larger long-term gains. Watkins and Rosegrant (2001: 65) state that this has been the case in the early stages of the Oslo peace process. The Israelis had to accept Arafat's return and a handover of territory in Gaza and the West Bank. Although this was a difficult decision on the part of the Israelis, and it certainly caused short-term problems, it was a necessary step for achieving longer-term interests.

Partisan perception, on the other hand, refers to the perceptions of the parties regarding the situation and each other's actions. The accumulated psychological residues, emotional associations, and expectations create perceptual distortions, alter the attitudes of the disputants, and may impede reaching an agreement. Groupthink refers to the internal cohesion that increases among groups with the outbreak of the conflict situation. Groupthink refers to the psychological process that distinguishes "us" from "them" and locks the parties in an in-group/out-group consciousness. Such an attitude discourages contact with the Other and creates mistrust while increasing in-group solidarity. Overcoming psychological barriers is exceptionally difficult but crucial to the negotiation process.

Institutional Barriers

During a negotiation process, internal political and organizational factors may impede reaching a negotiated agreement. This becomes especially significant in protracted and intractable conflicts where hard-liners or "spoilers" invariably seek to thwart the moderates' attempts to reach a negotiated settlement. Terrorist attacks by extremist groups, for example, can effectively undermine the negotiation process. When this is the case, leaders and moderates at all levels have to work hard to foster and sustain public support for the "peace process."

It is also crucial for a negotiation team to be well organized and to have the authorization to devote the necessary resources to the process. Being ready and well organized helps the parties, strengthens their strategic capabilities, and is therefore very important to the negotiation process.

Cultural Barriers

Although conflict resolution scholars tend to avoid culture as a dimension of conflict and conflict management, the alarming increase in ethnic and religious conflict has rendered its study inevitable and necessary. Culture plays a considerable role in the negotiation and bargaining process, and negotiators have recognized the importance of paying attention to cultural sensitivities and symbols.

Although culture may serve as a resource to resolve

conflicts (e.g., in cultures with authentic mechanisms and value systems that may promote peace), culture may also pose a barrier to a negotiated agreement. Conflict situations often enhance group cohesion, give rise to narratives of victimhood, and cement hostile images of the Other that justify the use of violence. This can lead to ethnocentric worldviews and, together with the psychological barriers mentioned earlier, contribute to stereotypical and dehumanizing perceptions of the Other. In this case, culture in the form of ethnocentrism becomes one of the main obstacles to overcome in negotiation and bargaining processes.

Culture also influences communication and decision-making processes in negotiation and bargaining. Different cultures may inhibit or sanction distinctive patterns of communication and decision making. Culture influences the symbolization processes and worldviews of the parties. For these reasons, understanding cultural traits and filters to recognize the ideas and behaviors of the Other makes distinguishing cultural diversity in the decision-making process easier. However, culture is not an answer to all the problems in a negotiation process. Human beings have the ability to learn and understand other cultures and develop better understanding of each other. In order to do that, negotiators must be acquainted with ways to analyze culture.

Understanding culture requires exploring the underlying assumptions that its members take for granted (Cohen 1991). For negotiators, the most germane cultural assumptions are those involving power and value. In order to develop an understanding of another culture one needs to analyze artifacts: the visible signs, symbols, and communication styles that demonstrate preferences for directness or indirectness, or use of nonverbal communication. One must also analyze social norms, the shared rules that guide behavior and attitudes toward time and timeliness, and assumptions, which are the deeper, often unspoken beliefs that infuse and underpin social systems.

Bargaining and Negotiation Strategies

Theories and approaches have been developed to analyze actual negotiation behavior in order to predict, or at least explain, negotiation behavior, as negotiation occupies an important practical and theoretical space in managing conflicts. Many of these approaches treat negotiation "as a way of waging a contest, and prescriptions are about how to win for yourself and your side" (Kriesberg 1998a: 265). Other conceptualizations consider negotiation "a way to reach mutually acceptable and even beneficial agreements, and prescriptions aim to efficiently and effectively attain such outcomes for all parties in negotiations" (265).

Generally, negotiations are viewed as the continuation of conflict by other means, since the parties attempt to maximize their gains and compel the other party to make concessions. This perception has led many theorists to develop a theoretical framework that aims to inform practitioners on how to maximize gains. This approach perceives conflicts as zero-sum, where concessions reflect weakness. Nevertheless, this perspective embraces the belief that a series of concessions by opposing sides will be made and an agreement reached somewhere between the opposing opening positions, around the midpoint between them (Kriesberg 1998: 266). In order to advance their own interests, the adherents of this approach suggest taking a hard-line position in negotiations, and they argue that firmly staking out a desired solution and embracing it will result in the maximization of advantages (266). According to this theoretical perspective, bargaining strategies, and the advantages of staking out a relatively high opening position are the center of attention. The use of threats and coercion to influence the other party is a common strategy advocated by this approach.

The critics of the aforementioned approach suggest that negotiations should instead be based on a problem-solving approach. In an attempt to introduce this perspective, Fisher and Ury (1981) developed the "principled negotiation" approach, which argues that with positional bargaining, negotiators will play either a soft or a hard game, but they should change the game and negotiate on merits. This approach suggests that negotiators should separate people from problems and focus on interests rather than positions. They suggest that this approach enables the negotiators to formulate options for mutual gain.

Furthermore, negotiators are advised to generate many possible options to solve the problem through brainstorming sessions, where all participants are encouraged to suggest alternative ideas and solutions. These ideas may then form the basis of new discussions that can lead to an agreement. Based on the same idea, Zartman and Berman (1982) proposed that under specific conditions a reconfiguration of the conflict may lead to mutually beneficial, or at least mutually acceptable, agreements. The reconfiguration must be based on joint action, as unilaterally imposed settlements are not feasible. This perspective suggests that reconfiguring the conflict in order to ensure it is no longer perceived as zero-sum will encourage the parties to formulate solutions that will be acceptable to both sides.

These two approaches are often complementary, and many negotiators regularly synthesize them. As Kriesberg (1998: 271) notes, "an analysis of the conflict that is to be subjected to negotiation, it is widely recognized, is an important first step to effective negotiation." Such analysis requires a careful examination of the available alternatives if a negotiated agreement cannot be reached. In this case, negotiators must prepare their best alternatives to a negotiated agreement (BATNA).

The major difference between these two approaches is that those who advocate maximizing interests believe in the necessity of changing the external reality by increasing the costs of the other side if they fail to reach an agreement. Problem solvers, in contrast, argue that changing the other side's BATNA may be affected by changing the frame within which the conflict is viewed. The proponents of this view suggest achieving that goal through persuasion and insights gained from exploring the perspective of the opposing sides (Kriesberg 1998). Those who argue that both approaches should be combined suggest that the problem-solving approach must be understood broadly to include strategies of constructive struggle that may foster conditions that encourage problem-solving negotiations and reaching outcomes that minimize injustice. However, these strategies may also include escalating the conflict by mobilizing broad support and adhering to policies that do not deny the humanity of the opponents (Kriesberg 1998).

Conclusion

This chapter has considered negotiations as a crucial response to conflict in any system of interactions, let alone the international system. The guiding assumption underpinning our analysis is that conflict is an inherent part of the human condition and that there are many ways of dealing with, or managing, conflicts. Whichever form of conflict resolution is adopted, it is clear that it will contain some elements of negotiation, whether explicitly or implicitly. Negotiation is central in conflict resolution. It is a universal process of conflict resolution. It is used by all societies and organizations, and it is embedded, legally or normatively, in many systems of relations (e.g., labor-management relations, international diplomacy). As a form of conflict resolution, negotiation represents the very essence of interactions between multiple, sovereign, and legally equal states in international relations.

Human relationships are so diverse and conflict behavior is so pervasive that it is naturally difficult to capture the complexity of this central process of interaction with a single, all-encompassing concept or idea. Indeed, many practitioners and observers of negotiation caution us against the practice of theorizing about such a complex process (Zartman 1975). Having discarded the notion that the negotiation process is beyond conceptualization, we have sought to understand the process of bargaining and negotiation by recognizing that personal, environmental, and systemic factors produce conflict and that these factors should be separated and studied whenever one approaches the subject of conflict and conflict management. Any approach that has its origins in this basis can help us to apply work from various fields and consolidate our cumulative knowledge. The social-psychological approach, as presented here, offers the prospect of a broader and more integrated framework on the nature, development, and outcomes of bargaining and negotiation.

The social-psychological approach is seen as the most suitable approach, not only because of its theoretical relevance but also because an assessment of bargaining determinants might move us closer to the task of offering policy recommendations to conflict management practitioners. A number of recommendations, derived from the writings of those who employ this approach, are worth highlighting.

1. Divide complex issues into smaller, more manageable issues
2. Deal with less contentious issues first
3. Concentrate on problems, not personalities
4. Accept third-party assistance, if offered
5. Do not overuse threats or commitments
6. Adopt a general definition before hammering out the details
7. Reciprocate concessions

These recommendations are equally applicable to interpersonal bargaining as they are to international negotiations.

The social-psychological approach, which can generate policy recommendations, can also generate hypotheses and advance further research on bargaining and negotiation. It tells us which cluster of variables account for specific aspects of bargaining and negotiation (e.g., increased responsiveness to role factors leads to increases in competitive behavior), and it tells us what might be done about these aspects (e.g., a strong third party that conveys its own proposals and facilitates secrecy can counteract high role-responsiveness). In sum, the social-psychological approach is the only one that *describes* how people behave and *prescribes* how they should behave; it is also the only approach with both heuristic and prescriptive value.

There are still big gaps in our understanding of conflict resolution, but the strategy of offering broad interpretations and blending them with empirical evidence can go some way toward the development of a theory of bargaining and negotiation. The analytical rigor of the social-psychological approach provides us with such a strategy. What is now required is further study of the relative importance of the clusters of factors and intervention strategies that are associated with successful outcomes. A long, major research effort should be undertaken before we can expect any significant gains. The task is a long-range one; the need, however, is immediate and overwhelming.

CHAPTER THREE

Mediation and International Conflict Resolution

When negotiations fail, or for some reason one or both parties in conflict refuse to communicate, states will often seek or accept mediation by an outside person, party, or organization to assist with their conflict resolution efforts. As a method of conflict resolution, the practice of settling disputes through intermediaries has had a rich history in all cultures, both Western and non-Western (Gulliver 1979). In the international arena, with its perennial challenges of escalating conflicts, an anarchical system, the absence of generally accepted "rules of the game," and an alarming growth in internal and ethnic conflicts, third-party mediation is as common as conflict itself. As a form of international conflict resolution, third-party mediation is particularly likely to take place when: (1) conflicts are long, drawn-out, and complex; (2) the parties' own conflict resolution efforts have reached an impasse; (3) neither side is prepared to countenance further costs or escalation; and (4) the parties are prepared to cooperate in an attempt to break their stalemate (Bercovitch 1984).

Mediation is fast becoming one of the most important methods of resolving international conflicts. Even a cursory survey of recent conflicts reveals the extent, and heterogeneity, of international mediation. In the last decade we have seen the involvement of the United Nations (in the Vietnam-Kampuchea dispute, the Falklands-Malvinas conflict, and the Afghanistan conflict), the pope (in the Beagle Channel dispute), African Union (in the Tanzania-Uganda dispute, the South West Africa dispute, and more recently in Zimbabwe), Economic Community of West African States (ECOWAS) in the Ivory Coast dispute, the Swiss-based Centre for Humanitarian Dialogue (in Aceh), the Organization of American States (in the Nicaragua dispute), the Arab League and the Islamic Conference (in the Iran-Iraq dispute), small states (Algeria's role in the U.S.-Iran hostage crisis, Norway in the Israeli-Palestinian conflict), and powerful states (numerous efforts by Condoleezza Rice in the Middle East). Systematic empirical studies suggest that mediation is used in about 70 percent of all conflicts and achieves some success in 34 percent of the cases (see Bercovitch and Gartner 2008). Less formal (e.g., Quakers' mediation) or institutionalized (e.g., mediation by individuals) mediation of international conflicts occurs on a daily basis. Whichever way we look at it, mediation has been, and remains, a central feature of interstate relations.

The challenges of the post–Cold War era, with its increased instability, sudden change in many of the accepted rules of the game, growing economic disparity and resource scarcity, the proliferation of intense ethnic and other identity-based conflicts, and the threats posed by different forms of terrorism, will no doubt require us to use mediation even more frequently than in the past. Mediation may be the closest thing we have to an effective technique for dealing with the complex, difficult, and asymmetric conflicts in the twenty-first century. It is suited to a heterogeneous environment, multiple actors, wide disparities, and insistence on some mythical equality and formalized rules of interaction. For this reason alone, it is essential that we study mediation seriously and systematically. In an increasingly interdependent world, conflicts affect us all; their proper resolution belongs to us all.

A Conceptual Framework for Mediation

For many years, the study of mediation has suffered from conceptual imprecision and a startling lack of information. Practitioners of mediation, formal or informal, in the domestic or international arena were keen to sustain its image as a mysterious practice, akin to some art form, taking place behind closed doors. On the other hand, scholars of mediation did not think their field of study was susceptible to a systematic analysis. In short, neither group believed that it could discern any pattern of behavior in the various forms of mediation, or that any generalizations could be made about the practice in general. Descriptive and ideographic approaches only characterized the approach to mediation.

The study of mediation in international relations and the development of a theory of mediation have been beset by two major problems: first, the difficulty of defining the subject matter; and second, the absence of empirically oriented studies. Both these matters need to be addressed if a conceptual framework is to be developed and the gaps in our knowledge closed. Mediation is the most common form of third-party intervention. However, it is not a discrete activity but rather a continuous process. It falls somewhere on a spectrum of behavior that ranges from the highly passive (e.g., go-between) to the highly active (e.g., putting pressure on disputants). The form and character of mediation in a particular conflict is determined by a range of factors including the nature of the dispute, the nature of the mediator, and a number of other cultural and contextual variables.

The prevalent agnosticism toward analysis and the desire to maintain the intuitive mystique of mediation are best exemplified in the comments of two noted American labor mediators. Arthur Meyer, commenting on the role of mediators, notes that "the task of the mediator is not an easy one. The sea that he sails is only roughly charted, and its changing contours are not clearly discernible. He has no science of navigation, no fund inherited from the experience of others. He is a solitary artist recognizing at most a few guiding stars, and depending on his personal powers of divination" (1960: 160). William Simkin, an equally respected practitioner of mediation, comments in a more prosaic but no less emphatic fashion that "the variables are so many that it would be an exercise in futility to describe typical mediator behavior with respect to sequence, timing or the use or non-use of the various functions theoretically available" (1971: 118). This kind of sentiment does not take us very far.

The most helpful approach to mediation sees it as an extension of negotiation, a closely related form of conflict resolution, but one with its unique features and conditions. The parameters of such an approach were established by Carl Stevens and Thomas Schelling. Stevens states that "mediation, like other social phenomena, is susceptible to systematic analysis. The key to analysis is in recognizing that where mediation is employed it is an integral part of the bargaining process. . . . [A]n analysis of mediation is not possible except in the context of general analysis of bargaining negotiations" (1963: 123). In a similar vein, Schelling notes that a mediator "is probably best viewed as an element in the communication arrangements, or as a third party with a payoff structure of his own" (1960: 22).

Definition of Mediation

Mediation differs from other accommodative strategies such as arbitration (in its nonbinding character) and negotiation (in its triadic rather than dyadic structure). Etymologically, mediation comes from Latin origin "to halve," but different definitions of mediation purport to: (1) capture the general picture of what mediators do or hope to achieve; (2) distinguish between mediation and related processes of third-party intervention (e.g., arbitration); and (3) describe mediators' attributes. It is worthwhile to examine some definitions of mediation and assess their implications.

Oran Young defines mediation as "any action taken by an actor that is not a direct party to the crisis, that is designed to reduce or remove one or more of the problems of the bargaining relationship, and therefore to facilitate the termination of the crisis itself" (1967: 34). In a similar vein, Chris Mitchell defines mediation as any "intermediary activity . . . undertaken by a third party with the primary intention of achieving some compromise settlement of the issues at stake between the parties, or at least ending disruptive conflict behavior" (1981: 287). In a more detailed fashion, Blake and Mouton define mediation as a process involving "the intervention of a third party who first investigates and defines the problem and then usually approaches each group separately with recommendations designed to provide a mutually acceptable solution" (1985: 15).

Other definitions are less outcome-oriented and focus on the act of the intervention itself. Christopher Moore defines it as "an extension and elaboration of the negotiation process. Mediation involves the intervention of an acceptable, impartial, and neutral third party who has no authoritative decision-making power to assist contending parties in voluntarily reaching their own mutually acceptable settlement" (1986: 6). And Linda Singer defines it as a "form of third-party assistance [that] involves an outsider to the dispute who lacks the power to make decisions for the parties" (1990, 20).

A range of definitions also focus on neutrality and impartiality as the distinguishing features of mediation. Gail Bingham defines mediation as the "assistance of a 'neutral' third party to a negotiation" (1985: 5). Jay Folberg and Alison Taylor see mediation "as the process by which the participants, together with the assistance of a neutral person or persons, systematically isolate disputed issues in order to develop options, consider alternatives, and reach a consensual settlement that will accommodate their needs" (Taylor 1984: 7). Finally, Spencer and Yang see mediation as "the assistance of a third party not involved in the dispute, who may be of a unique status that gives him or her certain authority with the disputants; or perhaps an outsider who may be regarded by them as a suitably neutral go-between" (1992: 1495).

Some may consider this quibbling over definitions as inconsequential, merely an exercise in academic nit-picking. It is most emphatically not so. The myriad possible mediators and the range of mediation roles and strategies are so wide as to defeat many attempts to understand the essence of mediation. In the absence of a generally accepted definition, there is a tendency to identify mediation with one particular role (e.g., a go-between) or a single strategy (e.g., offering proposals). This does not help us to understand the reality of international mediation. Assigning an exclusive role or strategy to one kind of mediation overlooks the dynamics of the process. It is also detrimental to the search for common and divergent dimensions of mediation in international and other social contexts, and the effort to draw general lessons from mediation experience. The reality of international mediation is that of a complex and dynamic interaction between mediators who have resources and an interest in the conflict or its outcome, and the protagonists or their representatives who wish to see their conflict resolved. In any given conflict, mediators may change, their role may be redefined, the issues may alter, and what is expected from a mediator may change at every phase of the conflict. At times even the parties involved in the conflict may and often do change. To understand this complex reality, a broad definition of the process is required. Mediation is defined here as a process of conflict management, related to but distinct from the parties' own negotiations, where those in conflict seek the assistance of, or accept an offer of help from, an outsider (whether an individual, an organization, a group, or a state) to change their perceptions or behavior, and to do so without resorting to physical force or invoking the authority of the law (Bercovitch 1992: 7).

This may be a broad definition, but it is one that can be generally and widely applied. It encourages us to recognize that any mediation situation comprises (1) parties in conflict, (2) a mediator, (3) a process of mediation, and (4) the context of mediation. All these elements are important; together they determine the nature, quality, and effectiveness of the mediation and indicate why some efforts at mediation succeed while others fail.

Characteristics of Mediation

Mediation is, at least structurally, the continuation of negotiations by other means. What mediators are able to do in their efforts to resolve a conflict may depend, to some extent, on who they are and what resources and competencies they can bring to bear. Ultimately, though, their efforts depend on who the parties are, the context of the conflict, the issues at stake, and the nature of their interaction. "Mediation," as Stulberg rightly notes, "is a procedure predicated upon the process of negotiation" (1981: 87). Mediation is, above all, adaptive and responsive. It extends the process of negotiation to reflect different conflicts, different parties, and different situations; to assume otherwise is to mistake wishful thinking for reality.

What, then, are the main features or characteristics of mediation across levels?

1. Mediation is an extension and continuation of peaceful conflict resolution.
2. Mediation involves the intervention of an outsider—an individual, a group, or an organization—into a conflict between two or more states or other actors.
3. Mediation is a noncoercive, nonviolent, and, ultimately, nonbinding form of intervention.
4. Mediators enter a conflict, whether internal or international, in order to affect, change, resolve, modify, or influence it in some way. Mediators use personal or structural resources to achieve these objectives.
5. Mediators bring with them, consciously or otherwise, ideas, knowledge, resources, and interests of their own or of the group or organization they represent. Mediators often have their own assumptions and agendas about the conflict in question.
6. Mediation is a voluntary form of conflict management.

The actors involved retain control over the outcome (if not always over the process) of their conflict, as well as the freedom to accept or reject mediation or mediators' proposals.

7. Mediation usually operates on an ad hoc basis only.

Elements of Mediation

Every mediation effort has four core elements: (1) the parties; (2) the issues or the nature of the dispute; (3) the mediator; and (4) the context. All the elements must be analyzed to understand the outcome in a particular mediation.

The Identity and Characteristics of the Parties

Conflict resolution by third parties can be effective only when the adversaries have well-defined and legitimate identities (by this we mean a legitimate authority in a country), or when the countries involved have similar political values and commitments (e.g., joint democracies). A mediator's job is most complex if the incumbent government of one of the adversaries is experiencing an insurgency, rebellion, or other serious internal threat. Mediation has a better chance of success when the adversaries are recognized as the legitimate spokesmen for their parties. Disunity or lack of cohesion within a state makes it difficult for both the adversaries and the mediator to engage in any meaningful form of conflict settlement because the state's representatives lack power or authority to make decisions or concessions. The repeated failure of mediation attempts in Lebanon, Cyprus, Sudan, Ethiopia, and Fiji illustrates this point only too well. The more clearly identifiable and united conflict parties are, the higher the chances of a successful mediation (Modelski 1964; Burton 1968).

Issues or the Nature of the Dispute

There is a general agreement in the literature that "the success or failure of mediation is largely determined by the nature of the dispute" (Ott 1972: 597). The importance adversaries attach to the issues in a dispute will naturally affect the choice of conflict management style and the chances of a successful mediation. When vital interests are at stake, such as issues of sovereignty or territorial integrity, intermediaries will be unlikely to have much impact on the dispute. Is it possible to go beyond this rather obvious point and identify some aspects of a dispute more specifically, then assess their effect on international mediation?

The literature on mediation abounds with notions linking its effectiveness to the nature of the issues in dispute. Mervin Ott sees the "absence of vital national security interests, particularly questions of territorial control" as a necessary precondition for successful mediation (1972: 616). Robert Randle contends that "should a dispute affect vital security interests of the parties, no amount of mediation by a third party is likely to prevent the outbreak of hostilities" (1973: 49). Arthur Lall, a practitioner as well as a student of international mediation, contends that "it is one of the principles of international negotiation that when territory is at stake, the party in possession tends to resist third party involvement" (1966: 100). What they all seem to suggest is that the parties' perception of the issues is a key factor in determining whether to accept a mediation initiative and whether it will have much success.

The Identity and Characteristics of the Mediator

Regarding the importance of the identity and characteristics of a mediator, academic opinion varies. Scholars such as Young (1967) see the nature of the mediator as a key predictor of success, while others including Ott (1972) relegate it to a secondary position. It seems possible to argue that the personal characteristics of a mediator differentiate effective from ineffective mediation or, alternatively, that personal traits are essentially irrelevant. It is, however, still useful to investigate the relationship between mediators' characteristics and effective mediation.

Mediation is a voluntary process. This means that mediators cannot mediate unless they are perceived as reasonable, acceptable, knowledgeable, and able to secure the trust and cooperation of the disputants. Elmore Jackson, an experienced international mediator, makes this quite clear: "It would be difficult, if not impossible, for a single mediator, who was distrusted by one of the parties, to carry out any useful function" (1952: 129). To be accepted by the adversaries, and to secure their positive attitudes and disposition, a mediator must be perceived as independent and credible. The adversaries' motivation to engage in conflict management and their confidence in a mediator will be enhanced if both sides see a mediator as an impartial yet skilled participant in the process.

Effective mediation is dependent on not only the mediator's knowledge and skill regarding conflict and conflict resolution but also their prestige and authority, originality of ideas, access to resources, and ability to act unobtrusively. Paul Wehr, in a theoretical discussion, lists the required attributes for successful mediation as including: (1) knowledge about conflict situations; (2) an ability to understand the positions of the antagonists; (3) active listening; (4) a sense of timing; (5) communication skills; (6) procedural skills (e.g., chairing meetings); and (7) crisis management (1979). A mediator is not expected to be an omniscient polymath or a modern version of a Renaissance man, but to be effective he or she should have at least a few of these traits.

The list of desired personal attributes for a successful international mediator is very long indeed. Among the attributes that experienced mediators cite as particularly important are intelligence, stamina, energy, patience, and a sense of humor (Bercovitch 1984). Such personal qualities are associated with success in other areas of human endeavor; they are, of course, no less important in international mediation. Trust, credibility, and a high degree of personal skill and competence are necessary preconditions for effective mediation (Landsberger 1960; Karim and Pegnetter 1983).

Another characteristic that has been traditionally cited as strongly associated with effective mediation is evenhandedness or impartiality. Young (1967: 81) claims that "a high score in such areas as impartiality would seem to be at the heart of successful interventions in many situations." His views are echoed by Jackson (1952) and Northedge and Donelan (1971), who claim that disputants will only have confidence in mediators who are impartial, both in their approach to mediation and in how they are perceived by the parties. Impartiality is thus presented as the key to successful mediation.

This is not very helpful. The traditional emphasis on impartiality stems from the failure to recognize mediation as a structural extension of bilateral bargaining and negotiation. It makes a lot of sense to see mediation as "assisted negotiation" (Susskind and Cruickshank 1987). To suggest that mediation is a totally exogenous input with no interests or preferences is both erroneous and unrealistic. A mediator engages in behavior that is designed to elicit information and exercise influence. To exercise any degree of influence mediators need "leverage" or resources. Leverage or mediator power enhances the mediator's ability to influence the outcome (Siniver 2006). The mediator's task is primarily one of reframing and persuasion, which is best achieved, as Zartman and Touval observe, not when a mediator is unbiased or impartial but instead when he or she possesses resources that either or both parties value (Zartman and Touval 1985, 2007). In short, effective mediation in international relations seems to depend more on resources (by which we mean diplo-matic, economic, status, and skills) than on impartiality (Brookmire and Sistrunk 1980).

Context

The final critical element of the mediation process is the context within which it takes place. Mediation cannot be viewed in isolation from the social and international context in which it is inextricably embedded. This context affects the nature as well as the outcome of the mediation process.

Context refers to such factors as the history of a conflict, the interaction between the parties, their relationship to the mediator, and the nature of the international environment in which it occurs. It also refers to the environment in which the mediation process takes place. Is it a formal diplomatic environment, or an informal and flexible environment? The environment influences the perceptions of the parties, as well as their reactions and options. Disparities between the power of the parties and the mediator are also part of this context, and they have a significant effect on the mediation process. The international economic, political, and social arena may pressure the parties to accept a resolution of their conflict and influence the conditions and choice of potential mediators.

Approaches to Mediation

The study of international mediation has attracted numerous scholars and produced a diverse range of approaches and perspectives (see Kolb and Rubin 1991). These approaches—a seemingly endless variety of them—include purely scholarly studies, policy implications, reflections of the mediators themselves, and studies suggesting that academics should act as third parties in mediation efforts. Some approaches offer prescriptive guidelines to practitioners, while others focus on descriptions and theory development. The following section identifies the three primary traditions in the study of international mediation.

The first group of studies is essentially prescriptive and is devoted to offering advice on what constitutes good conflict management in real-world situations (e.g., see Fisher and Ury 1981). These studies, mostly developed by scholars associated with the Program on Negotiation at Harvard University, generate books and manuals on how mediators and negotiators should behave, what constitutes good negotiation or mediation, and how conflicts—serious or otherwise—can be resolved.

Other studies of mediation (in a variety of contexts) are based on theoretical notions and the participation of academic practitioners in a variety of actual conflicts, with the aim of testing ideas and developing a generic theory for the resolution of social conflicts. These studies use a variety of interaction and problem-solving techniques to combine political action with scientific experimentation and thus contribute to the development of a set of rules that can address all (not just international) conflicts. Some of this research (see Burton 1969, 1972, 1984; Doob 1971; Fisher 1983; Kelman 1992; Bercovitch and Rubin 1992; Walton 1969) has generated valuable insights, but much of it is still resistant to any form of empirical analysis (by its very nature it has to be secret), and it is hard to assess its outcomes (as they are dependent on what the parties say or feel).

The third set of studies uses actual descriptions and empirical examinations of mediation cases. These studies seek to develop theories and to offer general guidelines through: (1) the detailed description of a particular case of international mediation (see Ott 1972; Rubin 1981); (2) laboratory and experimental approaches to mediation that examine how parties and mediators behave in controlled circumstances (see Bartunek et al. 1975; Rubin 1980); and (3) large-scale systematic studies that draw on numerous cases of international mediation to formulate and test propositions about effective mediation and to assess the conditions under which mediation efforts may be more effective (see Bercovitch and Rubin 1992; Touval and Zartman 1985). This tradition is arguably the most fruitful approach, producing the most relevant policy implications for decision makers.

The Contingency Approach

Neither the anecdotal nor the third-party consultation approach is quite satisfactory. The former emphasizes the objective aspects of a dispute, assuming that all cases are different and that nothing meaningful can be derived about kinds of mediation and dispute outcomes. The latter, concerning itself with the subjective elements of perception and communication, assumes that no conflict is too intractable and that experienced third parties can remove all the obstacles to a successful resolution. Neither approach has really stimulated much-needed empirical research to date. Therefore, a fourth and more promising method of analysis is one that we refer to as the "contin-

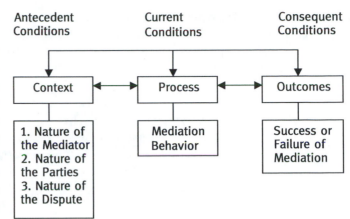

FIG. 5.   A contingency model of mediation

gency approach" to understanding mediation (fig. 5). This approach treats the outcomes of mediation efforts (be they successful or unsuccessful) as dependent, or contingent, upon the environment (or context) of a conflict and the manner of behavior within it (i.e., process). This approach holds that there are conflict situations where mediation can be an effective form of conflict resolution. Likewise, there are situations where mediation simply cannot achieve anything either proactively or reactively. A key task for the scholar is to distinguish between these two kinds of conflict. The contingency approach helps us address the two central questions in the study of international mediation: when to mediate and whether mediation is likely to be successful.

Factors Influencing Mediation

The different approaches to mediation outlined here often complement and sometimes contrast with one another. They can all, however, provide useful insights on the three most relevant questions in mediation: Why mediate? How does one mediate? When is mediation most likely to be successful? The following examines these questions in detail.

As a legitimate form of international peacemaking and an expression of the basic norm of peaceful resolution of conflicts, mediation is most likely to take place when: (1) a conflict is long, drawn-out, or complex; (2) the parties' own conflict-management efforts have reached an impasse; (3) neither party is prepared to countenance further costs or loss of life; and (4) both parties are prepared to cooperate, tacitly or openly, to break their stalemate

(Bercovitch 1984). When these conditions prevail, the parties may have a high motivation to resolve a conflict, and a potential mediator will find a strong motivation to settle immensely helpful.

Other factors, beyond those that relate to the conflict and how it is managed, have an impact on mediation, both on how it unfolds and its outcomes. These factors may be categorized as follows: personal and role factors, motivational factors, structural factors, and interactional factors.

Personal and Role Factors

As an instrument of diplomacy and foreign policy, mediation has become almost as common as conflict itself. Mediation is carried out daily by such disparate actors as private individuals; government officials; religious figures; regional, nongovernmental, and international organizations; ad hoc groupings; and states of all sizes. Different mediators bring their own interests, perceptions, and resources to the mediation situation. Each of them may adopt behavior that ranges from the very passive, through the facilitative, to the highly active.

Traditional approaches to mediation assume that conflict parties and a mediator share one compelling reason for initiating mediation: a desire to reduce, abate, or resolve a conflict (Horowitz 2007: 51–63). To this end, both sides may invest considerable personnel, time, and resources in the mediation. In reality, however, the mediation process is time-consuming, involves risks (of failure and uncertainty), and may result in failure (as it often does). Furthermore, not every actor can afford to mediate, or has the credibility and time. As a result, while a shared humanitarian interest usually does play a role in the decision to mediate, it is very rare that this is the only genuine reason for mediation; humanitarian interests are normally intertwined with other, less altruistic, motivations (Horowitz 2007).

Wall, Stark, and Standifer (2001) argue that interacting parties' motivation to seek assistance and the third parties' motivations to mediate are determined by "expected payoffs" that raise the participants' expectations regarding the benefits they will receive from the process. For a state in conflict, the payoffs may include increased financial or diplomatic support, or concessions for partaking in mediation (see Terris and Maoz 2005). For a mediator, improved relations with the competing parties, personal status, the prestige of being involved in the process, and a number of other payoffs may be motivating

factors (see Zartman and Touval 2007). For a mediator, mediation may well be seen as the continuation of foreign policy by other means.

Another factor that may affect mediation is the mediator's identity, experience, and skills. Mediation is a voluntary process, so only an appropriate, mutually acceptable mediator is likely to be effective. There is a consensus among scholars and practitioners that appropriate mediators should possess intelligence, tact, skills in drafting formal proposals, and a sense of humor, in addition to specific knowledge of the conflict at hand (Bercovitch 1997: 146). Mediators who possess these attributes are more likely to be acceptable to all sides in a conflict and hence overcome one of the main initial obstacles to successful mediation. But what of mediator identity itself? How do we approach this issue and analyze different mediators? The following threefold typology presents a useful way of thinking about and analyzing mediator identity.

Mediation by Individuals

The identity of a mediator may differ from case to case, and ranges along a spectrum from individuals all the way to international institutions. The traditional image of international mediation is usually that of a high-ranking official (such as Carter or Clinton at the Camp David meetings). The individual mediator normally represents his or her government in a series of formal interactions with high-level officials from the countries in conflict. This is a powerful image, much beloved by the media, but it is only partly accurate.

Individual mediation as discussed here refers to interventions conducted by individuals who are not government officials or political incumbents. Although individual mediation exhibits greater variety and experimentation than other forms of mediation, it essentially consists of only two kinds: formal and informal. Informal mediation refers to the efforts of mediators who possess a wealth of experience and commitment to international conflict resolution (e.g., the Quakers; see Yarrow 1978; Bailey 1985). Informal mediation also includes the efforts of knowledgeable scholars whose background, attitudes, and professional experience give them the opportunity to engage in mediation with real conflict parties (some notable examples are the efforts of scholars such as John Burton [1990], Leonard Doob [1974], and Herbert Kelman [1991]). These individuals approach a conflict as private citizens, not as official representatives. They utilize their academic competence, credibility, and experience to facilitate communications, gain a better understanding of the conflict, and work toward its resolution.

The process of informal mediation usually begins when mediators enter a conflict on their own initiative. The format and arrangements of such mediation are, to say the least, novel. Present in a personal capacity only, informal mediators tend to rely on communication-facilitation strategies; the whole tone of the mediation is free and flexible. This kind of process can serve as a useful precursor to a more formal mediation. The efforts of two Israeli academics, Ron Pundak and Yair Hirschfeld, as well as Norwegian Terje Roed-Larsen, exemplify the potential benefits of informal mediation; their efforts paved the way for formal discussions between the Israeli government and the Palestine Liberation Organization (Aggestam 2002).

Another example of informal mediation is the assistance given to parties in conflict by the International Negotiation Network (INN) at the Carter Center. This initiative was created by President Carter in 1986, with assistance from other international leaders, to fill a major mediation gap. Most states and international organizations are prevented from intervening in the internal affairs of another sovereign state. Yet, as the vast majority of recent serious conflicts have largely been internal rather than interstate, a clear need existed for an informal network of prestigious individuals (including former heads of state and UN secretaries-general) to offer additional mediation resources to disputants. The informal mediation conducted by the INN includes a range of methods such as clarifying issues, offering resources, and providing a face-saving option by bringing parties either into mediation or out of a conflict. The INN has been actively involved in various mediation and consultation efforts in Ethiopia, Liberia, Cyprus, Zaire, Burma (Myanmar), Cambodia, and Sudan (Spencer and Yang 1993). In short, the INN has shown just how much can be achieved through informal mediation by individuals.

Formal mediation, on the other hand, takes place when a political incumbent, a government representative, or a high-level decision maker acts in an individual capacity to mediate a conflict between the official representatives of other states. It invariably occurs within a formal structure, such as a conference, a political forum, or other official arena, and is much less flexible than informal mediation. Formal mediation is also less susceptible to the impact of personality. Its loss of flexibility, however, is more than matched by its immediacy of access to influential decision makers. For this reason, formal mediation is often indistinguishable from diplomatic activity; its range of roles is more limited than that of informal mediation, but its impact on outcomes is more direct. One of the more prominent examples of formal mediation is the effort undertaken by U.S. representative Richard Holbrooke, who conducted extensive and direct negotiations with Serbian leaders in 1995 during the Bosnian war, which resulted in the signing of a cease-fire agreement that effectively ended the siege of Sarajevo (Holbrooke 1999).

Mediation by States

Individual mediation, although significant, is not common at the international level. Most mediation efforts are carried out by states (or, to be more accurate, their representatives) and by regional and international organizations.

When a state is invited to mediate, or when it initiates mediation, the services of one of its top decision makers are usually engaged. In these cases, figures such as Henry Kissinger, Presidents Carter or Clinton, former secretary of state Warren Christopher; former assistant secretary of state Chester Crocker, or special representatives like Gunnar Jarring or Philip Habeeb all fulfill mediation roles, usually as representatives of their countries and under the glare and scrutiny of the international media.

When we talk about mediation by states, we normally distinguish between small states and large states, both of which claim legitimacy and authority based on different attributes. Small states such as Algeria, Norway, and Switzerland (see Slim 1992) have been involved in a disproportionate number of international mediations. Their very size and presumed lack of influence make them appear nonthreatening and ideally positioned to carry out mediations in certain types of conflicts. Small states usually wait for an invitation to mediate. When they do intervene, their efforts tend to be confined to regional conflicts, and their strategies tend to be mostly low-profile and commonly entail dialogue and communication (Touval and Zartman 2001: 430). This is where small states can be most useful in mediation efforts.

Large states, by contrast, often create the opportunity to mediate and use the mediation as a vehicle to protect or promote their own interests (Touval 1992a). Because of their global interests, large states become involved in many conflicts in various parts of the world. In the course of mediation a large state has access to a greater pool of resources and can select from a wide range of strategies. This enables them to wield a variety of carrots and sticks throughout the mediation process. They can generate and maintain momentum toward a political settlement by offering a neutral environment (e.g., Camp David or Dayton), pressing for concessions, offering proposals, or generally altering the parties' payoffs and motivations. A classic example of the type of mediation that can be conducted by large powerful states is Jimmy Carter's thirteen-day mediation between Egyptian president Sadat and Israeli prime minister Begin at Camp David. While Carter attempted to employ many problem-solving tactics, being the president of the United States meant that he was also able to utilize the sticks-and-carrots approach. "Carter offered both sides billions of dollars in aid and threatened dire consequences for not agreeing" (Princen 1991: 67).

Mediation, whether conducted by small or large states, is not prescribed by international law. States are advised to use it, but there are no norms governing its usage. It is unpredictable, continuously changing, and its precise form and characteristics are negotiated and renegotiated with each passing phase. There is little that is predetermined about its course or outcomes. There are however many factors that may help mediation, and just as many that may hinder. It behooves us to know the differences between them.

Mediation by Institutions and Organizations

The complexity of the international environment is such that states can no longer facilitate the pursuit of all human interests or satisfy demands for a shrinking range of public sector goods and services the world over. Consequently, we have witnessed a phenomenal growth in the number of international and transnational organizations, all of which may affect issues of war and peace. These organizations have become, in some cases, more important providers of services than states are. In the contemporary international system, they have also become very active participants in the search for mechanisms and procedures conducive to peacemaking and conflict resolution. We would expect these organizations to have a great impact on the mediation of international conflicts.

Three kinds of organizations play an important role in the area of peacemaking and conflict resolution: regional, international, and transnational. Regional and international organizations, such as the Organization of American States (OAS) and the African Union (AU), represent ensembles of states that have signified their intention to fulfill the obligations—including those of formal mediation—of membership as set forth in a formal treaty. Transnational organizations such as Amnesty International represent individuals from different countries who have similar knowledge, skills, or interests, and who meet on a regular basis to promote their common interests through various means, including informal mediation.

Of the international organizations now in existence, none has been more active in resolving conflicts through negotiations and mediation than the United Nations, whose charter (article 33/1) specifically commits it to address global issues pertaining to conflict and security. In the post–Cold War era, with the proliferation of low-level violence, civil wars, and ethnic conflicts, the United Nations is frequently seen as the only actor capable of resolving conflict independently. The *Agenda for Peace*, released by Secretary-General Boutros Boutros-Ghali (1995), recognizes the future challenges the United Nations is likely to encounter and places great emphasis on preventive diplomacy, peacemaking, and postconflict peacebuilding as priorities for the world organization.

Regional organizations, like the European Union (EU), the OAS, the AU, Association of South-East Asian Nations (ASEAN), and the Arab League, all adhere to the principles of negotiation and mediation as their preferred means of resolving conflicts. Because most conflict occurs between regional neighbors, it is not surprising that these organizations have always had great latitude in the field of conflict resolution (Thornton 1991). Some, like the EU and the Organization for Security and Cooperation in Europe (OSCE), have made conflict resolution a major component of their structure. Regional organizations usually engage in collective mediation; their strength undoubtedly is due to their members' common background, culture, and experience. They may not have the capacity or resources of the United Nations, but they are all involved in some current peacemaking activities: the EU in Bosnia, the AU in Somalia, Zimbabwe, and Ethiopia, and the OAS in El Salvador.

Transnational organizations, such as Amnesty International, the Quakers' Friends Peace Committee and Friends World Committee for Consultation, and the International Committee of the Red Cross, function independently of states and embody many of the elements commonly associated with impartiality. With limited resources and fewer strategies available to them, these organizations often find themselves involved in what are known as "humanitarian interventions" where the victims are hostages, refugees, or prisoners. When strict secrecy or a high degree of impartiality is required and when neither governments nor international organizations can gain access to a conflict, transnational organizations are an excellent option (Princen 1992). New organizations, such as the London-based International Alert, the Geneva-based Center for Humanitarian Dialogue, and the Atlanta-based International Negotiation Network, exemplify the growing number of institutions and organizations committed to peacemaking, mediation, and conflict resolution.

A related aspect of mediator identity that can help to account for effective mediation is that of mediator rank. It is important to recall that some high-status mediators, such as a president, a prime minister, or a secretary of state, are better equipped to marshal resources in the course of mediation than those of lesser stature. High-ranking mediators can be more persuasive than middle-level officials; they possess leverage and can use social influence that could be crucial in persuading the parties to make concessions or move toward an agreement. This notion is borne out in a series of empirical studies (Bercovitch and Houston 1993) that clearly show the positive association between high rank and successful mediation outcomes.

Motivational Factors

Given the diversity of conflicts, circumstances, and actors, there cannot possibly be a single right way to mediate international conflicts. However, it is possible to generalize from various studies on mediation and reflect on lessons learned in order to identify some factors and conditions that impede or support mediation.

The parties' motivation and commitment to accept and engage in mediation will undoubtedly affect the outcome. When disputants are unenthusiastic about mediation or believe they can get what they want through unilateral action, the likelihood of successful mediation is extremely low. Effective mediation requires mutual consent, acceptability (of mediator), high motivation, and active participation.

From the perspective of a would-be mediator, a number of features can be indicative of the parties' genuine motivation and serious commitment to mediation. Foremost is the receipt of a joint request. When one party only requests mediation or the mediator initiates the process, the chances of a successful outcome are slim. Mediation success is more feasible when it is wanted by both parties; a joint request may well be a prerequisite for effective international mediation (Bercovitch 1984; Hiltrop 1989).

When the mediator is an unofficial individual (e.g., former president Carter in North Korea in 1994), the motives for initiating mediation may include a desire to (1) be instrumental in changing the course of a long-standing or escalating conflict, (2) gain access to major political leaders and open channels of communication, (3) put into practice a set of ideas on conflict management, and (4) spread one's own ideas and thus enhance personal stature and professional status. The presence of one or more of these motives (which may be conscious or subconscious) in an opportune situation provides a very strong rationale for an individual to initiate unofficial mediation.

Where a mediator acts in an official capacity, representing a government or an organization, a different set of motives may prevail. Such persons may wish to initiate mediation because (1) they have a clear mandate to intervene in disputes (e.g., the charters of the Arab League, African Unity, and the Organization of American States each contain an explicit clause mandating that their members seek mediation in regional disputes); (2) they may want to do something about a conflict whose continuance could adversely affect their own political interests; (3) they may be directly requested by one or both parties to mediate; (4) they may wish to preserve a structure of which they are a part (e.g., the frequent mediation attempts by the United States in disputes between Greece and Turkey, two valued NATO member-states); or (5) they may see mediation as a way of extending and enhancing their own influence by becoming indispensable to the parties in conflict or by gaining the gratitude (and presumably the political goodwill) of one or both of the protagonists (e.g., the frequent efforts by the United States to mediate the Arab-Israeli conflict). A further example of the complex motivations behind mediation efforts can be seen in the decision by the Soviet Union to mediate the conflict between India and Pakistan. Their involvement stemmed from a desire to establish better relations with Pakistan, a country that at the time had better relations with the United States and China. Furthermore, the Soviet leaders also sought to establish a precedent that would justify future involvement in the region and therefore increase the breadth of Soviet influence (Touval and Zartman 2001: 429).

Mediators are political actors; they engage in mediation and expend resources because they expect to resolve a conflict or at least to stop it from becoming more violent, and thus gain something from the mediated outcome. For many actors, mediation is a policy instrument through which they can pursue some of their interests without arousing too much opposition (Touval 1992a). The relationship between a mediator and disputants is thus never entirely devoid of political interest. To overlook this aspect is to miss a key element of international mediation.

Parties in conflict may have different motives for choosing mediation: (1) mediation may actually help them reduce the risks of an escalating conflict and move them closer to a settlement; (2) each party may embrace mediation in the expectation that the mediator will be more sympathetic to their cause than their opponents'; (3) both parties may see mediation as a public expression of their commitment to an international norm of peaceful conflict management; (4) they may want an outsider to take much of the blame should their efforts fail; or (5) they may desire mediation because a mediator can be used to monitor, verify, and guarantee any eventual agreement (Touval and Zartman 2001: 432). One way or another, parties in conflict—and mediators—have compelling reasons for accepting, initiating, or desiring mediation.

Structural Factors

Various structural factors affect the mediation process. These factors include the physical, social, and interpersonal components of the mediation. When considering factors at the structural level, previous studies have determined that international mediation is likely to be more effective under some conditions and less effective under others. Conditions that are conducive to effectiveness include (1) relative power parity between the states or other actors in conflict (Quinn et al. 2006; Young 1967), (2) the absence of ideological issues, values, or beliefs (Bercovitch and Langley 1993), (3) a clear identification of the parties in conflict (which is not always as straightforward as it may appear), (4) the absence of severe internal disorganization or civil war in the country or countries where the conflict is taking place, (5) the exclusion of the nature and history of the parties' previous relationship from the mediation (Bercovitch 1989), (6) the presence of a ripe moment constituted by a "hurting stalemate" (Zartman 1985; see also Mitchell 2006), and (7) low-intensity conflicts.

Perhaps the two most important structural factors that may affect the success of mediation are the timing of mediation and conflict intensity. The timing of mediation is a crucial factor affecting the chances of its success. Conflicts, like all other social processes, have their own life cycles that may stretch across days, months, or years. There are times when a conflict is "ripe for mediation" (Zartman 1985) and times when mediation can only exacerbate a conflict and harm the credibility of the mediators (Haas 1990).

While it is generally accepted that in order to be effective, mediation must take place at a propitious moment, there is very little agreement on what constitutes, or how to recognize, such a moment. Frank Edmead claims that mediation is more likely to succeed if it is attempted at an early stage, and certainly well before the adversaries cross a threshold of violence and begin to inflict heavy losses on each other (1971). Others, like Northedge and Donelan, suggest that mediation can only be effective when a dispute has gone through a few phases and must certainly not be initiated before each side has shown a willingness to moderate its intransigence and revise its expectations (1971).

This divergence in opinion illustrates the difficulty of identifying conflict ripeness, which often varies from case to case and is dependent upon a range of dynamic factors. Yet the existence of a "hurting stalemate" (e.g., a military setback, a change in power relations, or a failure to impose a unilateral outcome) remains the best benchmark for deciding when to initiate mediation (see Zartman 1985, 2003). Disputants reach a mutually hurting stalemate when their own efforts to resolve a conflict have reached an impasse, when the costs, both human and material, of pursuing the conflict begin to outweigh the benefits, and when at the same time they both recognize some windows of opportunity.

An analysis of the mediation dataset and direct interviews with experienced intermediaries lend considerable support to this notion (Bercovitch 1984). Mediation, it seems, is more effective when it follows, rather than precedes, some test of strength between the parties. This is not meant to justify inaction on the part of mediators, merely to suggest that there are some moments in time when the process can be successful, and that these moments usually follow, rather than precede, the parties' own failed efforts. Of course ripeness and timing are matters of perception. When the parties perceive that a conflict is ready for mediation, they will accept an offer for mediation. Being able to identify precisely when these perceptions take hold is still a matter for much debate and uncertainty.

Closely related to this factor is the notion of intensity. Once again, the literature on mediation offers two contradictory notions. Jackson (1952) and Young (1967) suggest that the greater the intensity of a dispute, the higher the likelihood that mediation will be accepted and be successful (as a way of cutting losses, if nothing else). An opposite view contends that the greater the intensity and the higher the losses, the more polarized the parties' positions will become and the more determined each party will be to reject any mediation effort and to attempt to win at all costs (Modelski 1964; Burton 1969; Brockner 1982). In this view, mediation is more likely to be accepted and to be successful in low-intensity disputes, and protracted, intense international disputes are not particularly amenable to mediation or other forms of third-party intervention. What we find out is that high-intensity conflicts do indeed attract most mediation efforts (which stands to reason) but also show the lowest degree of successful mediation (Bercovitch and Gartner 2006).

The nature of a conflict, issues at stake, intensity, timing of mediation, and the mediation environment are all factors that have a significant effect on mediation. To increase the chances of success, potential mediators have to understand all the structural factors and make sure that as many of the initial barriers to mediation as possible are either removed or dealt with. Peacemaking of any form can not take place until and unless that happens.

Interactional Factors

Another factor that affects mediation concerns the nature of interaction between the parties. We refer to this as "interactional factors." These interactions may be secretive, zero-sum in nature in which little information is exchanged and no trust is built, or they may be of a different kind, where trust is built, information is exchanged, communication is in earnest, and the whole process is geared toward a win-win solution.

Interactional factors draw our attention to the important role of relationship between the parties and the nature of their interdependence. Mediators should consider these factors when they attempt to help parties resolve their dispute. Interactional factors play a major role in conflict resolution because they affect everything the parties do, think, or see, and they clearly can impede or facilitate effective mediation.

Understanding the nature of the interaction between parties and how best to change unproductive interactions is essential for a mediator. Based on this understanding, a mediator will choose an appropriate role, or strategy to work toward a successful outcome. As distributive interactions (e.g., low trust, low communication and information) make it more difficult for parties to understand each other's needs and interests, mediators may try to engage in behavior that can help the parties reframe issues, feel comfortable about exchanging information in private, find common interests, and generally control expressions of hostility. This may not necessarily get the parties to change their view of the conflict to a win-win perspective, but at least it may get them to understand the constraints that operate on each of them and the need to move away

from hostile exchanges. Mediators can bring to bear key resources (knowledge, information, communication channels, etc.) that may help to transform a hostile interaction into a more benign one.

Another important aspect of interactional factors is the power parity or disparity between the parties to the conflict. Both Ott (1972) and Young (1967) suggest that the smaller the power differences between the adversaries, the greater the effectiveness of international mediation. The idea that mediation is most effective in disputes involving adversaries with approximate power parity receives strong empirical support (Butterworth 1976). This is why we often refer to mediation as empowering. Mediation can place both parties on an equal footing, even if it is only for the duration of the process.

The previous relationship between the parties, suggested by Morton Deutsch (1973) as one of the main variables affecting the course and outcome of a conflict, has considerable influence on whether or not mediation would be *accepted* but seems to have no discernible impact on the *outcome*. The idea here is that parties in conflict learn norms of conflict resolution, and in each successive conflict they resort to more peaceful and cooperative means of dealing with their conflict. There is little empirical evidence supporting the idea that repeated conflict interactions improve conflict resolution (Bercovitch and Gartner 2006). There are indeed more mediation attempts in conflicts where parties had been engaged in conflicts before, but these efforts also show the lowest degree of successful outcomes. Having experience in previous conflicts makes it even harder to achieve a successful outcome in a current conflict.

Strategies of Mediation

Considerable attention has been devoted to the question of what exactly mediators do, what their role, functions, and behavior are, and how these might affect outcomes. It is possible to think of mediation behavior as the most important factor accounting for the success or failure of mediation. In an attempt to make some sense of mediation functions and behavior, James Wall (1981) identified more than a hundred specific functions and behaviors. All these forms of behavior arise from the fact that the negotiators concerned cannot reach an agreement, and their stated purpose is to change, modify, settle, or resolve a conflict. Enacting these behaviors constitutes the heart of mediation.

It is also possible to suggest a number of broad role categories that encompass related forms of behavior (Jabri 1990; Princen 1992). The late Jeffrey Rubin offered a comprehensive set of mediation roles. He distinguished between formal mediation and informal mediation; individual mediation (e.g., by Lord Owen) and mediation by a representative of a state (e.g., by the U.S. secretary of state); invited mediation and noninvited mediation; advisory mediation and directive mediation; permanent mediation and temporary mediation; and resolution-oriented mediation and relationship-oriented mediation. Each of these types of mediators has different interests, resources, and capabilities, and the behavior of each may lead to different outcomes (Rubin 1981). Joseph Stulberg, writing in a more traditional vein, lists the following as mediators' roles: (1) catalyst, (2) educator, (3) translator, (4) resource-expander, (5) bearer of bad news, (6) agent of reality, and (7) scapegoat (1987). Lawrence Susskind and Jeffrey Cruikshank, whose conception of mediation is that of "assisted negotiation," introduce a dynamic element into the discussion by identifying a number of roles such as representation, inventing options, or monitoring, and relating these to the various stages of the conflict (1987).

A different approach for categorizing what mediators actually do is that of a mediation strategy, which Deborah Kolb defines as "an overall plan, approach, or method a mediator has for resolving a dispute . . . it is the way the mediator intends to manage the case, the parties, and the issue" (1983: 24). Which, therefore, are the most important mediation strategies? Do different mediators choose different strategies? And does it matter which strategy a mediator chooses?

There are a number of ways of thinking about mediation strategies. Kolb distinguishes two kinds of strategies: deal-making strategies (affecting the substance of a conflict) and orchestration strategies (managing the interaction) (1983); similar to Rubin's resolution- and relationship-oriented roles. Janice Stein, in her study of successive American mediations in the Middle East, talks about incremental strategies (segmenting a conflict into smaller issues) and comprehensive strategies (dealing with all aspects of a conflict) (1985). Peter Carnevale suggests that mediators may choose from among four fundamental strategies: integration (searching for common ground); pressing (reducing the range of available alternatives); compensation (enhancing the attractiveness of some alternatives); and inaction (which, in effect, means allowing the parties to go their own way) (1986). Kenneth Kressel, in one of the most widely used typologies, presents three general strategies: reflexive (discovering issues, facilitating

better interactions); nondirective (producing a favorable climate for mediation); and directive (promoting specific outcomes) (1972).

Touval and Zartman's typology of mediation strategies is the most apposite for scholars or practitioners of international mediation. They identify three discrete categories of behavior on an ascending level of involvement that can describe the full range of mediation techniques. This typology is particularly useful because it is derived deductively from a general framework of mediation relationships that includes information, decision making, and influence. Above all, though, it includes dimensions of mediator behavior within three categories: communication, formulation, and manipulation (Touval and Zartman 1985).

The choice of any form of mediation behavior or strategy is rarely random. Rather, it is influenced by factors specific to the conflict and internal to the mediator. Mediators try to vary their behavior to reflect the conflict at hand. In low-intensity conflicts, for instance, communication strategies may be more effective; high-intensity conflicts may call for more active, manipulative strategies. Time pressure, mediator rank, and previous relations between the parties can all determine the choice of a strategy. To be effective, mediation strategies and behavior must be truly congruent with the nature of a conflict and the objectives and interests of a mediator.

Evaluating the relationship between what mediators do and the outcomes of their efforts is, on the whole, based on informal reflections from mediators (and they are usually quite reluctant to claim success or take responsibility for failure) or from direct observations of their performance. While conceptualizing or measuring mediator behavior is difficult, there are many who agree with Thomas Kochan and Todd Jick (1978) that this is the most critical variable affecting mediation outcomes.

It is impossible to deny that mediation behavior and strategies chosen will have a major impact on outcomes. Some scholars, including Burton (1969) and Kelman (1992), advocate communication-facilitation strategies as the most likely to achieve a successful outcome. Others (e.g., Touval and Zartman 1985) call for a more forceful approach to mediation involving formulation and manipulation strategies. Although much may depend on the nature and circumstances of a conflict, empirical analysis of mediation strategy suggests that mediation requires some leverage of one kind or another, and that high-ranking or more powerful mediators are more likely to be successful than other kinds of mediators (Bercovitch and Houston 1996). Further analyses of mediation have revealed that while communication-facilitation strategies are the most frequently utilized by international mediators, directive strategies appear to be the most successful (e.g., Bercovitch and Houston 2000; Gartner and Bercovitch 2006; Wilkenfeld et al. 2003). Active strategies can rely on the full scope of influence, using reward, persuasion, legitimacy, and information to affect an outcome (Bercovitch and Houston 1993).

Whichever intervention strategy mediators use, their underlying objective in any conflict is to change: (1) the physical environment of conflict management (e.g., by maintaining secrecy or imposing time limits, as President Carter did at Camp David); (2) the perception of what is at stake (e.g., by structuring an agenda and/or identifying and packaging new issues); and (3) the parties' motivation to reach a peaceful outcome by, for example, using subtle pressure. Any international conflict presents opportunities for some form of mediation. To be effective, however, mediation strategies must reflect the reality of the conflict and the resources of the mediator. In that sense, international mediation is a truly contingent and reciprocal political activity.

Evaluating Mediation

We have seen that numerous actors and organizations may undertake and initiate international mediation, but is there any way of assessing just how much these different mediators can achieve? Recent mediation efforts conducted in response to violent conflict in Sierra Leone provide an excellent example of some of the difficulties faced by those trying to assess the effectiveness of mediation. The conflict officially began in 1991, and what started as a relatively small incursion led to a severe conflict that displaced approximately half of Sierra Leone's already impoverished population (Keen 2003). In 1999, the Organization of West African States initiated mediation in an effort to stem the violence between government forces and the Revolutionary United Front (RUF). This mediation effort resulted in the signing of the Lomé Peace Agreement by both the government and the RUF. While this agreement initially led to a brief cessation of violence, the conflict soon regained its former intensity, and it was only after the arrival of well-equipped and well-trained British forces that the conflict was brought under control (Department of Peace and Conflict Research 2008). The fact that a peace agreement was signed could be construed as clear evidence of a successful outcome; however, the fact

that the agreement failed to hold would lead many observers to conclude that the intervention failed.

The mediation effort by the Organization of West African States in Sierra Leone illustrates the difficulties we face trying to evaluate mediation success: how can mediation outcomes be assessed, and how can the impact of a particular mediation be evaluated? If mediation is ultimately about changing or influencing a conflict or the way parties in conflict behave, can such changes be discerned? Furthermore, if change has been effected and a satisfactory outcome of sorts has been achieved, can this outcome be attributed to the wisdom and experience of the mediator or to the motivation of the parties? Conversely, if the conflictual relationship shows no signs of change, should we consider the mediation effort as a failure? How much time should elapse before we can realistically expect results from the mediation? Will the criteria change depending on the nature of the conflict, the parties, and the mediator? In short, evaluating success and failure in mediation poses serious conceptual and methodological challenges, and it is an issue that the field of conflict management has yet to address in a satisfactory manner (Stern and Druckman 2000a).

Because international mediation is not a uniform practice, it seems futile to draw up one set of criteria to cover the many objectives of all mediators. Individual mediators, for instance, may emphasize communication-facilitation strategies, be more concerned with the quality of interaction, and seek to create a better environment for conflict management. States, on the other hand, may seek to change the behavior of those in conflict and achieve a settlement of sorts. Such different objectives cannot be easily accommodated within a single perspective (d'Estree et al. 2001). To answer the question of whether mediation works, we need to know something about the various goals of mediation. Thus, we suggest that two broad criteria, subjective and objective, be used to assess the contribution and consequences of any form of international mediation.

Subjective criteria refer to the parties' or the mediator's perception (and, to some extent, that of other relevant external actors) that the goals of mediation have been achieved or that a desired change has taken place. Using this perspective, we can suggest that mediation has been successful when the parties express satisfaction with the process or outcome of mediation, or when the outcome is seen as fair, efficient, or effective (Susskind and Cruickshank 1987).

Fairness of mediation, satisfaction with its performance, and improvement in the overall climate of the parties' relationship are very difficult to measure, but they are undoubtedly consequences of successful mediation. They are subjective because they depend on the assessments of the parties in conflict. Even if a conflict remains unresolved, mediation—in any form—can do much to change the way the disputants feel about each other and lead, however indirectly, to both a long-term improvement in the parties' relationship and a resolution of the conflict.

Objective criteria for assessing the impact and consequences of mediation offer a totally different perspective. Objective criteria rely on substantive indicators that can be quantified empirically. Usually such criteria involve observations of change and judgments about the extent of change as evidence of the success or failure of mediation. Thus, one can consider a particular mediation effort successful if it contributed to a cessation or reduction of violent behavior and the opening of a dialogue between the parties. Alternatively, one can call a mediation outcome successful when the parties sign a formal and binding agreement that settles the conflict's issues.

Evaluating the success or failure of international mediation in objective terms is a relatively straightforward task. Here one can measure success or failure in terms of the permanence of the agreement achieved, the speed with which it was achieved, the reduction in the level of hostilities between the disputants, and the number of issues on which agreement was achieved. On the face of it, objective criteria seem to offer a perfectly valid way to assess the impact, consequences, and effectiveness of international mediation. Such criteria indicate (see Bercovitch and Gartner 2006) that overall mediation achieves an effective outcome in nearly 34 percent of all cases.

However, it would be unwise to rely solely on objective criteria. Different mediators, and indeed different parties in conflict, have different goals in mind when they enter the realm of conflict resolution. Changing the behavior of the parties could well be only one of many goals. Some international mediators may focus on the substance of interactions; others may focus on its climate, setting, and decision-making norms. These goals cannot always be evaluated easily. Perhaps each mediation case should be evaluated in terms of the criteria that are relevant to its own efforts. The questions of whether or not mediation works and how best to evaluate it can only be answered by collecting information and making judgments in specific cases. There are far too many concep-

tual problems with these questions, and it seems that, on this issue at least, our theoretical ambitions must be tempered by the constraints of a complex reality.

Conclusion

Mediation is a complex phenomenon. It is also one of the most important tools of international peacemaking. It is ideally suited to the reality of states and other diverse actors. There are many cases where parties, for a variety of reasons, do not choose negotiation and prefer mediation instead. The traditional reliance on power, deterrence, and coercion no longer works for conflict resolution. Negotiation and mediation have emerged as the most important tools of peacemaking in the latter part of the twentieth century. Even in the uncertain environment of post-2001 conflicts, with numerous new challenges facing policymakers, mediation remains one of the most valuable tools. Here we have looked at mediation and argued that the quest for a better understanding of the principles and practices of mediation can make sense only if it is conducted within some kind of an intellectual framework, one that can explain the logic and reasoning behind this method of conflict resolution, in which the mediator is neither directly part of a conflict nor totally removed from it. This chapter has sought to provide such a framework and assess its basic dimensions.

This framework reflects our conviction that mediation is an aspect of the broader process of conflict resolution and that, irrespective of what the conflict is about or who the mediators are, mediation involves the intertwining of interests, resources, and positions in an attempt to influence outcomes. This relationship is critical for analyzing the dynamics of conflict and assessing the prospects of successful mediation. Whether the parties involved are states or terrorist groups, it is important to know something about these features. We have tried to unravel the many aspects of this relationship and point out their influence on mediation. The foregoing analysis was by no means exhaustive, but it does integrate many findings that have a bearing on mediation and conflict resolution and provides answers to such questions as who may mediate conflicts, when mediation should be initiated, how it actually works, and how its impact can be evaluated.

CHAPTER FOUR

Arbitration, Adjudication, and International Law

International law–based methods of conflict resolution are a binding form of third-party intervention. Disputing states submit their claims to an impartial judicial body that makes a ruling on the basis of established international legal principles. Through adjudication, or judicial settlement, disputes are referred to an established court or standing tribunal, such as the International Court of Justice (ICJ) or the European Court of Human Rights (ECHR). Alternately, a dispute might be submitted to arbitration. This requires the parties themselves to set up the machinery to handle the dispute—the judges, procedures, and jurisdiction of the tribunal—as well as determine the scope or terms of the award. Historically, permanent judicial institutions developed out of the diplomatic practice of arbitration.

International law–based methods are, by and large, an efficient and rational means of dealing with a narrowly defined set of international disputes, namely, those that require a legal ruling, as opposed to a political settlement. They are also surprisingly effective; the vast majority of awards and judgments are adhered to (Merrills 1998). Unfortunately, the nature of international law—its historical development and its narrowly prescribed role—limits the efficacy of legal methods for dealing with the more contentious and potentially more destructive forms of conflict with which we are primarily concerned.

Any consideration of legal approaches to the maintenance of peace and order in international society runs the risk of falling into extremes. On the one hand, idealistic individuals concerned for international peace and order, as well as many international lawyers, see the establish-ment of international law as the panacea for international conflict. If states could be convinced or forced to submit their disputes to international courts or tribunals, the thinking goes, the peaceful rule of law would prevail. On the other hand, in avoiding the idealistic overestimation of international law, especially in its enforcement capacity, some have intentionally or unintentionally come close to denying any legal force at all for international law. Instead, they view it—cynically at times—as a convenient instrument of power politics (Delbruck 1987).

In avoiding these extremes, we suggest that international law plays a limited but important role in the range of conflict resolution methods available to international actors. It is a useful way of dealing with a certain class of disputes, which can, if left unresolved, lead to more serious conflict. And it has important normative functions relating to the maintenance of peace and order in the international system. In a negative sense, international law assists in preventing the growth of interests leading to strife. It does so by clarifying the values of the international society: what interests and goals may be legitimately pursued (a form of interest articulation); where the boundaries of respective spheres are delineated; and the allocation of rights and responsibilities (Starr 1997; Levi 1976).

In addition, international law creates situations for cooperation and adjustment: establishing and facilitating routine interactions among states; socializing decision makers as to the nature of the prevailing consensus in the international system and its expectations regarding the rights and duties of international actors; and regime and norm creation. Most important for our purposes, international law serves a variety of conflict-related functions, such as limiting the conditions under which a justified conflict can originate, regulating the legal means of pursuing the conflict, and serving a central role in the range of processes involved in conflict management and resolution (Starr 1997: 102).

In this chapter, we provide an overview and assessment of the main legal methods of conflict resolution. We do not consider humanitarian law or the legal processes of transitional justice such as international war crimes prosecution or quasi-legal truth commissions; these issues are covered in chapter 11. Instead, we focus on the institutions and processes that have emerged alongside the historical development of international law.

Conceptualizing Legal Methods of Conflict Resolution

The Nature of International Law

When we talk about law, we are referring to a "general rule which covers a specific class of cases, and which is backed by a probable sanction, stated in advance and widely accepted as legitimate" (Deutsch 1978: 201). International law may be conceived as "a body of rules which binds states and other agents in world politics in their relations with one another and is considered to have the status of law" (Bull 1977: 127). Looking at these definitions, a basic dilemma is immediately obvious. As neorealist scholars argue, the international system is anarchic, and there exists no legitimate authority above states to impose sanctions on lawbreakers. To realists, then, international law is most often irrelevant to the behavior of states because it lacks the centralized enforcement mechanisms and capability that are seen to represent law. According to this perspective, it is of no consequence because it is not really law in the true sense of the word.

This view is, in fact, one form of a simple criminal law approach that conceives of law as a series of commands that prohibit certain kinds of behavior under the threat of coercive force to ensure compliance (Starr 1997). There are two answers to this narrow conceptualization. First, law does not require command and coercive sanctions to be regarded as law. In fact, much of international law—and domestic law, for that matter—is devoted to facilitating coordination and cooperation in the exchange of goods, services, communications, and a multitude of other transactions. This kind of law does not require the threat of coercive force to function effectively.

A second answer is that international law does entail sanctions, albeit informal ones (Bull 1977). States obey international law for a variety of reasons. They may fear the consequences of precipitating (by example) widespread disobedience to the rule of law, which would in turn result in chaos. They may face a range of possible reprisals from aggrieved states or other international actors such as international organizations or multinational companies. They may perceive it to be in their interests to adhere to international law for reasons of reciprocity. From a positive perspective, compliance with international law can bring with it the reputation of being a law-abiding and trustworthy member of the international community, which in turn has its own rewards. For small states—the majority of nations in the international system—the practice of international law protects them from predation and coercion by more powerful states; a rule-based international system protects their interests by creating a level playing field. In other words, as with all legal systems, international law is based on a Golden Rule principle—rule-based behavior toward others will itself beget rule-based behavior (Kegley and Wittkopf 1992). As Joyner observes, "The reality as demonstrated through their behavior is that states do accept international law as law and, even more significant, in the vast majority of instances they usually obey it" (1992: 202). Even so-called rogue states like Libya have been persuaded to adhere to international law (regarding involvement in international terrorism in the 1980s) because they recognize the advantages that accrue from international acceptance and recognition.

The Functions of International Law

The functions of international law, and domestic law for that matter, are, first, to regulate interaction and interrelations in such a way that they can proceed in an orderly and efficient manner. In this sense, law plays a communication and facilitation role, establishing the rights and responsibilities of states in their daily interactions. Similar to the domestic rules of the road that let the driver know what should be done and what to expect others to do, international law facilitates routine dealings among states. For example, there are well-developed bodies of law regulating diplomatic relations, treaties, and commercial transactions.

Perhaps its most important function, however, is in the creation, maintenance, and operation of regimes. Regimes involve "the cooperation and collaboration of individuals or groups, without solutions imposed from some higher authority, and with the relevant participants willing to engage in self-regulation (and enforcement!) in order to achieve some good or to protect an existing common-pool resource" (Starr 1997: 103). The regulation of interaction and the creation of regimes provide a normative foundation for the necessary degree of stability within the system. The international system therefore can be understood as a legal order, a primary function of which is to provide mechanisms or procedures by which the system can adapt itself to changing circumstances without being violently disrupted (Delbruck 1987: 133). Fostering orderly change in the society of nations involves creating new norms of international law to deal with vital conflicts of interest, such as the distribution of resources not yet subject to the sovereignty claims of individual states or the contradictions between universalistic human rights claims and the right of sovereign states to conduct their internal affairs as they see fit. In recent years, this norm-creating task has been undertaken by quasi-legislative conferences, arguably the most important of which has been the Law of the Sea Conference.

The new treaty law—or customary law—emanating from international conferences provides an especially valuable contribution to conflict resolution because the new rules are usually accompanied by elaborate procedural means of dispute settlement. This is the third main function of international law, namely, limiting and controlling the destructive or disorderly effects of conflict on the system through the provision of conflict-resolution mechanisms. The legally based procedures and mechanisms for the resolution of international conflicts—arbitration and judicial settlement—are well developed and, for some types of disputes, successfully deployed.

Finally, from a sociological perspective, we might say that international law functions to identify and embody the idea of a society of sovereign states (Bull 1977), in much the same way that domestic law provides a sense of political identity and nationhood. Order is the basis of any society. Even though the order of international politics can be described as undeveloped, decentralized, or imperfect, it is order, nonetheless. Not only is there an international system, but there is also an international "society" because there is a legal and normative order based on widely accepted sets of expectations, rights, duties, and regimes.

The Development of International Law

Because rules are so vital to the existence of society (no society can exist without them), the history of international law is as old as the international system itself. Among the many elements contributing to the development of international law, the most fundamental are the need to limit the use of force and the need for cooperation (Fawcett 1971: 19–20). After the medieval feudal system disintegrated and the first European states emerged, states cooperated or fought as they saw fit. Although the international system in the seventeenth and eighteenth centuries has thus been called anarchic, despite the reign of sovereign monarchs, certain basic rules of conduct or rules of international law were developed and observed. These were formulated primarily to regulate mutual relations in peace and conflict.

In the nineteenth century, when the idea of the state really took hold, international rules of law developed at a fast pace. The Act of the Vienna Congress, the Peace Treaty of 1856 ending the Crimean War, the Acts of the Berlin Congress (1875, 1888), and the Act of the Brussels Congress (1890) were all important steps in codifying international relations. Furthermore, international rules of law provided criteria for settling disputes (Delbruck 1987: 128, 132). International law was refined and developed even further in the twentieth century. Most important, from the pioneering of the League of Nations following World War I, to the establishment of the United Nations in 1945, international law has sought to create centralized, authoritative mechanisms for regulating state relations and resolving conflict.

Contemporary international law, then, attempts to prohibit states from engaging in activities that are likely to disturb international peace and security. It also attempts to encourage those activities that are conducive to establishing a peaceful order, such as the regulation of economic, social, communications, and environmental matters (Delbruck 1987; Bull 1977).

Law-based Methods of Conflict Resolution

International law provides a variety of procedures and mechanisms for conflict resolution, ranging from established courts to ad hoc tribunals. At the more formal end of the spectrum are a series of well-established courts, such as the International Court of Justice (ICJ) or the Hague Permanent Court of Arbitration (PCA). Less formal practices include establishing commissions or tribunals for limited periods to hear specific cases or referring the dispute to a specially chosen individual, such as a foreign head of state or the pope. A relatively new and highly flexible form of judicial settlement can be seen in the 1991 OSCE Dispute Settlement Mechanism. The main task of the Mechanism is to act as a kind of conciliation commission, in particular, to assist the parties in finding an agreement of procedure for the settlement of the dispute. Although it is a nonbinding, voluntary form of third-party dispute facilitation, the stipulation that it be conducted "on the basis of international law" gives the Mechanism a unique legal character (Oellers-Frahm 1992). While it is sometimes difficult to draw clear conceptual distinctions between the different law-based methods, it is common practice to divide them into two groups—arbitration and adjudication (sometimes called judicial settlement).

International Arbitration

What Is Arbitration?

Article 37 of the Hague Convention for the Pacific Settlement of International Disputes (1907) offers the following definition: "International arbitration has for its object the settlement of disputes between states by judges of their own choice, and on the basis of respect for law. Recourse to arbitration implies an engagement to submit in good faith to the award." In reality, this definition is far too narrow to capture the various forms that international arbitration takes today. It is more generally conceived of as "the voluntary submission of a dispute to a third party for settlement by the making of an award which will bind the parties" (Wallace-Bruce 1998: 63). Arbitration therefore exhibits elements of both mediation and judicial settlement, and on a continuum of conflict resolution methods it would fall between diplomatic bargaining at one end and adjudication at the other. Historically, it was conceived as "diplomatic arbitration" whereby a trusted third party proposed a compromise. A binding award was only imposed failing acceptance of the compromise (Pinto 1990: 63). International arbitration has gradually assumed a more judicial character ever since the *Alabama Claims Arbitration* of 1872 between the United States and Great Britain. In spite of the pronounced judicialization of arbitration in contemporary international law (Wallace-Bruce 1998), it remains a flexible method of dispute resolution and can take place be-

tween states, between states and international organizations, between private individuals, or between a private individual and a state.

The History and Development of International Arbitration

While arbitration was employed by the classical Greek city-states and in medieval Europe, there is almost universal consensus that the foundations for modern international arbitration were laid in the provisions of the General Treaty of Friendship, Commerce, and Navigation signed in 1794 between the United States and Great Britain (Wallace-Bruce 1998; Rosenne 1995). Commonly known as the Jay Treaty (named after the then U.S. secretary of state, John Jay), it established three arbitration commissions to settle outstanding issues resulting from the American Declaration of Independence in 1776. Not entirely successful, the Jay Treaty nonetheless paved the way for the further development of interstate arbitration practice.

The next significant step was the refinement and development of the rules and practices of international arbitration following the *Alabama Claims Arbitration* of 1872, also between the United States and Great Britain. The *Alabama* case involved allegations that Britain had violated its neutrality during the American civil war by allowing two ships—*Alabama* and her supply ship, *Georgia*—to be built in British shipyards for use by the Confederate forces. Considered by many to be the high point of international arbitration, the *Alabama Claims Arbitration* ushered in a new epoch of interstate dispute settlement (see Wallace-Bruce 1998; Pinto 1990; Stuyt 1990). From this time onward, many bilateral treaties included procedures for arbitration along the lines of the *Alabama* case.

In 1899 and 1907 the First and Second Hague Peace Conferences were convoked by the Russian international lawyer F. F. Martens. At the first conference in 1899, the Hague Convention for the Pacific Settlement of International Disputes was signed. It recognized that for questions of a legal nature—in particular, the interpretation and application of treaties or international conventions—arbitration was the most equitable and effective means of settling disputes when diplomacy had failed. In recognition of this fact, Chapter II of the Convention established the Permanent Court of Arbitration (PCA) at The Hague, whose object was to facilitate "an immediate recourse" to international arbitration (Wallace-Bruce 1998: 55–56; Rosenne 1995: 8–12). The Second Hague Peace Conference in 1907 not only strengthened the operation of the Court, but it spelled out the rules to govern international arbitration, such as the definition of the dispute, the time allowed for the appointment of arbitrators, the form, order, and time for submission of pleadings and oral evidence, the responsibilities of the parties for defraying costs, and the competence of the Court itself.

Further important stages in the development of international arbitration took place when the League of Nations and the United Nations included it in, first, the 1928 General Act for the Pacific Settlement of International Disputes and, second, the Model Rules of Arbitral Procedure adopted by the International Law Commission in 1958. More recently, attempts have been made to revitalize the work of the PCA through international conferences in 1993 and 1999, its centenary year. However, throughout this period these institutionalized forms of arbitration were rarely employed by states, and arbitration in general—usually by ad hoc tribunals—was a relatively uncommon method of dispute settlement.

Forms of Arbitration

International actors who agree to resolve their dispute by arbitration must first decide what kind of tribunal or arbitrator to appoint. There are three main types. The first possibility is to appoint a commission of arbitrators, normally consisting of equal numbers of national arbitrators appointed by the parties, and a neutral member (or umpire) to whom the case can be referred in the event of disagreement. Alternately, the parties can refer the dispute to a foreign head of state or government. This form of arbitration derives from long-established interstate practice. During the medieval period, for example, the pope was often called upon to act in this capacity. Interestingly, both the queen of England and the pope acted as arbitrators for territorial disputes between Chile and Argentina during the twentieth century. These kinds of informal, ad hoc arbitrations are by far the most common form, as they give states more control over the process and greater flexibility than permanent, institutionalized arbitration.

Referring disputes to The Hague Permanent Court of Arbitration is a second type of international arbitration. Somewhat of a misnomer, the PCA is neither a "court" nor an "arbitral tribunal." Rather, it is an institutional framework designed to facilitate arbitration through providing a list of jurists and a bureau with premises, staff, and library (Butler 1992). The disputing parties can choose an arbitrator(s) from the general list of the Court.

From this point, the proceedings are fairly flexible, although the award is binding and not subject to appeal, and the parties share the expenses. The PCA has rarely been used, partly because it is expensive, formal, and rigid, and affords the parties less control over both the process and the outcome than other forms of arbitration.

The third type of arbitration is the international claims tribunal, the first of which was established in the Jay Treaty. The most common form of tribunal is the collegiate body consisting of an uneven number of persons—generally three or five—who decide the case by majority vote (Merrills 1998: 91). International claims tribunals are established by a treaty agreement between two or more states, usually to deal with a specific class of claims by nationals of one or both states. They are a hybrid mixture of purely "public" arbitrations and commercial, "private" dispute settlement; while the institution of claims settlement is a creature of international law, the actual substance of the process involves individuals and corporations making commercial claims (Bederman 1992: 162). Historically, they were typically constituted to obtain compensation in the aftermath of hostilities or revolutionary events, such as the American Revolution. A more recent example, the Iran-U.S. Claims Tribunal established at The Hague under the 1981 Algiers Accords, was constituted to deal with several thousand claims arising out of the U.S.-Iran hostage crisis.

How Does Arbitration Work?

The agreement to settle a dispute or class of disputes by arbitration may be contained in a pre-existing treaty or in a special agreement called a *compromis*. The compromis sets out how the arbitration is to proceed and what general principles must apply. The first principle is that, in contrast to the compulsory jurisdiction normally exercised by courts in domestic legal systems, international arbitration is entirely consensual. In other words, no dispute between states or international organizations can be submitted to arbitration, except with the consent of the parties. Once consent has been given, however, a state cannot resign from its obligation to submit to arbitration (Wallace-Bruce 1998: 64). The 1899 and 1907 Hague Conventions, and latterly the International Law Commission, lay down rules providing for the procedural framework of arbitration. Ultimately, however, it is for the parties to agree on the procedural arrangements in the compromis. In reality, they can exercise a high degree of control over the way their dispute is to be handled.

The first matter for negotiation between the parties is the membership and composition of the arbitral body. We have already discussed how the parties can choose various forms of informal arbitral bodies or formal institutionalized tribunals. The normal practice is to appoint equal numbers of "national" arbitrators, and then an agreed "neutral" member. Typically, reputable judges, international lawyers, diplomats, former government officials, or respected academics are chosen to serve on the tribunal. In rare cases, the appointment of the arbitrators is put into the hands of a third party, such as the president of the ICJ (Wallace-Bruce 1998: 66).

The second issue that must be agreed to in the compromis are the terms of reference. These procedural arrangements determine the way in which the arbitration is to be conducted, such as the number and order of the written pleadings, the oral stage of the proceedings, the important issue of time limits, how the tribunal will obtain evidence, and what language will be used. The compromis must also determine how the decision will be taken, whether it can order provisional measures, whether separate opinions are allowed, and whether the decision will be published. Last, the parties must determine where the arbitration is to be held and how it will be paid for (Merrills 1998: 95–99).

The third matter agreed to in the compromis involves the criteria that the tribunal must apply in making its decision and what the effects of the award are to be. A generally agreed principle is that arbitrators should apply international law in making their award. However, the parties can, if they so decide, invest the arbitrators with authority to decide their dispute in accordance with the municipal law of a particular country or to apply a combination of domestic and international law. There are four generally recognized sources of law that arbitrators or international jurists can draw upon in deciding cases: (1) international conventions that have established rules recognized by the states, usually contained in bilateral treaties, protocols, or agreements; (2) international custom, as evidence of a general practice that has over time become accepted as law; (3) the general principles of law recognized by "civilized nations," or the general principles common to national legal systems and international law; and (4) the judicial decisions and legal opinions of learned jurists and experts (Bull 1977: 17; Elias 1979: 116–20). Normally, an arbitral award is binding but not necessarily final. The parties may, for example, agree to take further proceedings or leave the way open to interpret, revise, rectify, appeal from, or nullify the decision (Merrills 1998: 105).

An Overview of Interstate Arbitration

How widespread is the resort to arbitration in international relations? The most authoritative scholarly study on the subject surveyed nearly 450 arbitrations from 1794 to 1989 (Stuyt 1990). Of these, the vast majority of cases—more than three-quarters—were ad hoc, informal arbitrations. In direct contrast, recourse to the PCA has been infrequent in the extreme. In the first hundred years of its existence, only twenty-five cases were considered by the Court or with the cooperation of its International Bureau: twenty-one were dealt with between 1902 and 1932, one in 1935, 1940, and 1956, and one in 1970 (Butler 1992: 43–44). Since 1999, the PCA has experienced something of a revival; it currently has a caseload of eight, the most important of which are the *Eritrea-Ethiopia Boundary* and *Claims Commissions,* which came out of their 1998 border war (see Hague Permanent Court of Arbitration 2008).

The employment of international claims tribunals has only been marginally higher, with around sixty-five of these bodies established since the Jay Treaty in 1794. However, it must be remembered that these commissions sometimes deal with substantial numbers of separate disputes. The Jay Treaty tribunal issued 536 awards over five years of operation, while the United States–Mexico Claims Commission created in 1868 dealt with over 2,000 claims between 1871 and 1876 (Bederman 1992: 161, 167).

In terms of their subject matter, the majority of arbitrations have been concerned with claims arising out of injuries to aliens, although these kinds of issues have been less evident in post–World War II cases. About a quarter of all cases were boundary and territorial sovereignty cases, while another fifth of the tribunals listed by Stuyt (1990) dealt with claims arising out of World War II. The remainder were largely concerned with some aspect of treaty interpretation (Gray and Kingsbury 1992: 61–62). Recent arbitrations at the PCA have dealt with issues of boundary demarcation, pollution, human rights, marine environment protection, and investment disputes.

Apart from the obvious preference shown by states for informal, ad hoc arbitration, the survey of interstate arbitration demonstrates its declining usage. While there were approximately 178 interstate arbitrations between 1900 and 1945, in marked contrast, there were only forty-three from 1945 to 1989 (Gray and Kingsbury 1992: 56) and less than twenty since. A few of these may be considered important, however: the 1968 *Rann of Kutch* arbitration (India and Pakistan); the 1977 *Beagle*

Channel arbitration (Argentina and Chile); the 1986 *Rainbow Warrior* arbitration (France and New Zealand); the 1988 *Taba Boundary* arbitration (Egypt and Israel); the ongoing U.S.-Iran Claims Tribunal established in 1981; and the *Eritrea-Ethiopia Boundary* and *Claims Commissions* established in 2000. Related to this is the striking contrast between the extremely high number of conciliation and arbitration treaties—hundreds have been signed since the beginning of this century—and the astoundingly low resort to arbitration in actual disputes. In essence, arbitration has proved to be perhaps the least popular method of conflict resolution for international actors in the postwar period, despite a small rise in its usage in the last decade.

International Adjudication

What Is Adjudication?

Adjudication (judicial settlement) involves the reference of a dispute or disputes to a permanent judicial body or standing tribunal for binding settlement. The primary difference between arbitration and adjudication, therefore, is that in adjudication the machinery and procedure of the tribunal, including the method of selecting the judges, are already established by existing international instruments, such as the Statute and the Rules of the ICJ (Bilder 1997: 161). Permanent judicial tribunals, such as the ICJ and the ECHR, are established to deal with a broad number and range of disputes, and they continue to operate beyond the final award in any particular case.

There are a number of reasons why states might submit their dispute to an established court, as opposed to an arbitral tribunal. First, established courts, already in existence and readily available, obviate the need for the parties to negotiate a compromis detailing procedures, judges, and jurisdictions. Second, the judges on a permanent court are usually professionals with considerable judicial experience, a special commitment to impartiality, and an interest in developing consistent jurisprudence (Bilder 1997: 165). In contrast, part-time arbitrators may be relatively unskilled and less insulated from partisan pressures. Third, the court's costs are borne by the international community, often making adjudication far less expensive. Last, international courts are seen to be more prestigious, creating greater pressures toward compliance.

The most important international court is the International Court of Justice, established by the UN Charter and seated at the Peace Palace. At present, it is the only inter-national court with a general and a global jurisdiction. In addition to the ICJ, however, there are several other important international courts: the European Union's Court of Justice and the Court of First Instance operating in Luxembourg; the European Court of Human Rights in Strasburg; and the Inter-American Court of Human Rights in San Jose, Costa Rica. Other continuing tribunals include the recently established International Tribunal for the Law of the Sea and the International Criminal Court (ICC), as well as adjudication machinery attached to the UN's specialized agencies—the International Labor Organization (ILO), the World Bank, and the International Monetary Fund, for example.

History and Development of Adjudication

Permanent international courts developed out of arbitration practice. Concurrent with efforts to institutionalize arbitration at the Hague Peace Conferences of 1899 and 1907, the first permanent international court—the little known Central American Court of Justice—was established by the Washington Peace Conference of 1907 between Guatemala, El Salvador, and Honduras. Even though it heard ten cases between 1908 and 1918, it was doomed to failure by the United States' steadfast refusal to participate.

Following World War I, Britain and the United States lobbied vigorously in the ensuing peace negotiations for the establishment of a League Court to settle disputes arising out of the forthcoming peace treaty and any other international disagreements. Consequently, provisions calling for such a court were included in the Treaty of Versailles. In 1920, a draft statute was prepared, and on 15 February 1922 the Permanent Court of International Justice (PCIJ) was formally inaugurated at The Hague under the aegis of the League of Nations. The PCIJ functioned from 1922 to 1940. Its reputation remained largely intact, in spite of the League's failure to prevent the outbreak of World War II. As a result, the Allies agreed that a new international court should be constructed in much the same form as the prewar Court (Janis 1992: 18). The International Court of Justice was established by the UN Charter as the principal judicial organ of the United Nations and the legal successor to the PCIJ in 1946. It is in many respects similar to the PCIJ and in most material respects reflects the provisions that constituted the PCIJ. With a shared and continuing jurisprudence, the two courts are usually treated as one continuous organization.

Since the establishment of the ICJ, a number of other

permanent regional and international courts have also come into existence: the ECHR in 1949; the European Union's Court of Justice in 1957 and the Court of First Instance in 1989; the Inter-American Court of Human Rights in 1969; the International Tribunal for the Law of the Sea in 1996; and the ICC in 1988.

The International Court of Justice

When most people talk about international adjudication, they are in fact referring to the ICJ. It is the most prominent and most important international judicial institution and the only one that presently exercises a general global jurisdiction. Established by the UN, it is governed by a special treaty called The Statute of the Court, which is annexed to the UN Charter and to which all 191 members of the United Nations are parties (Bilder 1997: 167).

Jurisdiction of the Court

The Court's powers to decide cases—its "contentious jurisdiction"—are defined in its statute. Like any other international judicial processes, the Court can only hear and decide disputes with the consent of the states involved. Unlike arbitration processes, however, the Court can only decide cases between states; neither the United Nations, nor other IGOs, NGOs, or individuals can bring contentious cases before the Court. There are several ways in which states can give their consent. The first and most common way for states to submit their cases is simply to conclude a special agreement providing for the Court to deal with an existing dispute (Bilder 1997: 168). The 1984 *Gulf of Maine* maritime boundary dispute between Canada and the United States was submitted by this voluntary method.

Second, states may include a "compromissory clause" or "jurisdictional clause" in any bilateral treaty. This type of clause gives the Court jurisdiction to decide any future dispute involving the interpretation or application of that treaty. There are some 300 treaties in force that include such jurisdictional clauses (ICJ 2008). The United States persuaded the Court to assert jurisdiction over Iran in the 1980 U.S.-Iran *Hostages* case on the basis of several relevant treaties that contained jurisdictional clauses.

Third, states may give the Court a form of compulsory jurisdiction to decide any dispute they may have in the future with any of the other states who have also given their consent. They do so by filing a declaration to this effect under the provisions of the "optional clause" of Article 36(2) of the Court's Statute.

> The States parties to the present Statute may at any time declare that they recognize as compulsory *ipso facto* and without special agreement, in relation to any other State accepting the same obligation, the jurisdiction of the Court in all legal disputes concerning:
>   (a) the interpretation of a treaty;
>   (b) any question of international law;
>   (c) the existence of any fact which, if established, would constitute a breach of an international obligation;
>   (d) the nature or extent of the reparation to be made for the breach of an international obligation.

As of 2008, there were sixty-five states who had conferred compulsory jurisdiction on the Court. Every state in this group has the right, in principle at least, to bring one or more other states belonging to this group before the Court.

In reality, however, most declarations accepting the Court's general compulsory jurisdiction are saddled with reservations that may include time limits or the exclusion of certain categories of disputes. The best-known example of such a reservation is the so-called Connally Amendment whereby the United States excepted from the Court's compulsory jurisdiction any "disputes with regard to matters which are essentially within the domestic jurisdiction of the United States of America as determined by the United States of America" (Janis 1992: 23). Others have filed reservations against disputes involving "national security." Some have even retained the right to exclude "any given category or categories of dispute" upon making an appropriate notification to the UN secretary-general (Bilder 1997: 169). In some cases—notably France in the *Nuclear Tests* cases brought by Australia and New Zealand, and the United States in the *Nicaragua* case—states previously submitting to Article 36(2) have subsequently withdrawn their consent to such general jurisdiction. Often, the Court has to go through a "jurisdictional" phase in which it decides whether both states have in fact, properly consented to its jurisdiction.

A final area of the Court's jurisdiction relates to its advisory role. Article 65 of the ICJ Statute states that the Court is competent to "give an advisory opinion on any legal question at the request of whatever body may be authorized by or in accordance with the Charter of the United Nations to make such a request" (ICJ 2008). That is, pursuant to the Charter of the United Nations:

(1) The General Assembly or the Security Council may request the International Court of Justice to give an advisory opinion on any legal question.

(2) Other organs of the United Nations and specialized agencies, which may at any time be so authorized by the General Assembly, may also request advisory opinions of the Court on legal questions within the scope of their activities.

This is a form of secondary jurisdiction and the word *advisory* was included to make it plain that such pronouncements by the Court are always nonbinding (Janis 1992: 28). In 1975, the Court handed down an advisory opinion on the *Western Sahara* case after the General Assembly had asked the Court to advise it on the legal status of the territory at the time of its colonization, and the nature of its "legal" ties to Morocco and Mauritania. More recently, in July 2004 the Court issued an advisory opinion on the construction by Israel of a security wall in the Occupied Palestinian Territory. It found that the wall was contrary to international law (ICJ 2008).

Composition of the Court

The Court is composed of fifteen judges, each from a different country. They are elected to nine-year terms by the United Nations General Assembly and the Security Council, voting every three years in staggered terms. Once elected, judges do not represent their governments but are independent magistrates chosen to reflect the "main forms of civilization" and the principal legal systems of the world (ICJ 2008). The judges are required to possess the qualifications necessary for appointment to the highest national judicial offices, or be jurists of recognized competence in international law. In early 2008, the Court was composed of judges from France, China, Japan, Madagascar, Slovakia, Germany, Sierra Leone, Russia, Britain, Venezuela, Jordan, Mexico, Morocco, New Zealand, and the United States. If the Court does not include a judge of the nationality of one of the disputing states, that state may appoint a person as an ad hoc judge for that case. Thus, there may be more than fifteen judges sitting on a particular case.

Procedures of the Court

The Court's procedures, unsurprisingly, are highly formal. Cases are brought by written application or notification of a special arrangement to use the offices of the Court, and the parties are allowed to retain counsel if they desire. There then follows a written phase of the proceedings, in which the parties have specified dates on which to submit written memorials, countermemorials, and replies supported by documents. This is followed by the oral phase, in which at a public hearing the Court hears witnesses, experts, agents, and counsel for both sides. After the hearings are closed, the Court deliberates in camera before making a majority decision. The judgment is delivered at a public hearing, following which the reasons for the judgment are published in an opinion. Dissenting judges are entitled to deliver separate opinions. The process is identical for requests for advisory opinions; every state or intergovernmental organization is entitled to submit its views in writing or orally.

The Court normally hears cases as a full court. However, under special circumstances, Articles 26 to 29 of the Statute provide for the creation of special chambers—composed of fewer judges who are acceptable to the parties—to deal with particular categories of cases, for the speedy dispatch of business or to deal with a special individual case (Merrills 1998: 140). Such special chambers were established in 1982, 1985, and 1987. In July 1993, in response to the growing saliency of international environmental issues, the Court established a special seven-member Chamber on Environmental Matters (ICJ 2008).

In deciding its cases, the Court must apply the applicable law. Article 38 of the Statute provides as follows:

1. The Court, whose function is to decide in accordance with international law such disputes as are submitted to it shall apply:

   (a) international conventions, whether general or particular, establishing rules expressly recognized by the contesting States;

   (b) international custom, as evidence of a general practice accepted as law;

   (c) the general principles of law recognized by civilized nations;

   (d) subject to the provisions of Article 59 (which prescribes that the Court's decision has no binding force except between the parties and in respect of that particular case), judicial decisions and the teachings of the most highly qualified publicists of the various nations, as subsidiary means for the determination of rules of law.

2. This provision shall not prejudice the power of the Court to decide a case *ex aequo et bono*, if the parties agree hereto. (ICJ 2008)

In other words, the Court applies the same sources of law that arbitration panels and other judicial bodies recognize.

Functions of the Court

The Court has two primary functions: to settle in accordance with international law cases submitted by states and to render advisory opinions on legal questions referred to it by duly authorized international organs and agencies. The Court is not authorized to hear cases brought by individuals or nonstate groups, nor can it exercise any criminal jurisdiction, having no authority to try to punish individuals for violations of international criminal law; it can only try cases brought by states and with their consent. Once a case has been tried, there is no appeal from its judgment; its decision is final and binding. Article 94 of the UN Charter adds weight to the Court's power, stipulating, "If any party to a case fails to perform the obligations incumbent upon it under a judgment rendered by the Court, the other party may have recourse to the Security Council, which may, if it deems necessary, make recommendations or decide upon reasons to be taken to give effect to the judgment" (ICJ 2008). There has in reality been little recourse to this provision, as most of the Court's judgments are adhered to.

The Court's other function—delivering advisory opinions—is both discretionary and nonbinding. It may refuse to give an opinion if it suspects that the request is an attempt by one party to obtain a legal ruling without the consent of the opposing party (Bilder 1997: 168). In almost all cases, however, the Court has complied with requests for advisory opinions. Unlike its judgments, the Court's advisory opinions are not legally binding and impose no obligation on the requesting organization or state to heed the Court's advice (Janis 1992: 29). In practice, advisory opinions are usually accepted in the same fashion as its judgments, apart from those cases involving intractable political conflict—the July 2004 opinion on Israel's security was immediately rejected by the Israeli government.

The Court's Work

Considering the elaborate organization and high professional quality of the Court, it has only a moderate record in conflict resolution and has been involved in none of the most serious conflicts of the twentieth century. In fact, the considerable attention it attracts is far greater than the sum of its practice might appear to warrant. In the twenty-five years from 1921 to 1945, the Permanent Court of International Justice issued thirty-one judgments, twenty-five substantive orders, and twenty-seven advisory opinions. This is roughly three or four decisions every year. In the years since 1946, the International Court of Justice has issued seventy-nine judgments, more than sixty substantive orders, and twenty-five advisory opinions. Taken together, the Court has averaged about two judgments or decisions per year, although there have been more or less busy years: no decisions were rendered in 1947, 1967, 1977, and 1983; seven or more decisions were rendered in 1950, 1956, and 1973 (Janis 1992: 19). In recent years, there has been something of an upsurge in the work of the Court, and in early 2008 there were some fourteen cases pending. Overall, however, in the context of the many hundreds of international disputes and wars over the last hundred years, the Court has taken only a minor role in interstate conflict resolution.

The Court's judgments have concerned disputes over land frontiers and maritime boundaries, territorial sovereignty, the nonuse of force, noninterference in the internal affairs of states, diplomatic relations, hostage-taking, crimes of genocide, the rights of asylum, nationality, guardianship, rights of passage, and economic rights. Importantly, in the majority of cases considered by the Court, judicial settlement has only been one part of the conflict settlement process, with negotiation, mediation, or referral to the United Nations sometimes preceding or following the judicial phase. In fact, judicial processes are virtually always accompanied by diplomatic attempts at settlement. While many of the cases considered by the Court have been of only minor importance, a number have been relatively significant both in terms of their usefulness in settling potentially dangerous disputes and for their impact in developing international law (Bilder 1997: 171). The Court, therefore, has been an occasional but real actor on the world stage.

The Court's advisory opinions have been somewhat underutilized in comparison to its judgments. The PCIJ handed down its first advisory opinion in 1922. In all, it delivered twenty-seven opinions, of which eleven concerned Poland and/or Danzig and six related to the International Labor Organization (Janis 1992: 28). The ICJ first rendered an opinion on *Conditions of Admission of a State to Membership in the United Nations* in 1948. Since then it has given twenty-five advisory opinions, although fifteen of these were given before 1961. This translates to about one every three years for the last four decades.

Evaluating Legal Methods of Conflict Resolution

Why do international actors choose legal methods to resolve their disputes? When will they be helpful and successful, and when will they be unhelpful? States and other international actors have to assess both the advantages and disadvantages of legal approaches compared to other methods like negotiation, mediation, or referral to the United Nations. Like other approaches, legal methods have a mix of strengths and weaknesses.

The Strengths of Legal Methods

In the first instance, legal methods are a rational and orderly way of dealing with disputes, providing a flexible framework in which each side can present its respective claims (Merrills 1998). Consequently, a greater understanding of each other's position may result, thereby facilitating the conflict resolution process. Related to this, arbitration and adjudication are dispositive and can be a useful way of settling troublesome issues, dispensing with the need to arrange further conflict resolution exercises and moving on to other issues (Bilder 1997: 174). In some instances, it can be a way of disposing of minor legal disputes which have the potential to grow into major problems if they are not dealt with swiftly.

Legal methods are also impartial and principled, being based on "the rule of law" rather than the respective power of the parties or the bias of government officials. This is a major advantage for small states that are vulnerable to coercion by more powerful nations. It also means that states can have confidence in the process, and decisions reached by impartial processes can assert a strong claim to both acceptability and legitimacy. Being based on the application of legal principles, arbitration and adjudication are authoritative processes, having respect from both the parties and the international community. This can also buttress expectations of and pressures for compliance with the award (Bilder 1997: 174).

The psychological effect of an impersonal legal process should also not be discounted. Legal methods provide states with a powerful face-saving device (Bederman 1992: 166). Governments can dispose of politically sensitive or highly charged issues without taking responsibility for losses or concessions. In addition, the duration of the legal process—usually years of dispassionate legal analysis

and adjustment—can buy time to seek a negotiated settlement and reduce tensions by effectively depoliticizing the issues (Merrills 1998: 161) or providing an opportunity to let off steam and permit tempers to cool (Elias 1979: 139).

The processes of arbitration and adjudication are generally understood to be complex, expensive, and somewhat intimidating. The proposal by one state or the wider international community to submit a dispute to legal settlement is therefore a powerful signal indicating the seriousness of the conflict. Consequently, the parties may be encouraged to redouble their efforts to find a peaceful solution through diplomatic means. In any case, the very existence of judicial processes or provisions for compulsory arbitration can discourage unreasonable behavior and prevent the escalation of conflict, even if they are not specifically invoked (Bilder 1997: 174; Merrills 1998: 117).

At the general level of international law, legal methods are important not only for settling individual disputes but also for guiding and clarifying rules for future behavior. The ICJ is particularly important in this regard. By far the bulk of the judicial work of the Court involves the interpretation and application of international conventions and various agreements. Its importance in ensuring uniformity, providing unity, and developing international legal principles cannot be overemphasized (Elias 1979: 120). In this regard, the Court has made a tangible contribution to the conduct of nations, including conflict regulation. In fact, the record shows that states, for the most part, adhere to judicial decisions. This has the effect of reinforcing the international rule of law. The normative function of international arbitration and adjudication is important and real, even if it is difficult to measure. When a legal system works well, disputes are in large part avoided (Higgins 1994: 1). The existence (and operation) of legal methods therefore acts as a normative framework for conflict prevention.

The Limitations of Legal Approaches

Despite their evident advantages, law-based methods of conflict resolution also have serious limitations, which are especially evident in three areas: enforcement, judicial scope, and the conservative nature of international legal processes (Bercovitch and Jackson 1997). International law differs from the domestic law of nations because it has no enforcement machinery. If a state is determined to violate international law, no central authority or coercive machinery exists to prevent it or punish that state. Only ad hoc (and necessarily selective) coalitions supported by powerful states, such as those organized against Iraq in 1991 and 2003, can enforce international law through military force. Critically, powerful states are immune even from this kind of ad hoc enforcement.

> The difference between international law and the domestic law of countries lie[s] not in their character as law or in the kind of order they are designed to support, but in the actual distribution of power in the countries they serve, and in the degree to which that distribution has itself been reduced to order. A national community is one in which there is a very large number of weak units of power, so that sanctions against breaches of the law are normally effective and easy to maintain. . . . The international community is one in which there is a small number of units of power, of which some are enormous, most are considerable, and none are negligible. (Fawcett 1971: 15)

This problem strikes at the very heart of international law. It means that observance of international law is based on considerations other than the threat of coercion. In international relations, self-enforcement proceeds from calculations about reciprocity, self-interest, and the threat of informal sanctions and negative world opinion. For extremely powerful states or states that feel vulnerable to their neighbors, considerations of national security may override other considerations like negative world opinion.

A second shortcoming of law-based methods of conflict resolution concerns judicial scope. Legal methods are rarely able to address political questions. Inasmuch as few disputes relate purely to legal questions, litigation is suitable for very few international conflicts. Tribunals have to focus on the narrow legal issues before them and ignore wider underlying causes and sources of tension. Where the legal dispute is a symptom of a far more complex problem, the judgment may not settle and may even exacerbate the conflict (Bilder 1997: 176). It can also be argued that as states are political entities, even strictly legal questions are never truly divorced from political considerations. The counterargument, of course, is that international law is a complete system, and if the parties have given their consent, there is no dispute that is beyond the jurisdiction or capacity of a court or arbitral tribunal. The World Court has never rejected a case on the grounds that it is "non-justiciable" and better dealt with by "political" methods. Nonetheless, most states are reluctant to use judicial methods where political interests are involved (Merrills 1998: 155–59), which excludes nearly every armed conflict in modern times.

The third limitation is that law is a very conservative creature that does not adjust easily to change. At a practical level, this means that judicial processes are inherently inflexible. Where states are bound in an interdependent relationship of continuous interaction, and where many problems are intrinsically resistant to all-or-nothing solutions, the necessarily zero-sum nature of judicial decisions may be profoundly unhelpful (Bilder 1997: 177). The arbitration or adjudication process may also freeze the dispute and lock the parties into hardened positions. This can narrow the space for compromise or maneuver, leading to long-term contention and conflict escalation.

More substantively, the many changes in the nature and makeup of the international system, as well as the rise of new forms of violent conflict, have not been matched by appropriate changes in international law. Lacking the legislative processes for amending or revoking the existing sources of law that domestic systems provide, international legal bodies inevitably perpetuate the status quo through their recognition of existing treaties and obligations. In a system characterized by conflict and change, international law is dangerously inflexible (Luard 1988: 247, 255; Ziegler 1987: 159). Thus, when one party is demanding a change in the law—perhaps with good reason—rather than the application of existing laws, international tribunals may provide an unsatisfactory solution (Bilder 1997: 177).

In addition, the main body of current international law originated in the European state system. For this reason, international law has marginal relevance for many new African and Asian states, who have only a weak cultural affinity with it. Also, most international law accepts only the nation-state as a valid subject of law, whereas the contemporary international system contains a multitude of important nonstate actors, such as international organizations, ethnic groups, liberation movements, terrorist groups, NGOs, and powerful multinational companies. Many of the actors involved in today's internal wars do not qualify as states and thus have little recourse to international law. It is due to this combination of factors—the political character of terrorism and the inflexibility and state-centrism of international law—that law-based methods for dealing with the challenges of international terrorism are highly limited (Nesi 2006).

Other potential problems with legal methods include the possibility that they may, in fact, fail to act impartially: the process of selecting judges may be influenced by political factors, and the national judges on the panel may be predisposed toward one party's position (Bilder 1997: 175–76). Furthermore, the act of "taking a state to court" may be regarded as a hostile and unfriendly act, thereby increasing tensions and escalating the conflict. Last, judicial settlement may be too precedential. That is, while the outcome of a particular minor dispute may be of little interest to the parties, its precedential effect on similar or analogous disputes or classes of disputes could be highly significant. This problem is directly related to the fact that the majority of judicial settlements are final and binding, and there is no way to challenge dubious or unsatisfactory awards (Merrills 1998: 119).

Conclusion

At the start of the chapter, we argued that it is easy to fall into the extremes of pessimism or overoptimism when assessing the role of law-based methods in international conflict resolution. We have attempted to walk a fine line between these positions, suggesting that international law has a real but limited role in the management of international conflict. Several other conclusions flow from the analysis.

First, legal methods are an important part of the *interstate* conflict resolution system. Used in conjunction with other established diplomatic processes, they are a useful way of dealing with a particular set of disputes—interstate legal and commercial issues—and may even be useful for some important political questions as well, such as territorial disputes. Interestingly, judicial methods have been important for settling a number of territorial disputes in Africa. As a consequence, despite the potentially large number of boundary conflicts in the region—due to the haphazard colonial boundary-drawing process of the late nineteenth century—such disputes have actually been rare in postcolonial Africa. Law-based methods have also been effective in settling commercial, trade, and some territorial disputes between the developed and liberal democratic OECD nations.

In this regard, law-based methods have a better adherence record than some other less formal methods of conflict resolution such as mediation or referral to international organizations. However, the most important function of legal methods is their normative, conflict-prevention function. Successful judicial settlement strengthens the rule of law in international society and discourages the kind of behavior that is likely to lead to serious interstate conflict in the first instance. Evidence for the ongoing efficacy and relevance of international law lies in the increasingly rare instances of serious interstate conflict, the 2003 Gulf War notwithstanding. Despite the rise in the number of states in the international system, the vast majority of international armed conflicts today involve subnational groups vying for power within states. In this respect, it is not too late to suggest that it will be important that the ongoing "war on terrorism" avoids undermining the institutions and norm-upholding functions of international law; sacrificing the international legal order for narrow conceptions of national security can only result in a weakening of international conflict resolution.

The strength of international law, however, is at the same time its greatest weakness. Having a well-developed set of procedures and a history of dealing with interstate disputes, international legal methods are poorly positioned to deal with international conflict and security issues like terrorism in the twenty-first century. A creature of the late nineteenth and early twentieth centuries, international law is severely limited in its ability to offer solutions to the kinds of intrastate conflicts and substate challenges that now predominate. This is not to say that it has no potential for contributing to the resolution of internal wars or terrorist campaigns; rather, it is to suggest that unless it can reform and shed its Euro-centric, state-centric biases it will be increasingly irrelevant to the resolution of serious international conflicts like those seen since the early 1990s. In this regard, the current articulation of human rights law and its accompanying prosecutorial instruments such as the ICC is a welcome development (Delbruck 1987: 139). By strengthening the emerging human rights regime, one of the primary sources of intrastate conflict can be dealt with, and one of the primary impediments to postconflict reconstruction—justice for human rights victims—can be neutralized. Thus, we see an important normative, conflict prevention role for international law–based methods, even if their conflict resolution potential is politically circumscribed in particular instances of conflict.

CHAPTER FIVE

International Organization
The United Nations

Resolving or managing conflict through the structures of international organizations such as the United Nations (UN) is a political approach that differs significantly from the diplomatic and law-based methods—negotiation, mediation, adjudication, and arbitration—we have already examined. In the multilateral context, disputing states have opportunities to explore their settlement options through a variety of open and closed forums, with or without the help of any number of intermediaries and with an expanded range of possible outcomes. At the same time, there are considerable risks in resorting to multilateral institutions. A state may face exposure to unwanted scrutiny and attention from outside powers, pressure to conform to international opinion, or collective expressions of disapproval. This potent mix of opportunity and risk means that states rarely submit their disputes to international organizations as a matter of first resort. In most cases they will attempt to deal with the conflict themselves and only avail themselves of multilateral channels if their own efforts fail or as an adjunct to other diplomatic processes. Nonetheless, the premier multilateral institution, the UN, has to some degree been involved in nearly every serious international conflict in the postwar period. In spite of numerous and at times spectacular failures, the UN has proved to be remarkably durable and flexible. With a clear mandate, an accompanying range of methods and mechanisms at its disposal, a strong record of involvement in crises, and near universal membership, the UN plays a central role in the institutional resolution of international conflict.

The legal and normative basis of the UN's role lies in Article 1 of the UN Charter, which defines the primary purpose of the Organization.

> To maintain international peace and security, and to that end: to take effective collective measures for the prevention and removal of threats to the peace, and for the suppression of acts of aggression or other breaches of the peace, and to bring about by peaceful means, and in conformity with the principles of justice and international law, adjustment or settlement of international disputes or situations which might lead to a breach of the peace.

Article 1 later speaks of the UN's secondary goal of promoting "international cooperation in solving international problems of an economic, social, cultural, or humanitarian character, and in promoting and encouraging respect for human rights." In other words, the primary task of the UN is the maintenance of a new framework for international security based on collective action and cooperation in areas that are likely to be the source of tension. The Charter gives the Organization two distinct responsibilities: to end armed conflict whenever it occurs and to assist states in conflict to settle their differences by peaceful means.

Occupying the central role in the institutional structure for dealing with international disputes, no other body has been quite so demonized, idealized, misrepresented, and misunderstood as the UN. It is, in fact, a misnomer to conceive of the UN as a unitary actor or a "body." It is, rather, an amalgam of actors, processes, and interests, lacking any real autonomy and more accurately described as an arena—a locus of action for states pursuing foreign policy aims (Zartman 1999: 68). In this sense, conflict resolution occurs "through" the UN rather than "by" the UN (see Merrills 1998), and only after member-states harmonize their foreign policy aims in a cooperative framework.

The notion of the UN as a kind of structured process through which states interact, rather than as an autonomous actor able to act with a degree of independence, makes evaluating its role in conflict resolution a problematic exercise. International organizations (IOs)—lacking the boundaries that define and distinguish a territorial entity, and with circumscribed decision-making processes, limited resources, and few autonomous implementation powers—cannot be evaluated on the same terms as governments. After all, the UN operates concurrently with governments and other actors it cannot control. It is only one element of the international conflict resolution system—albeit a central element—and usually works in tandem with the parties' own efforts, intervention by other intermediaries such as interested states, and even the involvement of other IOs like regional organizations. Attributing cause and effect, therefore, is extremely difficult, as is disentangling where and what role the "UN" played in a conflict.

As a consequence, the UN is regularly subjected to contradictory expectations about its ability to act autonomously and effectively and its aims and purposes. Such expectations produce contradictory assessments about the utility of the UN's procedures and the extent to which it should be involved in conflict resolution. Optimists tend to place unrealistic hopes in the Organization, evaluating it by standards unrelated to its actual capacities (Roberts and Kingsbury 1993: 14). For example, the UN is sometimes judged against the standard of a prototype world government dedicated to the elimination of war or as the embodiment of a higher international morality. Its inevitable failures in the face of such expectations can be the starting point for bitter criticism and disappointment. The UN is then criticized for its double standards—proclaiming one set of values while practicing another. Alternately, it is maligned for being the vehicle by which states, especially the most powerful states, pursue their own narrow interests. Both positions, of course, are founded on a misunderstanding of the workings of IOs in international relations.

In this chapter, we aim to provide a more realistic assessment of the UN's place in international conflict resolution, avoiding the extremes of overoptimism or undue pessimism. The following sections outline the methods by which the UN manages disputes, its advantages and disadvantages, and its overall record of conflict resolution. Before we look specifically at the UN, however, a general discussion of the role of IOs in conflict is necessary.

International Organization and the Resolution of Conflict

The UN is not, strictly speaking, a functionalist enterprise in the same way that the European Union (EU) is. It is not a supranational organization, and in the Charter the sovereign state remains the building block of international order. The UN's role in promoting peace and security, however, originates in functionalist principles. In addition to the peaceful settlement of disputes, the UN has other goals: the development of friendly relations between states; promoting cooperation and the harmonization of action between all members; enacting measures to strengthen universal peace; and practicing tolerance and peaceful coexistence (see Bennett 1988: 100). The functionalist approach recognizes that peace is only possible in the context of meaningful cooperation between states and dealing with the underlying economic, social, and ideological causes of conflict.

Functionalist theory argues that IOs are the primary means by which interdependence—economic, political, and environmental—can be managed. Cooperation within institutions over issues such as free trade or the global commons will produce, as a spillover effect, political cooperation and a commitment to the pacific settlement of disputes.

> The theory of *functionalism* in international relations is based on the hope that more and more common tasks will be delegated to such specific functional organizations and that each of these organizations will become in time *supranational;* that is, superior to its member governments in power and authority. In this way, says the theory, the world's nations will gradually become integrated into a single community within which war will be impossible. (Deutsch 1978: 208; emphasis in original)

Facilitating international cooperation is no easy task, however, and simply establishing an institutional framework is no guarantee of success. In the context of international relations, it is sometimes rational for states to enjoy public goods—such as the global commons, free-trade regimes, or international security—without contributing toward their costs. This is the so-called free-rider dilemma, whereby states adopt uncooperative postures so as not to be hurt by the defection or cheating of others (Gowa 1989: 309). In addition to the possible gains of defecting, the large number of actors in international politics creates uncertainty about the intentions, policies, and actions of other states. Cooperation therefore falls victim to calculations of self-interest in the context of uncertainty. It is not that states are unwilling to cooperate, but rather that "the structures of international relations preclude the generation or sufficient co-ordination of collective will for co-operation to emerge" (Van Walraven 1999: 15).

Normative and Constructivist conceptualizations of international relations suggest that cooperation is not necessarily a chimera, however, and IOs can play an important—if limited—role in mitigating these structural obstacles, thereby facilitating cooperation. First, it is argued that cooperation is possible if a powerful state or group of states provides unequivocal leadership in pursuing the attainment of the public good (Snidal 1985). Obviously, a precondition for the emergence of such leadership is a willingness on the part of the hegemon to bear the costs associated with such a role. In other words, cooperation emerges if a hegemon (or dominant hegemonic coalition) guarantees that agreements are kept, rules obeyed, and transgressors punished. In addition to the necessary capabilities for such a role, the hegemon must attain a certain degree of legitimacy. IOs provide both forums and processes by which hegemonic leadership can emerge or coalesce around dominant coalitions, and the UN Security Council was in fact designed to institutionalize such leadership in the area of international peace and security.

As the record of the UN demonstrates, hegemonic leadership is not always forthcoming, especially for conflicts in regions where the great powers have no direct interest and there is no direct threat to the stability of the entire system—such as Africa in the post–Cold War period. However, cooperation is still possible, even in the absence of hegemonic leadership, in the context of international regimes. Regimes are defined as sets of principles, norms, rules, and decision-making procedures that facilitate agreements between states in given issue areas (Krasner 1983: 1). They are not identical with international organizations but represent the decision of states to cooperate in the cadre of such organizations (Haas 1983: 190–91). International regimes facilitate cooperation by providing a forum for establishing contacts and formulating common postures, reducing transaction costs, mitigating the effects of international anarchy, clarifying standards of conduct and international norms, and improving transparency, which in turn reduces uncertainty. The UN has attempted to establish and maintain a regime based on the peaceful settlement of disputes and collective security management.

Nevertheless, the UN regime is for various reasons weak, and cooperation—especially in the area of security cooperation—is often difficult to attain. It is partly due to the very large number of actors, each with its own interests and concerns, interacting in the UN framework. Such a context makes it hard for states to identify all the different interests or anticipate the behavior of others, and thus relative anonymity goes up, the possibility of free-riding increases, and the feasibility of sanctions is reduced (Van Walraven 1999: 22). A strategy for affecting the behavior of states and engendering cooperation in such a situation is to involve fewer actors in a specific context, usually by decomposing the issue area or differentiating cooperative procedures. Actor reduction tactics increase transparency and enhance reciprocity. This is a common strategy for IOs, and the UN Security Council is an example of such a process in action. Here a select and relatively small group of powerful states has assumed responsibility for the security issue area.

In summary, IOs operate in a highly constrained environment. They possess little autonomy, and cooperation on important issues is not automatic. Nevertheless, there are means by which the structural impediments to international cooperation can be overcome, such as hegemonic leadership, regime creation, and actor reduction, among others. The position of the UN is similarly constrained, which, as will be demonstrated, helps to explain its patchy record in conflict resolution and some of its more obvious shortcomings.

The Basis of UN Conflict Resolution

The UN came into being on 24 October 1945 in the aftermath of World War II. As the successor to the League of Nations, and having learned from its failures, the UN was equipped with two main mechanisms for preserving peace: a collective security system and a set of procedures for the peaceful settlement of disputes. The essence of the collective security concept is that the threat of collective force will deter aggressors, or failing deterrence, that the actual employment of collective measures will defeat them. Chapter VII of the UN Charter establishes the basis of the collective security framework. It gives the Security Council wide-ranging authority to first, determine whether a threat to international peace exists (Article 34), and second, authorize preliminary measures (Article 40), sanctions (Article 41), or the use of force (Article 42) to deal with the threat. In addition, members of the UN are expected to support the Security Council's decisions (Article 43) or in some cases implement those decisions on behalf of the Security Council (Article 48). Last, Article 47 provides for the establishment of a Military Staff Committee, made up of representatives of the permanent members, whose purpose was "to advise and assist the Security Council on all questions relating to the Security Council's military requirements for the maintenance of international peace and security, the employment and command of forces placed at its disposal, and regulation of armaments, and possible disarmament." Since this book is concerned with peaceful methods of conflict resolution, it is not necessary to examine the coercive aspects of the UN system any further.

The basis for the UN's approach to conflict resolution lies in the obligation on member states to settle their disputes by peaceful means, to refrain from the threat or use of force, and to cooperate with UN-sponsored actions (Article 2). The Charter states, "The parties to any dispute, the continuance of which is likely to endanger the maintenance of international peace and security, shall, first of all, seek a solution by negotiation, enquiry, mediation, conciliation, arbitration, judicial settlement, resort to regional agencies or arrangements, or other peaceful means of their own choice" (Article 33). If the disputing parties fail in their own efforts, they are obligated to refer it to the Security Council (Article 37).

Of course, the Security Council does not need the consent of the parties to consider any conflict, which makes it rather unique among international conflict resolution methods. Under Article 34, "The Security Council may investigate any dispute, or any situation which might lead to international friction or give rise to a dispute, in order to determine whether the continuance of the dispute or situation is likely to endanger the maintenance of international peace and security." Although the Security Council has primary responsibility for ensuring peace and security, other UN organs also have important roles in conflict resolution.

UN Methods of Conflict Resolution

As we have stated, conflict resolution takes place primarily "through" UN structures, rather than "by" them. Three main organs—the Security Council, the General Assembly, and the secretary-general—play the most important roles in UN conflict resolution. Each has a number of available procedures for dealing with conflict. Over time, UN conflict resolution practice has had to adapt to changes in the international environment. One of the most important adaptations, and one not foreseen by the founders of the Organization, has been the emergence of peacekeeping.

The Security Council

Due largely to its enforcement powers, many consider the Security Council to be the most important organ in the UN conflict resolution framework. Disputes can be referred to the Security Council in three ways: by member states, usually one of the disputants or a Security Council member; by the General Assembly; or by the secretary-general. Unlike diplomatic or legal methods, the consent of the disputing states is not required for the conflict to be dealt with by the Security Council. Once a dispute has been referred to the UN, the Charter provides a logical progression of steps to be followed.

First, the issue will be adopted as an item on the Security Council's agenda. Usually there is a preliminary discussion about the legality, practicality, or wisdom of Security Council involvement. During this process, which might take days, some of the substantive issues at the heart of the dispute may be aired even if the agenda item is subsequently rejected (Bennett 1988: 103). Long-running disputes that have been previously adopted can be taken up at any time without this preliminary step. Once the dispute has been accepted onto the agenda, a Council meeting is held where the parties or sympathetic representatives each present their case. Any other parties whose interests may be affected will also be allowed to participate, and documentation, including communications between the respective governments, will be presented. At some point during the debate, one or more resolutions relating to the conflict will be introduced and voted on.

The Security Council, in dealing with a conflict, can either suggest the terms of settlement itself or pursue a form of pacific settlement. If it specifies a solution to the conflict, such as demanding a troop withdrawal by the invading side, it may employ its coercive methods to enforce the decision: imposing sanctions or authorizing a military action. Normally, the Security Council only recommends the terms of settlement when it is satisfied that the parties themselves have exhausted all peaceful avenues and the dispute is likely to escalate and endanger international peace and security (Murphy 1983: 14).

More commonly the Security Council will attempt to promote the peaceful settlement of the dispute. In these circumstances, there are a large number of methods it can call on. Often, its first action will be to make recommendations or call on the parties to observe a cease-fire, stand down their armed forces, withdraw from disputed territory, accept an offer of mediation, or initiate bilateral negotiations. If the facts surrounding the dispute are unclear or contested, the Security Council may authorize and dispatch a fact-finding mission, made up of either a special representative or a subcommittee. Clarifying the situation can in itself facilitate communication between the parties and promote dialogue. In addition to fact-finding committees, there may be a need to establish a special committee to assist the negotiations. These can take the form of good offices committees or a more formal conciliation commission.

One of the Security Council's most important roles is mediation, and this too may take several forms. It may formally appoint a mediator, such as the secretary-general or one of his officials, a prominent personality, or a high-ranking government representative to act as an intermediary on behalf of the Council. Alternatively, the Security Council might appoint an informal mediator who can act with a degree of latitude. In some cases, the Council itself will act as a mediator, either through a prominent member, such as the current president of the Council, or through informal consultations. This kind of "quiet diplomacy" often occurs in the private chamber of the Security Council, which is directly adjacent to the public chamber, and accounts for the vast majority of the Council's work (Fetherston 1994b: 5–6). In many cases, the open meetings are formalizations of informally agreed measures. Another form of mediation is convocation, where the Security Council brings together all the essential actors in a dispute in a round-table discussion (Zartman 1999: 71–73).

Other methods by which the Security Council can manage disputes include referral to other UN bodies, such as the ICJ in cases where there is a legal dimension to the conflict, or to regional organizations, such as the African Union (AU), the Organization of American States (OAS), the Arab League, or EU when local regional actors might be more appropriate. Last, the Security Council can authorize peacekeeping operations to oversee cease-fires, supervise troop withdrawals, provide a buffer between the two armies, assist in demobilization, or implement agreements.

The General Assembly

The basis of the General Assembly's role in conflict resolution lies in Article 10, which gives it the right to consider any matter within the purview of the Charter. Also, the Assembly has the right to make inquiries and studies that might lead to united action (Articles 13, 14) and to be kept informed (Articles 10, 11, 12). Furthermore, Article 14 states that the Assembly "may recommend measures for the peaceful adjustment of any situation, regardless of origin, which it deems likely to impair the general welfare or friendly relations among nations." Its general role, then, is to serve as a forum for public discussion and multilateral diplomacy aimed at the adjustment of unsatisfactory situations and the acceptance of cooperation.

In contrast to the Security Council, the Assembly's approach has always been more in the nature of persuasion than in authoritative decision making. This is due to the restrictions of the Charter and the Assembly's unwieldy size, cumbersome organization, and lack of enforcement powers. We have already noted that the Charter gives the primary responsibility for peace and security to the Security Council. This is reinforced in Article 12, which forbids the Assembly from taking any action on a dispute while it is being considered in the Security Council. When action is required to ensure international peace and security, the Assembly must refer it to the Security Council "either before or after discussion" (Article 11).

In practice, these restrictions mean that the General Assembly tends to deal with unresolved disputes that have become perennial problems, while the Security Council deals with new disputes, especially of a crisis nature (Bennett 1988: 129). Although they have been assigned different roles, in practice there is a great deal of cooperation and coordination between the Assembly and the Security Council. Many disputes have been handled by both bodies, and the Security Council is not averse to passing on responsibility to the Assembly if it feels there is an advantage to be gained.

The General Assembly has over the years played a larger role in conflict resolution than might have been anticipated, given its inherent limitations. The reasons for this lie in the devices by which the Assembly has encroached on the domain of the Security Council and expanded its own powers. First, the General Assembly has always given generous interpretation to its Charter powers and functions in the area of peace and security. In addition to passing frequent resolutions on conflict situations and contentious issues, it has called several special sessions to deal with disputes and threats to the peace.

Second, and most important, in 1950 the Assembly passed the Uniting for Peace Resolution. This resolution asserted the right of the Assembly to deal with disputes posing a threat to or breach of the peace, or an act of aggression, at a time when the Security Council was paralyzed by superpower competition and the promiscuous use of the veto. The Western powers first used this resolution to continue UN action in Korea in the face of Soviet opposition in the Security Council. The Assembly created the first UN peacekeeping force during the Suez Crisis of 1956, the United Nations Emergency Force (UNEF I), as well as the UN Operation in the Congo (ONUC) in 1960. In fact, the level of paralysis in the Security Council in the 1950s due to superpower rivalry created serious expectations that the Assembly might become the predominant agency for dispute settlement (Bennett 1988: 129). This did not eventuate, but the Assembly does retain a fairly significant role in conflict resolution as a consequence of these events.

Like the Security Council, a dispute can be referred to the Assembly by a party to the dispute, by the Security Council, or by any member or group of members of the Organization. Similarly, the Assembly can recommend terms for the settlement of the dispute, although unlike the Security Council it has no power to enforce its decisions. In 1948, for example, the Assembly set out an elaborate plan for the future of Palestine during the Arab-Israeli conflict. Normally the Assembly will attempt to assist the conflict resolution process using an array of peaceful methods similar to those of the Security Council. For example, the Assembly will often call on the parties to initiate a cease-fire, begin talks, or implement a peace plan. In unique circumstances it may also initiate a peacekeeping mission under the Uniting for Peace Resolution. The Assembly has established a Special Committee on Peacekeeping Operations to assist the UN's work in this area.

Fact-finding is another important method available to the Assembly, and in recent years there have been serious suggestions that a permanent fact-finding capability be established for Assembly use. Like the Security Council, the Assembly can also employ mediation, conciliation, and good offices, either formally in special bodies or informally through quiet diplomacy. Last, the Assembly can refer the dispute to regional organizations or other UN organs.

In addition to directly assisting the parties and passing resolutions on issues causing dispute, the Assembly plays an important role in attempting to deal with some of the underlying causes of tension in international relations.

Thus, it has for many years been active in promoting disarmament and arms control, environmental protection, the regulation of the small arms trade, the end of racial discrimination, fairer trade structures, and universal human rights, among other contentious issues.

The Secretariat

As the third pillar of the UN's conflict resolution structure, the secretary-general's position is one of the most visible and important of the entire UN system. The various secretaries-general have over the years forged a role that is relatively independent of the other two organs. The basis of this role lies first of all in Article 97, which provides that the secretary-general shall be the Chief Administrative Officer of the UN. As such, he is the focal point for the collection and distribution of information and helps prepare the ground for the decision-making organs. An important part of this administrative role is his annual report on the Organization's activities, which is often a vehicle for drawing attention to areas of conflict. Second, "the Secretary General shall act in that capacity in all meetings" of the General Assembly and Security Council, and "perform such other functions as are entrusted to him by these organs" (Article 98). In other words, the Security Council or Assembly may delegate certain tasks to the secretary-general, such as providing good offices, dispatching a fact-finding team, or overseeing a peacekeeping operation.

The secretary-general's most overtly political function and the source of his autonomy lies in Article 99, which states that he "may bring to the attention of the Security Council any matter which in his opinion may threaten international peace and security." This article gives him the authority to investigate any matter—not just open conflicts—which in his independent judgment may constitute a threat to peace and security, and place the matter on the agenda of the Security Council. By implication, he may even request the president of the Security Council to call a meeting (Skjelsbaek and Fermann 1996: 92). This, in one sense, can be construed as a kind of early warning function. In practice, however, the Secretaries General have used the powers of Article 99 to provide authority for a wider range of independent action than this (Cordovez 1987), such as fact-finding, mediation, and, in some cases, preempting the involvement of the Security Council by assisting the parties directly.

The level of autonomy and independence that gradually accrued to the secretary-general was largely unforeseen, the direct consequence of wider international developments combined with forceful leadership on the part of individual secretaries-general. As the effects of the Cold War began to be felt in the Security Council, the responsibility for peace and security fell to the Assembly, before decolonization—and the resulting influx of new members—reduced its effectiveness. With the Security Council deadlocked and the Assembly powerless, a disproportionate weight of responsibility fell on the secretary-general. In addition, a series of secretaries-general actively pursued and expanded their responsibilities in crisis management, often in the face of opposition by the Security Council members.

The methods of conflict resolution that the secretary-general can employ include both the delegated tasks he performs and his independent actions. First, the Security Council or Assembly may instruct the secretary-general to use his good offices, send personal emissaries, conduct inquiries through fact-finding, or supervise the implementation of agreements. He also plays an important role in providing information to decision makers and in coordinating the activities of the Security Council and the Assembly. One of his most important delegated functions is the organization and administration of peacekeeping operations. Once the Security Council has created and defined a peacekeeping mission, the secretary-general directs and manages the operation, then reports regularly to the Council on its progress. Specifically, with the help of the Department of Peacekeeping Operations (DPKO), the secretary-general is responsible for working out the terms of the operation, recruiting, deploying and supplying troops, arranging for financial support, negotiating the status-of-forces agreements that defined the terms of access, and overseeing operational control on a daily basis (Haas 1987: 42). Over the years, the secretary-general's role has been crucial to the success of UN peacekeeping.

Everything that he may be asked to do, apart from establishing a peacekeeping operation, the secretary-general can also do on his own. Typically, he will issue an appeal to the parties to instigate a cease-fire, initiate talks, or implement agreed terms. Given that he cannot personally devote himself to every conflict, he often sends special or personal representatives to act on his behalf. His role as mediator is very important, and may involve simply providing good offices or conciliation. Alternately, he is sometimes asked to suggest substantive proposals for settlement. In practice, much of his work occurs in quiet diplomacy, making the most of his central position, his discretion and impartiality, and the moral and politi-

cal status of his office. He also provides an important point of contact between governments that may not be able to meet directly, and sometimes even between governments and nongovernmental actors such as liberation movements. For example, he has at various times provided important contacts between the PLO and the Israeli government. In addition to fact-finding and conducting inquiries, the secretary-general has also been asked to act as an arbitrator, notably in the Rainbow Warrior case between New Zealand and France.

Peacekeeping

Along with the Uniting for Peace Resolution and the development of the role of the secretary-general, the emergence of peacekeeping has been a major innovation of the UN. In the next chapter, we provide a more extensive analysis of peacekeeping. Peacekeeping can be defined as "an operation involving military personnel, but without enforcement powers, under-taken by the United Nations to help maintain or restore international peace and security in areas of conflict" (United Nations 1990: 4). It emerged as a creative response to deadlock in the Security Council and was first developed to provide observer groups for conflicts in Kashmir and Palestine in the 1940s (Karns and Mingst 1994: 190). Later, it was used as a means of securing the withdrawal of British, French, and Israeli forces from Egypt during the Suez Crisis.

Based on the principles of impartiality, the consent of the parties, and the nonuse of force except in self-defense, peacekeeping can play a useful role in containing and defusing conflict, thereby providing breathing space for diplomatic negotiation or mediation. Specifically, peacekeeping operations involve a wide variety of tasks, depending on the nature of the conflict. First, they may involve an observation role, which can include the investigation of conflicts, cease-fire supervision, monitoring the terms of agreements, verification of troop withdrawals, and reconnaissance. Second, they may act as force separators in a buffer zone between conflicting parties. Third, peacekeepers are often called upon to guarantee law and order within a country, acting as a kind of international police force. In more recent years, peacekeeping has expanded its traditional tasks to include enforcement action and forms of humanitarian intervention (see chapter 8). In practice, peacekeepers are quite often called on to provide mediation and conciliation in zones of conflict, organize proximity talks, and arrange local truces.

UN Conflict Resolution since 1945: An Overview

The UN has been involved in nearly every major international conflict since 1945, either through direct action by the Security Council, formal or informal discussions in the Security Council and General Assembly, diplomatic activity by the secretary-general, peacekeeping operations, or simply through quiet diplomacy in the corridors and chambers of the Organization. An overview of disputes considered by the Security Council and the General Assembly between January 1946 and June 1986, for example, documents more than 170 disputes (Bennett 1988: 107–14). A number of studies have attempted to examine the UN's record of formal involvement in conflict resolution to see what kind of success it has had. There are a number of problems with trying to assess the UN's impact on cases of conflict resolution. First, the UN is often only one of several actors that may be actively involved in a dispute at any one time. It may simultaneously be considered along with other organizations, interested states, and individual mediators. Second, a great deal of conflict resolution occurs "through" the UN and not necessarily "by" it, in informal, quiet diplomacy. That is, the diplomacy that the UN provides is often an adjunct to processes ongoing elsewhere, and the extent to which any final agreement is the result of UN activities is often unclear.

Nevertheless, Haas (1987, 1989), examined 282 disputes that occurred between July 1945 and September 1981. He discovered that 40 percent of the disputes were formally referred to the UN. Moreover, when they were broken down into degrees of seriousness, it was found that 49 percent of the most serious disputes were formally dealt with in the UN. Overall, the UN's aggregate level of success—measured by its impact on the dispute—was 23 percent, although this score obscures wide fluctuations in the UN's performance over time and issues.

Haas found that the UN's success was lowest for conflicts during the most intense periods of the Cold War and in decolonization conflicts that involved serious civil war. It was most successful when the conflicts were at the less serious end of the scale and involved middle or small states from the same Cold War bloc or when they were both unaligned. Interestingly, joint leadership by the superpowers and the active intervention of the secretary-general also produced successful action.

Another study by Wilkenfeld and Brecher (1989) examined 160 international crises between 1945 and 1975. They found that the UN was directly involved in 59 percent of them and was effective in abating the crisis in 18 percent of the cases. Similar to Haas, they also found that UN involvement increased when the crisis involved large-scale military actions: in 32 cases of full-scale war, the UN was active in 29 of them. Interestingly, they also found that the UN's success rate in these serious cases rose to 45 percent. Like Haas, they discovered that success was correlated with high-level activity on the part of the Security Council and the General Assembly.

Our own empirical study focused on instances of UN mediation, rather than the entire range of possible UN activities (see Bercovitch 1996b; Bercovitch and Fretter 2004), and covered the 1945 to 1995 period. The UN actively mediated in 91 of the 295 conflicts during this period. Obviously, some disputes involved UN activities other than mediation. We found that of 355 instances of mediation by UN officials or bodies over this period (some disputes required numerous mediation attempts over many years), success—in the form of cease-fires, partial agreements, and full political settlements—was achieved in 35 percent of the cases (see table 2). This record compares favorably with mediation success rates in general (see chapter 3) and demonstrates that when the UN actively engages in conflict resolution, it can have a significant impact.

Table 3 shows that UN interventions and mediations

TABLE 2. Mediation Success by International Actors

Mediators	Number of Mediation Efforts	Proportion of All Mediation Efforts	Successful Mediation Efforts	Success Rate
United Nations	355	23.1%	127	35.7%
Individual	55	3.6%	16	29.1%
Regional Organization	174	11.3%	78	44.8%
NGOs	97	6.3%	25	25.7%
State	722	46.9%	244	33.8%
Mixed	135	8.8%	54	40.0%
Total	1,538	100	544	

Source: Data from authors' own research.

occur primarily in conflicts between states. This is not surprising given that the UN is an intergovernmental organization, but it is problematic in the sense that the vast majority of serious international conflicts since the early 1990s have been intrastate conflicts. The bad news is compounded in table 4, which shows that UN mediation in intrastate conflicts is considerably more unsuccessful than its efforts in international conflicts. Internal conflicts are by definition very difficult to resolve, and there are added problems when a state-centric organization such as the UN attempts to intervene in domestically based conflict in one of its members. Table 5 shows that the UN has been most active in conflicts in the Middle East, Africa, and East Asia. These regions have been the site of decolonization conflicts, superpower rivalry, and intense civil wars. Many of these conflicts have proved intractable, and often the UN has been called in only after other parties have failed to manage them effectively themselves. In fact, the data show that most UN mediations are initiated once a conflict has been in existence for three years or more. By the time it is submitted to the UN it may well have spread and escalated beyond the capacity of any conflict manager.

Related to conflict intractability is the level of intensity. Here our data show that over 70 percent of UN mediations took place in conflicts of the highest category of intensity, that is, where more than 10,000 people had already perished in the fighting. The more intense the conflict, the more difficult it is to manage and resolve, as the level of hatred and the resources the parties have committed to the conflict make them resistant.

It is generally agreed that the success or failure of conflict resolution is in no large measure determined by the nature of the issues in dispute. Mediation by the UN shows clear demarcation in effectiveness between issues: decolonization issues had a success rate of over 45 per-

TABLE 5. Regional Distribution of UN Mediation Efforts

Region	UN Mediation	(%)
North and South America	37	10.4%
Africa	102	28.7%
Southwest Asia	24	6.8%
East Asia and the Pacific	27	7.7%
Middle East	84	23.6%
Europe	81	22.8%
Total	355	100%

Source: Data from authors' own research.

cent; Cold War issues had success in only 22 percent of cases; internal issues, such as ethnicity, had success rates of 21 percent. Internal conflicts, rooted in identity politics and competition over state resources, and framed in zero-sum terms, are highly resistant to conflict resolution, especially traditional forms of diplomacy. State-centric organizations, often without the resources to apply leverage, struggle to find effective solutions. Fortunately, as we shall see in subsequent chapters, the UN is attempting to adapt to the challenges of managing internal conflict through new methods aimed at getting to their roots.

Evaluating UN Conflict Resolution

For the reasons suggested previously—contradictory expectations about the aims, functions, roles, and abilities of the UN—assessing the achievements or the potential of the Organization in conflict resolution is a tricky exercise. There are no agreed-upon standards by which to measure its successes or failures, and observers differ in their initial expectations about what the UN could or should attempt to achieve. For example, some commentators see the veto powers of the permanent members as a positive feature which keeps the major powers within the UN framework when they might otherwise abandon it, prevents the UN from damaging conflicts with its most important members and protects it from involvement in divisive and risky missions (Roberts and Kingsbury 1993: 41). Others would argue that the veto is an outdated relic of the postwar configuration of power and one of the main obstacles to more effective decision-making procedures in conflict situations. In the following sections, we try to present a balanced assessment that takes into account both sides of the argument. The UN has a mix of positive and negative characteristics, as do other mediators.

TABLE 3. UN Mediation and Conflict Type

	Interstate Conflict	Intrastate Conflict	Total
UN Mediation Frequency	253 (71%)	102 (29%)	355 (100%)

Source: Data from authors' own research.

TABLE 4. UN Mediation Success and Conflict Type

	Interstate Conflict	Intrastate Conflict	Total
UN Mediation Success	87 (68%)	40 (32%)	127 (100%)

Source: Data from authors' own research.

The Strengths of UN Conflict Resolution

The UN's record displays a number of genuine achievements. It has been instrumental in resolving several serious international conflicts, and the development of peacekeeping has been one of the great innovations of the international conflict resolution system. Peacekeeping operations have contributed to the stabilization of conflict situations and postconflict reconstruction on more than a few occasions. More specifically, the UN possesses a number of unique advantages over other methods of conflict resolution.

The Functions of IOs

In ways similar to the functions of international law, IOs contribute to conflict resolution through establishing norms by which states must abide in their mutual interaction. Distinguished from decision-making procedures and rules, norm-based standards of behavior encourage a certain approach to conflict resolution. In the case of the UN, they form the defining characteristics of the UN regime, thereby acting as intervening variables in international politics. For the most part, these norms have proved highly durable and relatively clear. The UN's norms revolve around Article 33(1) where states are encouraged to settle their disputes by the many peaceful methods we have described. Most IOs, of course, also provide specific machinery for dispute settlement.

The particular values of the UN regime—limitations on the use of force, international cooperation in economic and social issues, disarmament and arms control, peaceful settlement of disputes, the promotion of human rights—have the effect of mitigating anarchy and dealing with some of the underlying sources of tension in international politics. The international norms created and sustained by IOs also function to facilitate peaceful and orderly change in international relations. They provide a relatively benign framework for changes in ideologies and political systems (Roberts and Kingsbury 1993: 46), thereby reducing uncertainty, defusing tension, and mitigating potential sources of friction. Norm creation is also a source of international law, and IOs play an important role in codifying and enforcing international legal principles.

One of the most important roles played by IOs involves providing a forum and a venue for multilateral diplomacy. In addition to setting the terms of debates, IOs also act as communications links and a means of promoting transparency. In an environment where misperception and miscommunication can sometimes lead to war, the value of this role should not be underestimated. The daily opportunities for quiet diplomacy in the multilateral context can act as a safety valve in times of international tension: "The existence of the United Nations itself facilitates diplomacy by bringing together ambassadors in a setting in which unobtrusive contacts are easily arranged and outside states can make an effort to encourage settlement behind the scenes, without the publicity and complications of formal intervention" (Merrills 1998: 224). In some cases, dealing with a dispute in a structured forum can have the effect of isolating the conflict and halting its spread. Over the long term, the influence of the IO can help to stabilize the situation at a minimal level of conflict. The forum provided by IOs also acts as a process for mobilizing international resources, such as for peacekeeping operations or coordinating and harmonizing diplomatic exercises.

The Security Council

The UN possesses all the advantages of other IOs in international conflict resolution. It provides dispute resolution machinery and processes, a venue for communication and coordination, opportunities for quiet diplomacy, and a normative framework. In addition, and as a consequence, the UN wields a considerable amount of moral authority and imbues its conflict resolution efforts with a degree of legitimacy and respect not always accorded to other actors.

> The status of the council endows its actions with an aura of legitimacy that is often perceived as overriding the legitimacy of other actors. Thus decisions of the council defining or interpreting the principles according to which various conflicts ought to be resolved, as well as actions of mediators carried out under its auspices, are automatically perceived as legitimate by virtue of their emanating from the council. (Touval 1995: 208)

Its processes may also facilitate the mobilization of considerable resources, such as the initiation and management of large-scale peacekeeping operations. In cases of state collapse, large-scale multidimensional operations are a necessity for reconstruction but would be impossible without UN support.

In recent years, the UN has become a dumping ground for so-called orphan conflicts (Touval 1994)—those disputes that have become so intractable and destructive that no other actor has been able, or sometimes willing, to deal with them effectively. Many of these conflicts occur in other regions of the world, such as Africa, where the great powers in particular are unwilling to risk involvement. Without the involvement of the UN, many of these conflicts would remain unresolved and the burden of their destructive effects would have to be carried by neighboring states or regional bodies.

Unlike diplomatic and legal methods of conflict management, the Security Council—in theory—does not need the permission of the parties to deal with a conflict. According to the Charter, it can deal with any dispute that may threaten international peace and security. Furthermore, it can enforce its decisions if the parties are reluctant to comply. In some cases, the threat or use of sanctioning behavior is necessary to compel the parties to accept a peaceful solution and acts as an important source of leverage.

Finally, the veto power of the permanent members provides a safety valve for the great powers that keeps them within the multilateral context and protects the Organization from potential involvement in damaging conflicts. It relieves the Organization of pressures and tensions it could not sustain. Related to this, peacemaking through the UN can allow states to limit costs through collective burden-sharing and serve "as a buffer to protect states from the possibly damaging consequences of a failed peacemaking process" (Touval 1994: 50). It acts as a risk haven for great powers reluctant to act as "the world's gendarme" (Zartman 1999: 75), providing an environment for collective responsibility and multilateral safeguards that can dilute unilateral exposure.

The Secretary-General

The secretary-general, despite lacking disposable resources, possesses a number of advantages over other conflict resolution actors. First, the secretary-general's position in the UN system puts him in the best position to exploit the traditional methods of peacemaking diplomacy (Cordovez 1987: 169–70). At the center of the UN's administration, he has almost unlimited access to information and is a focal point for contacts between states, and even between states and nongovernmental actors. Almost uniquely among international actors, the secretary-general has access to all governments, and vice versa. Under Article 96, he also has direct access to the ICJ—he can request advisory opinions. Unlike the deliberative bodies, he can act swiftly as a helpful third party, offering a number of possible methods of adjustment to disputing parties. In addition, he is always available to member states, able to act as the quiet but active third party, and

he has procedures for utilizing resources in the area of humanitarian relief and economic development.

Second, the secretary-general has acquired a symbolic role as the embodiment of the basic purposes and principles of the Charter (Cordovez 1987: 172). The perceived objectivity, discretion, and independence of the secretary-general furnish the office with genuine credibility as an impartial third party. In practice, this authority facilitates both access to information in fact-finding that is unavailable to other actors, and acceptance of his role as mediator in disputes where the motives of other actors may be suspect. His authority also adds weight to public appeals. The confidentiality of the secretary-general's office, furthermore, provides an important face-saving option for states whereby agreements worked out by UN officials can be publicly attributed to the statesmanship of the disputing governments. This behind-the-scenes role, rarely visible to the public, is one of the most effective and important functions of the Office. As former secretary-general Perez de Cuellar observed, "No one will ever know how many conflicts have been prevented or limited through contacts which have taken place in the famous glass mansion which can become fairly opaque when necessary" (quoted in Franck and Nolte 1993: 144).

Third, the development of the secretary-general's role, and the latitude of Article 99, mean that he enjoys a flexibility and freedom not always available to other UN organs, which can sometimes be instrumental in bridging the gaps within the formal machinery of the Organization (Elaraby 1987: 198). Over the years, the secretaries-general have responded in a pragmatic and flexible fashion to the unique circumstances of conflicts that might otherwise have become bogged down in the Security Council or General Assembly. In short, due largely to the efforts of the secretary-general, "the whole is now a little greater than the sum of the parts and the institution has acquired a degree of authority in dispute situations" (Merrills 1998: 257).

The Challenges Facing UN Conflict Resolution

In spite of the UN's advantages and achievements in the area of conflict resolution, it also has a number of significant limitations. There are numerous serious conflicts that it failed to anticipate, prevent, or manage once fighting had erupted. Some of the UN's failures lie in the nature of IOs generally, while others are embedded in the Organization's own structures and processes. In some cases, the UN has failed to realize its own potential through shortsightedness or incompetence, and in others it has been the victim of internal and external factors beyond its control.

The Limits of International Organizations

While the existence and promotion of international norms of behavior encourages a certain approach to conflict resolution, the UN regime is relatively weak, and its ability to influence state behavior is circumscribed by a number of fundamental internal weaknesses: the simultaneous relevance of contradictory norms, such as the norm of noninterference in states' domestic affairs versus the promotion of human rights; some norms in the UN regime appear to be more effective than others, such as the aforementioned norm of noninterference versus the norm of pacific settlement; and policy processes in the UN impose limits on its ability to delegitimate state behavior in some cases, while allowing the promotion of double standards in others.

At a basic level, IOs are conservative creatures, oriented toward maintaining the status quo, particularly in terms of the interests of their members: nation-states. The UN in particular was a creature of the times in which it was established. Created by the victorious allies following World War II, it assumed that the primary threat to international peace would be aggression by states and that cooperation between the allies would continue to be an effective means of maintaining the peace. The evolution of the international system has, in many ways, outmoded the UN's underlying rationale. Now, in an international environment made up of a variety of actor types, and in which the dominant forms of conflict involve primarily nonstate actors, state-centric processes are not necessarily going to be effective. IOs then are limited by their membership and orientation; nonstate actors like liberation movements or rebel groups cannot utilize their dispute resolution machinery or play an active role in their deliberations. It is also unclear how effective IOs can really be in dealing with issues like international terrorism, transnational crime, nuclear proliferation and environmental conflict.

Another major problem lies in the UN's legitimating role, which in turn is dependent on the UN's effectiveness in enforcing its norms. The failure to consistently punish violators of the norms undermines the UN's effectiveness, and hence its legitimacy as norm upholder. Failures in Bosnia, Rwanda, the Democratic Republic of the Congo (DRC), and Darfur have been particularly damaging in recent years. At the same time, one of the key norms of IOs—the principle of nonintervention in the internal affairs of member states—has itself proved to be an obstacle to the resolution of international conflicts, particularly in the post–Cold War period when most conflicts have occurred within states and involved governments attacking their own citizens.

A particular problem for IOs involves disputes where the violation of one of its norms lies at the root of the conflict, such as when one state violates the territorial integrity of another or employs force in pursuit of its goals. By definition, the IO must be against the violator in these cases. This can marginalize the leverage of the IO—particularly if it cannot muster collective delegitimation and enforce its norm—while at the same time limiting its ability to act as a neutral or impartial intermediary. Weak regimes like the UN are also ineffectual in disputes involving issues that are perceived in zero-sum terms (Van Walraven 1999: 293). This is one of the reasons why the UN had such a poor record of dealing with Cold War conflicts. In other cases where the issues have involved gross human rights violations, for example, it is the perceived neutrality and impartiality of IOs like the UN that has proved problematic. By attempting to avoid partiality toward one side—in some cases, member governments, or in the case of collapsed states, competing factions—the UN has effectively legitimated and thereby strengthened the hand of elements antithetical to reconciliation and long-term conflict resolution.

As arenas of foreign policy, and lacking autonomous decision-making capabilities, IOs are vulnerable to the vagaries of the political will of their membership. They tend to work vigorously on issues only when hegemonic leadership or a dominant coalition emerges, which is usually in cases where great power interests are directly affected. The result is that paralysis often occurs when dealing with conflicts in other regions such as Africa. In these areas, there are rarely pressing interests for the great powers, and at the same time, the weak states of the region find it difficult to mobilize effective coalitions. Furthermore, the chances of cooperation are reduced by the large number of actors in the UN. The most obvious problem in this regard is the lengthy and cumbersome decision-making processes of the deliberative organs. In addition, in order to receive adequate support from the majority of members, UN resolutions are often so watered-down that they fail to deal effectively with the issues in dispute. This least-common-denominator approach, combined with the slow decision-making process, undermines the reputation of the UN as an effective conflict manager.

In other cases, an IO may become prisoner to the interests of one powerful member who through hegemonic leadership uses the organization to pursue its own foreign policy goals. This can damage the credibility of the organization in the eyes of the world, especially when UN-sanctioned actions become clearly identified with one or more of the great powers; the actions of the United States in the First and Second Gulf Wars have been thus characterized by some observers. The Security Council, dominated by the great powers who regularly block action that is not directly in line with their interests, is thus viewed with suspicion, especially by many small states who fear being victimized in this way. This is not surprising, because unlike many IOs, great powers cannot be impartial toward the issues involved in a conflict and must guard their interests closely (Thakur 1993: 16). It does, however, mean that IOs face inherent limitations on their freedom of action and that there is a tendency for issues to be excessively politicized.

Finally, the power and influence of IOs, particularly the UN, are often overestimated. Expectations are too high about what they can achieve; this has certainly been the case for the UN since the onset of the "war on terrorism." This can lead to unrealistic goal- and task-setting and to disillusionment and delegitimation when the inevitable failures occur. The failures in dealing with many of the orphan conflicts of the early 1990s (Bosnia, Somalia, Rwanda), along with the controversy surrounding the 2003 Gulf War, have seriously damaged the UN's credibility since then (Touval 1994). Part of the problem, particularly during the 1990s, occurred due to overstretch brought on by ambitious attempts to deal simultaneously with numerous complicated civil wars in Africa, Asia, and the former Soviet Union.

The Limits of UN Conflict Resolution

As an IO, the UN suffers from all the limitations inherent in this form of organization. In addition, states will not submit their disputes to the UN unless they can foresee some real advantage in doing so. States prefer to retain freedom of action over both the process and outcome of conflict resolution. Although the UN can consider a dispute without a state's permission, the world body has little real hope of resolving the conflict without it and can do little by itself to enforce the process or outcome of peaceful conflict resolution (Claude 1964: 209–10).

In spite of the UN's powers to investigate any matter that might be a threat to international peace and security,

historically it has a poor record of anticipating and preempting crises. Most often, it responds to crises that are already out of control, like the orphan conflicts of the 1990s (Sullivan 1999: 48). Part of the problem resides in the UN's information deficit, which is itself the result of two factors. First, the UN does not have the technical, human, or financial resources for the gathering and analysis of information that large states have, nor can it engage in techniques that employ secrecy, stealth, or anything that might be considered spying (Dorn 1996: 263). It lacks independent sources of information and must rely on media and governmental sources. Second, the UN is curtailed from investigating matters that could be construed as falling within the domestic affairs of a state, even if the issue has international repercussions. This is obviously a major disadvantage in the present security environment where many threats—like terrorism—emanate from the internal sphere and require timely intelligence to respond effectively.

There are also a number of limitations on the role of the secretary-general in conflict resolution. In spite of the relative autonomy he can exercise through the powers invested in Article 99, he must maintain the confidence of the Security Council by walking a delicate tightrope between respecting the wishes of the Council and engaging in conflict resolution activities that are not necessarily sanctioned by the Council. In addition, the independence afforded by Article 99 can be undermined by the responsibilities of Article 98. When the Security Council asks the secretary-general to carry out its wishes, it reduces his role to that of letter carrier. His reputation as an honest broker can be jeopardized when he is identified with the exercise of Security Council—and by definition, Security Council members'—power (Franck and Nolte 1993: 180). Furthermore, the failure of conflict resolution missions harms the office. It has been common to let the secretary-general take the fall for wider diplomatic failures. As the most visible symbol of the Organization, this can be damaging to its reputation.

There are also important limitations to UN peacekeeping, even though there is a common tendency to view peacekeeping as some kind of panacea for problem conflicts (see chapter 6). First, these missions are an improvised response to particular situations and have no clear constitutional basis or generally applicable model (Merrills 1998: 244). This often generates disagreements about the nature of their mandate, their financing and leadership (particularly in terms of the role of the secretary-general), and even their legitimacy. Second, it is sometimes forgotten that peacekeeping cannot by itself resolve conflicts. There is a danger that the interminable repetition of peacekeeping operations "may become in effect a substitute for a settlement, a perpetual treatment of symptoms rather than causes" (Merrills 1998: 257). Peacekeeping is, after all, only a prophylactic that may provide the foundation for a final settlement. The more important task is to deal with the underlying conditions that gave rise to the need for peacekeeping in the first place.

An examination of the UN's actual record in conflict resolution finds a number of negative features, in addition to the positive aspects we identified. According to Haas and others, the UN's overall effectiveness has declined over time, fewer serious disputes go to the UN, the UN's record in dealing with civil conflicts has been poor, and the Organization has a tendency to deal with only the proximate causes of conflict rather than their underlying causes (Haas 1987). The profile of disputes that the UN has been good at dealing with is, in fact, highly restricted. Wilkenfeld and Brecher found that high levels of UN activity in a crisis may actually prolong it (1989). Touval argues that UN mediation has extended or aggravated many of the intractable conflicts of the 1990s, because belligerents have been able to manipulate the Organization's obvious weaknesses (1994: 45). The practices that contribute to this situation include "the indiscriminate holding of special conferences, the toleration of forum shopping, and the acceptance of a double standard that denounces the use of armed force in general but legitimates it in the case of national liberation against a racist enemy" (Haas 1987: 46).

A related problem is that many of the lessons learned from the past have not been fully internalized, and familiar errors continue to be made. The reasons for this are inherent in the nature of the Organization: "There is no institutional memory of great power. Each generation of national and international decision-makers seems to be condemned to relearn the same old lessons" (Haas 1987: 55). In fact, some argue that a process of "negative learning" has taken place since the 1990s, with the Security Council becoming far more conservative and in one sense hostage to U.S. domestic concerns over the Organization's failure in Somalia—the so-called Somali Syndrome (Malone 1997: 404). Following the Brahimi Report on improving peacekeeping in 2000, DPKO added a Peacekeeping Best Practices Unit to analyze lessons learned and offer advice to new missions. It is still too early to tell whether its work, or the new activism of the United States, will counteract the inherent tendencies toward institutional memory loss.

The UN as Mediator

A problem of UN conflict resolution is that its mediatory capacity can be easily overwhelmed by the simultaneous eruption of several conflicts or the pace and scale of events. In such situations, its slow reactive capacities, lack of resources, and limited ability to focus on several crises at once mean that it must often delegate mediatory functions to other organizations or interested states. Furthermore, there is often an expectation for the UN to get involved in a conflict regardless of whether other non-UN mediators are already present. This raises the problem of coordination and can lead to a situation termed *crowdedness* (Khadiagala 2000), a process where mediators' leverage over the parties is cancelled out as the disputants can turn to different mediators in search of a better deal (Van Walraven 1999: 297).

A direct consequence of the UN's lack of resources for sidepayments and credible threats is its restricted opportunities for exerting influence. This often precludes a forceful posture, especially if relatively powerful countries are involved, and means that UN mediators act principally as communicators rather than as manipulators— a demonstrably less effective form of mediation in international politics (Bercovitch and Houston 1993; Van Walraven 1999: 293).

There are clear reasons why states are reluctant to allow the UN to act as a mediator in their disputes and prefer to rely on direct negotiation or non-UN mediation. First, there are risks in allowing a third party whose interests are not always clear to mediate. The interests of the UN are not always clear because the great powers sometimes use the UN as a means of realizing narrow self-interest, cloaking their goals in the statements and actions of the Organization. States prefer other states as mediators for the simple reason that their self-interests are relatively transparent. After all, states do not mediate unless there is some advantage to be gained.

Second, the UN is perceived as being above the states; it can hardly stand between the disputants and command confidence as an intermediary with its own self-interests. Third, in addition to its unwieldy structures and procedures, there is also a fear that the UN cannot avoid setting precedents, and it thus lacks the necessary freedom to maneuver. Once the UN has decided on a mediating proposal or framework, it effectively becomes locked into a fixed position. Modifying its principles in response to changing circumstances—a necessity in a dynamic negotiation process—is nearly impossible (Touval 1994: 53). If it goes as far as stating its position in a resolution, then it is well and truly locked into a single path from which there is usually no return. Fourth, proceedings in a multilateral context—such as in a Security Council meeting or a special committee—may be used to embarrass one party or may not allow for bargaining under the protection of face-saving formulas. Last, as Touval has argued, the UN does not serve well as an authoritative channel of communication, it has little political leverage, its threats and promises lack credibility and it is incapable of pursuing coherent, flexible, and dynamic negotiations guided by an effective strategy (1994: 45).

Conclusion

In this chapter, we have attempted to present a balanced assessment of the role of the UN in international conflict resolution. We have tried to avoid the extremes of over-idealization of the Organization or needless cynical pessimism. There is no question that IOs are now a permanent feature of international relations and that they have important roles to play in the regulation of international interactions, especially between states. The UN in particular is a crucial part of the international conflict resolution structures through which states settle their disputes. Nevertheless, international organization is by its nature limited in what it can realistically hope to achieve, especially in intractable intrastate conflicts or complex challenges like terrorism. It is too easy to criticize the UN for failing in tasks for which it is institutionally ill-equipped and ill-prepared by unwilling member states.

In fact, the UN has played an important role in international conflict resolution, and there is little doubt that the world is more peaceful than it might otherwise have been without its involvement. In particular, the Organization has been instrumental in helping states to behave in a less conflictual manner, cooperate more readily and regularly, and adhere to a set of shared norms (Thakur 1993: 10). In spite of its obvious limitations, the UN has at times proved to be adaptable and effective, and its record contains a number of impressive achievements. Furthermore, as the world's most respected and universal IO, it is strategically positioned to continue its central role in the international management of crises and conflicts.

The critical question, however, is whether the Organization is flexible enough to adapt its machinery and its processes to the realities and challenges of internally based conflicts and security threats such as terrorism. The kinds of conflicts that now dominate the global security agenda will require new ways of thinking and different kinds of approaches. Inevitably constrained by the major political forces of the post-1945 period—the Cold War and decolonization—the present international environment offers the Organization a new dispensation and expanded opportunities for cooperation. In fact, recognizing its limitations in dealing with intractable internal conflicts, the UN has embarked on a period of genuine and wide-ranging reform. An impressive array of new methods and procedures are being tried; the UN is even making a coordinated attempt to deal with the challenges of terrorism (Nesi 2006). In subsequent chapters we examine aspects of the UN's growing involvement in internal conflict resolution.

CHAPTER SIX

Peacekeeping

Peacekeeping is a fairly recent addition to the repertoire of international conflict resolution approaches. Unlike negotiation, mediation, and international organization, which have been used by states for settling disputes for hundreds of years, peacekeeping has only become an established method of conflict resolution since 1956. A form of peaceful third-party intervention, peacekeeping is designed to be more of a prophylactic course of action than a curative one. Typically, peacekeeping operations are dispatched *after* a cease-fire has been reached and with the agreement of both states. The role of the operation is to prevent the re-eruption of armed conflict and to oversee the implementation of a political settlement. It is an adjunct process to the diplomatic efforts—negotiation, mediation, or consideration in the UN—that attempt to resolve the underlying issues through dialogue. In other words, peacekeeping is aimed at controlling, or at least influencing, the violent manifestation of conflict; it is not a method for resolving the conflict itself. This is an important distinction, because it is easy to lose perspective and to expect more from peacekeeping than it is capable of delivering. When peacekeeping operations fail to prevent or resolve outbreaks of fighting, this is more likely to be due to the failure of diplomacy rather than the peacekeeping operation.

As an improvised mode of conflict resolution, peacekeeping has gone through several distinct phases since its inception. The first phase can be described as traditional or orthodox peacekeeping. It generally refers to UN operations between 1948 and 1988, although these kinds of peacekeeping missions continue to be mounted for some interstate disputes such as the present UN Mission in Ethiopia and Eritrea (UNMEE). This operation is overseeing a cease-fire and force disengagement process following a brutal border war in 1998–2000. The second phase of UN peacekeeping—so-called second-generation peacekeeping—occurred between 1989 and 1994, after which a third generation of peacekeeping operations is presently taking shape. Second- and third-generation peacekeeping is what we have chosen to call *humanitarian intervention* and is discussed in chapter 8. Other international actors, such as regional organizations and coalitions of willing states, have also been greatly involved in peacekeeping. In fact, such non-UN operations—sometimes called fourth-generation peacekeeping—have become an important feature of international security management in the post–Cold War period; we examine this kind of activity in chapter 9. Here, we focus exclusively on the first and original phase of peacekeeping—traditional UN peacekeeping.

Traditional peacekeeping is an ideal form of interstate conflict resolution because it operates on the principles of consent and impartiality. Peacekeepers can only deploy when they are invited and assured of full cooperation by the disputing states. When they are in the field, they must act as neutral observers. In this way, peacekeeping maintains state sovereignty and power and allows the parties a high level of control over the settlement process. As we have previously suggested, this is very important for states who like to retain freedom of action. For this reason, traditional or orthodox peacekeeping has been used—in most cases, successfully—in eighteen conflicts since the first full-fledged peacekeeping operation in 1956 (see table 6). Its inherent advantages, as well as its impressive record of success, means that it will continue to be an important part of the conflict resolution process for interstate conflict for some time to come.

Traditional Peacekeeping

Peacekeeping is a form of third-party intervention aimed at controlling the manifestation of violence, thereby facilitating the peaceful resolution of disputes between states by providing breathing space. It arose as a creative response by the UN to situations where the Security Council was unable to take effective leadership in conflict situations due to internal differences between the permanent members. It was never envisaged by the original architects of the UN who fully expected that allied cooperation would continue as it had during World War II and provide the basis for a functional collective security system. For this reason, peacekeeping is not even mentioned in the UN Charter. Lacking precise definition or prescribed procedures, peacekeeping has always been an improvised response to specific situations of conflict. It has evolved through different phases according to the security environment of the international system and represents an amalgam of procedures, processes, and principles worked out largely in situ. The historical origins of peacekeeping lie first of all in the experience of the League of Nations. International peace observation forces under the direction of the League were deployed in the Upper Silesia region between Poland and Germany, the Vilna province between Poland and Lithuania, and the Saar region in Germany (Diehl 1993b: 15–20). Second, following the 1948 war in the Middle East and the 1948–49 Kashmir conflict, the UN sent small unarmed observer forces to both these regions to monitor cease-fires, respond to complaints, and report back to the UN Security Council.

Based on these two antecedents of providing observer groups for states in conflict, UN secretary-general Dag Hammarskjöld, together with Canadian Secretary of State for External Affairs Lester Pearson, proposed a peacekeeping mission as a means of securing and overseeing the withdrawal of British, French, and Israeli forces from Egypt during the Suez Crisis of 1956. Wider than peace observation, this first full-fledged peacekeeping operation involved interposition between the conflicting states, verification of the cease-fire, and supervising the withdrawal of military forces. It was to be the blueprint for virtually all of the traditional peacekeeping operations that followed. Hammarskjöld aimed to develop the UN as an impartial instrument of what he termed *preventive diplomacy*, whereby the Organization actively intervened in conflicts before they became a major international problem (MacQueen 1999: 21). Peacekeeping would, in his view, play a vital part of this strategy. Peacekeeping was formalized as a recognized concept and method of the UN in 1965 when the General Assembly established the "Special Committee on Peacekeeping Operations." Importantly, peacekeeping was originally designed as an interstate method of conflict resolution; it was not envisaged that it would be used to deal with the complex and intractable intrastate wars most visibly seen since the 1990s.

Defining Peacekeeping

Broadly speaking, peacekeeping can be defined as "the prevention, containment, moderation, and termination of hostilities between or within states, through the medium of a peaceful third-party intervention, organized and directed internationally, using multinational forces of soldiers, police, and civilians to restore and maintain peace" (IPA 1984: 22). Marrack Goulding, a former undersecretary-general for Peacekeeping Operations, gives more specifics.

> Field operations established by the United Nations, with the consent of the parties concerned, to help control and resolve conflicts between them, under United Nations command and control, at the expense collectively of the member states, and with military and other personnel and equipment provided voluntarily by them, acting impartially between the parties and using force to the minimum extent necessary. (1993: 455)

However, these definitions fall somewhat short of describing the day-to-day realities of peacekeeping, nor do they provide a concrete link to broader processes of conflict resolution. A clearer picture of peacekeeping emerges when we examine its origins and functions in more detail.

The Basis of Peacekeeping

For many years, the precise Charter basis of peacekeeping remained ambiguous. Broadly speaking, peacekeeping falls within the purview of Article 1, which states that the UN's primary purpose is to "maintain international peace and security" through "effective collective measures for the prevention and removal of threats to the peace." It differed from the collective efforts suggested under Chapter VII, however, which are based on the concept of collective security—the nonconsensual use of preponderant force—and aimed at defense against an expansionist military power. Peacekeeping operations, by contrast, are more appropriately thought of as a Chapter VI mechanism, coming under "other peaceful means" among a range of peaceful options (Article 33). Based on the consent of the parties, strict neutrality, and the minimum use of force, traditional peacekeeping is a noncoercive tool of third-party diplomacy.

Actually, it is sometimes referred to as a "Chapter-six-and-a-half" activity, suggesting that it falls somewhere between Chapter VI—the "Pacific Settlement of Disputes"—and Chapter VII—"Action with Respect to Threats to the Peace, Breaches of the Peace, and Acts of Aggression" (Roberts 1996: 298). This particular characterization is perhaps a more accurate description of current "muscular" peacekeeping (so-called humanitarian intervention), which in addition to normal peacekeeping duties often involves the use of force authorized under Chapter VII. It is less applicable to traditional or orthodox peacekeeping, which remains essentially noncoercive and consensual.

How Does Peacekeeping Work?

Peacekeeping operations can be requested by the disputing parties themselves, the secretary-general, or an interested third party such as a mediator. Once the conflicting parties have given a clear statement of consent, the Security Council will authorize the mission, establish its mandate and duration, and make a request for member states to contribute forces. The secretary-general will then be instructed to oversee the day-to-day running of the operation and make regular reports back to the Security Council. The financing for peacekeeping comes from assessed contributions by members based on their regular budget contributions. Peacekeeping operations are normally applied after a peace settlement has been agreed to and are frequently part of the implementation package. They are, therefore, improvised to suit the specific requirements of the parties and the nature of the conflict to which they are dispatched. In this sense, each operation is unique, specially designed for local conditions. For ex-

ample, peacekeeping has been used in interstate conflicts over territory or to oversee the withdrawal of troops following an invasion, in civil wars, and in transfers of power following decolonization struggles. The size of the forces that have been deployed has varied according to the mandate and scope of the operation, ranging from less than 100 troops for small observer-type missions to over 10,000 military personnel for complex decolonization operations such as the UN Operation in the Congo (ONUC) in the early 1960s (see table 6).

One of the key tasks of traditional peacekeeping (as well as more recent humanitarian peacekeeping) is *observation*. Observers, by their mere presence and as a result of their international standing and their monitoring and reporting function, can have a salutary effect on the dispute, discouraging unreasonable behavior by the parties and building confidence. In addition, they provide the international community with firsthand and up-to-date information, which may be useful in ongoing diplomatic efforts or for the preparation of a large-scale peacekeeping operation. Military observer missions typically involve conducting vehicle patrols, manning observation posts, inspecting weapons sites, investigating incidents of alleged cease-fire violations, maintaining liaison between the various parties and their headquarters, and negotiating local cease-fires between opposing commanders.

Another key function of peacekeeping is the *separation of forces,* or *interposition* between the conflicting armies, usually in some kind of buffer zone. Physically separating the opposing forces discourages cease-fire violations or the escalation of shooting incidents and can act as a deterrent to the renewal of full-scale fighting. In other words, interposition forces can provide "a moral barrier to hostile action" (Diehl 1993b: 10), confronting the disputing states with the realization that they would have to pass through UN forces to attack their opponent. Last, in a number of decolonization conflicts, UN peacekeepers have been called upon to ensure *law and order* and take over *temporary administration* of the territory. This is usually only for the relatively short transition period between colonial rule and self-government.

Three key principles lie at the heart of traditional peacekeeping operations. For observers and participants alike they are the sine qua non of successful peacekeeping, and it is strict adherence to these principles that gives orthodox peacekeeping its distinctive character. In fact, humanitarian intervention (third- and fourth-generation peacekeeping) can be distinguished from traditional peacekeeping by the fact that it challenges every one of these founding principles. The first principle is the *consent of the parties* to the establishment of the operation, its mandate, its composition, and its leadership. Consent is normally given in a "Status of Forces Agreement" between the parties and the UN, which guarantees UN personnel freedom of movement in the territory they occupy and freedom from interference in the carrying out of their duties. The requirement of consent distinguishes peacekeeping from Chapter VII enforcement actions and locates it firmly in Chapter VI of the Charter—the "Pacific Settlement of Disputes." It also distinguishes it from the humanitarian interventions of the 1990s where consent was not always sought and where the absence of consent did not prevent the deployment of peacekeepers.

The second principle of traditional peacekeeping is its *strict impartiality,* both in terms of its force composition and its actions in the field of operations. Impartiality has been called "the oxygen of peacekeeping" by some observers, because "the only way peacekeepers can work is by being trusted by both sides, being clear and transparent in their dealings, and keeping lines of communication open" (Tharoor 1995–96: 58). For this reason, it is also vital that the contributing troops come from neutral countries and are broadly representative. In practice, this meant that for many years the UN tried to avoid using personnel from either the permanent members of the Security Council—who might attract Cold War rivalry, or in the case of decolonization conflicts, interfere in their former territories—or neighboring states that might have regional interests. Instead, for the most part, peacekeeping forces were drawn from small, nonaligned countries. The neutral composition of peacekeeping troops must be reinforced by neutral behavior, meaning that its actions should not favor one side over the other. While in some cases neutral action can be difficult to define or implement, nonetheless, traditional peacekeeping operations have always sought to stay within the strict confines of impartiality. Again, this is in contrast to humanitarian operations that have—as in Somalia when the UN tried to arrest the warlord Mohammed Aideed or in Bosnia where the UN authorized NATO bombing of Serbian forces—abandoned all pretense of neutrality.

The third principle of peacekeeping is the *nonuse of force,* except in the natural right of self-defense. In practice, this means that peacekeepers are always lightly armed and have little or no offensive capabilities. Conceptually, the principle of nonuse of force distinguishes peacekeeping from combat operations under Chapter VII, while in a practical sense, it protects what are relatively small and vulnerable forces from attack by not allowing them to be drawn into the original conflict. There

is a close link to the principle of consent: "The assumption has been that parties to a conflict would be more likely to accept a UN operation if the latter had neither offensive intent or capability, and would under no conceivable circumstances pose a threat to them" (Malan 1997: 5). Humanitarian operations, by contrast, often have fairly robust rules of engagement that allow UN forces to use force offensively.

In summary, traditional peacekeeping is perhaps best described along the following lines.

> Peacekeeping is therefore the imposition of neutral and lightly armed interposition forces following a cessation of armed hostilities, and with the permission of the state on whose territory these forces are deployed, in order to discourage a renewal of military conflict and promote an environment under which the underlying dispute can be resolved. Peacekeeping functions include observation, interposition, maintaining law and order, and humanitarian activity. These functions are not mutually exclusive; depending on the type of conflict, some or all may be part of the peacekeeping mission. In any case, peacekeeping operations are conceptually and operationally distinct from collective security and peace observation missions, although they share some commonalities and have similar historical roots. (Diehl 1993b: 13)

We consider peacekeeping to be distinct from both small peace observation missions (and small political missions, such as sending special representatives or maintaining small liaison offices) and the more complex humanitarian operations we examine in chapter 8. These three categories—observer missions, traditional peacekeeping operations, and humanitarian intervention—can also be described as observer, force-level, and multidimensional peacekeeping operations (Fetherston 1994a: 4). While the tasks of traditional peacekeeping at times overlap with peace observation and humanitarian intervention, the underlying ethos, as well as the aims, functions, and practice of peacekeeping, make it fairly distinctive. For this reason, we do not include small peace observation missions or complex humanitarian operations in table 6, as some authors are apt to do.

An Overview of Traditional Peacekeeping, 1956–88

The origins of peacekeeping can be found in prototype peacekeeping operations undertaken by the League of

Nations, most notably in the administration of the Saar region; the failure of the UN's collective security system due to the rapid breakdown of superpower cooperation after 1945; the lessons of early observer missions in 1948–49; and the enthusiasm, ideas, and leadership of the UN secretary-general of the time, Dag Hammarskjöld. The United Nations Truce Supervision Organization (UNTSO) mission to the Middle East in 1948 and the United Nations Military Observer Group in India and Pakistan (UNMOGIP) in 1949 were important antecedents of peacekeeping. Designed to fill the void left by collective security, these small operations relied on observation and moral presence rather than active peacemaking. Their tasks included reporting on troop movements, investigating complaints, and monitoring the state of the cease-fire. With a limited function and only a small number of unarmed personnel, they were unable to prevent later outbreaks of fighting, and their overall contributions to peace efforts have been marginal at best. In fact, both missions have become permanent features of the UN's peace efforts in the Middle East and Kashmir. The mixed record and clear limitations of peace observation combined with the Suez Crisis in 1956 to create the impetus for a new approach, which is today known as peacekeeping.

The UN Emergency Force (UNEF I) was the first true peacekeeping operation. It was an impromptu response to both the insufficient political consensus for Chapter VII–based collective action against France, Britain, and Israel, and the inherent limitations of peace observation. After all, UNTSO was already in the region but had failed to deter the war (Diehl 1993b: 28–30). Security Council Resolution 998 authorized the secretary-general to dispatch a UN force to the region, and in conjunction with the Canadian foreign minister, Lester Pearson, these two set about designing a framework for the operation. It differed from previous peace observation operations in a number of crucial respects. First, unlike peace observation missions where units were directed by their own national commanders, UNEF I was under the direction of the secretary-general who appointed the field commander and oversaw the entire operation. Second, UNEF I included no forces from the major powers. This was to become an essential feature of all subsequent peacekeeping operations and was a crucial ingredient of its impartiality. Third, the force was designed to be strictly neutral in both action and purpose, in no way altering the existing military balance. Last, UNEF I acted as an interposition force between the parties, something that a small peace observa-

tion mission would have been unable to achieve (Diehl 1993b: 31). In effect, various aspects of peace observation were combined with a set of new principles to form the new strategy of peacekeeping.

The first elements of UNEF I arrived in the Canal Zone on 15 November 1956 and remained in place until May 1967. During this time, the UN troops monitored the cease-fire, supervised the withdrawal of French and British forces, and acted as a buffer against future Arab-Israeli confrontation. Importantly, UNEF I did not attempt to move beyond its assigned tasks into peacemaking activities. It was successful in virtually all aspects, performing its roles through interposition and moral authority rather than the use of force (MacQueen 1999: 27). It dampened and contained conflict in a highly unstable region and did so without entanglement in the superpower confrontation. UNEF I was also important not just as the first peacekeeping mission but also because its mode of operation became the primary model for all traditional peacekeeping operations that followed, and its principles remain at the heart of peacekeeping doctrine today.

Table 6 describes every traditional UN peacekeeping operation since 1956. We have excluded a number of peace observation missions, as by virtue of their small size, limited mandate, and unarmed status, they do not fit our conception of orthodox or force-level peacekeeping. Most of the operations described in table 6 involved interstate conflicts or tasks involving traditional military activities. For example, in the Angolan civil war, UN Angola Verification Mission I (UNAVEM I) was tasked with overseeing the withdrawal of Cuban troops; this contrasts with later missions in Angola that saw the expansion of peacekeeping activities into areas like election monitoring and humanitarian activities. Traditional peacekeeping operations dominated the period until 1988, when expanded UN operations—what we have chosen to call humanitarian intervention—began to be increasingly employed as an alternative form of UN military intervention. At present, both traditional peacekeeping and humanitarian operations are used by the UN for conflict resolution. Importantly, traditional peacekeeping is used almost exclusively in interstate conflicts, while humanitarian intervention is engaged to deal with the more complex challenges of internal or intrastate conflicts. For example, as we noted earlier, UNMEE (established in 2000) is a traditional peacekeeping operation designed to oversee a cease-fire, act as an interposition force, and supervise the demarcation of the international border between the two states.

TABLE 6.   Traditional UN Peacekeeping Operations, 1956–2007

Name of Mission	Location	Start/End Date	Personnel Strength	Function
UN Emergency Force I (UNEF I)	Suez Canal and Sinai Peninsula	November 1956–June 1967	6,000	Supervision of cease-fire between Israel and Egypt, and withdrawal of Anglo-French forces from Canal Zone.
UN Observation Group in Lebanon (UNOGIL)	Lebanon-Syrian Border	June 1958–December 1958	600	Prevention of hostile infiltration into Lebanon.
UN Operation in the Congo (ONUC)	Republic of Congo/Zaire	July 1960–June 1964	20,000	Initially to supervise withdrawal of Belgian troops; expanded to include law and order and administrative functions.
UN Security Force in West New Guinea (UNSF)	Dutch New Guinea/Irian Jaya (Indonesia)	October 1962–April 1963	1,600	Law and order, transitional administration of the territory during transition to Indonesian rule.
UN Yemen Observation Mission (UNYOM)	Yemen	July 1963–September 1964	200	Supervise withdrawal of Saudi and Egyptian forces.
UN Peacekeeping Force in Cyprus (UNFICYP)	Cyprus	March 1964–present	1,200	Interposition force between Greek and Turkish Cypriots; supervise cease-fire line after 1974 Turkish invasion.
UN India-Pakistan Observation Mission (UNIPOM)	India-Pakistan border west of Kashmir	September 1965–March 1966	100	Supervision of cease-fire following 1965 India-Pakistan war.
UN Emergency Force II (UNEF II)	Suez Canal and Sinai Peninsula	October 1973–July 1979	7,000	Interposition force, supervise cease-fire following Israel-Egypt 1973 war.
UN Disengagement Observation Force (UNDOF)	Golan Heights (Syria-Israel border)	June 1974–present	1,000	Interposition force, supervise disengagement of Israeli and Syrian forces following 1973 war.
UN Interim Force in Lebanon (UNIFIL)	Southern Lebanon	March 1978–present	4,600	Supervise Israeli withdrawal following 1978 invasion, administrative assistance.
UN Good Offices Mission in Afghanistan and Pakistan (UNGOMAP)	Afghanistan, Pakistan	May 1988–March 1990	50	Supervise implementation of peace agreement and Soviet withdrawal from Afghanistan.
UN Iran-Iraq Military Observer Group (UNIIMOG)	Iran, Iraq	August 1988–March 1990	400	Supervise Iran-Iraq cease-fire.
UN Angola Verification Mission I (UNAVEM I)	Angola	January 1989–May 1991	70	Supervise Cuban troop withdrawal following cease-fire.
UN Iraq-Kuwait Observation Mission (UNIKOM)	Iraq-Kuwait border	April 1991–October 2003	1,200	Monitor demilitarized zone.
UN Observer Mission Uganda-Rwanda (UNOMUR)	Uganda-Rwanda border	June 1993–September 1994	80	Prevent border infiltration of military supplies and personnel.
UN Observer Missions in Georgia (UNOMIG)	Georgia	August 1993–present	140	Verify peace accord; later to monitor CIS peacekeeping in Georgia.
UN Observer Mission in Liberia (UNOMIL)	Liberia	September 1993–September 1997	160	Support and monitor ECOMOG peacekeeping operation.
UN Mission in Ethiopia and Eritrea (UNMEE)	Ethiopia, Eritrea	July 2000–present	3,800	Interposition, supervise cease-fire, border demarcation.

Source: Data from MacQueen 1999; Berman and Sams 2000; and United Nations 2008.

Evaluating Traditional Peacekeeping

Evaluating the success of traditional peacekeeping as an approach to conflict resolution is a challenging task. Most often peacekeeping has been applied in conjunction with other methods and approaches, usually after the worst of the fighting had stopped. In many cases, a renewal of armed hostilities was avoided. At the same time, however, the conflict itself often remained unresolved, and peacekeepers were required to stay in the zone of conflict for several decades. Peacekeeping operations are normally assessed on two criteria: the extent to which they contribute to the limitation of armed conflict and their ability to promote resolution of the underlying issues (Diehl 1993b: 167). For those who define success according to the first criterion—in terms of ending armed hostilities and preventing their renewal at least for a period of time—then every operation except the UN Interim Force in Lebanon (UNIFIL) can be described as at least partially successful. If on the other hand, success is considered to be the peaceful resolution of conflict, then only UNEF II and perhaps the increasingly strained UNMEE falls into this category (Karns and Mingst 1994: 198). UNEF II was an important factor in facilitating the Israeli-Egyptian peace agreement signed at Camp David in 1979, while UNMEE has been critical to the stabilization if not the settlement of the border dispute between Eritrea and Ethiopia. Nevertheless, beyond these broad categorizations, there are a number of distinct advantages and disadvantages associated with traditional peacekeeping as a method of conflict resolution.

The Strengths of Traditional Peacekeeping

The advantages and achievements of traditional peacekeeping, although modest, are genuine. First, peacekeeping is an ideal form of interstate conflict resolution because it allows states to retain control over both the process and the outcome of the settlement. It maintains state sovereignty and power, which is very important for state actors. States are far more likely to accept peacekeeping than adjudication, for example, because it is a voluntary and consensual process.

Second, UN peacekeeping has proved effective in freezing a number of conflicts, limiting their spread, and deterring the renewal of hostilities—even if it was unable to resolve the underlying dispute. In some cases, peacekeeping reduced the risk of competitive intervention by neighboring states or major powers (Roberts 1996: 299). There is no doubt that UN peacekeeping in the Middle East, Cyprus, and Kashmir, while it may have failed to address the underlying issues, did help to normalize to some degree the regional international relations of these areas. The presence of peacekeeping forces can have the effect of stabilizing fragile cease-fires and ending open conflict, thereby giving the parties the confidence and space to pursue peaceful talks in an atmosphere free from the pressures of open warfare. Acting as an international witness to events in a particular conflict, peacekeeping operations can also constrain the more bellicose behavior of the parties. In addition, most orthodox peacekeeping operations have generally been well prepared, have kept more or less to schedule, and have stayed within budget (McLean 1996: 325). Peacekeeping is actually a relatively cost-effective method of managing conflicts that can be highly destructive in physical and human terms. Certainly,

peacekeeping is far less expensive than collective enforcement actions, for example.

Third, the principle of impartiality led to the general practice of not using troops from the five permanent members of the Security Council or forces from neighboring states. In this manner, conflicts were insulated from both Cold War rivalry and regional hegemony. For example, in the Congo, ONUC prevented the direct involvement of the superpowers from supporting local factions. Despite the carnage in that country between 1960 and 1964, it never reached the level of destruction seen in neighboring Angola where the superpowers simply backed their own local clients, and the UN was unable to intervene effectively (MacQueen 1999: 82).

Fourth, peacekeeping has facilitated the implementation of peace agreements, giving states a face-saving exit strategy and raising the confidence of the parties that the settlement would be adhered to. In fact, peacekeeping has been most successful when it is deployed following a settlement and in conjunction with other diplomatic efforts. Because it requires the consent of the parties and acts in a neutral manner, there is at least a nominal commitment to cooperate with the peacekeeping forces. Furthermore, unlike collective security, no aggressor need be identified and no single party is singled out for blame. It remains, therefore, the most viable form of international military involvement in interstate conflict.

Fifth, peacekeeping was important to the UN as an organization, going some way toward rescuing it from military irrelevance following the onset of the Cold War (MacQueen 1999: 80). The failure of the collective security framework and the deadlock in the Security Council threatened to push the Organization to the margins of international security affairs. Peacekeeping, along with other developments we have described, allowed the UN to forge an important role in international security management, preventing its marginalization.

Last, UN peacekeeping has acquired an important reputation for impartiality and professionalism. It is accepted and trusted in many parts of the world where other forms of intervention, including regional peacekeeping, are not. This reputation is built in part on its record of success. The UNEF I and UNEF II operations helped to avert war between Israel and its neighbors and probably contributed to the Camp David Peace Agreement. The UN Disengagement Observation Force (UNDOF) has certainly played an important role in keeping the Golan Heights quiet since 1974. The ONUC operation in the Congo prevented the secession of Katanga and helped to restore a semblance of order to that country. In Cyprus, UNFICYP has prevented the reignition of open warfare between the Greek and Turkish communities. Several other UN operations—such as UNGOMAP, UNIIMOG, UNAVEM I, UNIKOM, UNOMUR, and UNMEE (see table 6)—have been instrumental in facilitating orderly troop withdrawals, preventing cross-border infiltration, and guaranteeing cease-fires.

In short, traditional peacekeeping has proved itself to be an effective tool in the resolution and management of interstate conflicts in particular. And in the absence of a consistent and effective system of collective enforcement, it is likely to remain at the center of multilateral intervention. In other words, it is now a permanent addition to the repertoire of tools for international conflict resolution, its main advantage being that it sits at the "conjunction between the best possible and the most desirable" (MacQueen 1999: 85).

The Challenges and Weaknesses of Traditional Peacekeeping

In spite of its obvious merits, traditional peacekeeping is no panacea for international conflict, not least because it cannot by itself deal with the underlying causes of any conflict. It is not designed for such a task, and in fact it is misplaced to blame peacekeeping for failing to find political solutions to disputes. Nevertheless, peacekeeping does face a number of problems and limitations that constrain its utility. First, at a conceptual level, it has been argued that by freezing the conflict, peacekeeping takes away much of the immediacy from the situation and removes the incentive for negotiations (Diehl 1993b: 102). Cease-fires can dissipate the internal political and moral pressures to end the conflict, and once peacekeeping forces are in place, bargaining positions can harden. In this sense, preservation of the status quo becomes an acceptable alternative to either renewed hostilities or serious negotiations. This criticism has been leveled at UN forces in Cyprus, which seem to have reinforced the stalemate and by default allowed the Turkish Cypriots to establish a de facto state.

Second, in spite of a number of recent internal reforms, the UN still faces an institutional capability deficit in regard to peacekeeping. The Organization lacks a satisfactory command system that is capable of rapid decision making and effective coordination of the many different types of forces and contingents involved. Added to this, UN peacekeeping has always lacked effective military planning, intelligence, logistics, and communication capabilities. This is largely due to the fact that for most of its life, the Organization had no formal structures or machinery for peacekeeping and had to improvise peacekeeping operations when and if they were needed. It is only fairly recently that the UN has accepted that peacekeeping operations are likely to be one of its permanent functions, requiring institutionalized procedures, capabilities, and support structures (United Nations 2000). The establishment of the Department of Peacekeeping Operations (DPKO) is a direct consequence of this new recognition. In addition, because each operation is a temporary, ad hoc organization, little institutional learning takes place, and experienced personnel are rarely retained. Rather, each new operation is cobbled together from scratch, as it were. Again, as we noted in the previous chapter, even though a Peacekeeping Best Practices Unit has now been created within DPKO to study and document past and ongoing operations, it is too early to ascertain how effective it will actually be in institutionalizing lessons learned from field experiences. Related to this, there is little sign that UN peacekeeping has evolved a satisfactory peacekeeping doctrine or set of operating procedures beyond the general adherence to the principles we have discussed—although the Brahimi Report of 2000 has gone some way forward in this regard.

Third, peacekeeping operations, by their very nature, pose a bewildering array of practical and operational problems that have on occasion led to serious problems in the field. A peculiar form of military arrangement, peacekeeping operations involve unfamiliar tasks and often confusing command structures. Force components come from different countries with disparate military traditions and styles, equipment, capabilities, and training standards. Unlike national military structures or intensively trained collective security formations such as NATO, peacekeeping forces cannot be expected to cohere as easily (McLean 1996: 324). A particular problem is the relationship between UN and national commands. States that supply forces, as well as their commanders in the field, tend to retain independence of decision making and are often reluctant to defer to UN command. This is particularly problematic in dangerous and complex operations where clear and rapid decision making is critical.

Fourth, the UN has always struggled with the problem of finances for peacekeeping. In the early 1960s, disputes over members' obligations led to a major crisis that was not resolved until the International Court of Justice ruled that peacekeeping expenses should be borne by all UN members (Karns and Mingst 1994: 210). Despite this ruling, members' contributions to the peacekeeping budget have consistently been in arrears—in 1994 peacekeeping arrears reached more than $1 billion for the first time—and as more operations have been launched, the financial strains have mounted ever higher. By 2004, outstanding contributions to peacekeeping were around $2.5 billion. The cost of peacekeeping has steadily risen: it was $233 million in 1987, $421 million in 1991, $3.5 billion in 1993–94, and $4.5 billion in 2004–5. Financial constraints prevent the speedy deployment of peacekeepers while funds are gathered and may also limit the numbers and types of peacekeepers that can be deployed.

Fifth, as the previous chapter demonstrated, the UN has a number of inherent organizational shortcomings. To be effective, peacekeeping operations require a clear and achievable mandate and the resources to complete their tasks. Like all IOs, the UN has to operate on the principle of building consensus for its decisions. For this reason, it is subject to the competing interests of its members. This means that frequently mandates reflect the need to maintain unstable and fragile coalitions or do not have the full support of key states. Sometimes there are disagreements about the scope and even the legitimacy of an operation. For these reasons, a number of UN peacekeeping operations have been criticized for their vague and unclear mandates and for failing to provide the necessary resources for fulfilling those mandates. At a more fundamental level, the UN has failed to act altogether or made an entirely inadequate commitment to conflicts desperately in need of intervention, due to blocking actions by great powers that have interests of their own to pursue. This has led to charges of inconsistency and selectivity in applying peacekeeping to regional conflicts. During the 1990s, for example, UN peacekeeping in Angola constantly suffered from inadequate institutional support due to the special relationship between the United States and UNITA (Uniño Nacional para a Independência Total de Angola).

Sixth, peacekeeping is frequently limited by its own established principles. The need for impartiality may have insulated local conflicts from Cold War rivalry and regional hegemony. At the same time, however, it also denied UN forces the authority and strength that a great power might have provided, or the local knowledge, interest, and staying power that a neighboring force might have had (Roberts 1996: 299). Similarly, the principled reliance on host state consent was at times cruelly exposed—such as when UNEF I was expelled from Egypt in 1967; and peacekeeping forces could not always prevent the breakdown of order or the invasion of foreign forces. In more recent operations, limitations on the use of force placed peacekeepers in harm's way and allowed atrocities to occur in plain view of UN soldiers who lacked the authority and hardware to intervene.

Last, and most important, traditional peacekeeping is designed for interstate conflict. It is ill-equipped to deal with the intrastate or civil conflicts which have come to dominate the international security agenda in recent times.

> UN peacekeeping operations were most effective when conflicts involved legitimate governments that decided to settle their disputes by peaceful means. . . . Traditional peacekeeping has been least problematic when parties have agreed to end their conflicts and only need the UN to help them keep their word, where the consent and cooperation of the parties can be assumed and the impartiality of the peacekeepers is not challenged, where there are low risks and little or no need to use force, where the tasks of the peacekeeper are limited to those compatible with basic military skills, and where the limited resources of the UN are adequate for the task at hand. (Malan 1997: 6)

Unfortunately, the vast majority of international conflicts since the end of the Cold War have not belonged to this category. Rather, they have been complex and intractable civil wars, often involving multiple factions, massive human rights abuses, major humanitarian crises, and sometimes the complete breakdown of state structures. The principles of peacekeeping—consent, impartiality, and the nonuse of force—are under these circumstances almost impossible to apply. Sometimes there is no functioning government to give consent, the factions are unwilling to cooperate with the UN, human rights abuses against civil populations require the UN to condemn and act against one side, and continuing attacks necessitate higher levels of military force to protect UN troops. In other words, traditional peacekeeping is not the right method for dealing with civil wars. It does not have the conceptual basis, the military preparedness, the resources, the institutional structures, or the skills required for the expanded tasks of managing civil wars. For that, the UN has had to adapt peacekeeping approaches to humanitarian intervention (see chapter 8).

Conclusion

Traditional peacekeeping remains an important part of the interstate conflict resolution system. It has a number of inherent features that make it an attractive method for controlling conflict between states, and it will no doubt continue to be employed for overseeing cease-fires and interposition. It was developed as a realistic alternative to the failures of collective security and the limitations of small peace observation missions (Diehl 1993b). However, more improvements, particularly at the institutional and operational levels, are needed to make traditional peacekeeping more efficient. Systematic planning, logistics, and command and control must take the place of ad hoc, improvised operations. In addition, despite their limitations, adherence to the principles of consent, impartiality, and the nonuse of force must be maintained at all costs. The erosion of these principles will herald the death of traditional peacekeeping and deprive states of a useful alternative to violent confrontation. Fortunately, the UN has in recent years begun to address some of these concerns.

In other words, it is vital that traditional peacekeeping in interstate conflicts be distinguished from the "wider peacekeeping"—what we call humanitarian intervention—in internal conflicts (see chapter 8). The two concepts apply to contrasting situations. Traditional peacekeeping takes place under an entirely different set of circumstances from humanitarian intervention; and its mode of operation, its ethos, and its principles need to be distinguished and maintained. What some have referred to as the "crisis of expectations" about peacekeeping is in many respects really the failure to accept the functional differences between peacekeeping and humanitarian intervention. Applying traditional peacekeeping to internal conflicts is almost certainly a recipe for failure, but in interstate conflicts it remains an important option.

Traditional peacekeeping, furthermore, must never be used as a substitute for diplomacy. On its own, it cannot bring about political settlement, nor was it designed to do so. It should always be used judiciously and in concert with an overall diplomatic program. The UN—and the wider international community—must continue to rely on its broad repertoire of methods in dealing with interstate disputes and should not try to apply old solutions to new problems. A small rise in the number of interstate wars in the late 1990s and early 2000s suggests traditional interposition peacekeeping will continue to be an important part of international peacemaking efforts for the foreseeable future.

PART TWO

Twenty-first Century Methods and Approaches

CHAPTER SEVEN

Preventive Diplomacy

By the end of the twentieth century, the most violent and destructive period in all of human history, we had witnessed some of the most radical changes in the international environment—changes that should have given cause for unrestrained optimism. Economic advances have taken place nearly everywhere; East-West conflict and the threat of a nuclear holocaust came to an end; Eastern Europe, for so many years the focus of superpowers' conflict, is now merely a historical memory. A new spirit of superpower cooperation in the United Nations and elsewhere resulted in a greater consensus on the need to strengthen international and regional organizations, and a commitment to deal effectively and peacefully with many conflicts. In such a context, talk of a "New World Order," particularly in the wake of the first Persian Gulf War in 1991, seemed both apposite and timely.

Alas, in many ways such perceptions have proved to be merely illusory. Though we may well live in a "New World," it is a one in which order is perennially precarious. The international environment of the twenty-first century is as frightening and dangerous as that of the last century. The threat of nuclear war may have subsided, but conflict and violence are still very much with us. More than 80 conflicts, in two dozen locations, involving at least 64 governments, took place in the immediate few years following the end of the Cold War. Of these conflicts, 35 resulted in large-scale fatalities of 1,000 deaths or more. Most of those killed were civilians; in 1992–93 alone, close to one million people died because of conflict, and 20 million refugees had to flee from the effects of conflict. The United Nations was involved in more than thirteen peacekeeping operations during that year alone—the most in its fifty-year history. This "New World," which emerged in the shadow of the Cold War, was one of conflict, aggressive nationalism, chaos, and instability.

By any conceivable standard, the presence and intensity of conflict in the post–Cold War era has been remarkably high; the geographical area involved has been considerable; and the number of people affected by it has been truly significant. Conflicts since 1989 have occurred not between states, but within states. Of the 94 conflicts since 1989, only two were of the traditional interstate kind; all the others involved civil conflicts or state formation conflicts (Wallensteen and Sollenberg 1995: 2000). More recent reports find that interstate wars now constitute less than 5 percent of all armed conflicts (Human Security Centre 2005). Ethnic, communal, religious, or secessionist conflicts have shaped the new international environment and dictated the need to devise new and more effective strategies of cooperation and conflict resolution. The threats to international peace and stability may have changed the nature and location of conflict, yet they remain as menacing as ever. Unless we learn to deal with these new threats to peace, the international community may well face a new period of increased violence and destruction in many places across the globe. The traditional tools of conflict resolution such as negotiation, mediation, and arbitration may just not work in this new international environment.

Ethnic or communal conflicts—such as those in the

former Yugoslavia, Ethiopia, parts of the fragmented Soviet Union, the Sudan, Somalia, Sierra Leone, the Democratic Republic of Congo, Burma, Rwanda, Iraq, or Bangladesh—entail high human costs, much of it borne by the civilian population. In such places as Rwanda or the former Yugoslavia, civilian populations were targets of horrific violence, resulting in ethnic cleansing and huge refugee flows. Scholars and diplomats describe these types of conflict as "intractable" because they are notoriously resistant to a political solution (Crocker, Hampson, and Aall 2004: 7). In addition to the human suffering and material devastation that these conflicts cause domestically, they also invite intervention by neighboring states. These neighboring states may intervene by supporting the secessionist demands of one ethnic group or another, or because they fear spillover effects (refugees, illegal trade, etc.) of the conflict into their own territory. All this exacerbates conflicts and may cause them to escalate into serious interstate and even regional wars.

The potential escalation of ethnic and communal conflicts and their dire consequences have prompted wide and intense interest among officials and scholars in redefining the new peace and security agenda, and devising ways of dealing with, or better still anticipating, the occurrence of these extremely complex and serious conflicts. Furthermore, the post–Cold War period has seen a proliferation of "weak" or "failed states," such as Somalia and Afghanistan, where calamities of one sort or another are most likely to occur. This phenomenon has led some scholars to link preventive diplomacy (or conflict prevention since these terms are used synonymously) to the daunting problem of state failure (Carment 2004). Preventing the collapse of a state where the infrastructure is under immense strain can save a country from mass slaughter of civilians, violent conflict, and gross abuses of human rights. Thus, prevention is tied in to the need to avoid human suffering in certain states, and the need to prevent violence from taking place. As far back as 1992 the UN secretary-general, Boutros Boutros-Ghali, brought this concern into focus with the publication of *An Agenda for Peace,* which articulated a novel and proactive vision of the UN. The UN, in this view, moves beyond merely keeping the peace in the aftermath of violent conflict, and becomes a central agent in the development of early warning systems in particular and in the practice of conflict prevention in general. Preventing conflicts from taking place is preferable to trying to resolve them once violence has begun. It may all be quite a simple idea, but it is a novel and radical one in international relations (see George 2000).

What measures, therefore, can be undertaken by the UN and others when violent conflict appears imminent in order to preempt this escalation? If we could understand conflict and its root causes, we might well be able to devise ways of stopping it before it occurs or before it escalates. This chapter will address this question by situating the concept of preventive diplomacy in the context of conflict escalation, defining the term, outlining the components of an effective conflict prevention regime, and, last, by exploring various obstacles to preventive diplomacy.

Conceptual Framework for Preventive Diplomacy

Traditionally, we think of conflicts as social processes that have political, ideological, or economic causes, and that escalate, stagnate, or terminate. The life cycle of a conflict begins with the phase of conflict formation, where the parties emphasize their differences. It then goes through maturation and escalation, where various violent or nonviolent means are employed, and then terminates with a resolution or renewal of conflict.

The prevailing approach in international conflict resolution has always been framed in terms of responding to (or dealing with) a conflict once it has occurred, after the violence and human suffering have begun. Given the intractable and destructive nature of ethnic and communal conflict, new approaches are required to reduce the likelihood of widespread violence and fragmentation of societies. We need to devise ways and means of dealing with conflict in the post–Cold War era that are not merely reactive but rather aim to predict and prevent conflict (George 1999). The purpose and practice of preventive diplomacy, with or without the help of a third party, purport to achieve this objective.

Although the range of possible responses to conflict and the tools of conflict resolution seem broad, they have not been particularly adequate in the post–Cold War era. A better understanding of the different measures that may prevent or halt conflicts—and the possible complementary use of these approaches—might help us to strengthen mechanisms of conflict resolution and face the challenge of conflict in the new millennium more effectively.

A number of approaches may be relied upon to manage or resolve conflicts. Former UN secretary-general Boutros-Ghali (1992) in identifying four broad approaches was the first to draw serious attention, at an official level, to the idea of conflict prevention. The four approaches he notes are (1) peacemaking; (2) peacekeeping; (3) peacebuilding; and (4) preventive diplomacy.

Peacemaking is an approach to conflict that seeks to bring hostile parties to an agreement by peaceful means. Peacemaking techniques rely on the traditional tools of negotiation, mediation, conciliation, arbitration, adjudication, or any other peaceful means the parties may choose. Peacemaking may be further enhanced by mobilizing resources and financial assistance to get the parties, especially fragile states, to commit to a peaceful settlement and to stick to it. Peacemaking efforts have for centuries been the way the international community sought to limit violence. Alas, such efforts cannot tackle the more serious issues of ethnic conflicts, human rights abuses, or the economic collapse of a country. Clearly, other forms and tools of conflict resolution may be needed in such cases.

Peacekeeping, one of the most important innovations of the UN, is an approach designed to separate hostile parties, contain the severity of a conflict, reduce tensions, and provide opportunities and incentives for resuming negotiations. Peacekeeping is in effect an attempt to interpose between the combatants and thus stop further escalation. Because of the 1956 Suez Crisis, the UN is frequently credited with inventing modern peacekeeping to cope with new security challenges. As an international response to conflict, peacekeeping is predicated on parties' consent and use of force in self-defense only (this is what makes it acceptable to parties in conflict). Peacekeeping has become so popular that it has stretched UN organizational, financial, logistic, and personnel resources to its limits. Peacekeeping by the United Nations has been particularly popular in the post–Cold War era. The UN launched a similar number of peacekeeping operations within three recent years as were launched in the previous forty-five years.

Peacebuilding measures, on the other hand, include efforts that go well beyond limiting violence and securing a political settlement. Peacebuilding includes measures to identify the root causes of conflict and create structures that will support a sense of certainty, confidence, and security between hostile parties. Peacebuilding measures are designed to be applied at the postconflict phase to prevent the recurrence of violent conflict. Such measures usually take the form of concrete cooperative projects from which all parties involved may benefit, joint programs that reduce hostility and foster a commitment to peace and economic development, and the development of many sectors of a civil society. Once peacebuilding measures take hold, they produce an environment that ensures security, justice, and well-being for all, and one in which conflict resolution can be self-sustaining.

Preventive diplomacy is a very different approach to conflict. It has a strong emphasis on prevention rather than cure, and it involves actions that aim to identify a place where a conflict is likely to take place, create mechanisms to warn the international community against it, and marshal political will to stop the conflict from unraveling. Central to preventive diplomacy is the desire to reduce the potential for violence, make it an unreasonable option, and create conditions that encourage peaceful resolution of political differences (e.g., deal with underlying injustices and inequalities that make people resort to violence).

If the international community is serious about moving beyond the current ad hoc and largely reactive approach to conflict to a more proactive approach, it must deploy an array of policy tools for preventive diplomacy and gain significant support for such a policy. There is a clear need to strengthen the international community's methods of identifying potential conflicts and warning against them. This need, it seems, can best be met by having at our disposal a range of effective policies for the *prevention* of conflict. Now, with so many new features of conflict, and with internal conflicts becoming so destructive, only conflict prevention policies offer a chance to forestall human suffering, save countless lives, and stop large-scale violence.

Defining Conflict Prevention

Preventing war and limiting the destructive effects of conflict is not a new endeavor. For instance François de Callières in eighteenth-century France explored how crises can be dealt with before they turn into war (Lauren 1983). In addition, the Vienna Congress of 1815 attempted to limit the negative effects of wars. The prevention of violent conflicts has gained renewed importance given the changing nature of conflicts in the twentieth century. As conflicts these days can involve weapons of mass destruction, increased elements of ethnicity, and religion, and many are likely to spill over to neighboring states, international bodies such as the UN have been at the forefront of attempts to develop new approaches to prevent such deadly conflicts.

Conflict prevention is essentially about means and ends: how to identify situations that might become dangerous, violent, and very destructive, and how to stop them from becoming so. It is not about preventing normal everyday conflicts but rather trying to avoid the descent into violence and destruction. This is not an easy matter in international relations. The term *conflict prevention* can be defined both narrowly and widely; each definition will have different policy implications, of course. Within a narrow definition, conflict prevention is seen as a range of actions undertaken to prevent a potential conflict becoming violent before the deployment of forces or forceful intervention by an international or regional organization. Michael Lund limits the definition of preventive diplomacy to the phase of the conflict where serious violence has not yet occurred. He calls this stage "unstable peace" (1996: 37). I. William Zartman, however, defines conflict prevention as "providing diplomatic assistance in conflict situations as a strategy to prevent renewed outbreak of conflicts that are protracted in nature" (1983: 361–64). By defining it this way, Zartman limits the term to the diplomatic instruments involved in preventing the next round of violence. This narrow definition of conflict prevention is the one that is most widely recognized and suggests the employment of diplomatic strategies "through a mixture of coercion and cajoling, usually political and often high-profile" (Dwan 2000: 11). These strategies also include the enforcement of sanctions and embargoes on one or both of the parties. However, these measures are often challenged in international forums and are often not considered very effective (De Jonge Oudraat 2007).

In order to develop a more effective approach to preventing conflicts, Louis Kriesberg has proposed a broader definition of preventive diplomacy to include not only measures designed to prevent a conflict but measures to remove the conditions that lead to the outbreak of conflict in the first instance (Kriesberg 1998b). This can be done by distinguishing between proactive policies that reduce the underlying structural conditions that lead to violence, and preventive policies that address the immediate sources of conflict (Ackerman 2000). Carment and Schnabel (2003) define conflict prevention broadly as "long term proactive operational or structural strategy undertaken by a variety of actors, intended to identify and create enabling conditions for a stable and more predictable international security environment" (11). A broader definition of conflict prevention expands the domain of policy measures to include addressing structural causes of conflict such as poverty, social, political, and economic inequality; and corrupt governance. This approach to conflict prevention goes beyond trying to avoid situations of potential physical harm. It adopts a more holistic understanding of conflict and argues that conflict must be prevented by transforming its underlying sources. Clearly, this approach poses a serious challenge to the very foundation of an international community of states, insofar as it challenges the inviolability of the notion of sovereignty, and consequently a consensus on appropriate measures and policies may be hard to get. Furthermore, conflict prevention defined this broadly entails a new set of values and beliefs about the nature of domestic as well as international order, and legitimates, if not mandates, international actors to act on those values (Dwan 2000). At the heart of these values and issues is the relationship between the rights of the states and the rights of individuals. This trade-off where the rights of individuals override the rights of states to maintain their sovereignty has been labeled the "Responsibility to Protect" (ICISS 2001).

Definitions of terms have policy consequences; it is not merely an academic exercise. Regardless of whether conflict prevention is defined narrowly or broadly, the concepts and the practice are primarily concerned with the intentional use of various policy tools and instruments in order to prevent a violent conflict from emerging or escalating, and to create the conditions for long-term peace and stability. Thus, we can think of conflict prevention in terms of short-term effects where preventive measures are undertaken to prevent the occurrence of violence, or as structural prevention, where measures are undertaken to ensure the long-term resolution of a conflict and a radical restructuring of the elements that cause the incompatibility in the first place (see Miall 1999 on different definitions and approaches). Thinking about conflict prevention as a set of immediate and operational tools to avoid violence, and long-term structural measures to address the failures in governance, institutions, and practices that give rise to conflict in the first instance, takes us some way toward articulating coherent policies that can gain national and international support.

Components of an Effective Conflict Prevention Regime

Preventing a violent conflict from emerging or an existing conflict from escalating, which is the fundamental aim of conflict prevention, can be achieved through a number of means and methods. These generally fall under three main categories: (1) early warning and response systems, (2) confidence-building measures, and (3) other diplomatic missions.

Early Warning and Response Systems

Early warning is a concept that is usually used in the context of avoiding a natural disaster, such as flooding, drought, earthquake, or food shortages. The concept has become central in the study of preventive diplomacy too. Preventive action to address conflicts before they erupt into violence depends on knowing something about where and why violent conflicts might occur. Thus, predicting conflicts on the basis of identifying some structural conditions that are generally conducive to violence becomes central to any set of diplomatic efforts designed to prevent serious destruction of any sort, or higher levels of conflict. Prediction of this kind requires understanding the causes of conflicts and recognizing early signs of potentially destructive conflicts. The earlier we recognize these signs the earlier we can take action to prevent violence, and thus have a better chance to succeed (Zartman 2005). Early warning systems are therefore composed of both a warning and response components.

Conflicts do not occur randomly. They take place within certain kinds of structures or systems of relationships (inequality, economic deprivation, human rights abuses, failed states, etc.). Any attempt to prevent conflict should at the very least identify the possible causes of a conflict. Early warning is thus about knowledge about causes of conflict in general, identifying the presence or absence of such causes in a particular situation, issuing public warnings to concerned states and agencies predicting the outbreak of conflict and violence, and hoping that some action will be taken to stop the conflict from becoming violent. The causes of conflict tend to be multiple, interrelated, and mutually interactive over a long period (Collier et al. 2003). Accurate assessments of conflicts and credible early warnings may, in some cases, lead to early preventive responses. Early warning is thus about the systematic collection, analysis, and risk assessment of structural and proximate conditions that may accelerate the escalation and level of violence in a conflict.

Effective early warning requires an integrated strategy across different sectors (e.g., diplomacy, military, economic, political, and social) and periods of engagement (Lund 2003: 47). These strategies must be targeted at specific conflict variables or causes. They may differ from one another and may be initiated by any state, the United Nations, regional organizations, or any of the numerous nongovernmental organizations (e.g., International Crisis Group, Centre for Humanitarian Dialogue, Amnesty International, Human Rights Watch).

It is not always easy, however, to identify with complete certainty where a particular competitive situation might escalate into a violent conflict, nor which strategy is best for that particular dispute. The major problems in determining where and when to act are the ability to forecast the internal dynamics that can lead to violence and the reluctance of the political actors to act. As it is expensive to invest in preventive diplomacy, political actors, including the United Nations, are frequently unwilling to intervene and invest unless they have sufficiently reliable information that a particular dispute may escalate into a conflict. This is one of the major reasons for the failure in the international arena to act in preventing conflicts. To overcome this problem, there is a need to develop better "early warning and response systems."

Developing improved early warning and response systems requires an increased knowledge of the causes and dynamics of conflicts. In order to develop an effective preventive strategy, it is imperative to understand what causes the conflict in the first place. Anne Marie Gardner identifies two points of convergence in the conflict studies literature, although different conflicts emerge due to different reasons (2002). The first point of convergence, called "key variables," includes insecurity, inequality, private incentives, and hostile perceptions. These key variables are what Michael Brown (1997) calls "proximate" or "trigger" causes of conflict that fuel escalation and determine if a conflict will become violent. These variables must be identified and their precise nature understood in the course of a program of early warning and preventive intervention.

The second point of convergence concerns structural and mobilizing causes of conflict. Structural and mobilizing causes of conflict are typically the underlying, embedded causes of conflict that create the conditions necessary for a conflict to emerge. These two points are closely interwoven, and effective conflict prevention should therefore be multidimensional and combine security, economic, and other concerns into a coordinated approach (CIIAN 2006). Moreover, the approach taken should address the underlying factors with long-term prevention strategies and the proximate causes with short-term preventive strategies.

Key Causal Variables

What should a successful program of early warning warn us about? According to Gardner, some of the issues and areas that deserve the most serious attention and should be monitored include government collapse, the inability of a state to protect all groups within its borders, human rights violations, refugee flows, ethnic tension, high military expenditure, and dominance of one ethnic group at the expense of other ethnic groups (Gardner 2002). The issues pose a serious security dilemma and create a set of circumstances where the likelihood of violent conflict becomes very high (Posen 1993).

Another key variable that may trigger serious conflict is inequality. Although it is not a sufficient cause of conflict in itself, inequalities within a society can underpin grievances and facilitate conflict escalation. Economic deprivation is a major source of tension within any country; it is often linked to conflict and security issues, and is seen as one of the main reasons for conflict escalation (see Gardner 2002; Stewart 2002; Collier et al. 2003).

Private incentives can also lead to conflict according to Gardner (2002), as local leaders may be motivated by political or economic gains (Mueller 2004). Ethnicity and ideology can become instruments for these leaders toward achieving their own goals, benefiting from the continuation of the conflict rather than its cessation. When that is the case, the private incentives of leaders and their followers must be addressed within the conflict prevention strategies.

Perceptions, which include group identity and the degree of group cohesion, is also one of the key variables that may cause conflict escalation and expansion. Hostile perceptions may be expressed by the media or political leaders in a given country, but they are dangerous because such perceptions can be intensified and used by unscrupulous political leaders when there is a dispute (Kaufman 2001). Thus, any program of early warning must be able to identify hostile perceptions and build an effective program of prevention around them.

Structural and Proximate Causes

If preventive diplomacy is to be successful, the structural and proximate causes of a conflict must be identified and addressed. The structural and proximate causes are the underlying conditions that create the conflict in the first place, what Michael Brown (1997) calls "permissive conditions." Structural causes of conflict may include issues such as poverty, weakness of international or regional institutions, weak governments, ethnic discrimination, denial of human rights, and low political participation. The existence of these factors does not necessarily lead to conflict. In addition to structural factors, other factors such as proximate ones (e.g., incipient crisis, promulgating

discriminatory policies, a political assassination, threats of force against an ethnic community) have to be present for a conflict situation to turn violent. Proximate factors can be economic, political, cultural, or perceptual. When they are present and are there in tandem with structural conditions, the potential for violent conflict is very high, and that in itself should trigger many alarm bells among states and organizations in the international community.

There is clearly a need for a better understanding and transmission of knowledge and information about structural and proximate causes of conflict. The international community in the twenty-first century must learn to fully identify root causes of conflict, warn about the serious cases, and mobilize resources to pursue effective preventive strategies. The UN and the major Western powers can take a lead in this role.

Early Warning Signs and Indicators

Understanding what may cause conflict, however, is only the first stage. As stated previously, conflicts do not emerge suddenly or randomly. There are usually various early warning signs that indicate that violence might erupt in a troubled area. Understanding these signs is crucial for conflict prevention. The early warning signs can be analyzed under two categories. The first category includes *indicators*. Indicators refer to certain numerical figures, which if monitored, inform us about the changes in political and economical conditions. The indicators may include, but are not restricted to, unemployment rates, crime rates, forms of political expression, and association. The second category includes *signs*. Signs are shorter-term indicators, not necessarily regular, but their existence signals fundamental deterioration or changes in terms of the situation in a country. These may be a sudden increase in protests, ethnically or religiously motivated attacks on other groups, or other kinds of violent outbreaks.

These early warning indicators and signs can be studied within various groupings (table 7). The first group of indicators and signs are demographic, such as sudden demographic changes, the displacement or movement of groups, or the increasing territoriality of peoples. The second group is the economic group, which includes short- or long-term changes in economic performance, increase in poverty or inequality, rise of unemployment, or financial crises. The third group includes policy-related issues. These include destruction or desecration of religious sites, passing of discriminatory legislation favoring one group over others, destabilizing elections, or government clampdowns. The fourth group consists of social factors such as the rise of social intolerance and demonstrations. Finally, the fifth group, external indicators and signs, includes intervention or support of one group by an external actor, such as a foreign government, the spillover of ideologies or the conflict into neighboring states, or the influx of refugees into other countries.

These early warning signs and indicators must be monitored and administered accurately and judiciously. For that reason, gathering the right type of information is important. To be useful, early warning requires three types of information: (1) information on the conflict history and its context; (2) information on each party's status, traits, and objectives; and (3) information on ethno-communal groups and their grievances. This information (much of which already exists in slightly different forms in various research institutes) on the major elements of destabilization in world politics provides the basis of a model of risk assessment of communal, civil, and other conflicts.

An effective early warning system requires that a host of relevant sources—including academics, nongovernmental organizations, national governments, regional organizations, and the United Nations—work together to collect the necessary information and to develop reliable conflict analyses. At this stage, local organizations and nongovernmental organizations play an essential role, given that they often have better access to local networks, educational institutions, and political associations. Early warning findings should then be presented, with contingency plans for preventive action, to national decision makers, or to the UN Office of Political Affairs, which will have a mandate to develop policy options and recommendations.

The causes of conflicts, both internal and external, are usually complex and multilayered, but they are pretty well understood by most scholars and policymakers. Understanding the causes of conflict makes it possible to assess risk factors and prevent a conflict from taking place in the first instance, or from further escalation and expansion. Early warning is thus not unlike a system of monitoring structural and behavioral conditions, and making an intelligent assessment of the risks of conflict on that basis. It involves qualitative assessments of perceptions, and quantitative assessments of land distribution, access to resources and policy-making, and patterns of interactions between groups within a given country. It is an attempt to identify sources of tension, based on knowledge of conflict causes, and to warn against them, in the sincere hope that such warnings will be heeded. The benefits of prevention may well lie in the future, but the costs of not preventing conflicts, not heeding early warning signs, are too high to be borne by the international community.

From Warning to Response

There is a strong feeling among scholars and policymakers that the challenge for conflict prevention is not a lack of adequate warning, but the reluctance of governments or other political actors to take these warnings seriously, or take any concrete preventive action (Hampson 2002). This has been termed the "warning-response gap" (George and Holl 1997), and the existence of this gap is often attributed to a lack of political will. It is of course the main reason why preventive diplomacy may be considered a failure by some.

A "lack of political will" is consistently cited as a cause of failed prevention, but its meaning and the ways it might be influenced are seldom discussed (Woocher 2001: 181). A closer examination of this concept finds that a more useful definition of *political will* would consider if the necessary amount and type of political will are available for undertaking preventive action (Woocher 2001). Understood this way, a more accurate explanation of unsuccessful prevention would be that there is a lack

TABLE 7.   Early Warning Indicators and Signs

Demographic	• Sudden demographic changes and displacement/movement of people • Increasing territoriality of groups/people
Economic	• Short-term and long-term changes in economic performance of a country or region • Increase in poverty or inequality • Rise of unemployment • Economic shocks or financial crises
Policy-Related	• Deliberate acts of governments against a specific group or region • Destruction or desecration of religious sites • Active discrimination or legislation favoring one group over another • Potentially destabilizing referendums or elections • Goverment clamp-downs
Public Opinion or "Social" Factors	• A rise in societal intolerance and prejudice • An increase in number of demonstrations or rallies
External	• Intervention or support on behalf of one of the parties/groups by an external actor • Diffusion or contagion of ideologies or conflicts in neighboring regions • An influx of refugees from a conflict in a neighboring country

of the sufficient amount and correct type of political will to initiate a new preventive intervention. If the correct amount and type of political will exist, on the other hand, a global program of conflict prevention mechanisms based on good information, clear communication, credible early warnings to concerned audiences, and relevant responses may well come into being under the auspices of a separate office within the United Nations. In other words, an effective early warning system that consistently leads to early responses would be created; the gap would be bridged.

In conclusion, the need to monitor the growing number of internal conflicts and human rights abuses and to develop consistent and meaningful policies that can be realistically pursued by the international community is at the heart of a reliable early warning and response system that can deal with the growing number of internal conflicts occurring around the world. The UN has taken some important steps in that direction (see UN General Assembly Resolution A/60/891 of 18 July 2006). Individual states now have to embrace the principles articulated in that resolution. The human costs (in terms of deaths, destruction, injury, and refugees) of not doing so are simply too high.

Preventive Diplomacy: Actions

Preventive diplomacy depends ultimately upon a core set of activities that may be undertaken by states or international organizations, and that are designed to prevent violence in a target country or prevent it from spreading to other areas. To achieve that, a number of policy tools are available. They range from official diplomacy (e.g., negotiations and consultations), through nonofficial methods (e.g., Track II efforts), to economic measures (e.g., economic assistance, joint projects), and military measures (e.g., preventive deployment, demilitarized zones). In the next section we highlight some of the most important of these policy tools.

Confidence-Building Measures

Confidence-building measures play a very different role from early warning and response systems in preventing violent conflict. Uncertainty, anxiety, reciprocal fears, and misperceptions between conflicting parties pose a great threat to peace and security. These factors may fuel escalation or drive parties inadvertently toward violence because they increase tensions. Confidence-building mea-

sures are designed to lower the uncertainty, reduce the anxiety, and eliminate the misperceptions inherent in any unstable structure. Simply put, they strive to reduce the otherwise unchecked escalation of tensions between the conflicting parties. When parties have confidence in each other's intentions and future behavior, various events that could likely trigger the emergence of violent conflict can be prevented from materializing.

Reducing and managing the sources of tension between the parties by fostering a relationship of trust and confidence is an important requirement for conflict prevention (United Nations 2006: 14). However, trust and confidence are notoriously difficult to establish when parties are engaged in an internal conflict and when each side tends to emphasize the differences between itself and the other side (Ben-Dor and Dewit 1994). To create the political dynamics of trust and confidence, four types of measures may have to be adopted.

1. Joint and explicit declaration on an internationally accepted code of conduct (respect for noncombatants, prohibiting the use of chemical and biological weapons, etc.);
2. Agreement on information exchange and increased communication to assuage each party's fears about military intentions and activities;
3. Observations and inspections, through the exchange of military officers or the use of low-orbiting satellites, to ensure genuine transparency of intentions; and
4. Mutual agreement on measures of constraints (each party in a potential conflict binds itself not to use force under some specified circumstances, to ban certain kinds of weapons, or to establish buffer zones).

All these measures can prevent a tense situation from escalating into a full-blown conflict. The greater the level of participation by all political communities and domestic constituencies, the higher the likelihood that certain problems can be alleviated before they turn into serious and irresolvable conflicts. Successful confidence-building measures create a commitment to nonviolence and openness in dealing with any conflict. For these reasons, they are an important component of an effective conflict prevention regime.

Examples of concrete confidence-building measures can be found in many regions of the world. In Europe the Helsinki and Stockholm models focus specifically on promoting a convergence of expectations through knowledge and transparency regarding the organization and preparation of armed forces. In Southeast Asia, the Asia Regional Forum (ARF) meets every two years to discuss all current political issues and recommend a series of measures that might reduce hostility in any emerging conflict. Even in a conflict-prone area such as the Middle East, there are a variety of confidence-building measures, especially in the realm of physical separation, constraints on certain weapons, agreement on demilitarized zones, and acceptance of UN peacekeeping forces to promote transparency and provide early notification of possible instability.

Diplomatic Efforts

The third component of an effective conflict prevention regime entails a wide variety of instruments and tools that can be used to prevent violent conflict. These include coercive diplomacy, fact-finding, mediation, and negotiation.

Coercive diplomacy can be defined as a technique of statecraft that attempts to get a target (i.e., state, group within a state, or nonstate actor) to change its behavior through the threat to use force or through the actual use of limited force (Art and Cronin 2007: 299).

A number of scholars argue that sufficiently credible threats and the use of military force can make a crucial difference in preventing conflicts (see Hampson 2002). However, coercive diplomatic efforts do not remove the causes of the conflict; they only suppress them. Once the threat of force has ceased, the conflict will most likely erupt again. It is therefore necessary to consider alternative methods of preventive engagement.

Positive political, economic, or social incentives and inducements that encourage behavior that is more cooperative may be helpful. Targeted economic assistance, aid and developmental packages, trade agreements, or access to advanced technology may help to create a positive environment, which might lead to cooperation rather than competition between the conflicting parties. Frequently, therefore, mixed strategies that combine coercive measures and inducements have been viewed as the most effective approach.

Another conflict prevention instrument is fact-finding, which involves the investigation of a particular issue by a neutral international organization or a committee within the conflict areas. However, fact-finding missions only report their findings; they do not have the power to offer solutions or convince the parties to negotiate. In addition, such missions are frequently undermined by the unwillingness of the conflict parties to cooperate, and they are often accused of bias toward one party by the other.

Negotiation and mediation undertaken in the early stages of conflict is another conflict prevention instrument. The practice of preventing disputes through intermediaries has a rich history in all cultures, both Western and non-Western (Gulliver 1979). This approach suggests that, after observing signs of an emerging dispute, third parties may get involved in a mediation process to prevent the escalation of the dispute into a violent and destructive conflict. Bercovitch and Langley (1993), in their study of 97 disputes involving 364 mediation attempts, find a declining success rate for mediation as fatalities escalate. This finding suggests that mediation might have a greater chance of being successful if it is undertaken before the disagreement escalates into a conflict. However, the parties may not be interested in a mediated or a negotiated solution before they face the costs of war and realize the limits of what they can achieve. For that reason, they might not opt for mediation until and unless the conflict reaches a hurting stalemate.

Policymakers would benefit greatly if these tools were embedded within a framework that could guide their decisions regarding which of the tools to use and when. However, because each conflict has a life of its own—its own unique dynamics—developing a framework that can be applicable to all cases is not feasible. Instead, for conflict prevention efforts to be successful, there is a need to develop a contextual approach that permits the evaluation of each case on its own terms, then develops adequate preventive strategies that take into account the distinctive features of each case.

Factors Influencing the Success of Conflict Prevention

Although conflict prevention is not unique, its renewed importance in the twenty-first century requires an in-depth analysis of the factors that influence its success. This section will focus for the most part on the nature of the intervening actors (i.e., those third parties undertaking the preventive efforts), interactional factors, structural factors, and the timing of preventive interventions, among the various factors that have an impact on the success of conflict prevention.

The Nature of the Intervening Actors

In addition to the parties to the dispute, those actors who attempt to prevent it from escalating into violent conflict are very important for the success of preventive efforts. Four different kinds of actors may initiate preventive diplomatic efforts in conflict hot spots: (1) individuals, (2) states, (3) international and regional organizations, and (4) nongovernmental organizations.

Although some individuals may initiate preventive efforts, usually this is not a sufficient condition for success. Therefore, the support of the wider international community or a major actor is required for the preventive effort to be successful in these cases.

Likewise, unless it is a superpower, a state, represented by either diplomatic corps or high-level officials, also requires the support of the international community. However, these actors still contribute to conflict prevention by way of initiating dialogue, aiding in power sharing, and fostering a willingness to consider various solutions.

The third group of actors—international and regional organizations such as the UN, OAS, or EU—are the most common actors that undertake preventive measures. These international and regional organizations can prevent the escalation of conflicts by facilitating dialogue through the creation of specialist forums: providing economic, developmental, and humanitarian assistance; undertaking fact-finding and monitoring missions; helping to maintain dialogue between different groups; providing information to the involved parties; and assisting the development of legal and human rights standards. However, the role of the individuals representing international and regional organizations and their leadership and personal commitment to preventive diplomacy is significant in successful conflict prevention (Ackerman 2000). Moreover, the legitimacy and effectiveness of these actors are enhanced if they are well-recognized international or regional organizations, such as the United Nations or the European Union.

Finally, the last set of actors that can play a constructive role in preventive diplomacy are nongovernmental organizations and other grassroots organizations. These can include religious, civic, environmental, and humanitarian groups. In fact, NGOs have a crucial function to perform in preventing violent conflicts from emerging, as they are often already working with grassroots and civil society organizations within communities (Aall 2001). This means that they are often privy to local information concerning potential conflicts and can therefore provide early warning of impending conflict (Aall 2001: 379). Moreover, this established relationship with different community leaders enables NGOs to have greater access to these local leaders. Due to the nature of the work they do within these communities, these NGOs have a better chance of earning the trust of the local population and leaders. They also tend to exhibit a richer understanding of the needs and frustrations on the ground.

Because of this unique position, NGOs can play a major role in preventive diplomacy. They may provide education in conflict management and conduct training projects for different sectors of the community, such as students, children, government officials, and journalists. NGOs may also initiate community-building projects that deal with socioeconomic problems (e.g., jobs, education) concerning the entire society. They may conduct educational and cultural projects that strive to reduce prejudice, teach nonviolence, and rehumanize the other.

In sum, it is not possible to discern which actors are best equipped to help prevent violent conflicts, but it is not difficult to see how each comes equipped with its own resources, strengths, and shortcomings. Often a dominant international actor must initiate, or at least support, the initiative of preventive diplomacy. In addition, the support of major political powers or of a superpower such as the United States may be crucial for the preventive effort to be successful (Lund 2003: 49). More specifically, after the preventive effort has started, the support of the major actor or the regional or international institutions must continue in the implementation of the preventive measures (Zartman 2005: 201–2). Therefore, a multidimensional and coordinated approach that involves all the aforementioned actors undertaking different roles at different stages yet complementing each other is preferable. However, this requires good organizational skills, coordination, and a strong commitment to preventive diplomacy on the part of the international community.

Interactional Factors

In order for preventive efforts to be successful, there is a need to gain a deeper understanding of the interactional factors affecting the process. Interactional factors include the relationship between the disputants, distribution of power among the parties, and the behavior of the domestic leaders.

Studies show that intractable conflicts involving a long history of animosity between the parties will create a negative impact on the successful resolution of that conflict. Conflicts involving ethnic or religious identity issues, where there has been a deep-rooted animosity between the communities, are considerably harder to manage once they have begun. They are also much more difficult to prevent from escalating into destructive conflicts. However, even if there is a long history of animosity dating back to the period before state formation, that does not mean that preventive efforts will be ineffective.

Some scholars who examine the preventive efforts in Rwanda and former Yugoslavia argue that ethnic identity is innate and fixed. Human beings are inevitably driven to defend their ethnic groups, often by resorting to the use of force. In this view, therefore, international efforts to prevent ethnic conflicts are pointless (Ackerman 2000). Other scholars stress that ethnic conflicts are far too complex for outsiders to resolve and therefore any preventive efforts place unacceptable risks onto third parties (Ackerman 2000). However, Ackerman disagrees with these arguments and suggests that failed efforts in conflict prevention are due to the inability of the international community to act in a timely fashion. In addition, if or when the international society acts preventively, it is possible to avoid even complex conflicts such as ethnic conflicts (Ackerman 2000: 25).

In addition to the importance of the nature of interaction between the parties, another important interactional factor involves the behavior of leaders. Moderate behavior in domestic leaders is more responsive to preventive efforts than more extremist behavior. Moderate behavior here refers to moderation in pursuit of nationalist agendas, use of rhetoric, or avoidance or misuse of historical events and religious or national symbols; leaders who are more open to power sharing, information sharing, and who are willing to cooperate and contribute to the success of the preventive efforts. The ability of a leader to have the legitimacy to represent and speak on behalf of the public as well as control the extremists and opposition within the community is very important for the success of preventive diplomacy.

Structural Factors

Structural factors that influence the process of preventive diplomacy include the nature of the conflict and psychological and procedural factors.

Factors related to the nature of the conflict such as the size of a country in terms of population and geography, the distribution of ethnic groups, or level of economic development or underdevelopment may affect the success of preventive efforts. In addition, as mentioned before, if the dispute between the parties involves resources and is viewed from a win-win perspective, then preventive efforts have a greater chance of success. If the dispute involves identity issues based on ethnic or religious differences, it is more difficult to manage.

Understanding psychological factors is important in order to develop better strategies for preventing violence between two communities. Psychological factors help explain the mobilizing causes of conflict and are deep-rooted in the consciousness of the communities. They involve the dehumanization of the Other, the articulation of the dichotomy between us and them, and images of their own group and other groups. When this dichotomy is wide and deeply entrenched, it is much harder to succeed in the prevention of violence, as the Israeli-Palestinian, Greek Cypriot–Turkish Cypriot, and Muslim-Hindu conflict in Kashmir vividly demonstrate. In addition, traumatic experiences such as genocide or mass expulsion hinder preventive efforts. The case studies that Ackerman has investigated show that "the absence of a history of extreme individual and collective victimization and the presence of a peaceful self-image for ethnic groups are vital to the prevention of violence" (Ackerman 2000: 72).

A number of procedural factors can influence conflict prevention efforts. In broad terms, preventive diplomacy must be well coordinated and include varied and multifaceted actions, instruments, and strategies (Ackerman 2000). This is of particular importance when a situation of impending violence prevails. In addition, the conflict prevention process should reflect and be based upon the specific features of the target country or region, utilize a solidly based but flexible operational plan, engage and stimulate the capacity of locally affected people and their governments, and be responsive to matters of timing (CIIAN 2006: 16).

The Timing of Intervention

A crucial factor that affects preventive diplomacy is the timing of the prevention effort. Preventive diplomacy is more likely to be successful if it takes place in the early stages of the conflict before it escalates into violence (Zartman 2005: 201). This becomes especially vital where a spillover of violent conflict may negatively affect the balance of the region, therefore, identifying hot spots and initiating early responses soon thereafter is important for successful prevention. These preventive initiatives must take place immediately and address grievances and demands of the parties involved. To this end, Kriesberg (2001: 85) asserts that preventive policies "introduced early in response to emerging demands for greater political or economic rights may effectively prevent an intractable conflict from developing." In this sense, regional or international organizations or strong states must act promptly to prevent the conflict before it escalates. The failure to do so may result in the failure to prevent violent conflict.

Following that idea, Connie Peck suggests that the creation of dispute resolution services for use by UN members would allow them to comply with their obligations under Chapter VI of the UN Charter, by providing skilled third-party assistance through good offices and mediation as early as possible in a dispute (Peck 1996: 131).

However, timing is a difficult notion in conflict prevention as each case has its own internal dynamic and conflict cycle. Different conflicts move along different paths, and not all early intervention strategies will be successful in every case.

Obstacles to Preventive Diplomacy

The idea of preventing conflicts before they turn into all-out wars is crucial if we are to reduce human suffering, death, and destruction. Being proactive in the area of conflict resolution is certainly better than being reactive. However, it is easier said than done, and a recent report from the UN secretary-general lamented the unacceptable gap between conflict prevention rhetoric and reality (United Nations 2006). While the number of UN preventive diplomacy missions increased sixfold between 1990 and 2002 (Mack 2001: 527), there are a number of obstacles that render the preventive endeavor less than successful. Understanding these obstacles thus becomes important for both overcoming them and developing better preventive approaches.

One of the main obstacles to preventive diplomacy is that it is difficult for third parties to influence or manipulate domestic politics within the countries where a violent conflict is to be prevented. Preventive diplomacy requires the identification of the problem areas, then a timely intervention by appropriate third parties in order to reverse the course of the conflict. The adversaries, however, may perceive this as an intervention into their internal affairs, and therefore totally and utterly unwarranted and unjustified. To respond to a potential conflict situation before it becomes manifest means to trample on the norm of sovereignty, and this is no easy thing to do in international relations. By the time resources for preventive diplomacy are marshaled, it may well be too late, and too difficult to influence the leaders of conflict parties. Even if the third parties succeed in influencing the leadership, ex-

tremist groups may mobilize the support of the population against any outside intervention. Timely intervention in the case of preventive diplomacy means very early intervention by third parties; yet early intervention may violate the inviolable principle of sovereignty. This is a major dilemma with all aspects of this approach.

Another obstacle to preventive diplomacy is that it is not always easy to sustain the long-term support needed for it to succeed. It is important to bear in mind that conflict prevention is a long, costly, and fragile process that, even with initial successes, can be easily derailed, especially if the root causes of the conflict are not addressed. Zartman (2005: 201) reminds us that at every step of the process there are difficult decisions to be made that require taking risks, and that the safest choice is usually to do nothing. However, even in cases where the difficult choice to initiate action is made, "the greatest cause of preventive failure once action has begun has been intervenor fatigue and premature satisfaction with results" (Zartman 2005: 201–2). For this reason, once the initial preventive effort is initiated, the interested parties must follow up on that process. Therefore, long-term strategies and instruments are necessary to prevent a relapse into violence (Paris 2004). Preventive diplomacy requires strategic and operational resources; it requires attention to many problems. It is not a cheap investment. On the contrary, many of the institutions that are best suited to undertake preventive measures (e.g., regional and international organizations) do not have the resources to maintain their support for following up or establishing long-term strategies, especially when there are so many conflicts with the potential to become violent occurring in the world.

This point leads to another crucial obstacle to preventive efforts: the logistics. Although preventive efforts usually tend to be much less costly than massive reconstruction or humanitarian projects in the aftermath of conflict, it is not always easy to mobilize the resources necessary to undertake preventive efforts. Who will lead the efforts in prevention? Who will shoulder the financial burden of a given preventive effort? Who will decide how the resources are to be spent? These are but some of the daunting questions confronting the practice of conflict prevention. Preventive efforts require the development of systematic and coordinated long-term engagement, as well as the integration of political, social, economic, military, and human rights measures. Such coordination is hard to achieve and costly to maintain. There are no guarantees of success, and few institutional incentives to facilitate the practice of conflict prevention.

The fourth obstacle facing preventive diplomacy is the difficulty of assessing when preventive efforts are no longer necessary. When has preventive diplomacy been successful? How can we determine when the policy goals of prevention have been achieved? It is easy in such cases to think of failures, but impossible to think of success (how can we identify the nonoccurrence of an event as successful?). As the preventive effort is a continuous process, and assessing when the effort should be considered successful is problematic, it becomes difficult to evaluate the process itself and when it should be terminated. In addition to the difficulty of determining the duration of the effort, it is also hard to determine which third party should undertake the lead in prevention, what criteria should be used to make such a decision, and which actors should decide whether these criteria are met (Ackerman 2000).

Another major obstacle to preventive efforts, as Kofi Annan suggests in his Millennium Report, relates to the new norms and values that are increasingly shared by the international community. These new norms allow international organizations such as the UN to assess global trouble spots and then act upon these evaluations. It also asks the international community to unite to prevent deadly conflict by intervening into the domestic politics of countries where there is a danger of an escalation in conflict. This new approach, "the responsibility to protect," emphasizes human sovereignty and puts it on par with state sovereignty. It broadens the UN mandate and sets precedents for other countries to engage in domestic politics under the name of preventive diplomacy, which poses a serious challenge to established international norms and concepts of state sovereignty. As the idea of the "sovereignty of states" is one of the building blocks of international law and the international system, countries are wary about the consequences of any precedent that might undermine this norm. Thus, many states are hesitant to allow such intervention to become a norm, especially as no country is immune to conflict.

Above all, though, the major obstacle to preventive diplomacy is a lack of political will. There seems to be an opposition to the use of force internationally even in cases where humanitarian crises are obvious (e.g., Darfur, Zimbabwe). Those countries most vulnerable to conflict, those most in need of development, aid, civil society, and effective governance, are also the very same states that would resist any assistance or interference in their affairs. The wealthy Western powers who may undertake preventive efforts are usually reluctant to do so lest they offend political sensibilities. Early warnings are there aplenty, but international organizations do not have sufficient resources to undertake serious preventive measures, developing countries resent such measures, and Western countries show little will or determination in wanting to lead such efforts. They are all busy doing something but not necessarily preventing a conflict.

While these obstacles to prevention are serious impediments, it should be noted that in the major cases of state collapse during the post–Cold War era specific actions identified and discussed at the time could have been taken to prevent these costly catastrophes from occurring (Zartman 2005: 1). This suggests, once again, that *the* greatest obstacle to successful conflict prevention is mobilizing the international community to consistently undertake timely preventive efforts and sustain them for the required periods of time.

Conclusion

To return to the question originally posed at the start of this chapter—what can be done to prevent violent conflict?—the short answer is "quite a lot." Most, if not all, of the components of an effective conflict prevention regime are in place. Policymakers have abundant tools, mechanisms, and instruments to choose from; some of these, such as confidence-building measures, are safe choices because they are not highly controversial and would not put the intervenor into a high-risk, high-stakes position; whereas, should these less invasive actions fail to prevent the escalation of violent conflict, the intervenor can then apply other tools, such as coercive diplomacy, which entail a greater level of investment and risk assumed by the intervenor.

Although the importance and value of preventive diplomacy have been recognized internationally, many tools and instruments for conflict prevention have been adequately developed, several early warning systems are in place and operational, and the theory guiding conflict prevention interventions is becoming more refined, various concerns voiced by governments and the obstacles mentioned here have seriously impeded consistent practice in the international arena. Based on these concerns, defining what preventive diplomacy is and what it is not—meaning, to draw its boundaries—has been an important endeavor for many states.

That same concern has stopped many countries from taking preventive action and has thus undermined the necessary consensus and commitment to prevent conflicts.

For preventive diplomacy to be rooted deeply and firmly within the consciousness of the international community, there is a need to clarify what the term means, what that definition allows in terms of rules of intervention, and how that may impact the international system in the long run.

As conflicts are becoming progressively more costly for the affected states and the entire international community, with their attendant economic, political, and military spillover effects, there is an urgent need to further develop approaches and practices that may prevent serious conflicts from turning into deadly wars. This chapter argues that these approaches and practices to conflict prevention must be developed in a manner that would make them more attractive options to leaders of states and other potential intervenors, thus creating more consistent, timely, and long-term conflict prevention interventions.

Despite the widely publicized instances when prevention fails, there are indications that "a new international norm may be receiving gradual acceptance: if violent conflicts are not inevitable and can be prevented with reasonable effort, international actors [are] morally bound to act to do what is possible wherever situations could very likely lead to massive violence" (Lund 2004: 123). The key challenge for undertaking more effective prevention in the future lies in having this norm widely adopted and consistently acted upon. Somehow we have to move beyond verbal exhortations into actual policies.

CHAPTER EIGHT

Humanitarian Intervention

Humanitarian intervention is a recent and highly visible method of conflict resolution that recasts the traditional third-party intervention role into novel and highly controversial forms. On one level, it is an extension of preventive diplomacy; it involves attempting to stop large-scale human rights abuses or to prevent the outbreak of conflict and create the conditions for a durable, positive peace. A special form of peacekeeping, humanitarian intervention takes a multidimensional approach to conflict and involves a range of civilian and military actors and processes. It combines diplomatic-level and local-level mediation and conciliation, an expanded range of peacekeeping activities, administration and governance, relief and humanitarian action, and postconflict reconstruction. A series of successfully adapted peace support operations in Namibia, El Salvador, Cambodia, and Mozambique in the early 1990s saw humanitarian intervention quickly take over as the UN's primary method for dealing with complex and intractable civil wars. Today, humanitarian intervention is at the center of any international discussions about how to respond to the outbreak of serious internal conflict.

Initially, humanitarian intervention promised to be the silver bullet for an international conflict resolution system under strain from a series of vicious and bewildering internal conflicts in the former Soviet Union and Africa. These "new wars" (Kaldor 1999) proved resistant to traditional methods of conflict management—negotiation, mediation, involvement by international organizations, peacekeeping—and posed a complex array of security management challenges. Multidimensional humanitarian operations that simultaneously tackled the political, humanitarian, and economic aspects of conflict appeared to offer an alternative and potentially more effective approach. At the same time, international conditions permitted an unprecedented level of cooperation within the UN Security Council.

With its newfound freedom, buoyed by early success, the UN embarked on a spectacular expansion of its activities, applying various types of humanitarian peacekeeping missions as its new conflict resolution tool of choice. Between 1948 and 1988, the UN had launched a total of twelve peacekeeping operations (plus two small observer missions); but from 1989 to 2004, twenty-nine new operations were initiated (United Nations 2008). In 1988, there were just five peacekeeping missions involving 9,950 military personnel from twenty-six contributing countries; only five years later, the UN had eighteen ongoing operations involving 80,000 troops from seventy-six different member states (Findlay 1996: 2–3). Following a period of retrenchment in the late 1990s, the UN's involvement in peace support operations grew once more, and in November 2007, the UN had seventeen UN operations deploying 100,500 military and civilian personnel (United Nations 2008). In addition, the UN currently has eleven smaller "political and peace-building missions" operating in countries such as Somalia, Burundi, Guinea-Bissau, Nepal, and Tajikistan (United Nations 2008).

Regrettably, and some would say inevitably, the UN's initial enthusiastic burst of activity culminated in a series of devastating failures in Somalia, Bosnia, and Rwanda, as well as an inevitable overstretch of the Organization's conceptual and institutional resources. The effect of these failures initially cast doubt on the effectiveness of humanitarian intervention as a conflict resolution method and led to a period of retrenchment and intense self-reflection (see Boutros-Ghali 1995). In many ways, the UN was ill prepared for the challenges thrown up by the security environment of the post–Cold War system, lacking both the necessary conceptual and legal-normative framework for intervening in domestic conflicts, as well as the organizational capacity for launching so many complex, multidimensional operations. As we write in 2009, we find ourselves in a period of transition—an interregnum—for UN peacekeeping and conflict resolution, as it struggles to develop more appropriate forms of humanitarian intervention that can effectively cope with the challenges posed by intractable internal wars.

In this chapter, we assess the present operation of humanitarian intervention as a form of international conflict resolution, cognizant that current theory and practice are in a state of flux and that the fundamental legal-normative issues raised by its practice are highly contested. Humanitarian operations can be undertaken by a number of different actors—individual states, coalitions of willing states, regional organizations, or the UN. In fact, subcontracting all or parts of humanitarian operations to other international actors has been suggested as a way of relieving some of the pressure on the UN to deal with the numerous internal conflicts presently affecting large parts of the world. It should also help to overcome the reluctance of the great powers to intervene in peripheral regions where they no longer have significant interests. In this chapter, however, we concentrate primarily on UN-directed humanitarian intervention; task sharing or subcontracting by regional actors will be examined in chapter 9. Humanitarian operations also entail the significant involvement of NGOs in both relief and development activities, and in post-conflict reconciliation processes. We examine these roles in chapter 10.

Humanitarian intervention evolved from and is an adaptation of traditional UN peacekeeping to the specific challenges involved in dealing with complex internal conflicts. It entails an expansion—both conceptually and on the ground—of peacekeeping activities, functions, and roles. However, the exact dimensions of humanitarian intervention are both ill-defined and highly contested, and there is little agreement on its conceptual basis, its legal and political foundations, its normative aims, or how to evaluate it.

Conceptualizing Humanitarian Intervention

We conceive of humanitarian intervention as a special form of peacekeeping that emerged after 1989. Like traditional peacekeeping, humanitarian intervention is a form of third-party conflict resolution that involves attempts by external actors to deescalate the conflict and facilitate pacific settlement. Critically, in contrast to traditional peacekeeping, humanitarian intervention does not necessarily entail the consent of the disputing parties. In this sense, its orientation is closer to arbitration than mediation, although the full range of third-party roles is usually present in any one operation. It represents a united international community acting like an impartial judge in the first place and a law enforcement officer in the second.

Defining Humanitarian Intervention

In its most general conception, humanitarian intervention has been described as "employing military means for humanitarian ends under a UN sanction" (Whitman 1995: 7) or "the external use of force to stop genocide or widespread human rights abuse" (Pugh 1997: 135). These definitions highlight an important underlying motivation for international intervention, but only touch on one dimension of what the term describes. We suggest that humanitarian intervention refers to "complex, multifunctional operations . . . designed to supervise transitions from conditions of social conflict to minimal political order" (Chopra 1998: 6). Weiss describes humanitarian intervention in slightly more detail as "operations that combine military, civil administration (including election and human rights monitoring and political support), and humanitarian expertise with political negotiations and mediation" (1995: 1). Importantly, the UN conceives of humanitarian intervention as complex peace operations that combine *peacemaking* (using diplomatic methods to bring conflicts to a halt, such as mediation), *peacekeeping* (military operations designed to oversee cease-fires or the implementation of peace agreements), and *peacebuilding* (a range of activities designed to address the roots of conflict and create the conditions for a consolidated and stable peace) (United Nations 2000: 2–3). We would add that humanitarian operations sometimes also include *peace-enforcement*, so-called muscular peacekeeping, which involves using offensive military force to achieve humanitarian or political goals.

In this chapter, we conceive of humanitarian intervention in its descriptive—as opposed to normative—aspect. In other words, we are trying to describe actual UN operations, rather than some kind of ideal type. It is highly contested whether any genuinely *humanitarian* interventions have ever taken place, and there is no agreement on which cases might be included; disagreements still rage over whether India's intervention in Bangladesh, Vietnam's intervention in Kampuchea, Tanzania's intervention in Uganda, France's intervention in Rwanda, or NATO's intervention in Kosovo should be treated as humanitarian interventions. Humanitarian intervention is also different from humanitarian assistance. Intervention is coercive and implies the use of force for humanitarian aims; assistance, on the other hand, is associated with the provision of relief (Pieterse 1998).

A special kind of peacekeeping operation, humanitarian intervention can be distinguished from traditional peacekeeping along several key dimensions: actors, tasks, aims, principles, and context. First, humanitarian operations involve a significant expansion of the range of actors. In addition to traditional military contingents, these operations also include a wide range of UN civil agencies, UN aid agencies, and international and national NGOs working in concert. Second, the tasks of traditional peacekeepers are expanded beyond military activities such as cease-fire oversight to include humanitarian and political activities like the delivery of emergency aid and election monitoring. Third, the aims of humanitarian operations take on a much more overt political orientation. Instead of being directed toward acting as a neutral interposition force, for example, humanitarian operations are often directed at preventing human rights abuses, mitigating humanitarian crises, delivering aid, capturing war criminals, or even enforcing peace through combat operations. This makes them intensely political affairs. Fourth, the principles that have guided traditional peacekeeping for several decades—consent, impartiality, and the nonuse of force—have all been eroded in humanitarian operations. Often, state institutions have broken down and there is no effective authority to grant consent to the peacekeeping force, but the need to protect civilians from human rights abuses involves offensive military actions. Obviously, this may mean acting against one or more of the parties to the conflict. Last, the context of humanitarian intervention is different from traditional peacekeeping. For example, it tends to occur during the active phase of the conflict rather than after the fighting has ended, and to date, every operation has taken place in intrastate as opposed to interstate conflicts. In addition, humanitarian intervention takes place in so-called complex emergencies where state collapse, humanitarian disaster, human rights abuses, and ongoing factional fighting create an unstable and dangerous environment.

The Basis of Humanitarian Intervention

Like traditional peacekeeping (chapter 6), the Charter basis of humanitarian intervention is ambiguous, lying somewhere in the gray zone between Chapter VI and Chapter VII. In fact, the willingness to intervene in a sovereign state without clear consent and to employ offensive military force on occasion has made humanitarian intervention one of the most controversial and intensely debated subjects in international relations today. Its coercive and humanitarian aspects raise important legal, normative, and global governance questions that have yet to be fully addressed. The basis of humanitarian intervention therefore is both unclear and highly contested, and represents a tension between the principles of human rights, state sovereignty, and international order. Part of the challenge of making humanitarian intervention a more effective method of conflict resolution will be clarifying its legal, normative and political basis—developing a doctrine of humanitarian operations, in other words. Nevertheless, it is possible to discern the outlines of the political, legal, and theoretical basis of humanitarian intervention.

The *political basis* of humanitarian intervention lies in the end of the Cold War and the vast expansion of the UN's role in international conflict resolution, seen most visibly in the explosion of UN peacekeeping after 1988. This expansion of activities was itself the result of a unique coincidence of factors. First, the end of superpower hostility gave the Security Council a newfound capacity for cooperative action, as well as a new kind of collaboration between the secretary-general and the Security Council. Second, the freedom of action in the UN occurred at the same time that the need for international peacekeeping increased dramatically. The demand for impartial international forces came from a series of regional peace agreements between 1985 and 1991 in Afghanistan, Southern Africa, Central America, and Cambodia. In addition, the collapse of the Soviet Union and Yugoslavia in eastern Europe and the end of superpower patronage in Africa coincided with a wave of new conflicts. Third, a widespread mood of optimism that the UN could and should play a much more central role in international security quickly became evident, driven largely by a series of peacekeeping successes that had culminated in the 1988

Nobel Peace Prize being awarded in recognition of UN peacekeeping (Roberts 1996: 300). Finally, increasingly politicized humanitarian aid operations in Southern Sudan (Operation Rainbow and Operation Lifeline Sudan) and Angola (Special Relief Program for Angola) had been taking place since the mid-1980s. In these operations, the UN had attempted to deliver aid in the absence of a formal cease-fire (Duffield, Macrae, and Zei 1994: 228). Humanitarian intervention in the "complex emergencies" of the "new wars" was in this sense a linkage of humanitarian concerns with peace and security issues, and a process that had been under way for some time.

The *legal-normative basis* of humanitarian intervention lies in changes to the international legal and norm-based order. The direction of this change is clear but its content is still contested. In the first place, during this period there were efforts to "reorient military forces for peace-keeping and peace-enforcement in the expectation that humanitarian intervention would represent the enforcement component of global security" (Kaldor 2000: 2). That is, the enforcement provisions of Chapter VII were enlarged from collective self-defense to dealing with complex emergencies and their accompanying human rights abuses, refugee flows, or breakdowns of state institutions. In Haiti, the lack of democracy was interpreted as a "threat to international peace and security," widening the applicability of Chapter VII even further. Second, attempts to establish universal human rights gained momentum in the early 1990s. The human rights consensus that emerged, and that is still being negotiated, undermined the existing principle of nonintervention in the internal affairs of states. The scope of this principle has now been modified, and the scope for justified resort to force has expanded accordingly (Semb 2000: 470; see also Report of the International Commission 2001). Although the contents of the emerging principles for justified intervention are highly contested, the practice of UN authorization thus far suggests that states lose their right to nonintervention when: (1) a state engages in widespread and systematic human rights abuses; (2) a state collapses and humanitarian catastrophe results; or (3) the government of a state is illegitimate and as a consequence poses a threat to international peace and security. It remains to be seen whether a fourth condition, harboring international terrorists, gains widespread international acceptance, notwithstanding the so-called Bush doctrine of preemption.

The *theoretical basis* for greatly expanded and more complex peacekeeping operations developed out of the practical problems associated with peacekeeping operations from 1988 through 1992 in Namibia, Mozambique, El Salvador, and Cambodia. The peace settlements in these conflicts involved the implementation of complex transitional arrangements, which in turn necessitated expanding the roles that peacekeepers normally played. The lessons that the UN took from these operations included: efforts to resolve the underlying causes of conflict should be embedded in the peace process itself to forestall a return to violence; peace operations had to extend beyond the narrow parameters of traditional peacekeeping or diplomatic peacemaking to include political, social, and economic aspects; and coordination of political, economic and social strategies was essential, as was the close cooperation between the key actors (IPA 1996). Implementing these lessons thus involved the development of a wider, more comprehensive concept, namely, humanitarian intervention. The concept was given theoretical content in Boutros-Ghali's *An Agenda for Peace* (1992) and later the Report of the International Commission on Intervention and State Sovereignty, *The Responsibility to Protect* (2001). These documents argued that military force could play an important role in implementing coordinated strategies of peacemaking, peacekeeping, and postconflict peacebuilding. Each of these components was required to ensure that the conflict could be controlled and the re-eruption of violence avoided. The success of applying the new concepts in these initial operations raised expectations that an effective method of dealing with internal wars had been found.

In short, humanitarian intervention emerged in a specific historical context that has to a large degree dictated the content of the emerging humanitarian intervention discourse. The combination of political-historical, legal, and conceptual factors that coalesced around a set of specific operations in the period 1988 through 1992 set the scene for the evolution of humanitarian intervention. Furthermore, the circumstances from which it emerged have subsequently structured the debate over the legality and efficacy of humanitarian intervention.

How Does Humanitarian Intervention Work?

Humanitarian operations are initiated, formed, and dispatched in the same way as traditional peacekeeping missions. They may be requested by the disputing parties, the secretary-general, the Security Council, or some other interested third party. In some cases, however, the pressure for the UN to act may come not from the parties or international officials but from media attention and public opinion—the so-called CNN effect. Once a need has been identified, the Security Council will then authorize the mission, establish its mandate, and make a request for contributions by member states. The management of the operation will fall to the secretary-general who will be responsible for supervising the implementation of Security Council resolutions. He will normally be assisted by a secretariat, a team of military advisers drawn from members' national armed forces, and three main UN departments: the Department of Political Affairs (DPA), the Department of Peacekeeping Operations (DPKO), and the Department of Humanitarian Affairs (DHA). Once contributions have been received and plans for the operation have been finalized, the peacekeepers will normally deploy first to secure the safety of civilian workers.

As we have already suggested, the range of actors engaged in humanitarian intervention has expanded since the earlier forms of peacekeeping. Each operation is likely to include a variety of actors performing a diverse range of tasks: military units, police units, diplomatic officials, humanitarian relief and development NGOs, UN agencies, international financial institutions (IFIs), religious bodies, human rights advocacy groups, and professional groups. The specific tasks undertaken by peacekeepers in humanitarian interventions have also expanded greatly, especially in comparison to traditional peacekeeping operations. An examination of the operations launched by the UN since 1989 reveals the range and extent of tasks that peacekeepers now undertake.

- electoral preparation, organization, supervision and monitoring, or generally restoring or establishing democracy;
- information dissemination and public education;
- repatriation of refugees and displaced persons;
- humanitarian assistance, including establishing secure conditions for the delivery of aid, direct delivery of logistics, health or infrastructure support, and overseeing long-term development assistance programs;
- rebuilding infrastructure such as roads, bridges, airports, and essential utilities;
- demining activities, including training and education;
- ensuring law and order;
- guaranteeing and/or denying movement, such as protecting designated "safe areas" or at-risk groups in a defined area, mounting blockades, sanctions enforcement, and guaranteeing free passage—establishing "corridors of tranquility";
- establishing buffer or military exclusion zones, such as no-fly zones, and separating forces;
- political administration or trusteeship, including reconstructing governmental functions, regional interim administration, and local civil society capacity-building;
- advising, training and assisting police;
- observation and verification of cease-fire agreements;

- mediation and conciliation activities, including staffing local conflict resolution centers;
- boundary demarcation;
- facilitating and overseeing foreign troop withdrawals;
- human rights monitoring, training, and enforcement;
- capturing war criminals and securing and gathering evidence of war crimes;
- preventive deployment in zones of potential conflict— "trip-wire" peacekeeping;
- overseeing demobilization, including the collection, custody, and decommissioning of weapons;
- disarming combatants, especially paramilitary forces and private and regular armies;
- the integration of opposing forces into a new national army, including retraining and refitting rebel and regular forces.

The new tasks obviously entail much greater risks and potential pitfalls in many aspects, require greater levels of basic resources and higher standards of training for personnel, and necessitate a much higher level of overall coordination and control. They also require a greater commitment on the part of the intervening forces, and operations usually last for several years.

In contrast to traditional peacekeeping, there is great disagreement over the principles that are meant to guide peacekeepers and the other actors in humanitarian operations. While some argue that they should adhere to the tried-and-true principles of consent, impartiality, and the nonuse of force, others argue that this is naive in the context of the widespread human rights abuses and social disorder that characterize contemporary conflict. Besides, it is not always possible where states have collapsed and are highly dangerous for lightly armed and vulnerable peacekeepers. In some cases, impartiality may even be seen as collusion in human rights abuses, particularly if peacekeepers fail to act against a side that is committing atrocities. Following embarrassing failures in Somalia and Bosnia, which many concluded were the result of trying to apply principles that were unworkable in those kinds of conflicts, the UN Security Council has more frequently provided humanitarian operations with the mandate to use force under Chapter VII.

An Overview of Humanitarian Intervention since 1989

It is widely accepted that the new generation of multifunctional peacekeeping operations—what we have called humanitarian intervention—began with the mission in Namibia (UNTAG) in 1989 (Graeger 2000: 178). First-generation peacekeeping refers to traditional peacekeeping between 1948 and 1988, as we described in chapter 6. Second-generation peacekeeping is the term given to the expanded peacekeeping operations launched between 1989 and 1994 (the first phase of humanitarian intervention), while third- and fourth-generation peacekeeping describes the current phase of humanitarian intervention since 1994 (see Chopra 1998; Graeger 2000; Malan 1997, 1998).

Second-generation multifunctional operations began with the operations to oversee the end of regional civil wars in Namibia, Mozambique, El Salvador, and Cambodia (see table 8). These UN missions marked a new evolution in peacekeeping. They were characterized by an initial expansion of traditional peacekeeping tasks beyond cease-fire observation and interposition and in the context of the end stage of complex internal wars. For example, the UNTAG mission saw peacekeepers expand their usual roles to include ensuring law and order, some transitional administration tasks, public information, and electoral supervision; the ONUSAL operation in El Salvador was pathbreaking in its human rights observation role; in Mozambique, the UN was responsible for an ambitious demobilization program; and UNTAC in Cambodia was given effective responsibility for administering the country during an eighteen-month transition period, including direct control over Cambodia's defense, foreign relations, finance, and public security. In each case, the UN continued to adhere to the fundamental tenets of peacekeeping—consent of the parties, strict impartiality, and the nonuse of force. They were initially successful because the operations were applied in the context of a general peace agreement and there was a genuine willingness on the part of the protagonists to implement political settlements. Second-generation operations therefore represent a transition from traditional peacekeeping to humanitarian intervention because they involved the old reliance on the principles of traditional peacekeeping but took place in a new context involving a new range of tasks. The novelty of the new peacekeeping should not be overemphasized, however. Three earlier operations during the Cold War presaged the type of mission that would come later—ONUC in the Congo, UNSF/UNTEA in Irian Jaya, and UNIFIL in Lebanon.

Third-generation operations after 1994 differed from second-generation missions in several ways. In the first place, they tended to take place in a new context, namely, during the hostilities phase of the conflict rather than in the posthostilities phase. Whereas second-generation peace-keeping was applied in situations where an agreement had already been reached, third-generation operations tried to more actively create the conditions for peace through a combination of peacemaking and peace-enforcement activities. From a humanitarian perspective, the reasons were clear. The international community could not always wait until a political settlement had been reached before intervening, as by then it might be too late to prevent a humanitarian catastrophe.

Second, they entailed an even greater expansion of tasks beyond the second-generation operations. In Iraq and Bosnia, for example, they involved establishing military exclusion zones, blockades, and sanctions enforcement. In the former Yugoslavia and recently in Timor-Leste and Kosovo, they have also included capturing war criminals and gathering evidence of war crimes. Expanding the tasks that peacekeepers performed was an operational as well as normative imperative. In some cases, it was driven by the need to deliver emergency assistance or protect at-risk groups. It was recognized that resolving complex civil wars was not possible without a multidimensional approach that could deal with the causes and consequences of conflict on multiple levels. In other words, a more comprehensive approach that included peacemaking, peacekeeping, and postconflict peacebuilding was required.

The third-generation operations also involved the adjustment of all the principles of traditional peacekeeping. In particular, they entailed expanding the use of force for humanitarian and political ends such as establishing "corridors of tranquility," creating safe havens, enforcing sanctions, and maintaining blockades and military exclusion zones. It was deemed necessary to give the UN operations teeth in order to prevent the kinds of humiliations they had suffered in Bosnia and Somalia. In the early part of these operations, the disputing parties had regularly prevented the distribution of aid to suffering populations, maintained crippling sieges, and committed war crimes—such as ethnic cleansing and genocide—in full view of powerless peacekeepers. However, while using force for humanitarian ends overcame some of the weaknesses of previous operations, it also created its own set of problems, as we shall see.

Another key principle—consent—was also downgraded in third-generation humanitarian interventions. This was largely because in these kinds of conflicts consent is always likely to be partial or temporary. In cases of state collapse, it may be entirely nonexistent. Operationally, it is not practical to have the continued existence of a peacekeeping force dependent upon the whim of

TABLE 8. UN Humanitarian Interventions, 1989–2004

Name of Mission	Location	Start/End Date	Personnel Strength	Function
UN Transitional Assistance Group (UNTAG)	Namibia	April 1989–March 1990	8,000	Law and order, transitional administration, election supervision.
UN Observer Group in Central America (ONUCA)	Costa Rica, El Salvador, Guatemala, Honduras, Nicaragua	December 1989–January 1992	1,000	Supervise regional peace agreement, prevent cross-border infiltration, disarmament, demobilization.
UN Mission for the Referendum in Western Sahara (MINURSO)	Western Sahara	April 1991–present	2,500	Supervise cease-fire and force disengagement, prepare referendum on territory's future.
UN Angola Verification Mission II (UNAVEM II)	Angola	May 1991–February 1995	350	Supervise cease-fire, oversee national elections.
UN Observer Mission in El Salvador (ONUSAL)	El Salvador	July 1991–April 1995	1,000	Supervise cease-fire, oversee national elections.
UN Protection Force (UNPROFOR)	Bosnia, Croatia, Serbia, Montenegro	February 1992–December 1995	39,000	Securing "safe havens," security for humanitarian aid, monitor air-exclusion zones; replaced with NATO-led Implementation Force after Dayton Agreement.
UN Transitional Authority in Cambodia (UNTAC)	Cambodia	March 1992–September 1993	22,000	Supervise implementation of 1991 peace agreements, interim administration, administer national elections.
UN Operation in Somalia I (UNOSOM I)/Unified Task Force (UNITAF)	Somalia	April/December 1992–March 1993	28,000	Restore peace and stability, secure the distribution of humanitarian aid.
UN Operation in Mozambique (ONUMOZ)	Mozambique	December 1992–December 1994	7,000	Oversee implementation of peace accord, supervise national elections, demobilization, humanitarian assistance.
UN Operation in Somalia II (UNOSOM II)	Somalia	March 1993–March 1995		Create the conditions for peace and security, distribute humanitarian aid, disarmament.
UN Mission in Haiti (UNMIH)	Haiti	September 1993–June 1996	1,200	Training Haitian security forces; following 1994 U.S. intervention, electoral assistance.
UN Assistance Mission for Rwanda (UNAMIR)	Rwanda	October 1993–March 1996	5,500	Implement peace accords; overtaken by 1994 genocide; later given humanitarian mission.
UN Verification Mission in Angola III (UNAVEM III)	Angola	February 1995–June 1997	7,000	Supervision of 1994 Lusaka peace agreement.
UN Mission in Bosnia and Herzegovina (UNMIBH)	Bosnia	December 1995–present	2,500	Implementation of 1995 Dayton Agreement, including elections, humanitarian assistance, human rights.
UN Observation Mission in Angola (MONUA)	Angola	June 1997–February 1999	2,500	Continue UNAVEM III efforts to implement Lusaka Agreement.
UN Interim Administration Mission in Kosovo (UNMIK)	Kosovo	June 1999–present	7,800	Law and order, administration, human rights, humanitarian assistance.
UN Mission in Sierra Leone (UNAMSIL)	Sierra Leone	October 1999–present	10,000	Implementation of peace accord, law and order, demobilization, humanitarian assistance.
UN Transitional Administration in East Timor (UNTAET)	East Timor	October 1999–May 2002	12,000	Interim administration, law and order, humanitarian assistance, postconflict reconstruction.
UN Organization Mission in the Democratic Republic of the Congo (MONUC)	Democratic Republic of Congo	November 1999–present	5,500	Monitor cease-fire, demobilization, human rights, and humanitarian assistance.
UN Mission in Liberia (UNMIL)	Liberia	September 2003–present	15,000	Monitor cease-fire, demobilization, humanitarian and human rights support, security reform support, transitional government support.
UN Operation in Côte d'Ivoire (UNOCI)	Ivory Coast	April 2004–present	6,240	Monitor cease-fire, demobilization, humanitarian support, human rights assistance, restoration of law and order, peace process implementation.
UN Stabilization Mission in Haiti (MINUSTAH)	Haiti	June 2004–present	8,300	Security stabilization, national police reform, demobilization, human rights assistance, assisting political process.
UN Operation in Burundi (ONUB)	Burundi	June 2004–present	5,800	Monitor cease-fire, demobilization, humanitarian assistance, demining, electoral support.

Source: Data from United Nations 2008; Weiss 1995.

every local warlord or faction leader. Given the offensive use of force and the abandonment of strict adherence to notions of consent, the impartiality of third-generation peacekeeping has also been compromised. In Somalia, the UN deliberately attacked General Aideed's forces following an attack on Pakistani peacekeepers. The question is, should the peacekeepers be partial toward the belligerent parties or to the civilian victims of aggression? Is it possible to remain nonpartisan toward groups that flaunt the rules and are guilty of violating international norms and laws? The principle of impartiality is in the process of being reformulated in humanitarian intervention.

Last, unlike the relative successes of second-generation operations, third-generation operations have been characterized by major problems and embarrassing failures, particularly in Somalia, Bosnia, and Rwanda. Even in more recent operations, such as UNAMSIL in Sierra Leone, the UN initially failed to protect its personnel from capture or effectively establish even minimal levels of law and order. What is most disappointing is that the UN has so far failed to fully take on board lessons from its experiences in Somalia and Bosnia. The reasons for these systematic failures can be found in the conceptual, legal-normative, political, and institutional weaknesses that lie at the heart of humanitarian intervention.

Assessing Humanitarian Intervention

Assessing humanitarian intervention is fraught with difficulties because there is little agreement on its normative foundations, which in turn produces competing expectations about its goals and outcomes. In addition, it is a highly politicized process that touches on fundamental political values and issues about which there is little agreement. There are also the usual problems with assessing the outcomes of conflict resolution. Should success be measured on a long-term or short-term basis? Should it be assessed from the perspective of the parties to the conflict, the citizens of the state, the intervening parties, or the wider international community? What criteria are appropriate? Should normative values, such as fairness, social justice, legitimacy, and satisfaction, be applied? In practice, the success of humanitarian operations is usually considered at two basic levels: first, saving lives and mitigating the disastrous effects of conflict; and second, creating the conditions for a lasting political solution to the violence that put lives at risk in the first place. The optimal situation is where humanitarian intervention

both improves the lives of suffering people and facilitates a lasting solution to the conflict, thereby creating the conditions for a lasting and stable peace. In fact, it makes little sense to alleviate human suffering in the absence of an overall framework that can deal with the sources of conflict. It is no accident that the most successful UN humanitarian operations—El Salvador, Cambodia, Mozambique, and Namibia—all involved the implementation of carefully negotiated settlement plans, as well as measures to relieve human suffering and promote long-term development (Crocker 1996: 195).

Consequently, the overall record of humanitarian intervention is mixed. There are some important successes, as we have said, as well as some spectacular failures. Unrealistic expectations that humanitarian intervention would be a panacea for the internal conflicts of the 1990s was fed partly by the hyperoptimism engendered by the UN's role in the 1991 Gulf War. In fact, given the conditions and structures of the post–Cold War system—as well as the almost insuperable challenges involved in peacemaking in intrastate conflicts anyway—it is not surprising that humanitarian operations produced such a patchy record of achievement. First, in the early 1990s the UN was the victim of its own success. The number of negotiated settlements began to outstrip the willingness of members and the capacity of the small Secretariat staff to provide and organize the necessary forces to oversee the implementation of these new and complex agreements (Mackinlay and Chopra 1997: 179). International organizations are inherently limited in the number of crises they can focus on at any one time, and by 1994 when it had nearly 80,000 peacekeepers deployed worldwide and was peacemaking in more than a dozen different conflicts, the UN was seriously overstretched. Inevitably, its efforts in places like Angola, Somalia, and Rwanda began to suffer.

Second, as we noted earlier, the UN's peacekeeping capabilities were adequate for the conditions of the Cold War, and there was little incentive to alter them. The new challenges posed by intrastate conflicts—the expanded range of tasks demanded of peacekeepers and the dangerous and difficult conditions of internal wars—came as a complete surprise and forced the UN to improvise in situ. The ad hoc military organization in the UN Secretariat may have been appropriate for the relatively uncomplicated and benign operations during the Cold War, but it was always going to take time to adapt to the requirements of post–Cold War operations. It is not surprising therefore that the evolving humanitarian enterprise has been a stop-start affair, with the usual mix of blunders and triumphs.

The Strengths of Humanitarian Intervention

Similar to traditional peacekeeping, humanitarian intervention can be an effective way of freezing a conflict, limiting its contagious spread, and deterring the renewal of hostilities. It can stabilize a fragile cease-fire and provide a calm environment in which talks can take place, helping to create the conditions for peacemaking. That is, it has "proven to be remarkably resilient as a circuit-breaker in a spiraling cycle of violence. If a military solution proves illusory but peaceful settlement remains elusive, then peacekeeping forces are needed, wanted, and a useful instrument of conflict management" (Thakur 1995: 22). The presence of peacekeeping forces can have the effect of ending open warfare and constraining the more bellicose behavior of the parties. Moreover, the large-scale involvement of an international force can be a useful way of insulating the conflict from regional or wider international interference.

However, humanitarian intervention differs from peacekeeping, not least in the area of consent and the limited use of force. While some might suggest that abandoning these principles is dangerous and undermines the traditional utility of peacekeeping, it is also possible to argue that the need to obtain and retain consent was itself one of its primary weaknesses. Similarly, limiting the use of force to self-defense relegates peacekeepers to impotent witnesses in civil war situations—as the experience of UNAMIR in Rwanda so vividly demonstrated. In other words, it can be argued that abandoning the necessity of consent (or renegotiating its content) and giving peacekeepers enforcement capabilities has liberated peacekeeping to the point where it can now play a substantive, rather than marginal, role in international peacemaking efforts.

Beyond the general advantages of peacekeeping, however, humanitarian intervention—and third-party intervention in general—is indispensable in the majority of conflicts taking place around the world, which are in the main located in developing regions. Very few developing societies possess the capacity—in terms of civil society institutions, mediation and negotiation skills, or human and material resources—for solely indigenous peacemaking and reconciliation.

> Outsiders will be needed for the foreseeable future to move peacemaking forward—by undertaking direct actions and diplomatic initiatives, defining the parameters of tolerable behavior, and legitimizing principles for settlements and for membership of the global system. Often, as in Mozambique during the 1992–1994 settlement process, they are needed to translate a "ripening" situation into the essential building blocks of the transition from war to peace. Without outsiders to provide much of the pressures, ideas, concepts, resources, deadlines, and inducements, there would have been no settlement. Without outsiders to sustain the settlement through arduous years of implementation, the underlying agreements would have quickly collapsed. (Crocker 1996: 193)

The cost of providing this kind of assistance, furthermore, is relatively low compared to the alternatives. In both economic and human terms, the costs of allowing these kinds of conflicts to remain unchecked far outweigh the direct financial costs of large-scale humanitarian intervention.

More specifically, we would argue that humanitarian intervention has great potential to facilitate conditions of positive peace, because, as a broadly constituted conflict resolution process, it tackles both the long- and short-term causes and consequences of conflict (Fetherston 1994a: 3, 12). Ideally, humanitarian intervention brings together into a coordinated, multilevel, and multifunctional operation all the important actors and resources for alleviating the short-term humanitarian crises, as well as the long-term societal inequalities and grievances that caused the initial outbreak of conflict. Conceptually and intuitively, combining peacemaking, peacekeeping, and postconflict peacebuilding into a single approach would seem to be the logical answer to the complex and intertwined causes of today's "complex emergencies."

In terms of the two levels at which humanitarian intervention is normally assessed—saving lives and mitigating the disastrous effects of conflict, and creating the conditions for lasting political solutions to violent conflict—there have been clear cases of success. The operations in Namibia, Mozambique, El Salvador, and Cambodia have all been fairly successful to date in dealing both with the humanitarian situation and in creating the conditions for a durable peace. In the Somalia operation, which many consider to have been a major disaster for the UN, it is estimated that 250,000 lives were saved from famine through securing the delivery of relief supplies (Patman 1996: 12). Given the prevailing conditions, this was no small achievement. Humanitarian operations in Haiti, Sierra Leone, and Timor-Leste have without any doubt contributed significantly to an improvement in the security situation and improved the well-being of large portions of the population through the stabilization of the security situation and the delivery of humanitarian assistance.

In many parts of the world, UN peacekeepers are accepted in a way that other actors—such as regional organizations and single states—are not. During the Liberian civil war, for example, Charles Taylor, the leader of the main rebel faction, specifically requested UN peace-keepers because he rightly perceived that ECOWAS troops, dominated by Nigerian forces, would be biased against his group. A UN operation may sometimes be the only realistic and acceptable option for international assistance. In many ways, the UN's reputation as an impartial and legitimate third party is unrivaled. In internal wars, these qualities are essential for any intermediary.

Last, humanitarian intervention plays an important role in enforcing and establishing international human rights standards. By intervening forcefully in situations where human rights are being abused, the international community signals its concern. In particular, the prosecution of war crimes serves as an informal enforcement mechanism for international law and strengthens the overall human rights regime. By strengthening international norms of justice and human rights, humanitarian intervention contributes directly and indirectly to the alleviation of one of the primary sources of internal conflict.

The Challenges of Humanitarian Intervention

Humanitarian intervention represents a quantum improvement in traditional peacekeeping in terms of its applicability to internal wars. In spite of some real successes and its undoubted potential as a systematic approach to internal war conflict resolution, it is, nonetheless, an imperfect method. There are a number of very serious legal, normative, conceptual, political, and operational challenges facing the practice of humanitarian intervention. The issues revolve around two fundamental questions. First, under what conditions should the international community intervene in internal conflicts? Deciding *whether* to intervene has a number of serious legal and normative implications. Second, how is humanitarian intervention best carried out? Deciding *how* to intervene involves conceptual, political, and operational issues. Some of these problems are embedded in the very nature of international organizations and interstate politics, while others are specific to the unique challenges of intervening in internal war situations. Even though we consider them under separate headings, ultimately these problems intersect and overlap in important ways.

Legal Issues

The most significant legal issue raised by the practice of humanitarian intervention relates to the principle of non-intervention in the internal affairs of a state, which until now was considered to be the most appropriate principle for the regulation of international relations. The practice of humanitarian intervention—which often involves the use of military force in a sovereign state without first obtaining consent—has altered the scope of this principle and, correspondingly, the scope for justified use of force. The basis for the UN's increased intervention is thought to be the Grotian view that forcible intervention is justified if states undertake it to protect people from genocide or other crimes against humanity (Pugh 1997: 140). However, the Grotian right of intervention is not an established custom in international politics and gives rise to several further problems. For example, many states fear that by softening the principle of nonintervention and expanding the scope for justifiable use of force, the UN—and the international community at large—may get on a slippery slope of forcible interference in the internal affairs of states. This could undermine the state-centered international order and the UN itself. From this perspective, there is a real question whether the violation of state sovereignty is more destabilizing than large-scale human rights abuses themselves. As the 1999 UN General Assembly debate showed, most states are nervous about establishing a right to intervene for humanitarian purposes (Oudraat 2000: 422). They fear that such a right would lead to even greater meddling in their domestic affairs. They also fear abuse of the humanitarian principle by great powers like France and the United States, when ulterior motives like maintaining friendly regimes, protecting oil supplies, or imperial expansion are disguised by UN sanction. Virtually every humanitarian operation since the early 1990s has involved small, developing countries, and naturally they feel most threatened by the erosion of a legal principle that has until now given them some degree of protection against outside interference. The "war on terror" has greatly added to this sense of unease, particularly in its attempt to make preemption of terrorism an additional basis for intervention.

Thus far, attempts to clarify the exact conditions under which intervention is permitted, such as the principles outlined in *The Responsibility to Protect* (2001), have failed to reassure many of these smaller nations. There are two situations where humanitarian intervention is relatively unproblematic: in the case of genocide, there is a legal obligation to intervene under the Genocide Convention; and in cases of complete state failure, there is no real sovereignty to violate. However, most cases are not so clear-cut. In the Balkans, for example, the evidence for genocide was somewhat ambiguous, and the state had not entirely collapsed. The real problem lies in determining the threshold that will trigger intervention. How many lives must be lost before genocide is determined to be taking place? What number and type of victims make up "large-scale" human rights abuses? How ineffectual must state institutions become before they are considered completely failed? And who exactly is to make these determinations? These are more than theoretical concerns; the refusal to recognize that genocide was under way in Rwanda in 1994 meant that intervention came too late for nearly a million people. Similarly, exaggerations of the extent of human rights abuses in Kosovo in 1999 triggered an intervention that many feel could have been avoided through negotiation and that may have actually exacerbated the level of human suffering.

However, even if a legal framework could be agreed upon that sets out the criteria for intervention, this would be no guarantee that the international community would act in the next case of genocide. The right to intervene, in other words, does not necessarily imply the obligation to intervene. As we have already suggested, the UN can only act when its members agree to act, which is a politically necessary precondition. In short, "every approach that would allow for humanitarian intervention contains possibilities for abuse, and none provides a guarantee to future victims of genocide or gross violations of human rights" (Oudraat 2000: 421).

A related legal conundrum arises in exactly those cases where the UN Security Council is unable to provide the necessary authorization for humanitarian intervention due to divergence among the permanent members. In such cases, it is questionable whether other actors—regional organizations, single concerned states, or coalitions of the willing—should be allowed to act unilaterally and without UN authorization. To a degree, the interventions in Bangladesh, Uganda, and Kampuchea during the Cold War highlighted precisely this problem, although in each of these cases, the issue was circumvented when the intervening state justified its involvement on the grounds of national security rather than humanitarianism. Related to this, the intervention in Kosovo in 1999 raised the question of the legal foundations of humanitarian intervention when NATO acted without prior UN approval. Once the UN is deprived of its sole authority to authorize humanitarian intervention, the legal bases for such actions are greatly complicated and prone to abuse.

Normative Questions

Closely related to the legal issues facing humanitarian intervention lies a complex set of normative questions. The most important normative issues revolve around the moral injunction that the intervention does not create a greater injustice or cause more suffering than the initial crisis that warranted the intervention in the first place. At the root of this problem is the very real dilemma that "humanitarian war" is an oxymoron (Slim 1995: 1). Making war to enforce peace is at best, morally ambiguous, and at worst morally indefensible. From one perspective, there is a real danger that the use of coercive peacekeeping could increase levels of international conflict, particularly if it becomes an option of first rather than last resort (see Chandler 2001).

At a microlevel, it is now well established that humanitarian operations can exacerbate, and have in several instances exacerbated, the conflicts they were trying to mitigate. For example, they can contribute to the establishment of so-called war economies (Berdal and Keen 1997; Keen 1998) by providing warlords and militia groups with employment as security guards for relief operations. The hard currency they receive allows them to purchase more weapons for continuing the conflict. This was a common problem during the intervention in Somalia. On the government side, particularly since the 1980s, the imposition of fixed exchange rates has allowed regimes to tax relief inputs; large-scale relief operations therefore have provided regimes at war with precious hard currency (Duffield, Macrae, and Zei 1994: 227). It is also widely acknowledged that food aid is regularly raided or diverted for military purposes. Part of the price that relief organizations pay for access to needy populations is sometimes that they pay part of the relief aid to the armed groups who control the territory. This places a heavy moral burden on humanitarian organizations, as neither alternative—providing relief aid, which might indirectly contribute to the long-term continuation of the conflict, or not providing relief aid, which could lead to immediate large-scale human suffering—is an ethically acceptable outcome. Furthermore, the consequences of relief aid may not be obvious at the time to those responsible for evaluating the situation, but later it is difficult to then withdraw aid from suffering people.

At another level, some have suggested that the provision of relief contributes indirectly to the continuance of the conflict by relieving both government and nongovernment factions of the burden of assistance. This in turn frees up local relief resources for the war effort. In fact, relief operations may actually give support to counterinsurgency tactics. For example, military forces may be encouraged to maintain the levels of hunger and suffering at critical levels to ensure the continuation of large-scale outside relief or to herd civilians into closed camps—as Sudanese factions did during the 1980s. Certainly, international efforts to help refugees relieve governments of the need to deal with the problem.

The humanitarian component in some recent interventions has also impacted negatively on remaining civil institutions. The provision of humanitarian aid via parallel networks for the supply of food, health care, and education has undermined the legitimacy and role of the state and other social institutions in a number of cases (Duffield, Macrae, and Zei 1994: 227; Dzelilovic 2000: 109). The refusal to work with local institutions in Somalia and Mozambique, for example, limited the development of national capacity and undermined indigenous attempts to rebuild shattered civil institutions. In essence, the provision of relief frequently undermines local coping strategies.

The humanitarian-military interface can also cause problems. Delivering aid through military force is often not welcomed by relief workers because it undermines their intention to work impartially. The International Committee of the Red Cross (ICRC), for example, works to alleviate the suffering of all victims, even those attacked by the intervention force (Pugh 1997: 140). Coming under the protective umbrella of peacekeepers in such a situation can appear to align the relief agencies with one side to the conflict.

Politically, humanitarian interventions have been guilty of legitimating local warlords and war criminals, mainly through official recognition during political negotiations. This practice is part of the traditional diplomatic paradigm that views the military leaders in civil conflicts as being the most important focus of peacemaking efforts: if only they could be brought into a political deal, the fighting would be controlled. However, in the new wars, this approach has merely strengthened the forces of disorder and, in some cases, rewarded their strategies of terror. In the Dayton Agreement in 1995, the political deal between the Bosnian factions seemed to reward earlier strategies of ethnic cleansing and systematic human rights abuses. A similar process occurred in Afghanistan following the collapse of the Taliban regime. However, it is difficult to conceive of an approach that avoids legitimating the armed factions while at the same time securing their cooperation. At the very least, humanitarian intervention freezes the conflict, thereby reinforcing the status quo; depending upon the timing of the intervention, this may benefit one side, which can then regroup and rearm.

The UN's experiences in Bosnia highlighted a number of the normative dilemmas posed by third-generation peacekeeping. At times, peacekeepers were forced to call in air strikes on the very people among whom they were deployed and upon whose cooperation they were dependent (Malan 1997: 10). UN safe areas and their vulnerable inhabitants could only be supplied and protected with Serb consent. International pressure to punish the Serbs for transgressions risked the termination of their cooperation and hence the safety of the refugees in the safe havens. In short, "it is no easy task to make war and peace with the same people on the same territory at the same time" (Tharoor 1995–96: 60). On the humanitarian side of the operation, the blockade of aid convoys to Muslim areas in Bihac by the Krajina Serbs in March 1995 caused a similar dilemma. The UN responded to the Bihac blockade by suspending humanitarian assistance to the Serb population in Krajina as a means of pressuring the Serbs into reopening aid corridors. Clearly, the use of humanitarian pressure—employing relief as a weapon—as a means of achieving a humanitarian goal involves conflicting moral imperatives (Thornberry 1995: 5).

Conceptual Challenges

One of the greatest challenges to humanitarian intervention is the necessity of devising an appropriate conceptual framework. There is widespread agreement among both scholars and practitioners that there is a "crisis of theory" in current UN practice (Slim 1998: 10) and that "future conceptual clarification thus seems as important as institutional reform" (Vogel 1996: 6). There are several aspects to this problem. First, at its broadest level there is the problem of embedding any theory of humanitarian intervention in competing paradigms of world order. Some view humanitarian intervention as a crucial part of the emerging system of global governance and wish to see it codified in international law and institutionalized in practice as a means of establishing universal human rights. Others view it more critically as a part of the existing system of great power domination, whereby powerful states employ militarized peacekeeping as a means of achieving strategic objectives and enforcing a neoliberal economic order (Pieterse 1998; Ramsbotham 2000; Ramsbotham, Woodhouse, and Miall 2005). Clarifying its normative purposes will be essential to articulating a more coherent theory of humanitarian intervention.

Second, UN peacekeeping was designed primarily to deal with interstate conflicts and is ill-equipped—conceptually and institutionally—to deal with civil wars. There has been a reluctance to see complex emergencies as a new development or to distinguish between traditional peacekeeping tasks in the buffer zone experience and the challenges of dealing with complex civil wars. That is, in the multifaceted and unstable circumstances of a complex emergency "peacekeepers now face a doctrinal void in which the principles that dictated their previous success are invalid" (Mackinlay 1995: 54). Questions about the nature of impartiality (e.g., who should the peacekeepers be impartial toward?), the limits of consent (how much consent is enough?), and the distinctions between peacekeeping and enforcement have not been answered at the conceptual level. Clinging to these principles as a conceptual foundation for dealing with the new wars is an exercise in fallacious logic (Malan 1997: 11) and can lead to serious moral and legal dilemmas for peacekeepers on the ground. Before a more coherent approach to humanitarian intervention can be devised these kinds of questions will need to be addressed in a clear conceptual framework. Although the Report of the Panel on United Nations Peace Operations (United Nations 2000) has gone some way toward addressing these issues (discussed later), much still remains to be done.

Third, there is a major conceptual challenge in understanding the nature of internal conflicts. The UN has until recently displayed a tendency to interpret the new wars in traditional Clausewitzean and positivist terms and has not come to grips with the qualitative changes in modern warfare (Fetherston 1994a: 10). Misdiagnosing the causes of internal conflicts has resulted in inappropriate solutions based on traditional interstate models (Kaldor 2000). As a consequence, humanitarian operations have frequently opted for conflict control over conflict resolution, and substituted political settlement for reconciliation and the construction of sustainable cultures of peace. Moreover, they have tended to take a short-term, exit-oriented approach rather than the long-term capacity-building approach that could avert future bloodshed. The result has typically been a state of ongoing tensions, held in check only by thousands of well-armed peacekeepers or the reeruption of fighting once the peacekeepers leave.

In short, there needs to be an acknowledgment—based on a theoretical grasp of the nature of the new wars—that "complex emergencies" require "complex responses" (Greenaway 2000: 4). The typically ad hoc and uncoordinated responses have become unsustainable as the need for larger and more sophisticated peacekeeping missions has grown. Multilevel operations that involve myriad actors, each with particular expertise and resources, and acting in concert, are necessary for dealing with the prosaic causes of internal conflicts. In sum, peacekeeping—traditionally a conflict-settlement approach—needs to be radically reconceptualized into a conflict resolution activity (Fetherston 1994a: 12).

The Report of the Panel on United Nations Peace Operations, also known as the Brahimi Report (United Nations 2000), has acknowledged the need to "fine-tune its analytical and decision-making capabilities to respond to existing realities" (para. 9) and for "a doctrinal shift" (ix) in the way it conceives of peace support operations. It concedes that the key conditions for success include "a sound peace-building strategy" (para. 4), as well as political support and increased institutional capacity. Developing a sound strategy requires a solid grasp of the new security environment, and the report suggests that it is "important that negotiators, the Security Council, Secretariat mission planners, and mission participants alike understand which political-military environments they are entering, how the environment may change under their feet once they arrive, and what they realistically plan to do if and when it does change" (para. 26). In an important conceptual turnaround, the report concedes that "human rights components within peace operations have not always received the political and administrative support that they require" (para. 41). It goes on to recommend that hitherto peripheral conflict resolution activities—such as reconciliation activities, human rights monitoring, good governance programs, demobilization and reintegration programs, and police force capacity building—be brought into the mainstream through an overall multidimensional approach that combines peace-building and peacekeeping.

When complex peace operations do go into the field, it is the task of the operation's peacekeepers to maintain a secure local environment for peace-building, and the peace-builders' task to support the political, social, and economic changes that create a secure environment that is self-sustaining. Only such an environment offers a ready exit to peacekeeping forces, unless the international community is willing to tolerate recurrence of conflict when such forces depart. History has taught that peacekeepers and peacebuilders are inseparable partners in complex operations: while the peacebuilders may not be able to function without the peacekeepers' support, the peacekeepers have no exit without the peacebuilders' work. (para. 28)

Part of this overall rethink on the part of the UN is the recognition that there has been a "prevailing view of peacekeeping as a temporary aberration" when it should now be considered "a core function" of the Organization (para. 133).

Nevertheless, there is some way to go before a theory of humanitarian intervention will emerge, and in its absence practice will continue to be improvised in situ with all its concomitant risks. A common criticism of the UN's peacekeeping record is that it fails to learn lessons from previous operations. This is partly the result of the UN practice of initiating and operating each operation from scratch and partly the result of the old mind-set that sees it as a short-term, one-off event. It was only in 1995 that a "Lessons Learned Unit" was created in the DPKO for assessing the performance of completed operations (Pugh 1997: 147).

Political Problems

Humanitarian intervention faces a number of key political problems that are to some extent embedded in the nature of international relations and international organization. At the very least, humanitarian intervention is a profoundly ideological notion (Pieterse 1998: 3). First, states guard their power jealously, as we have said. Any method that undermines the process and outcome control that states normally like to hold over the conflict resolution procedure is likely to be eschewed in favor of those methods that retain their control. Humanitarian intervention undermines state power by weakening the nonintervention norm, thereby giving the international community the means and the justification for intervening directly in the internal affairs of states in conflict.

Furthermore, recent humanitarian practice has been to enforce certain political forms, namely, liberal democracy, on target states. The intervention in Haiti in 1994 was particularly important in this regard. There is genuine concern in some quarters that the language and practice of humanitarian intervention is being used by the great powers to disguise geostrategic and imperial interests—that what looks like humanitarian intervention is really European and American neoimperialism in disguise. This was one of the main criticisms leveled at France's intervention in Rwanda at the height of the 1994 genocide, and at interventions in Afghanistan and Iraq after 2001. For this reason, there seems little prospect of an emerging consensus on the principles of humanitarian intervention or agreement on a doctrine of humanitarian intervention, despite efforts such as *The Responsibility to Protect* (2001).

Second, the UN—as we suggested in chapter 5—is an international organization with all its accompanying limitations and defects. IOs must construct dominant coalitions for initiating large-scale action, and the larger the number of actors the more difficult this can be. Differences of perceptions and interests continue to be pronounced in international affairs and make united action on security issues uncertain and difficult. For UN humanitarian intervention, it means that there is usually a considerable time lag between the identification of a need for concerted action and the deployment of such a force. The glaring failure to engage forcefully in Darfur from 2004 onward graphically illustrates this problem. More generally, it means that UN Security Council policy is heavily influenced by the foreign policies and interests of its permanent members, who can, and still do, veto decisions.

Dominant coalitions—which are necessary for initiating and leading humanitarian operations—can rarely be constructed unless there is a synthesis between humanitarian concerns and the interests of the leading states. This is the problem of selectivity, where some conflicts receive no international attention because there is no coincidence of interest and compassion, while other conflicts do. For example, the UN has sent peacekeepers to deal with ethnic conflict in Rwanda, but not to Darfur; and it agreed to assertively protect humanitarian operations in Somalia, but not in neighboring Sudan. The perception that the process of selection of strategy is driven primarily by political factors (such as great power interests), and not by the needs of the conflict-affected populations, undermines the UN's credibility as the guarantor of international security. Reinforced by the lack of clear criteria and legal provisions for intervention, it paints the UN as a rich states' club unwilling to get involved in "the poor man's conflict" unless great power interests are directly affected.

Another problem inherent to international organization lies in the need for political compromise to build coalitions. The most common result of this is that mandates for action have to be watered down to accommodate wide-ranging interests, as noted in the Brahimi Report.

> The compromises required to build consensus can be made at the expense of specificity, and the resulting ambiguity can have serious consequences in the field if the mandate is then subject to varying interpretation by different elements of a peace operation, or if local actors perceive a less than complete Council commitment to peace implementation that offers encouragement to spoilers. (para. 56)

A seminar on the lessons learned from the UNOSOM operation in Somalia suggested that one of the primary problems faced by peacekeepers on the ground was that the operation's mandate was vague, it changed frequently according to circumstances, and it seemed to be open to myriad different interpretations (Malan 1998: 3).

International organizations are a problematic instrument for dealing with internal wars because they are interstate entities and thus have a built-in bias toward state actors. UN intervention in particular raises the political conundrum of how a world body committed to maintaining the territorial integrity of its members will decide when and how to support a regime that is attempting to protect itself from attempts at secession, for example (Thakur 1995: 11). In some cases, therefore, UN peacekeepers can be seen as biased against nonstate actors who feel that they have a genuine case for breaking away from an oppressive regime.

Third, the nature of the large states that contribute most of the core personnel and equipment for humanitarian operations is a limiting factor. These states are particularly sensitive to domestic opinion, and the U.S. failure in Somalia in particular reinforced the growing reluctance of Western states to risk casualties in the enforcement of UN mandates. This is the problem of mobilizing the political will of the key states to commit the moral and material resources necessary for a successful humanitarian operation. The Brahimi Report suggests that an emerging risk aversion has "grown since the difficult missions of the mid-1990s, partly because Member States are not clear about how to define their national interests in taking such risks, and partly because they may be unclear about the risks themselves" (para. 52). In any case, the result has been that the United States issued Presidential Decision Directive 25 (PDD 25) in May 1994, which laid down the criteria for U.S. involvement in UN operations. The criteria included the need for clear U.S. interests to be at stake and a limited time frame for each engagement—so-called sunset clauses (Slim 1995: 7). A major criticism of PDD 25 is that the combination of U.S. anxiety about sustaining casualties and working out in advance an end point to the operation can actually encourage local leaders and warlords to be obstinate, knowing that they only have to outlast an uncertain peacekeeping force (Roberts 1996: 310). At the same time, reflecting the U.S. government's post-Somalia disillusionment, the United States unilaterally decided to reduce its assessed share of peacekeeping costs (Pugh 1997: 146).

Related to this, the conduct of humanitarian operations—the peacekeepers on the ground—has been heavily influenced by the political will of the great powers. The problem is that states like the United States do not want to cross the Mogadishu line between classical defensive peacekeeping roles and the offensive enforcement roles that are often necessary in the implementation of a strong mandate. In practice, this means that humanitarian operations are conducted in a "post heroic," "casualty-averse fashion" (McLean 1996: 327). It can also impact negatively on the perception that local actors have of the willingness of the UN forces, which may in fact put them at greater risk. Beyond the broad problem of political will, domestic concern also explains why policymakers generally propose gradual and incremental policies, opting for half-measures and thinking in terms of best-case scenarios (Oudraat 2000: 425).

Fourth, there has been a crisis of expectations, combined with some spectacular failures, which has undermined the international consensus that characterized the immediate post–Cold War period. Overstretch and failure followed the zeal to intervene everywhere in the 1989–95 period and led to a retrenchment of UN peacekeeping that may only now be abating. The image of the UN is, in the eyes of many, now somewhat tarnished. Organizing large-scale humanitarian interventions is much more difficult today than it was at the beginning of the 1990s. This is the problem of "peacekeeping fatigue," which has affected mainly the large states, tired of pouring resources and troops into seemingly intractable civil wars.

Last, humanitarian intervention or "band aid" relief can be used as a substitute for resolving conflicts politically (Pugh 1997: 146). Dealing with the humanitarian crisis of a conflict often covers the lack of genuine political engagement. This is the "fig-leaf theory" (Slim 1998: 6). It suggests that humanitarianism is being overemphasized by the great powers to cover up the lack of real political concern and a policy vacuum for dealing with intrastate conflicts in peripheral regions.

Operational Challenges

There are too many operational challenges to cover here. We will describe them in very broad terms and under four main headings: institutional limitations, resource issues, training, and coordination. Generally, operational problems are the result of the ad hoc approach to humanitarian intervention—the same problem that has beset traditional peacekeeping since its inception. In some ways, they are also results of the inadequate conceptual and normative basis of humanitarian intervention and the related political weaknesses of managing complex peace operations from within the confines of an international organization.

First, the UN's institutional capacity for complex peace operations is generally underdeveloped. The task of maintaining up to eighteen complex missions in the field would stretch the capacity of any organization, but there are also problems specific to the UN structure. Systems of intelligence and command and control are fairly primitive, and the creation of the Situation Room at UN headquarters in 1993 only goes part way toward resolving the problem. It is understandably the result of bureaucratizing the long-standing operating procedures of traditional peacekeeping missions.

> Because peacekeepers, in principle, had no enemies in their area of operations, there was little pressure on them to be militarily effective. In the field, there was no need for total operational reliability day and night, and gaps in logistic arrangements were tolerated because they did not diminish results. This in turn removed pressure on the Secretariat to maintain an effective staff capability in New York. There was seldom any need, or facility, to maintain elaborate map rooms, with 24-hour vigilance and daily situation briefings. When the need arose, contingency planning could be carried out by co-opted staff officers who came and went on an ad hoc basis. Operational lessons were lost, UN equipment became obsolete, and military functions were largely conducted by a largely civilian Secretariat. (Mackinlay and Chopra 1997: 177–78)

Since the onset of more complex multifunctional missions, however, these administrative and institutional weaknesses have become a major source of frustration for mission personnel. Essentially, despite some recent improvements, the UN still lacks a satisfactory command system capable of military planning, logistics management, communication, efficient decision making, and coordination of the many different types of forces deployed. In addition, competition between departments and agencies remains an issue.

Second, as we have suggested, the UN lacks the resources for mounting complex humanitarian operations. Peacekeeping has been in a continuous state of financial crisis for many years, and the problem has only been exacerbated by the need for more and more large-scale operations. Typically, humanitarian operations run into the hundreds of millions of dollars. The U.S. decision to cut back its contributions to peacekeeping has further hurt the Organization, as the United States is one of the main contributors.

Third, there are huge problems with both the need for experienced administrative personnel and the varying levels of training for troop contributors. In terms of staffing

levels, the Brahimi Report argues that "it is clearly not enough to have 32 officers providing military planning and guidance to 27,000 troops in the field, nine civilian police staff to identify, vet, and provide guidance for up to 8,600 police, and 15 political desk officers for 14 current operations and two new ones, or to allocate just 1.25 per cent of the total costs of peacekeeping to Headquarters administrative and logistics support" (United Nations 2000: xiii). It is also a commonly recognized problem that the personnel for humanitarian operations—civilian and military—vary considerably in terms of standards of professionalism, levels and kinds of training, experience, military doctrine, and levels of equipment (Fetherston 1994a).

In addition to the problems of personnel, there are the normal problems involved in integrating into an overall operation different national forces who speak different languages, have different structures and traditions, and who are unfamiliar with each other. There are problems of equipment interoperability, especially between the forces from developing and developed countries. A key issue of second- and third-generation peacekeeping is that there has been a vast increase in the number of countries contributing forces to UN operations, and many of these new peacekeepers have very little operational experience. In other words, "lacking the experience and training of the 'old' peacekeepers, the newcomers have been thrown into the peacekeeping enterprise just as its boundaries have been widened, its content vastly expanded, and some of its previous norms and assumptions called into question" (Findlay 1996: 14).

Fourth, there are a number of issues around coordinating multifunctional operations that involve a wide range of actors. In the military sphere, command and control problems in the field have also continued over from traditional peacekeeping operations. In general, states are reluctant to transfer control over their armed forces to the UN because of doubts about the Organization's capacity for managing military operations (Thakur 1995: 12). As a consequence, long and complex decision-making procedures that involve clearance from national headquarters, as well as UN headquarters, can slow down the response time of military units in what are inevitably fluid and constantly changing security environments. Inefficient decision-making procedures also heighten the possibility of mistakes. The issue of multiple chains of command and the kinds of problems this can generate were clearly highlighted in Somalia, particularly when national contingents came under fire.

One of the most pressing problems lies in coordinating the military and humanitarian sides of operations (Thornberry 1995). Traditionally, humanitarian assistance and military protection have been approached as separate activities, carried out by very different kinds of actors (Minear 1995). The operational environment for both sets of actors is unfamiliar, and cooperation is difficult due to contrasting organizational cultures, ethos, mandates, funding, and political turf to protect. In fact, there is often a great deal of suspicion and rivalry between humanitarian and military organizations in peace support operations (Pugh 1997). In many cases, they also have conflicting interests. Military personnel can find it difficult to adapt to the humanitarian tasks they have to undertake, while humanitarian organizations find the security environment challenging. Maintaining strict neutrality, for example, is a problem for agencies that must at the same time rely on heavily armed UN peacekeepers for security.

In addition, the sheer number of tasks and the different groups needed to fulfill them requires an organizational capacity still lacking in the UN (Mackinlay 1995). As the Brahimi Report has noted, at present there is "no integrated planning or support cell in the Secretariat that brings together those responsible for political analysis, military operations, civilian police, electoral assistance, human rights development, humanitarian assistance, refugees and displaced persons, public information, logistics, finance, and recruitment" (United Nations 2000: xiii). Also, unclear command arrangements can allow separate agendas to emerge, as each agency is driven by its own operational imperatives while maintaining independent command lines to overseas headquarters.

Conclusion

In this chapter, we have attempted to provide an overview and assessment of the present state of humanitarian intervention. It is important to try to keep a sense of perspective, as the system remains in a profound state of flux despite efforts to refine its theory and practice. Humanitarian intervention has developed in dramatic fits and starts since the early 1990s leading to significant loss of perspective in terms of what it can and should achieve in the way of conflict resolution. A number of tentative conclusions follow from our discussion.

First, it has been suggested—due in part to a sense of disillusionment with some of the more spectacular failures in places like Bosnia and Somalia—that "international peacekeeping is in a state of crisis" (Malan 1998: 4). We disagree. Second- and third-generation peacekeeping—what we have called humanitarian intervention—is simply in its infancy. As an international instrument for the management and resolution of internal conflict, humanitarian intervention is still in a formative state. Efforts are continuing—in official reports, such as the Brahimi Report, in UN departments, among humanitarian organizations, and in numerous policy-making and academic circles—to refine the concept of humanitarian intervention, establish its legal and ethical basis, improve the institutional capacity of the UN, learn the lessons of past failures, and improve its operation in the field. The obstacles, as we have examined, are imposing, but they are not insurmountable. In fact, a number of lessons have already been learned, and some important steps have been taken; collective learning by the UN and the wider international community is slowly but surely taking place.

Second, in any event, it seems clear that humanitarian intervention is here to stay. It will continue to be employed by the international community in cases of intractable internal conflict, even if it is still an imperfect technique. In a real sense, it has now been institutionalized as one of the international community's primary responses to conflict. The fact is that very few conflict-torn societies have the internal resources to create the conditions for peace without external assistance, and there are some notable cases where humanitarian intervention has made a real difference in creating the conditions for long-term positive peace—Namibia, Mozambique, El Salvador, Cambodia, and Timor-Leste. At any rate, the UN is subject to powerful pressures from governments and global public opinion that make its involvement almost a sine qua non, especially in conflicts where large-scale human suffering or human rights abuse takes place. However, we do expect that in the absence of an agreed and institutionalized legal framework humanitarian intervention will continue to be practiced on a selective, case-by-case basis.

Third, humanitarian intervention will continue to be an appropriate method for managing and resolving conflict, provided it is properly conceived and implemented. It will be vital in the implementation of the agreements phase and in the postconflict reconstruction phase. However, it must be guided by a clear set of principles and objectives; be part of a coordinated, overall peace process; and be authorized and overseen solely by the UN. Humanitarian operations should not be a substitute for other peacemaking activities but rather a part of the overall package, including preventive diplomacy, mediation, reconciliation, and postconflict reconstruction. In other words, humanitarian intervention is not a panacea for internal conflict and should not be used in isolation.

Last, the greatest obstacle facing humanitarian intervention lies in the conceptual challenge. Recognizing the unique security challenges posed by new wars and developing the theoretical framework and concepts to understand these challenges will involve a profound paradigm shift. On the one hand, new ways of thinking about the causes and nature of conflict will be essential. This is vital if effective overall strategies are to be developed. On the other hand, broader theoretical and conceptual frameworks will be needed to integrate the multiple actors and activities in humanitarian operations. An ad hoc, piecemeal approach will no longer suffice. Integrated, multilevel, long-term approaches are required. For this, a comprehensive and coherent theory of humanitarian intervention must be articulated, codified, and institutionalized.

Humanitarian intervention is at the heart of the emerging international system for dealing with internal conflict. It provides the umbrella and the central organizing concept for an overall approach that tackles both the causes and the consequences of conflict. In the future, humanitarian operations will be the context in which regional bodies work together with the UN in "task-sharing" (see chapter 9) and in which nonofficial actors take on more mainstream roles in conciliation and postconflict reconstruction (see chapter 10). Central to the whole process, and vital to creating the conditions for long-term peace, will be local and national reconciliation and justice (see chapter 11) and long-term, multidimensional peacebuilding (see chapter 12).

CHAPTER NINE ⬦══════════════════════════════

Regional Task-Sharing

══⬦

Regional task-sharing—the devolution or "subcontracting" by the United Nations of conflict resolution tasks such as peacekeeping or peace-enforcement to regional actors—has emerged as a key plank in the post–Cold War international security management platform. Also referred to as "security regionalism" (Alagappa 1998), it recasts the traditional third-party intervention role into novel and controversial forms in much the same way that humanitarian intervention does (see chapter 8). On the one hand, it represents one of the relatively new conflict resolution approaches adopted by an international community cognizant that intractable intrastate conflicts cannot be dealt with using traditional diplomatic methods; on the other, it is an attempt to finally operationalize the provisions regarding regional organizations in Chapter VIII of the UN Charter that were curtailed by the onset of the Cold War.

Predicated on notions of complementarity, the task-sharing approach envisages the construction of a partnership between the UN and regional actors in a kind of "peace pyramid," in which the universal body—the UN—sits at the apex, authorizing and overseeing the efforts of regional actors who take primacy in dealing with local disputes. The regional actors may include regional intergovernmental organizations such as the African Union (AU, formerly the Organization of African Unity or OAU), the Organization of American States (OAS), the North Atlantic Treaty Organization (NATO), the European Union (EU), and the Arab League; or they may be informal coalitions of willing states or even single powerful states—such as the French-led Operation Turquoise in Rwanda in

1994. Recent UN task-sharing operations include the NATO-led International Security Assistance Force (ISAF) that has been operating in Afghanistan since December 2001, the French-led Operation Licorne in Ivory Coast since 2002, the EU-led Operation Artemis in the Democratic Republic of Congo (DRC) in 2003, and the Economic Community of West African States (ECOWAS) military force—ECOMIL—deployed in Liberia following the departure of Charles Taylor in August 2003.

Although regional organizations have always played an important role in diplomatic conflict resolution, before the 1990s there were very few examples of large-scale regional peacekeeping operations. Moreover, of the five cases during this period, only the Arab League's intervention in Kuwait in 1961 and the OAS operation in the Dominican Republic in 1965 could be considered in any way successful (see table 9). In contrast, since 1990 there have been more than twenty task-sharing operations, several of which—the ECOWAS operations in Liberia and Ivory Coast, Operation Alba in Albania, the Inter-African Mission to Monitor the Bangui Accords (MISAB) in the Central African Republic, NATO's involvement in Bosnia and Kosovo, the Southern African Development Community (SADC) intervention in Lesotho, the International Force East Timor (INTERFET) and Operation Artemis in the Democratic Republic of Congo (DRC)—were relatively successful.

The initial impetus for the revival of the "regional option" lay, paradoxically, in the expansion of UN peacekeeping in the early post–Cold War period. The humiliating failures in Bosnia, Somalia, and Rwanda in the early

1990s, the subsequent unwillingness of the great powers to get involved in complex internal wars, and institutional and conceptual overstretch convinced senior policymakers that the UN was unable to deal with the burgeoning number of regional conflicts on its own. The Organization began to explore the possibility of devolving responsibilities to other subuniversal actors. At the same time, the end of superpower competition in Africa and Asia and the collapse of the Soviet Union freed regional bodies from the crippling effects of the Cold War rivalry. Not only were regional organizations now able to take a nonpartisan approach to conflict regulation, but the conflicts themselves were thought to be more amenable to peaceful settlement in the absence of superpower interference.

The intervention by ECOWAS in Liberia in August 1990 proved to be a turning point in security regionalism. It was prompted not only by the intense brutality of the war and its regional spread through the movement of refugees, but also because no peace proposals or solutions were forthcoming from the OAU, the UN, or the United States (Conteh-Morgan 1993: 38–39). ECOWAS, therefore, did what no other international actor was capable of or willing to do, namely, intervene in an internal conflict. The UN Security Council backed the ECOWAS operation by imposing a Chapter VII arms embargo against the rebel forces, which represented "the first major UN effort to promote peacekeeping by a regional organization" (Henrikson 1995: 148). The willingness of ECOWAS to act, as well as the strong UN support for its efforts, gave added impetus to similar institutional adaptations that were starting to take place in the regional organizations of Europe, South America, and Asia.

Since then, regionalism has (re)emerged as one of the most important trends in international relations, and its corollary, security regionalism or task-sharing, has become one of the most important developments in international conflict resolution since the end of the Cold War. Much like the emergence of humanitarian intervention, however, it remains a controversial and, with few exceptions, little studied process (see Diehl 1993a; Alagappa 1995; Acharya 1995; Henrikson 1995; Goodpaster 1996; Weiss 1998). In spite of the apparent success of some task-sharing operations, there is scant evidence that regional actors are any better than the UN at dealing with the new wars. In this chapter, we provide an overview and assessment of regional task-sharing as a form of international conflict resolution. The term *task-sharing* is also used to describe the UN's subcontracting of elements of peace support operations to NGOs, particularly in relief and development activities and postconflict reconstruction; we

examine the role of NGOs in chapter 10. Here we concentrate solely on regional security management.

Conceptualizing Regional Task-Sharing

Regional task-sharing refers broadly to the emergence in the post–Cold War period of a two-tier conflict resolution system or a "global-regional peacemaking system" where regional organizations or groupings of states assume primary responsibility for preventive diplomacy, mediation, peacekeeping, peace-enforcement, and peacebuilding activities within their geographical area (Merrills 1998: 284). It has also been described as "subcontracting," "subsidiarity," "security regionalism," the "peace pyramid," or the "supervised devolution" of international conflict resolution—among other terms. The UN is at the apex of this system, providing authorization, legitimacy, monitoring, advice, and, where needed, diplomatic and material support.

Regionalism and Regional Organizations

Regionalism is a contested concept, and a precise meaning is difficult if not impossible to pin down. Nonetheless, it is important to provide a general theoretical context for assessing regional security task-sharing. A *region* may be defined as a geographical identity whose components share attributes or interactions—cultural, economic, political—that distinguish them from entities beyond the boundaries of the region, and where the level of interaction within the region is more intense than interactions between states inside and outside the region (MacFarlane and Weiss 1994: 19). Regional interaction is primarily focused on promoting cooperation between states for mutual benefit. *Regionalism*, therefore, describes "cooperation among governments or non-governmental organizations in three or more geographically proximate and interdependent countries for the pursuit of mutual gain in one or more issue-areas" (Alagappa 1998: 6). More specifically, a *regional organization* can be defined as "a segment of the world bound together by a common set of objectives based on geographical, social, cultural, economic, or political ties and possessing a formal structure provided for in formal intergovernmental agreements" (Bennett 1988: 350).

Regional organizations fall into three main categories: multipurpose organizations, alliance-type organizations, and functional organizations (Bennett 1988:

356). Another important distinction that has gained some currency in recent years is the new breed of geographically defined units known as "subregional" organizations, such as the Gulf Cooperation Council (GCC), the Inter-Governmental Authority on Development (IGAD), ECOWAS, and SADC. However, functionally and theoretically there is no reason to make any distinction between regional and subregional organizations. Multipurpose regional organizations are established by treaties and normally provide a broad framework within which a range of regimes and accompanying bureaucratic organizations in a number of issues and issue areas can operate (Alagappa 1995: 364). For example, most regional organizations include human rights, security regulation, and conflict resolution regimes, as well as provide for political, economic, and cultural cooperation. Some of the most important multipurpose regional organizations include the EU, the OAS, the AU, the Arab League, the Association of South-East Asian Nations (ASEAN), the Commonwealth of Independent States (CIS), the Commonwealth, and the Organization of the Islamic Conference (OIC).

Alliance organizations are either collective self-defense arrangements designed to confront a specific external threat or collective security arrangements for maintaining order among members. Nearly all of these types of bodies originated during the Cold War. The most important alliance-type organizations include NATO, the now defunct Warsaw Treaty Organization (Warsaw Pact), the Western European Union (WEU), the Australia-New Zealand-USA Pact (ANZUS), and the Organization for Security and Cooperation in Europe (OSCE). Also gaining in importance is the ASEAN Regional Forum (ARF), an emerging forum for security cooperation and confidence building in the Asia-Pacific.

Functional organizations are designed to promote fairly narrow economic, social, or political goals and generally have limited regard for security issues. There are a vast number and range of functional intergovernmental organizations. Some of the most important include the Organization of Petroleum Exporting Countries (OPEC), ECOWAS, SADC, the Organization for Economic Cooperation and Development (OECD), and the Asia-Pacific Economic Co-operation forum (APEC). Interestingly, some of these functional organizations are in the process of normative and organizational adaptation toward the inclusion of wider security matters. ECOWAS and SADC, for example, have been expanding their institutional frameworks to include significant security aspects for some years now. In the future, it is likely that they will more closely resemble and overlap with the multipurpose organizations.

Task-Sharing: Definitions, Types

Task-sharing involves regionally based (formal or informal) coalitions of states undertaking peacekeeping and/or peace-enforcement operations with UN approval and in concert with other UN conflict resolution efforts. There is obviously a fine line between the UN's own operations and task-sharing operations, as both rely on contributions by member states. However, we consider task-sharing to involve situations where significant aspects of decision making, especially in regard to security and the use of force, fall to the regional organization or regional coalition of states rather than to the UN secretary-general or the Security Council. Furthermore, responsibility for the success or failure of the operation or initiative is seen to lie with the regional actor, rather than with the UN. A key aspect of task-sharing is the notion that the (universal) UN devolves responsibilities toward institutional units that are "lower" or less universal on a hierarchy of international institutions (Smith and Weiss 1998: 227). In addition, task-sharing—in its ideal form—is an international division of labor that takes advantage of the different capabilities and resources of the different kinds of institutions.

Broadly, regional task-sharing falls into three main forms. First, regional intergovernmental organizations, such as the OAS, the AU, the Arab League, NATO, or the OSCE, can be tasked with peacekeeping or peace-enforcement actions or general responsibility for diplomatic peacemaking efforts. Examples of this variety of task-sharing include peacekeeping in West Africa by ECOWAS, peace-enforcement and peacekeeping by NATO in the former Yugoslavia and Afghanistan, peacekeeping by the CIS in Georgia, and peace-enforcement by the EU in DRC (see table 10). Second, ad hoc coalitions of willing states, which are also called multinational forces (MNFs), can be asked by the UN to deploy peacekeeping or peace-enforcement forces. MNFs differ from UN and regional peacekeeping in that they have no ties to any specific international organization and are often led and dominated by a single powerful state. Examples of this type of force include the Australian-led INTERFET in East Timor, MISAB in the Central African Republic, the U.S.-led Multinational Force (MNF) in Haiti, and the Italian and Greek-led Operation Alba in Albania (see table 11). Third, on rare occasions a single powerful state can be authorized to undertake a peacekeeping or peace-enforcement operation, such as the

French-initiated Operation Turquoise in Rwanda, Britain's Operation Palliser in Sierra Leone, and France's Operation Licorne in Ivory Coast. In this chapter, we focus primarily on the first two types of task-sharing operation.

In practice, the UN refers to regional task-sharing as "hybrid operations" (Jones 2004) and conceives of four main types of field mission: *integrated operations* have different regional organizations and the UN operating within a single or joint chain of command; *coordinated operations* occur when the UN and regional actors have separate but coordinated command structures; *parallel operations* involve the UN deploying alongside another organization's force but without any formal coordination; and *sequential operations* have the UN preceding or following a regional deployment. Furthermore, each of these categories in turn can be broken down into regional organization-led, MNF-led, or single state–led operations.

The Origins and Basis of Task-Sharing

The origins and basis of the (re)emerging security regionalism and task-sharing framework lie in three main factors: a unique combination of political factors, mainly in relation to the end of the Cold War; the efforts of the then UN secretary-general, Boutros-Ghali, to reinvigorate the existing Charter basis for regional delegation; and the perceived advantages that regional actors are thought to possess. As is the case with humanitarian intervention, the Charter basis of task-sharing is somewhat ambiguous and poses serious implementation difficulties. Guidelines developed by Secretary-General Boutros-Ghali and others in the UN DPKO only go so far in establishing a sound conceptual and operational basis for the partnership. In fact, the perceived advantages of task-sharing with regional actors are far more real in theory than they are in practice.

The Political Context

At a general level, the regionalization of international security management is in large part the result of the dramatic changes in the dynamics of the international political system. The collapse of the bipolar post–World War II security architecture and the subsequent search for a new world order has so far failed to provide a state or organization capable of effectively managing the challenges of the post–Cold War world (Alagappa 1995: 359). For a variety of reasons, including a new set of security imperatives derived from the "war on terror," the United States

has neither the will nor the resources to become the world's police officer; even in areas of vital interest—such as Europe and Asia Pacific—it is urging regional powers and organizations to carry more of the burden in maintaining peace and security. In peripheral regions like Africa, the United States is reluctant even to get involved, and almost the entire burden for security is being carried by regional actors. At the same time, the UN's role in security management has been greatly expanded due to rising demand. In other words, the reinvigoration of the UN and "the regional option" are both linked to the search for a new post-bipolar international order. This task has been further complicated by developments since the terrorist attacks on America in 2001.

The end of bipolarity enhanced the operating autonomy of regional actors in what were previously Cold War–protected reserves and removed some of the external obstacles to more effective regional organization. In the past, regional political processes and agencies had provided the superpowers with convenient pretexts for keeping disputes out of the UN. In Central America, for example, the United States relegated the conflicts in Cuba, Panama, and the Dominican Republic to the OAS. Likewise, the crises in Hungary and Czechoslovakia were dealt with by the Soviet Union through the Warsaw Pact (MacFarlane and Weiss 1994). Many regional organizations, such as the OAS, the OAU, and ASEAN therefore found a new lease on life and a renewed sense of purpose that was a direct result of the expanded opportunities for cooperation in the absence of superpower rivalry (Tascan 1998). Enhanced self-confidence and greater self-reliance in security matters were also spurred on by the processes of economic regionalism, particularly the demonstration effect of the Maastricht Treaty (Alagappa 1995: 360–61). Combined with the successes of certain regional efforts at conflict resolution—the OAS in Central America, ECOWAS in West Africa, ASEAN in Cambodia—the regional approach gained in both acceptance and its attraction for policymakers.

At the same time, the unprecedented wave of violent and seemingly contagious intrastate conflicts that swept across eastern Europe, central Asia, and Africa in particular forced regional organizations to confront the issue of conflict regulation in their own backyards. In effect, not only did the end of the Cold War free regional bodies for autonomous action, but the dramatic rise in the number of crises demanding attention—combined with UN overstretch and U.S. unwillingness to take the lead in international security—created the ideal moment for regional actors to come of age in terms of security management.

A related factor fueling demand for security regionalism lay in the concerns of many developing countries that the UN was dominated by a handful of powerful Western countries. The Security Council appeared—at least in the early 1990s—more willing to sanction international intervention in internal conflicts, the majority of which were located in developing countries (Acharya 1995: 211). This was a worrying trend for weak and vulnerable states that had suffered continual interference in their internal affairs throughout the Cold War. In the absence of an expansion in the membership of the Security Council to include representatives from other regions, developing countries began to see regional organizations as the kind of forum in which they could exercise greater control over security and conflict resolution. The rush to establish peacekeeping and security mechanisms in regional organizations—such as the 1993 OAU Mechanism for Conflict Prevention, Management, and Resolution, and the 1996 SADC Organ for Politics, Defense, and Security—was a reflection of the desire of peripheral states to take over responsibility for security issues in their regions. In addition, the resolute and purposeful intervention by ECOWAS in the Liberian conflict demonstrated that regional actors could take a lead in dealing with local conflicts without UN involvement.

The idea of contracting out major UN military operations to multinational coalitions or regional organizations was also partly due to the singular success of the United States in forming a viable multinational force during the first Gulf War in 1990 (Van der Donckt 1995). NATO in turn, contributed to the idea through its interlocking institutions concept for European security. Related to this, the broader process of security regionalism occurred as a natural outgrowth of increased UN-regional cooperation in Europe, Central America, and Central Africa. For example, the UN and the EU together convened the International Conference on the Former Socialist Federal Republic of Yugoslavia in London, with cochairs and "equal responsibility" during the early part of the Balkan conflict (Henrikson 1995: 157). Greater levels of cooperation between the UN and NATO in Bosnia occurred later, leading to full-scale task-sharing with the deployment of the Multinational International Force (IFOR) and the multinational Stabilization Force (SFOR). In Central America, a joint civilian operation between the UN and OAS in Haiti in 1993 (MICIVIH) proved that cooperation was both viable and mutually advantageous. In 1997, Mohammed Sahnoun was appointed as a joint UN-OAU Special Representative for the African Great Lakes region, the first such joint mediation effort between the two bodies.

The origins of the emerging two-tier task-sharing system also lie in the resource constraints imposed by an overload of UN commitments in the 1989–94 period and the failure of large-scale UN peace enforcement in Somalia and Bosnia. The widening gap between the expectations placed on the UN and what it could realistically achieve given its political, financial, and logistical constraints led to a major crisis of credibility in the mid-1990s. Obliged to acknowledge its limitations, and with a significant loss of confidence following the humiliations of Bosnia, Somalia, and Rwanda, the UN was forced to appeal to regional organizations for assistance. The Somali experience in particular was a devastating psychological blow for U.S. peacekeeping policy and partially accounts for subsequent U.S. reluctance to take the lead in matters of international peace and security.

The Charter Basis

The UN Charter basis for security regionalism and task-sharing lies primarily in Chapter VIII. Broadly speaking, Chapter VIII outlines five important principles that are to guide UN-regional relations. First, the Charter recognizes the right of regional organizations to exist and to be involved in security issues. Article 52(1) states that "nothing in the present Charter precludes the existence of regional arrangements or agencies for dealing with such matters relating to the maintenance of international peace and security as are appropriate for regional action, provided that such arrangements or agencies and their activities are consistent with the Purposes and Principles of the United Nations." Importantly, the reference to "arrangements or agencies" is broad enough to also include ad hoc groupings. Second, members of the UN are encouraged to make "every effort to achieve pacific settlement of local disputes through such regional arrangements or by such regional agencies before referring them to the Security Council" (Article 52). This article reinforces Article 33(1), which also exhorts states to resort to regional arrangements if their conflict threatens international peace and security. In fact, Article 52(3) states that the Security Council should "encourage the development of pacific settlement of disputes through such regional arrangement."

Third, the UN Security Council may in turn employ regional organizations for the settlement of local disputes: "The Security Council shall, where appropriate, utilize such regional arrangements or agencies for enforcement action under its authority" (Article 53). In other words, the Security Council can authorize regional agencies to undertake enforcement action under a Chapter VII mandate, as it did in Bosnia and East Timor—among others. Fourth, in safeguarding the overriding authority of the Security Council, Article 53(1) states that "no enforcement action shall be taken under regional arrangements or by regional agencies without the authorization of the Security Council." Last, regional organizations have a responsibility to keep the Security Council informed of their activities in this area: "The Security Council shall at all times be kept fully informed of activities undertaken or in contemplation under regional arrangements or by regional agencies for the maintenance of international peace and security" (Article 54).

An important modification of the Charter basis for regional organizations developed through interpretation and state practice in regard to Article 51, which states: "Nothing in the present Charter shall impair the inherent right of individual or collective self-defense if an armed attack occurs against a Member" (Bennett 1988: 354–55). The major powers in particular have interpreted this clause as justifying the creation of military security alliances, and the establishment of NATO, the Warsaw Pact, ANZUS, SEATO, and others has been the result. The existence of these collective security arrangements has often complicated the process of developing guidelines for UN-regional cooperation. NATO has argued, for example, that it is not a regional arrangement as defined by Chapter VIII and therefore is not subject to the authority of the Security Council.

An Agenda for Peace

In spite of the Charter foundation for security regionalism, the envisaged partnership never fully materialized. It was not until the end of the Cold War that the "regional option" was seriously contemplated as a necessary part of the international security framework. Invigorating the "hidden potential" of regional organizations for security management and conflict regulation fell to the then UN secretary-general, Boutros Boutros-Ghali (Leurdijk 1998: 50). In consecutive annual reports, he paid special attention to the possible functions that regional organizations could perform. In his 1992 annual report, Boutros-Ghali spelled out his view of the emerging role of regional actors.

> My aim is to see that in any new division of labor, the United Nations retains its primacy in the maintenance of international peace and security, while its burden is lightened and its mission reinforced and underlined by the active involvement of appropriate regional agencies. The exact modalities of this division of labor remains to be worked out, as regional organizations, no less than the United Nations itself, redefine their missions in the post–cold-war period. (1992: 44)

The potential role of regional bodies was discussed most fully in the secretary-general's *An Agenda for Peace* (1992) and *Supplement to An Agenda for Peace* (1995). In the first of these statements, the potential complementarity between the UN and regional organizations was identified. Boutros-Ghali argued that regional arrangements and agencies had an important role to play in preventive diplomacy, peacekeeping, peacemaking, and post-conflict peacebuilding. Furthermore, he outlined the potential advantages of such regional roles: "Regional action as a matter of decentralization, delegation and cooperation with United Nations efforts could not only lighten the burden of the Council but also contribute to a deeper sense of participation, consensus and democratization in international affairs" (1992: paras. 63–64).

The *Supplement* goes even further in outlining the specific forms that task-sharing could take (Boutros-Ghali 1995: section IV). The first form is broadly conceived of as *consultation,* where views could be exchanged on conflicts that both the UN and the regional organizations may be attempting to resolve. A second form is mutual *diplomatic support* for each organization's efforts, either by direct diplomatic initiatives or through technical support. The OSCE's advice to the UN on constitutional issues relating to the breakaway Georgian region of Abkhazia is an example of the latter. Third, the UN and regional organizations could reciprocate with *operational support,* such as the provision by NATO of air power to support the UN Protection Force (UNPROFOR) in the former Yugoslavia. Fourth, they could engage in the *co-deployment* of forces, as in the UN field missions deployed in conjunction with the ECOWAS forces in Liberia and the CIS in Georgia. Last, it was envisaged that the UN and regional organizations could mount *joint operations.* The point of departure here was the UN Civilian Mission in Haiti in 1993, where staffing, direction, and financing were shared between the UN and the OAS. The *Supplement* went on to argue that while a universal model for the relationship between the UN and regional organizations was not appropriate (given their heterogeneity of structures, mandates, decision-making machinery, and capacity), it should, nonetheless, be based on agreed principles for consultation, the primacy of the UN, a clearly defined division of labor, and the maintenance of consistency in joint operations or task-sharing situations.

The Perceived Advantages of Task-Sharing

A final factor in the revitalization of the regional bodies option was that they were seen to possess certain innate advantages for conflict resolution. In the first place, regional actors have a deep interest in conflict regulation in their respective regions, as the deleterious effects of conflict are most acutely felt by neighboring states. The explosion of conflict in Africa since the early 1990s had become a major concern to all the states of the region and pushed security issues to the top of the agenda in the AU, ECOWAS, and SADC. Following from this, it is often only states that are directly affected by the impact of a crisis in their locality that are willing to invest the resources and exhibit the staying power needed to sustain long-term operations. Outside actors, such as the United States in Somalia or the United Kingdom in Sierra Leone, may lack the necessary willpower for such a long-term commitment. Last, it is believed that regional actors can provide a sense of legitimacy to conflict resolution processes not always available to foreign powers. In addition, they possess local knowledge and experience, personal contacts with state leaders, proximity, and some resources, especially in the form of personnel.

An Overview of Task-Sharing

The history of task-sharing falls neatly into two periods. During the Cold War, UN-regional cooperation was limited and, more often than not, highly competitive (Acharya 1995). There were very few examples of task-sharing in the sense of UN-delegated peacekeeping operations, although there were some cases of autonomous regionally based operations. The real start of task-sharing begins in the immediate post–Cold War period when a large number of subcontracted peacekeeping and peace-enforcement operations were undertaken within a relatively short period. At the same time, a range of institutional developments in the UN and regional organizations began to provide a formal framework for the new cooperative relationship. The task-sharing ideal finds its strongest expression in the African region, the site of the most conflicts, the largest number of task-sharing operations, and a range of new institutions for UN-regional cooperation. While it is premature to speak of a "global-

regional peace-making system" (Merrills 1998: 284), the building blocs of such a system are rapidly falling into place.

Task-Sharing during the Cold War

All the main regional organizations incorporated conflict resolution and security regulation procedures into their formal machinery, and some like the OAU (now the AU) and the OAS included it as a major institutional objective. The machinery of the OAS, for example, includes the 1948 American Treaty on Pacific Settlement (or Pact of Bogota) and the 1970 Inter-American Committee on Peaceful Settlement. These bodies were designed to assist in the resolution of disputes through inquiry, mediation, and recommendations on appropriate means of settlement. The OAU originally included the Commission of Mediation, Conciliation, and Arbitration as one of its major organs, although it was never enacted. Similarly, in 1956 the North Atlantic Council passed a resolution committing NATO to the settlement of disputes within the organization and authorized the NATO secretary-general to offer his good offices and to use inquiry, mediation, conciliation, or arbitration in settling conflicts between members.

In spite of their conflict resolution mechanisms, Chapter VIII regional organizations played a much smaller role than the architects of the UN Charter had envisaged. They were not employed as a first port of call or as "shock absorbers" and tended to grow apart (Henrikson 1995: 132–33). At times, they acted in a highly competitive manner, and the superpowers tended to use the regional bodies as gatekeepers to their own spheres of influence. The United States dominated the OAS and used it to keep the UN from interfering in anticommunist struggles in Latin America. Similarly, NATO encouraged its members to settle their disputes within the organization, obviating the need for UN involvement. For its part, the Soviet Union used the Warsaw Pact to settle disputes and keep its allies in line. In particular, a perennial problem of UN-regional cooperation has been the question of supremacy. No organization will easily compromise its autonomy or independence, and as demonstrated in previous chapters, the UN has struggled to establish its authority as the leading actor in international peace and security.

There were a few cases of regionally organized peacekeeping operations during this period (see table 9). For the most part, however, regional involvement in peacekeeping was both infrequent and relatively unsuccessful.

This was a reflection of the smaller number of peacekeeping missions in general, the UN's unwillingness to delegate operations and the failure by regional actors to develop the necessary mechanisms and capabilities for peacekeeping (Acharya 1995: 208–9). The embarrassing failure of the OAU peacekeeping force in Chad in 1981 clearly highlighted the institutional and resource deficiencies of regional organizations in peacekeeping, and it discouraged other regional actors from attempting similar operations. Similarly, the OAS peacekeeping operation in the Dominican Republic in 1965 was criticized for legitimating what was essentially U.S. military intervention and led to a deep mistrust of regional peacekeeping among Latin American nations (Acharya 1995: 210).

As a consequence, regional organizations largely confined their activities to mediation and conciliation. Interestingly, they tended to rely not on their formal conflict resolution machinery but on ad hoc and informal diplomatic processes. The main form of OAU mediation was the ad hoc mediating committee usually made up of several African heads of state, while the Commission on Mediation, Conciliation, and Arbitration was never used in any conflict resolution effort. In the OAS, the Inter-American Peace Committee was highly successful until it was replaced by a formal mechanism in 1970, after which time it was rarely employed (Scheman and Ford 1985).

Empirical studies during this period show that while regional organizations dealt with far fewer conflicts than the UN, their success rate was comparable, and in the case of the OAS, much higher. Haas examined 282 international disputes between 1945 and 1981 and found that of these, 123 were placed on the agenda of the UN, while 28 went to the OAS, 25 to the OAU, 22 to the Arab League, and 5 to the Council of Europe (Haas 1989: 193). In terms of success rates, Haas found a 23 percent success rate for the UN compared to 34 percent for the OAS, 20 percent for the OAU, 15 percent for the Arab League, and 18 percent for the Council of Europe (Haas 1989: 195). However, a closer look at the cases reveals that typically the conflicts dealt with by regional organizations were of a lower intensity, had not spread beyond the protagonists' borders, and involved small or middle powers not aligned to one or other of the superpowers. There is also a clear trend toward lower levels of success as the Cold War progresses. The OAS, for example, had been highly effective before the 1965 peacekeeping operation in the Dominican Republic. Following this intervention, the consensus in the organization collapsed, and it became a virtual bystander in inter-American conflicts until the end of the Cold War.

The Post–Cold War Experience

Task-sharing emerged as an important new approach for dealing with internal conflicts after 1990. Following publication of *An Agenda for Peace,* the UN significantly expanded its cooperation with regional organizations. It endorsed, either tacitly or with explicit Chapter VII authorization, major peacekeeping operations by regional organizations in Liberia, the former Yugoslavia, Tajikistan, the Georgia-Abkhazia civil conflict, the Sierra Leone civil war, the Guinea-Bissau civil war, and the Kosovo conflict, among others (see table 10). It also accorded several MNF operations with Chapter VII authorization, most notably in Somalia, Rwanda, Haiti, Central

TABLE 9.   Regional and MNF Peacekeeping Operations, 1945–89

Conflict	Force Name and Size	Primary Actors	Dates of Operation
Kuwait Independence	Arab Security Force in Kuwait; 3,000 troops	Arab League; Saudi Arabia	September 1961– February 1962
Dominican Republic Civil War	The Inter-American Peace Force (IAPF); 23,000 troops	U.S.; OAS	April 1965– September 1966
Lebanon Civil War	Symbolic Arab Security Force, later the Arab Deterrent Force; 2,500 troops	Arab League; Syria	June 1976– September 1982
Chad Civil War	The Inter-African Force (IAF); 3,500 troops	OAU; Nigeria; France	November 1981– June 1982
Lebanon Civil War	Multinational Force (MNF I, II, III); 2,500 troops	U.S.; France; Italy	August 1982– February 1984

Source: Data from authors' research.

TABLE 10. Regional Organization Peacekeeping Operations, 1990–2004

Conflict	Force Name and Size	Primary Actors	Dates of Operation	Level of UN Cooperation
Liberia	ECOWAS Cease-fire Monitoring Group (ECO-MOG); 15,000 troops	ECOWAS; Nigeria	August 1990–October 1999	Tacit endorsement of ECOMOG; establishment of UN Observer Mission in Liberia (UNOMIL)
Georgia/South Ossetia	CIS Peacekeeping Force; 1,500 troops	CIS; Russia	July 1992–present	Tacit endorsement of CIS PKO
Moldova/Trans-Dniester	CIS Peacekeeping Force; 1,800 troops	CIS; Russia; Moldova; Trans-Dniester	July 1992–present	Tacit endorsement of CIS PKO
Bosnia	NATO sanctions monitoring missions; Stabilization Force (SFOR)—followed by Implementation Force (IFOR); 60,000 troops	NATO	July 1992–present	Full subcontracting to NATO under Ch. VII; full cooperation with UNPROFOR and UNMIBH
Tajikistan	CIS Collective Peacekeeping Force; 10,000 troops	CIS; Russia; coalition of willing states	September 1993–June 2000	Tacit endorsement of CIS peacemaking efforts; UN Military Observers in Tajikistan (UNMOT) mission established to monitor CIS PKO
Georgia/Abkhazia	CIS Peacekeeping Force Georgia; 1,100 troops	CIS; Russia	June 1994–present	UN approval of CIS force; establishment of UN Observer Mission in Georgia (UNOMIG) to monitor CIS mission
Sierra Leone	ECOMOG II; 15,000 troops	ECOWAS; Nigeria; Sandline	May 1997–October 1999	Tacit endorsement of ECOMOG; establishment of UN Mission of Observers in Sierra Leone (UNOMSIL); replaced by UN Mission in Sierra Leone (UNAMSIL)
Democratic Republic of Congo	SADC Force; 15,000 troops (estimated)	Zimbabwe, Angola, Namibia, SADC	August 1998–present	None
Lesotho	SADC Force; 800 troops	South Africa, Botswana, SADC	September 1998–May 1999	None
Guinea-Bissau	Coalition of Local States Monitoring Group; ECOMOG Interposition Force; 600 troops	ECOWAS	February 1999–May 1999	Endorsement of ECOMOG peacekeeping; establishes small Post-Conflict Peace Building Support Office in Guinea-Bissau (UNOGBIS)
Kosovo	Kosovo Force (KFOR); 40,000 troops	NATO; OSCE; EU	June 1999–present	Full subcontracting to NATO under Ch. VII to provide security for UN Interim Administration Mission in Kosovo (UNMIK)
Afghanistan	International Security Assistance Force (ISAF); 6,500 troops	NATO; willing states	December 2001–present	Full UN Ch. VII mandate; full cooperation between ISAF and UN Assistance Mission in Afghanistan (UNAMA)
Ivory Coast	Joint mission by French forces and ECOWAS Peace Force for Ivory Coast (ECOFORCE); 3,000 French troops in Operation Licorne and 2,000 ECOWAS troops	ECOWAS; France	September 2002–present	Post hoc Ch. VII endorsement of force; establishment of UN Mission in Ivory Coast
Democratic Republic of Congo (DRC)	EU expeditionary force/Operation Artemis; 2,200 troops	EU; France	June 2003–September 2003	Full UN authorization of EU-led interim emergency multinational force; mission taken over by UN Mission in the Congo (MONUC)
Solomon Islands	Regional Assistance Mission to the Solomon Islands (RAMSI); Operation Helpem Fren; 2,300 troops	Pacific Island Forum (PIF); Australia; New Zealand	July 2003–present	UN endorsement of PIF peacekeeping operation
Liberia	The ECOWAS Military Mission to Liberia (ECOMIL); 3,600 troops	ECOWAS	August 2003–September 2003	UN authorization for ECOMIL; replaced by UN Mission in Liberia (UNMIL)

Source: Data from authors' research.

African Republic, Albania, and East Timor (see table 11). Apart from the increasing tendency to use MNFs, the most active regional organizations in task-sharing have been ECOWAS, NATO, and the CIS. Actually, it is in Africa that regional task-sharing has been most prominent and where its machinery is most developed (see Jackson 2000). In contrast, the OAS remains reluctant to engage in peacekeeping and confines itself to civilian-based operations, or observation and verification missions.

In most cases, these regionally led operations involved the subcontracting of the peace-enforcement or security phase of the operation, followed by a handover to more traditional UN peacekeeping operations once a secure environment had been achieved. In other words, the most dangerous part of the overall humanitarian intervention was being given to regional actors, and the UN was returning to its more traditional Cold War role of peacekeeping in the posthostilities phase of the conflict. The UN subcontracted this part of the operation largely as an attempt to overcome the problems of political will among great power states. In the post-Somalia environment, these states would be unlikely to authorize a peacekeeping mission that could be dangerous, but they might agree to one that subcontracted the dangerous phase to regional actors or willing coalitions. This model seems likely to continue in the post–September 11 period, particularly with the armed forces of several leading Western states committed to operations in Iraq and Afghanistan. The UN will mount complex, multidimensional humanitarian interventions in select cases, but only when re-

gional actors agree to take on the initial security stabilization phase of the operation. In the three years since the terrorist attacks, this has been the pattern in Ivory Coast, DRC, and Liberia. In each case, a regional force was used for security stabilization until an expanded UN operation could deploy.

Accompanying the rise in regional peacekeeping operations has been a series of institutional developments in both regional organizations and the UN designed to facilitate greater UN-regional cooperation and security regionalism. There is not the space to describe all of these developments here; a few important examples will suffice. Since 1992, NATO has expressed its willingness to engage in peacekeeping, and this has been followed by a series of concrete measures designed to expand its capabilities in this area. In 1993, for example, the North Atlantic Cooperation Council (NACC) established an Ad Hoc Group on Cooperation in Peacekeeping to set the basis for NATO involvement in peacekeeping. NATO has since participated in UN task-sharing in Bosnia, Kosovo, and Afghanistan following the Bonn Agreements of December 2001.

Another European organization, the Conference on Security and Cooperation in Europe (CSCE), changed its name to the Organization for Security and Cooperation in Europe (OSCE) in 1994. This was in recognition of its transformation from a loose arrangement of conferences to a fully functioning Chapter VIII–type regional organization oriented toward security and conflict resolution. Earlier in 1992, the organization had created a permanent

TABLE 11.   MNF Peacekeeping Operations, 1990–2004

Conflict	Force Name and Size	Primary Actors	Dates of Operation	Level of UN Cooperation
Somalia	UNITAF/Operation Restore Hope; 37,000 troops	U.S.; coalition of willing states; UN	December 1992– May 1993	Security Council Chapter VII endorsement; succeeded by UN Operation in Somalia (UNOSOM II)
Haiti	Multinational Force (MNF)/Operation Uphold Democracy; 20,000 troops	U.S.; coalition of willing Caribbean states	September 1994– March 1995	Security Council Chapter VII endorsement; succeeded by UN Peacekeeping Mission in Haiti (UNMIH)
Papua New Guinea– Bougainville	South Pacific Peacekeeping Force (SPPKF); Operation Lagoon; 200 troops	Australia; New Zealand; coalition of willing Pacific states	October 1994	Tacit UN endorsement
Central African Republic	Inter-African Mission to Monitor the Bangui Accords (MISAB); 1,100 troops	France; coalition of willing states	February 1997– April 1998	Post hoc Chapter VII endorsement; succeeded by UN Mission in the CAR (MINURCA)
Albania	Operation Alba; 7,000 troops	Italy; Greece	April 1997– August 1997	Security Council Chapter VII endorsement
East Timor	International Force, East Timor (INTERFET); 10,000 troops	Australia; coalition of willing states	September 1999– February 2000	Security Council Chapter VII endorsement; succeeded by UN Transitional Authority East Timor (UNTAET)

Source: Data from authors' research.

Forum for Security Cooperation (FSC) at the Helsinki Summit, which it was envisaged would lay the foundation for OSCE peacekeeping and conflict prevention activities. Shortly after, the OSCE declared itself a regional arrangement within the scope of Chapter VIII, and in May 1993, it signed an agreement with the UN laying the foundation for security cooperation and coordination (Acharya 1995: 220). The UN and OSCE have since sent joint observer and mediation missions to conflicts in the former Soviet Union, among others. In November 1999, the OSCE established an Operations Center for the planning and deployment of field operations.

Established in 1991, the CIS had been involved in peacekeeping operations in Tadjikistan and Georgia since 1993, based on the 1992 Agreement on Military Observers and Collective Peacekeeping. In 1996 the CIS Council adopted a statute on collective peacekeeping, establishing their legal basis, composition, training, and other related matters (Merrills 1998: 271). At the same time, the CIS set out arrangements for cooperation with other international organizations, in particular the UN and the OSCE. Similar to the OSCE, the CIS has also declared itself a Chapter VIII regional arrangement.

Last, the UN itself has sought to expand cooperation with regional organizations. In August 1994, Secretary-General Boutros-Ghali convened a meeting between himself and the heads of the CIS, the Commonwealth, EU, LAS, NATO, OAU, OAS, OIC, and WEU. The aim of the meeting was to discuss ways of encouraging closer cooperation between the UN and regional organizations, particularly in the area of joint peacekeeping training and peace support operations (Henrikson 1995: 162–63). Since then, the UN has held annual meetings between the secretaries-general of the UN and various regional organizations and established special UN representative offices at the headquarters of regional bodies like the AU.

Evaluating Regionalism and Task-Sharing

At a general level, assessing the role of regional actors in task-sharing involves the same criteria as for peacekeeping operations and humanitarian intervention, that is, saving lives and mitigating human suffering, and creating the conditions for a lasting solution to the violence. Obviously, we are dealing with a variety of different actors, and the effectiveness of regional organizations will be contingent on the type of institution, its capacities and resources, its legitimacy and credibility, the nature of the

conflict, and the degree of commitment to the process from its members. Some regional arrangements will be more effective than others. In addition to these unique features, regional actors—both formal intergovernmental organizations and ad hoc coalitions—possess a series of advantages and disadvantages that are innate to their particular form of international organization.

The Strengths of Regional Task-Sharing

The obvious advantages of task-sharing, especially for the UN and the international community, are that it relieves an overburdened UN and provides an alternative avenue for conflict resolution in the absence of strong UN or U.S. leadership. As we noted in chapter 6, the expansion of peacekeeping in response to rising demand has placed the UN in an almost impossible situation. Both regional and MNF task-sharing can help to ease the financial and material burden. Intuitively, it also makes sense that regional organizations and the UN would have comparative advantages in peacemaking, and a more logical division of labor would relieve both of having to undertake tasks for which they are ill suited. In addition, the process of delegating conflict regulation tasks to regional actors could "contribute to a deeper sense of participation, consensus, and democratization in international affairs" (Boutros-Ghali 1992: paras. 63–64). Beyond these generalities, however, there are a number of specific ways in which regional actors can add value to the processes of international conflict resolution.

The Advantages of Regional Organizations

Regional organizations—as a form of international organization (IO)—have many of the same strengths as the UN (see chapter 5). For example, they mitigate anarchy through the creation of international norms, facilitate the construction of security communities, provide a forum and venue for multilateral diplomacy, act as a communications link, reduce uncertainty, mobilize resources for peace processes, and have a range of institutional machinery for conflict resolution. The strategies available to them include norm-setting and regime creation, assurance, community building, deterrence, nonintervention, isolation, fact-finding, mediation, judicial settlement, peacekeeping, peace-enforcement, and internationalization (Alagappa 1998: 10). In other words, they institutionalize the opportunity to resolve disputes among members through their ability to provide an immediate hearing to aggrieved parties or dispatch observers to the scene of the problems.

> In contrast to traditional mediation, international organization reflects the nations' desire for pre-established machinery that will help avoid the uncertainties of ad hoc arrangements in the heat of conflict. In many cases, machinery motivates nations to mediate their own conflicts. Thus, the international machinery is most useful not for any action of its own, but just because it exists. It is, in reality, a type of safety net. (Scheman and Ford 1985: 226–27)

The collective legitimation of norms, such as the nonintervention norm, as well as specific collective declarations of nonintervention by the organization, can also prevent or discourage disputes from arising in the first place or prevent further escalation (Merrills 1998: 270). As such, regional organizations—in their wider normative orientation—play an important conflict prevention role. There is no question that regions like Africa, the Americas, and Southeast Asia are more stable and peaceful for having the AU, the OAS, and ASEAN than they otherwise would be.

Regional arrangements also have a relatively strong record of conflict resolution in comparison to the UN and have played important roles in dampening and isolating some potentially serious situations. For example, the OAS was very successful in dealing with conflicts in the Western Hemisphere, particularly (but not only) prior to 1965. It played an important role in settling the so-called Soccer War between El Salvador and Honduras in 1969, for example. The OAU, on the other hand, has been successful at reinforcing norms of the nonviolent resolution of interstate disputes (Wolfers 1985: 189). In a continent replete with potential territorial and resource disputes stemming from arbitrary (and often irrational) colonial boundary delineation, there have been surprisingly few violent border conflicts, and most disputes have been settled through international legal processes. This is in no small measure due to the AU's norm-setting role in inter-African affairs.

In addition to their "safety net" role, there are also numerous unique advantages for regional organizations in conflict resolution. In the first instance, regional organizations, in theory at least, can facilitate greater consensus in collective conflict regulation than the much larger and more diverse UN (Diehl 1993a: 212). This is a function of their smaller size, which facilitates coalition-building and the harmonization of interests. At the same time, regional

organizations have a much more manageable security agenda than the global organization, and resources can be concentrated in areas of concern instead of having to be spread out over numerous crises. Greater consensus is also thought to be possible because regional organizations are more homogeneous—states in the same region have similar cultures, share historical roots, are at roughly the same developmental stage, and have similar political outlooks due to facing common problems. In comparison to the UN, regional organizations—by virtue of their proximity—are also better positioned to provide early warning, information and intelligence gathering, and fact-finding. In all, these factors should create the ideal conditions for speedy, decisive, and clearly articulated mandates with few conditions. One consequence is that in regional peacekeeping operations (or in general peacemaking efforts), the support given to them by the local populations and the disputants should in theory be greater than for UN operations (Diehl 1993a: 213). This is because outsiders may be viewed with suspicion, while regional actors, who have a natural affinity with those in that region, may command greater legitimacy.

Related to this, regional organizations provide an important forum for facilitating dialogue and conflict resolution. Regular sessions furnish opportunities for leaders of states in conflict to meet without loss of face or bargaining positions, and if necessary, in informal corridor diplomacy. At the same time, the presence of other leaders means that there are numerous potential third parties for mediation and conciliation (Amoo and Zartman 1992: 136). In Africa and other developing regions of the world, political rule tends to be personalized, and foreign policy is often a function of individual leadership rather than institutional processes or collective interest aggregation. When interpersonal conflict between leaders forms a major component of interstate conflict—as it frequently does—regional organizations can play an important role in facilitating leadership conciliation.

Another important advantage is that regional organizations may be better able to secure the support of interested third parties (Diehl 1993b: 125–26). Third parties can easily spoil peacekeeping or peacemaking efforts, as happened with Syria in Lebanon or Turkey in Cyprus. In part, this is because they are not included in the debate and authorization stage of the proposed operation in the Security Council. In regional peacekeeping, these third parties will often play an important part in the construction of the terms of the mandate, the force composition, and its overall objectives. Such participation can secure at least tacit support from the third party and circumvent damaging opposition.

In the area of internal conflicts, regional organizations have played an important indirect role in the promotion of human rights and good governance, the lack of which can often be the source of conflict. The AU, for example, has observed over forty elections and referenda in recent years (Bakwesegha 1997: 89). In many of these countries—Lesotho, Togo, Congo, and Gabon—potential conflicts have been diffused and stabilized before the outbreak of violence. The OAS has been similarly involved in the Americas. Perhaps the best example of this principle is the OSCE's High Commissioner for National Minorities (HCNM), which has played an essential role—through long-term missions and visits by the High Commissioner—in helping to manage the delicate and potentially explosive citizenship issues in Latvia, Estonia, and many other ex-Soviet republics. The HCNM's work has greatly contributed to European conflict prevention and stability.

The Advantages of MNFs

One of the key advantages of MNFs is precisely the fact that they are not international organizations and thus do not face the same problems of lack of autonomous decision making, coalition building, free riders, lack of political will, and institutional inertia. By definition, they are highly motivated, strongly interested, and willing states who have the autonomy and usually the capabilities—most often based on the military leadership of a single strong state—to do the job. Relying on a leading state's existing military systems for deployment patterns, supply of materials, and modes of operation means that when the mission is authorized the managerial components already exist. A smooth and rapid deployment is then possible. A consequence of this is that MNFs have fewer problems obtaining resources and materials and therefore a greater measure of financial stability. In addition, they do not face the same kind of institutional demands that UN or regional peacekeeping does; UN and regional peacekeeping serves many masters, and changes in mandates often occur as a response to changing political winds (Diehl 1993a: 221). Australia's leadership of INTERFET is a useful example in this respect. Based on the existing force structures of the Australian army, and with preplanning for just such a contingency in the region, INTERFET deployed far quicker than a UN force would have been able to do and faced fewer problems of resources, consensus, or mandate interpretation.

The Challenges of Regional Task-Sharing

Regional organizations face two main sets of challenges. First, as a form of international organization regional bodies face all the same limitations that the UN does. For example, they face the same problems of coalition building, resource constraints, Charter restrictions, competing norms and principles (noninterference versus human rights), and lack of autonomy from member state interests. In addition, regional organizations are in no better position to overcome the primary legal, conceptual, operational, and political constraints that we described in terms of humanitarian intervention (chapter 8). Second, regional organizations face a unique set of problems that are directly related to their subuniversal character and their often peripheral status in world politics. Task-sharing with MNFs also entails a set of unique problems, which we discuss in a separate section later.

The UN Charter

One of the most serious challenges confronting the future development of security regionalism lies in its slightly unclear Charter basis. The provisions for regional agencies were adopted after much compromise, and as a consequence, the final articles contain a number of ambiguities and contradictions. For example, while Articles 33(1) and 52(2) would seem to give regional arrangements priority of action in regard to "local" disputes, Articles 34 and 35 (together with Articles 24 and 39) appear to give the Security Council overall supremacy, if not ascendancy (Henrikson 1995: 129–30). The vagueness of this division of labor has colored UN-regional relations ever since. In addition, there is no clear definition of what a "regional arrangement" actually is, particularly in the light of the collective defense organizations that have evolved under Article 51. NATO in particular (along with certain other collective defense arrangements) has deliberately avoided defining itself as a regional arrangement under Chapter VIII because it wanted to avoid any connotations of subservience to the UN Security Council (Smith and Weiss 1998: 235). In other words, the evolution of myriad forms of multilateral institutions, interactions, and practices may have outstripped the usefulness of the undefined Charter term *regional arrangements*.

The protection given to the inherent right of collective self-defense under Article 51 has also muddied the water of appropriate regional action. The scope of possible action under Article 51 is ambiguous, especially when one considers that the customary concept of self-defense permits the use of preemptive military force. It is conceivable that regional arrangements could intervene in a local conflict and then apply for Security Council endorsement retrospectively. In the event that they fail to win UN authorization, they could claim legality under Article 51. To many, the 1999 NATO air campaign in Kosovo crossed this murky line, as having failed to obtain a Chapter VII authorization from the Security Council, NATO officials consistently stated that the action was in the interests of wider European security—self-defense—as well as for humanitarian reasons.

A related problem lies in the fact that in any region there are often several regional bodies with overlapping responsibilities, and it is neither possible nor appropriate to determine in advance which institution will be the most appropriate under the Charter (Alagappa 1998: 5). There is also the possibility that the existence of a "smorgasbord" of regional arrangements could lead to buck passing instead of decision making (Smith and Weiss 1998: 230). Alternatively, it could lead to multiple, uncoordinated, or even competitive peacemaking efforts—the problem of third-party "crowdedness" (Khadiagala 2000). In other areas such as the Middle East, there are no organizations that span the entire region and include every state. Those regional arrangements that do define themselves under Chapter VIII, such as the OSCE, find themselves encouraged to deal with matters that are "appropriate for such action" without anything to indicate precisely what matters would be appropriate. While the tendency has been to simplistically assert that regional arrangements should deal with conflicts in their region—"African solutions for African problems," for example—there is a danger that this could result in a kind of "tribalization of peacekeeping" (Otunnu 1995) or the revival of the old "spheres of influence" politics, albeit with UN oversight (MacFarlane and Weiss 1994: 27–28). By granting some recognition to regional task-sharing under Chapter VIII, therefore, the Charter may have enhanced the legitimacy of regional actors even when they engage in actions not specifically authorized by the world body (Smith and Weiss 1998: 235).

The lack of a clear Charter basis for task-sharing can result in unilateral actions by regional actors—such as both ECOWAS and SADC operations—with UN endorsement sought retrospectively. Post hoc authorization by the Security Council in turn begs the question of the necessary mechanisms of accountability (Broad 2000). In the event of a regional operation that clearly violated international norms of human rights, for example, the UN's leverage is limited to withdrawing its legitimating authority and mobilizing international opinion against the regional actor. There is no agreed framework for managing such a situation, and it is unclear what the long-term effects of such an event would be.

Conceptual Challenges

The conceptual challenge of task-sharing originates in both its weak Charter basis and the rapidity with which the regional security framework has evolved. The enlarged international security agenda, combined with UN overstretch, has led to the rapid development of new structures but without a clear conceptual framework or any kind of strategic design. There are two key aspects to the conceptual challenge. In the first instance, as we noted in chapter 8, humanitarian intervention and peacekeeping in general lack a conceptual framework—regardless of whether it is undertaken by the UN or regional organizations. There are serious questions about the role of third-party intervention in internal conflicts, and in the case of peacekeeping there are particular questions about the nature of consent, the role of peace-enforcement, issues of coordination, and conflict management versus conflict resolution. As yet, there is no widely accepted "theory of peacekeeping" that could guide regional, MNF, or UN peacekeeping.

Second, apart from the broad guidelines in *Supplement to An Agenda for Peace*, there is no clear conceptual framework for the division of labor between the UN and regional arrangements. Presently, task-sharing operations are designed and implemented largely in situ, which can lead to unforeseen problems. A potential difficulty arises when both the UN and regional actors enter into a partnership seeking additional resources, but without a reduction in their autonomy (Broad 2000). Interorganizational competition and conflict can result from each party wanting the benefits of partnership without compromising their independence. This is largely a question of the primacy of the respective organizations in terms of who has priority or who is ascendant at that particular time (Henrikson 1995: 124). The highly publicized conflicts between NATO and the UN over the "dual key" arrangement in Bosnia, and between the UN and United States over post-Saddam Iraq, illustrate this pitfall. As we have seen, the unclear Charter basis for task-sharing and the involvement of collective defense arrangements like NATO in peacekeeping has muddied the waters even further.

At the same time, there are no guidelines for ensuring the accountability of regional forces to overall Security Council authority beyond the injunction to keep the UN informed of their activities. When the UN sends observer missions to regional peacekeeping operations, there are sometimes problems of access and freedom of movement. In Tajikistan, for example, UN military observers could not speak Russian and faced serious obstacles in their efforts to observe Russian decision making and mission functioning (Weiss 1998: 36). In UNOMIL, only 300 observers were deployed, far too few for effective oversight by the world body. In most cases, UN observers do not operate jointly with regional powers and maintain separate command structures. While efforts are now under way within DPKO to conceptualize and formalize roles during so-called hybrid operations (see Jones 2004), it is too early to tell how effective such guidelines will be in practice.

Practical and Operational Problems

As with UN peacekeeping, regional missions face the same kind of practical and operational problems associated with deploying, managing, coordinating, and supplying a military force made up of different nationalities and with both civil and military components. Even more than the UN, however, regional organizations lack the institutional capacity and experienced personnel for complex multifunctional missions. Most of the regional institutional instruments for peacekeeping have only been adopted in the past few years and are for the most part rudimentary and underdeveloped. Even military organizations like NATO are beginning to realize that the Alliance's military structures—designed for collective defense—may not be entirely compatible with peacekeeping requirements (Van der Donckt 1995). In fact, compared to the regional organizations, the UN has far more practical experience, relatively well-developed institutional capacities, and a wider resource base to call upon. Regional organizations also tend to have laborious decision-making procedures and lack executive decision-making bodies like the UN's Security Council. This can make regional operations even slower to deploy than UN operations, despite their geographical proximity.

The devolution of peacekeeping operations to regional arrangements also does not address the paucity of resources available to most regional actors (Broad 2000). Peacekeeping operations incur huge financial and resource costs; at the regional level there are necessarily fewer states to bear the burden of these costs. In addition, there is as yet no precedent for UN financing of non-UN commanded operations (Van der Donckt 1995). Outside of Europe, most regional arrangements do not have the resources to mount large-scale military operations, and when they

do—as in the MISAB operation in the Central African Republic—they are unsustainable over the medium to long term. Even with French support, the MISAB mission soon had to be replaced by a UN operation when it became obvious that contributing states could not afford to continue. The OAU's failure in Chad in 1981 was largely attributable to the lack of resources; of an estimated $162 million needed for the operation's budget, the OAU only managed to secure a meager $400,000 (Acharya 1995: 210). One result of the lack of resources is that regional groupings tend to be dominated by a local hegemon who can manipulate power asymmetries to its own advantage or may be prone to interference by powerful outside actors.

The Political Context

One of the most serious disadvantages of regional actors, particularly in managing the kinds of intrastate conflicts that have come to dominate the post–Cold War security agenda, is the question of whether such bodies can act, or be perceived to act, as neutral or impartial parties in internal conflicts. As Alagappa puts it: "To the extent that regional institutions do have a role in domestic conflict management, their status quo character leads them to favor incumbents. Governments tend to support one another" (1998: 17). In some cases, proximity may mean that neighboring states are actually significantly involved in the conflict. Therefore, the corollary to the advantages that regional organizations are thought to possess—genuine interests in the conflict, geopolitical proximity, and indigenous knowledge of the terrain—is that they are often liable to be too close to the issues and too interested in the outcomes (Hutchful 1999). In any event, such complications may preclude the emergence of the necessary cohesion and consensus needed to intervene in the first place (Hurrell and Fawcett 1995: 315).

For example, the record clearly demonstrates the bias of the AU toward state actors. In virtually every intrastate conflict in the 1990s, the OAU (as it then was) condemned the actions of nonstate actors, such as coup leaders, rebel groups, or irregular militias, and sided with the incumbent ruling elite. The OAS shows similar tendencies toward regime maintenance in the Latin American region, especially in its post–Cold War efforts to provide leadership in restoring democracy. It condemned the coups in Guatemala, Haiti, and Peru and applied economic sanctions to back its demands for a return to democratic rule (Tascan 1998: 92–93). How regional arrangements can expect to act as neutral mediators in such situations is problematic. In fact, the status quo character of regional intervention may contribute to the prolongation and intensification of domestic conflicts (Alagappa 1995: 375). By strengthening the hand of the government regional support may increase the regime's harsh treatment of substate groups seeking political change.

It is difficult to conceive, for example, of a situation where an intervening regional organization would help dismember one of its members if that was a necessary part of the final settlement. The secession of Eritrea from Ethiopia in 1993 is an example where such a solution was viewed as necessary. In the early stages of the Liberian conflict, Charles Taylor rightly perceived that the ECOMOG forces would be biased against the NPFL and instead requested UN peacekeepers. In reality, all ECOWAS operations—Liberia, Sierra Leone, Guinea-Bissau, and Ivory Coast—have been directed toward maintaining incumbent regimes. Similarly, interventions by SADC in Lesotho and DRC were intended to prevent the overthrow of the existing governments by rebel forces, as was the CIS intervention in Georgia in 1993. This is not really surprising given that regional organizations are designed to promote the interests of their members, namely, governments. Their character is to promote norms of territorial integrity, selective self-determination, and the promotion and protection of incumbent regimes, which by definition militates against secession or violent domestic political change. In short, the nature of regional organizations—their inherent predispositions and proclivities—severely limits their role in the resolution of internal conflicts.

The problem of regional bias against nonstate actors in conflict can also have serious implications for wider international efforts and for the collective international security framework in general. In Liberia during the early 1990s, the UN aligned itself with ECOMOG, deferring to the much-disputed ECOWAS Peace Plan and relying on ECOMOG troops for protection. The effect was to compromise the perceived neutrality of the world body and at the same time foster the impression that the UN was either incapable or unwilling to engage in peace-enforcement actions in Liberia (Adibe 1998). In more extreme cases, the credibility of the UN is damaged when the regional organization with whom they are task-sharing fails to protect civilians or engages in acts of human rights abuse. Such a situation occurred in Abkhazia where civilians were murdered while CIS and UNOMIG (UN Observer Mission in Georgia) personnel stood by (MacFarlane 1998: 127).

A related problem is that most regions outside of Europe lack the resources required to deal decisively with such conflict situations. Thus, peacekeeping operations are liable to fall victim to a regional hegemon using power asymmetries to dominate regional or subregional organizations for self-interested objectives. That the UN Charter is vulnerable to being sidestepped by dubious regional arrangements raises awkward questions about Security Council overview of such interventions in both Europe and Africa. It is particularly evident in West Africa with ECOWAS's dominance by Nigeria, and to a lesser extent in SADC, especially in South Africa's manipulation of SADC to justify its intervention in Lesotho. The role of Russia in CIS peacekeeping operations in the "near abroad" is similarly suspect (MacFarlane 1998). A very real danger, therefore, is that regional actors may seek UN endorsement under the task-sharing arrangement in an effort to "cloak proposed actions in a collectively validated legitimacy" (Smith and Weiss 1998: 237). This is another expression of the fig leaf problem of humanitarian intervention we described in chapter 8.

Another problem facing many regional organizations is that they are primarily economic cooperation organizations. Extending economic cooperation to military cooperation leads to ambiguity and confusion about essential institutional purposes. It is not possible to maintain effective coherence by drafting an additional protocol to incorporate political and security dimensions or mechanisms for the prevention, management, and resolution of conflict (Malan 1998). This procedure, in both ECOWAS and SADC, for example, added a military dimension to existing rivalries contained in the economic organizations. The reality is that as intergovernmental actors, regional organizations are really only good at dealing with a narrow range of conflicts, namely, conflicts between member states over an issue of claims that can be settled by appeal to normative principles (Wolfers 1985: 186–87). The kinds of conflicts which have come to dominate the current international security agenda—complex internal conflicts, collapsed states, terrorism—are beyond the abilities of most regional arrangements. Internal conflicts, impinging as they do on issues of state sovereignty, are often very divisive and can strain the bounds of regional cohesion and consensus. This is especially true in regions dominated by weak states and where multilateralism is relatively shallow.

The Limits of MNF Peacekeeping

Obviously, MNF peacekeeping operations face most of the same problems faced by formal regional organizations in terms of their legal basis, conceptual framework, and operational challenges. However, they also face a number of unique obstacles. One of the main weaknesses of MNF task-sharing is the lack of binding ties between ad hoc coalition members (Goodpaster 1996: 20). In the absence of strong organizational and historical ties there is a constant danger of coalition disintegration if the political and operational pressures become too great. In addition, the lack of an established or appropriate military structure may cause operational problems. MNFs organize themselves with little or no precedent and often without existing peacekeeping support structures (Diehl 1993b: 137–38). This is not a problem when a powerful state uses its own military structure as the focus of organization, such as Australia's leadership in INTERFET, but in the Central African Republic the more diverse MISAB forces faced just these kinds of difficulties. A reliance on traditional military structures, however, can also mean using troops with no peacekeeping training or experience, which carries its own set of obvious problems.

Constructing a coalition around a single powerful state can also magnify the problem of power asymmetries and hegemonic dominance. MNF operations, as much as regional organizations, face the problem of perceptions of bias and impartiality. An operation dominated by the troops of one large state can begin to resemble a national operation, leading to claims of imperialism or worse. Last, in the absence of a regionwide or global coalition, MNFs are necessarily built on a fragile domestic consensus and thus can be more prone to the effects of public pressure.

Conclusion

In this chapter, we have attempted to provide an overview and assessment of the evolving conflict resolution method of regional task-sharing. Our task has not been easy, given the rapidity with which the task-sharing framework has evolved and its as yet undefined contours. Nonetheless, a number of important conclusions follow from our analysis. In the first place, task-sharing is undoubtedly here to stay. For the foreseeable future it is likely that most UN peacekeeping operations will involve some level of regional task-sharing (Jones 2004). The UN is overstretched, and in the absence of international leadership by the United States (absent except for situations directly linked to the "war on terror"), regional actors have no choice but to take responsibility for conflicts in their own localities. Thus, it is no longer a question of whether or not task-sharing is a good idea. Rather, the questions are primarily normative: What form should task-sharing take? What is the appropriate division of labor between the UN and regional bodies? What role can or should regional organizations play in conflict resolution? How can their efforts be improved? How can regional actors be held accountable to the wider international community?

Second, in spite of the wholehearted and enthusiastic adoption of the task-sharing framework, and in spite of its unquestioned importance for global governance, it is clearly no panacea for the problem of internal conflict, and there can be no automatic presumption in favor of the advantages it offers (Hurrell and Fawcett 1995: 314). The record of regional actors in post–Cold War conflict resolution is mixed to say the least, and the rhetoric of security regionalism is far ahead of the reality on the ground. Furthermore, the weaknesses of regional arrangements—organizational, structural, conceptual—while not immutable, are unlikely to change significantly in the near future. Regional actors will always be severely limited as agents of internal or domestic conflict resolution for the reasons we have outlined. They also would appear to face a comparative disadvantage in terms of peacekeeping and peace-enforcement, and are not a proven supplement to current UN arrangements (Diehl 1993b: 131). In fact, we would suggest that regional humanitarian intervention should be avoided if at all possible. Where it cannot be avoided, serious attention needs to be given to the question of how the Security Council and international community in general can restrain the illegitimate use of force by regional hegemons who try to cloak their self-interested designs in collective regional action.

In spite of the many problems and constraints facing regional bodies there are some important roles that they can and should play in international conflict resolution. Obviously, there is no question that regional arrangements have an important role to play in dealing with interstate disputes through diplomatic peacemaking, and in this regard they have a relatively strong record of success. In relation to internal conflicts, however, we suggest that regional arrangements can play an important role in the lower end of the conflict spectrum. Physically and culturally closer to the ground, regional organizations are ideally placed to facilitate early warning and preventive diplomacy, and in this aspect, they have a comparative advantage over the UN. Once a conflict is under way, however, regional organizations are likely to prove less able in conflict containment and even weaker in conflict termination. The UN and other actors should take the lead at this stage, although regional officials may still play a role in facilitating dialogue. The role performed by the joint UN/OAU representative to Africa's Great Lakes, Mohammed Sahnoun, might prove informative in this regard.

In the postconflict stage regional organizations can also play an effective role. Dealing with the roots of internal conflicts and preventing their reoccurrence involves moving beyond Track I diplomacy toward a range of Track II activities that can promote reconciliation, nation building, and durable human security. Here regional organizations can be involved in promoting Track II dialogue and reconciliation talks, human rights monitoring and training, election monitoring and good governance training, community development initiatives, economic reconstruction, and a range of other civilian tasks. In other words, regional organizations can be usefully employed in peacebuilding activities (see chapter 12). The OAS's role in monitoring elections in Nicaragua through the UN Observer Mission (ONUVEN) and in helping to disarm and reintegrate the Contras is informative here (Tascan 1998). Thus, while military aspects of security and peacekeeping should ideally be undertaken by the UN, civilian tasks can be coordinated and controlled by regional organizations. In Haiti, for example, the OAS/UN International Civilian Mission in Haiti (MICIVIH) apportioned all military activities to the UN, leaving the OAS responsible for civilian activities such as human rights observation, election monitoring, and restructuring the Electoral Tribunal (Tascan 1998).

These kinds of divisions of labor would seem to be a more appropriate model for dealing with internal conflicts in the post–Cold War security environment. If appropriate arrangements and mechanisms for UN-regional cooperation can first be conceptualized, then successfully institutionalized, security regionalism holds genuine potential for the more effective management and resolution of contemporary internal conflicts.

CHAPTER TEN ═══════════════════════════════

Nonofficial Diplomacy

Broadly speaking, there are two types of intervening actors in international conflict: official, diplomatic, and governmental actors (Track I diplomats) and informal, nonofficial, and private actors (Track II diplomats). Nonofficial or Track II diplomacy, once virtually invisible in international conflict resolution, is now a critical aspect of peacemaking efforts in virtually every internal war around the world. A facet of the democratization of world politics—the expansion of the nongovernmental sector into all aspects of global governance—the benefits of citizen-based peacemaking were most dramatically illustrated in the Rome Agreement in 1992 between the Mozambique rebel group Renamo (Resistencia Nacional de Mocambique) and the Frelimo (Frente da Libertacao de Mocambique) government, in the Oslo Accords of 1993 between the PLO and the Israeli government, and in the Inter-Tajik Dialogue in 1994. In each of these celebrated cases, private individuals acting in an unofficial capacity played key roles in gaining the trust of the parties and mediating peace agreements in conflicts that had thus far been resistant to traditional diplomacy. These examples clearly illustrated the ability of nonofficial mediators to gain entry into intractable intrastate conflicts and the potential synergies that can be achieved when official Track I and citizen-based Track II diplomats coordinate their activities into a single peacemaking effort.

Since the late 1980s, there has been a proliferation of NGOs established specifically for the task of conflict resolution in war-afflicted countries. By the mid-1990s, the Carter Center in Atlanta listed more than eighty international NGOs working specifically in conflict prevention and resolution. Many have large budgets and work simultaneously in dozens of countries. A well-known directory indicates that the twelve largest conflict resolution NGOs (those dedicated solely to conflict resolution activities, such as the Carter Center, Conflict Management Group, the Institute for Conflict Analysis and Resolution, International Alert, the International Crisis Group, the Institute for Multi-Track Diplomacy, Search for Common Ground, and the United States Institute for Peace) had a combined budget of $136 million in 2000 (Aall, Miltenberger, and Weiss 2000). In addition to these single-purpose organizations, thousands of humanitarian and relief assistance, human rights, environmental, civil society–and democracy-building NGOs, as well as churches, civic associations, and concerned individuals, have also started to incorporate conflict resolution training and conflict prevention and peacebuilding activities into their everyday work. Publications by the European Centre for Conflict Prevention describe 100 nongovernmental organizations working in the fields of conflict prevention and peacebuilding in Africa, 187 in Central and South Asia, and over 300 in Europe and Eurasia (Mekenkamp, van Tongeren, and van de Veen 1999, 2002; Van Tongeren, van de Veen, and Verhoeven 2002).

At the governmental level, foreign affairs departments and international organizations have begun to establish sections and units to liaise with NGOs working in areas of conflict. The United Kingdom, Canada, Switzerland, Netherlands, Finland, and Sweden, among others, have created peacebuilding units in their foreign ministries, allocated funds for conflict resolution activities, organized conferences for NGOs in conflict resolution, and in some cases, created special ambassadors with conflict resolution responsibilities (Peck 1999). The U.S. State Department encourages dialogue between official and unofficial diplomats through regular lunchtime meetings, while the Canadian government has sponsored numerous meetings between government officials and NGO representatives to discuss Asia-Pacific security (Chataway 1998: 282). Since the Oslo success in 1993, the Norwegian government has institutionalized its relationship with NGOs working in conflict resolution through the creation of the Norwegian Emergency Preparedness System and the Norwegian Resource Bank for Democracy and Human Rights (Lieberfeld 1995). These mechanisms involve a series of standby arrangements through which close cooperation takes place between NGOs, the Ministry of Foreign Affairs, and academic institutions in a wide variety of settings involving peacemaking and humanitarian assistance.

The UN has a long-standing relationship with NGOs through Article 71 of the Charter and the work of the Economic and Social Council (ECOSOC). NGOs can be accredited to the UN through the NGO and Institutional Relations section of the UN Department of Public Information (DPI). There are now more than 20,000 NGOs from every part of the world that have entered into some type of relationship with the UN system (Mawlawi 1993). Many of these work in the area of conflict resolution and are increasingly involved in UN peacekeeping operations. NGOs have also been heavily involved in UN Conferences, such as the four UN World Conferences on Women and Development (among others), and in 1997 senior representatives from CARE, Médecins sans Frontières, and OXFAM were invited to brief the UN Security Council on the conflict raging in Africa's Great Lakes region (McDonald 2003). More specifically, international organizations in general are increasingly meeting with NGOs to coordinate their conflict resolution activities. The OSCE, for example, cohosted a meeting with the Institute for Resources and Security Studies in 1995 to clarify and strengthen relationships between the OSCE and NGOs working in conflict resolution (Gutlove and Thompson 1995). Similarly, in the UN there is now an annual DPI-NGO conference, weekly briefings for NGOs, and quarterly workshops on issues of mutual interest.

In fact, nonofficial diplomacy has become an increasingly important facet of the emerging conflict resolution system for internal conflicts, even if its role is still little understood or appreciated by governmental officials. While NGOs are well known as essential players in the international response to humanitarian emergencies, human rights abuses, and physical and societal reconstruction efforts, their conflict resolution activities remain somewhat below the diplomatic radar. Recent publications by conflict resolution organizations (Mekenkamp et al. 1999, 2002; Van Tongeren, van de Veen, and Verhoeven 2002) are beginning to provide important accounts of the range of both official and nonofficial diplomatic efforts to resolve internal conflicts. Often working on the front line in a humanitarian capacity, and respected by all sides for their neutrality, NGOs are ideally placed to play a conflict resolution role and can have significant advantages over official diplomats.

In this chapter, we outline the functions, roles, and activities of NGOs and other nonofficial actors in the resolution of internal conflicts. We assess their advantages and disadvantages and suggest that they have a critical part to play in all phases of conflict resolution, from prenegotiation to mediation and into the implementation and postsettlement phases. In particular, the coordination of Track II diplomacy with official Track I efforts in the mediation stage offers tremendous possibilities for settling contemporary internal conflicts. Nonofficial diplomacy is an essential element of the kind of multidimensional approach that is necessary to resolve the deep roots of intractable internal wars.

Nonofficial Diplomats and International Conflict Resolution

The dramatic emergence of nonofficial diplomacy as an important strand of the emerging system for dealing with internal conflicts can be attributed to several key developments. First, at a broad level, there has been since the 1970s a democratization of global governance whereby nongovernmental actors—individuals, associations, organizations, religious groups, multinational companies, social movements—have come to play a more active role in both negotiating and implementing global governance policies. In the late 1990s, the Union of International Associations reported a total of 16,586 international NGOs (INGOs) of which about 50 percent were Northern-based organizations working in developing countries and supporting thousands of other local organizations (Aall, Miltenberger, and Weiss 2000: 89). It is estimated that there are now more than 50,000 NGOs worldwide (Van Tuijl 1999: 493). This represents a doubling of NGOs since 1978, and twenty times the 1951 number. This process has been facilitated by advances in communication and transportation that have made it easier for private citizens to become involved in the conduct of interstate relations. In addition, nongovernmental actors have intensified their activities in response to the political opportunities provided by the end of Cold War hostilities (Aall, Miltenberger, and Weiss 2000: 92). International organizations and diplomatic agendas are no longer off-limits to nonaligned or neutral actors like NGOs. The rise of issue areas demanding genuine global cooperation (as opposed to unilateral state action), such as environmental pollution, nuclear proliferation, disease control, and transnational organized crime (among others), combined with the erosion of the boundaries between high and low politics, has also created the space for concerned citizens to become involved in what were traditionally seen exclusively as interstate concerns.

In fact, the role of NGOs in supporting the efforts of international organizations has to a large extent now been institutionalized, one consequence of which has been a softening of official attitudes. Many diplomats are no longer inclined to hold the view that nonofficial actors are just "meddlers" in international politics. Rather, they now accept that NGOs are important for initiating and conducting research, formulating policy alternatives, monitoring policy implementation, and providing operative assistance (Berman and Johnson 1977: 21). Some even suggest "it is unlikely that modern-day conflicts can be resolved without some combination of Track I and Track II initiatives" (Chataway 1998: 272). As a result, there has been something of a proliferation of international institutions, conferences, and think tanks outside of official policy-making circles devoted to dealing with global governance issues, including, at an ever-increasing rate, conflict resolution.

Second, the high-profile successes of the Rome and Oslo Accords had a powerful demonstration effect, not only for the involvement of nonofficial actors in conflict resolution but also for the potentiality of combined Track I and II initiatives. The Community of Sant'Egidio, for example, successfully mediated the Mozambique peace process and has since launched similar peacemaking efforts in Kosovo, Algeria, and Guatemala. Similarly, Norway has attempted to employ the same kind of mediation approach—secret negotiations combining Track I and Track II processes, sometimes referred to as "Track 1.5"—in the Sudan and Sri Lanka. The success of the quasi-official Oslo talks made a strong impression on the views of diplomats about the possibilities of official and nonofficial cooperation in mediation (Chataway 1998: 273). At the same time, a large number of specialist NGO agencies have been established to promote peacemaking in internal conflicts through research and policy advice, direct mediation, problem-solving workshops, peace education activities, human rights advocacy and training, reconciliation, conflict prevention, and postconflict reconstruction work.

Nonofficial efforts at peacemaking have to a large extent been spurred on by the dismal record of traditional diplomatic mediation in protracted conflicts. It took three separate agreements—the Cotonou Agreement in 1993, the first Abuja Agreement in 1995, and Abuja II in 1996—brokered by international mediators (the first two failing completely) to finally bring a respite in the fighting to Liberia. This was followed by seven years of political instability and growing insurgent violence; even after Charles Taylor was exiled from Liberia in 2003, peace remained extremely fragile. In Angola, a full and final peace settlement was mediated in the 1991 Bicesse Peace Accord only for the fighting to reerupt in 1992 at an even greater level of ferocity than before. The pattern of diplomatically mediated agreements followed by further fighting continued in Angola for another decade until the death of UNITA's leader, Jonas Savimbi. In Somalia, the U.S./UN peace effort succeeded in bringing together warlords and faction leaders for mediated talks in several rounds in 1993–94. International mediation failed to settle the conflict, however, and the U.S./UN-led peace effort collapsed in ignominy in 1994. Mediation in the Balkans—at least a partial success in some eyes—failed to solve any of the underlying issues, and an uneasy peace is maintained by the presence of tens of thousands of heavily armed NATO troops. In Rwanda the mediated agreements in the Arusha Accords of 1993 were at the very least incapable of preventing the subsequent genocide, and at worst partly responsible for it. In numerous other internal conflicts—Kenya, Burundi, Democratic Republic of Congo, Ivory Coast, Myanmar, Kashmir, Israel-Palestine—international mediation failed (and continues to fail) to make a significant difference to the course of the conflict. Unsurprisingly, this sad litany has engendered a growing sense of pessimism about the ability of official third parties to deal effectively with contemporary conflict (Hampson 1997: 727) and encouraged nonofficial mediators to try their hand.

Fourth, the increased demand for humanitarian assistance in internal conflicts and the problems of mobilizing the official resources necessary for long-term reconstruction have led to a growing interest in the potential for nongovernmental conflict mitigation activities (Rouhana 1995). The UN estimated that there were 20.3 million refugees in 1999 and 20 to 30 million internally displaced persons (Aall, Miltenberger, and Weiss 2000: 92). A large proportion of these are located in Africa, the site of over a dozen internal wars in the 1990s and a region consistently marginalized in international policy-making circles. In other words, as violent civil conflicts have proliferated, particularly in peripheral areas of the world, so has the need grown for organizations specializing in humanitarian relief, conflict resolution, human rights protection, refugee assistance, and postconflict reconstruction. The flexibility of NGOs compared with official agencies means that they can more rapidly respond to emerging crises, quickly closing the gap between diplomatic recognition of a humanitarian disaster and the formulation of an international response. For example, in July 1994 at the height of the genocide there were only 3 international NGOs providing relief in Rwanda; by 20 September 1994 there were 106 (Aall, Miltenberger, and Weiss 2000: 93). Few official agencies—including the UN—could deploy to a remote developing country so rapidly.

Conceptualizing Nonofficial Diplomacy

We use the term *nonofficial diplomacy* to describe broadly the activities of private, nongovernmental actors seeking to prevent, resolve, or ameliorate violent political conflicts. Other terms used to describe the array of activities that fall outside official intervention include *Track II diplomacy, unofficial diplomacy, back-channel diplomacy, face-to-face diplomacy, problem-solving approaches, multitrack diplomacy, citizen-based diplomacy, nongovernmental diplomacy, nonofficial mediation,* and *interactive conflict resolution.* These terms tend to be used interchangeably, even though interactive conflict resolution and problem-solving approaches are really a subset of the broader category of nonofficial or Track II diplomacy. In interactive or problem-solving initiatives, trained scholar-practitioners run special conflict analysis workshops to facilitate dialogue between influential people from the societies in conflict (see Kelman 1992; Saunders 1987). The underlying assumption is that increased communication and understanding between middle-level leaders will permeate both upward to the Track I level and downward to the level of community reconciliation.

We conceive of nonofficial diplomacy as a broader concept, "encompassing the many kinds of nonofficial interaction between members of adversary groups or nations which aim to develop strategies, influence public opinion, and organize human and material resources in ways that might help resolve conflict" (Chataway 1998: 270; see also Montville 1987). In other words, it is defined by the nature of the intervention—aimed specifically at the resolution of conflict, rather than at mitigating humanitarian crises, for example—and the nature of the third party—an individual or organization not representing governments or official international bodies (Rouhana 1995: 257).

The Basis of Nonofficial Diplomacy

A basic premise of nonofficial diplomacy, long held by religious groups and gradually accepted in the 1980s by the wider conflict resolution community, is that conflict resolution expertise is not the exclusive domain of diplomats and government representatives, and private citizens acting in a nonofficial capacity have a great deal to offer. In fact, as the 1990s opened and official intervention in the bitter civil wars in Liberia, Somalia, and Bosnia failed to halt the carnage, conflict resolution activists and scholars started to assess the relative strengths and weaknesses of official and nonofficial diplomacy in internal conflicts. They came to the conclusion that resolving these "new wars," which were a different kind of conflict from the traditional interstate disputes of the past, required a multidimensional approach involving a range of actors, both official and unofficial. The multiple causes of internal conflicts required multiple conflict intervention tracks to resolve them.

The foundation of nonofficial diplomacy is the notion of complementarity and relative advantage. As the Carnegie Commission on Deadly Conflict put it, "the prevention of deadly conflict is, over the long term, too hard—intellectually, technically, and politically—to be the responsibility of any single institution or government, no matter how powerful. Strengths must be pooled, burdens shared, and labor divided among actors" (Carnegie Commission 1997). Not only do nonofficial diplomats have strengths and abilities in internal conflicts that official diplomats lack, but internal conflicts also require a range of activities at different social levels in order to be resolved, many of which are best (or sometimes only) undertaken by nonofficial actors. Diplomats, for example, cannot invest the necessary time and resources required to promote long-term societal reconciliation, whereas nonofficial actors are often in a better position to undertake such tasks.

A final assumption of nonofficial diplomacy is that conflict and conflict resolution have their roots in psychological processes (Montville 1991) and that resolving conflict therefore involves undermining manifestations of violence by altering the psychological climate between the antagonists. A psychologically based approach, nonofficial diplomacy assumes that altering the perceptions of both individuals and society at large, and meeting the psychological needs of the parties, are necessary for genuine conflict resolution over the long term (Burton 1979, 1987).

The Roles and Functions of Nonofficial Diplomacy

Nonofficial diplomats play a wide variety of roles in conflict resolution, many but not all of which remain in the background of official efforts. In the context of dealing with internal conflicts, however, they are no less important for sometimes being below the official radar. The following quote from the European Platform for Conflict Prevention and Transformation illustrates the wide variety of possible nonofficial conflict resolution activities.

> A freedom fighter, struggling against the military occupation of his land, is encouraged by a religious-based peace mission to try another approach. He puts down his weapons and opens a center for conflict resolution, to mediate local disputes and promote dialogue and nonviolence. A village elder, with modest financial help from an international agency, arranges a traditional ceremony of reconciliation to re-integrate child soldiers who committed atrocities, under duress, against their own families during a recent civil war. Mid-level community and political leaders attend a series of facilitated discussions with their counterparts across the communal divide of their conflict. Several years later, many are in important government positions, and ideas generated in those conversations begin appearing in the political discourse. An influential journalist meets with his colleagues from "the other side" of an ethnic conflict in an NGO-sponsored dialogue, and subsequently refuses to use stereotypical or derogatory language about "them" in his news coverage. (Diamond 1999)

In addition to activities that might be described under the general peacebuilding rubric—humanitarian assistance and emergency relief, human rights promotion, civil society and democracy building, resource mobilization—nonofficial actors play a number of targeted conflict resolution roles, including early warning and conflict prevention, national-level diplomatic mediation, local-level peacemaking, problem-solving or Track II work-

shops, building peace constituencies, conflict resolution training, peace education, and societal reconciliation.

The Institute for Multi-Track Diplomacy states that nonofficial diplomacy has three broad aims:

1. To reduce or resolve conflict between groups or nations by improving communication, understanding, and relationships;

2. To decrease tension, anger, fear, or misunderstanding by humanizing the "face of the enemy" and giving people direct personal experience of one another; and

3. To affect the thinking and action of Track One by addressing root causes, feelings, and needs and by exploring diplomatic options without prejudice, thereby laying the groundwork for more formal negotiations or for reframing policies (Diamond and McDonald 1996: 2).

Among nonofficial diplomats, religiously motivated actors have been described as having four kinds of conflict intervention roles (Sampson 1997: 279–80). First, as advocates they are primarily concerned with empowering the weaker parties, restructuring relationships, and working to transform unjust social structures. Second, nonofficial intermediaries devote themselves to peacemaking, through acting as a channel of communication or by bringing the parties together to facilitate dialogue. Third, observers act as a physical and moral presence in the conflict in an attempt to prevent further violence and transform the underlying conflict dynamics. Last, educators attempt to lay the groundwork for conflict transformation by changing people's perceptions through peace education and training programs.

An Overview of Nonofficial Diplomacy

While nonofficial diplomacy has certainly proliferated in the 1990s, it has in fact been an adjunct to international diplomacy for many decades. Although somewhat invisible until recently, nonofficial diplomacy has been reported in, among others, the Arab-Israeli conflict (Kelman 1979; Kelman and Cohen 1974; Rothman 1992; Rouhana and Kelman 1994; Watkins and Lundberg 1998; Corbin 1994; Aly 1994), the U.S.-USSR conflict during the Cold War (Chufrin and Saunders 1993; Saunders 1991), the Biafran war (Yarrow 1978; Sampson 1994), the Cyprus conflict (Doob 1974; Volkan 1988; Fisher 1992), India-Pakistan (Yarrow 1977; Fisher 1980), the Zimbabwean war of independence (Kraybill 1994), the Falklands-Malvinas conflict (Azar 1991), the conflict in Northern Ireland (Doob and Foltz 1973; Turner 1990), the Lebanonese civil war (Azar 1990), the Argentina-Chile Beagle Channel conflict (Princen 1987), the Nicaraguan civil war (Nichols 1994), and the Sri Lanka-Tamil conflict (Tiruchelvam 1996; Coy 1997; Goodhand and Lewer 1999). Many other efforts have no doubt gone unreported and unseen in the international conflict resolution literature.

The earliest and most prominent nonofficial diplomats were religious and spiritually oriented NGOs, many of them motivated by deeply held convictions and values and already working at a grassroots level in conflict-afflicted countries. Since World War II, for example, the American Friends Service Committee and the British Friends—otherwise known as Quakers—have mediated in several prominent international conflicts, sometimes even seconding their professional conciliators to the UN (Mawlawi 1993; Bailey 1985). Their conflict resolution roles grew out of their humanitarian activities and allowed them to intervene as trusted third parties in the Middle East (1955, 1967), between the two Germanys (1962–73), during the India-Pakistan war (1965), and in the Biafran civil war (1967–69). Other nonofficial diplomats have included: journalists (in the Cuban Missile Crises and during the Vietnam War, for example), lawyers (during the Iranian Hostage Crisis), retired diplomats (former President Jimmy Carter in Bosnia, Haiti, and Sudan), academics (in the Arab-Israeli conflict and the Vietnam War), the pope (in the Beagle Channel dispute), humanitarian NGOs (the ICRC in the Biafran conflict), and peacemaking NGOs (Moral Re-Armament in Zimbabwe).

As we have stated, nonofficial diplomacy has proliferated since the early 1990s as part of the democratization of global governance. Nonofficial diplomats are working in nearly every internal conflict in a wide variety of capacities from peace education to international mediation and reconciliation (see Mekenkamp et al. 1999, 2002; Van Tongeren, van de Veen, and Verhoeven 2002). The extent of nonofficial diplomacy in contemporary internal wars can be graphically illustrated by a partial listing of the internal and external religiously motivated groups who were working in fact-finding, consultation, facilitation of inter-religious dialogue, nonviolence training, and trauma healing in the former Yugoslavia in the late 1990s: the Center for the Promotion of Interreligious Dialogue, Justice, and Peace (Sarajevo); the Franciscans (Bosnia); Christian Information Service (Zagreb); Peace and Justice Institute of the Evangelical Theological Faculty (Osijek, Croatia); Conference of European Churches; World Council of Churches;

International Fellowship of Reconciliation; Pax Christi; World Conference on Religion and Peace; Mennonites, Quakers, and Methodists; Council of Churches for Britain and Ireland; Conflict Resolution Training Committee of the University of Bradford (Britain); Religion and Conflict Resolution Program of the Center for Strategic and International Studies (Washington, DC); International Orthodox Christian Charities (Baltimore); Appeal of Conscience Foundation (New York); and Catholic Relief Services (Baltimore) (Sampson 1997: 305–6). A careful examination of any of the world's current internal wars would reveal a similar list of nonofficial involvement.

Nonofficial Diplomacy in Mozambique

The story of the Mozambique peace process is a unique instance of international mediation in a regional conflict because it is one of the few cases where nonofficial diplomacy supplanted official Track I diplomatic efforts as the primary site for negotiations (Jackson 2005). Toward the conclusion of the talks, international diplomatic officials were brought back in to the process to add legitimacy, provide expertise, and add the kinds of resources unavailable to the nonofficial mediators. This coordination of unofficial and official diplomacy was a rare example of synergism in international mediation. There are in fact relatively few success stories in the mediation of intractable civil wars of the kind experienced in Mozambique and even fewer instances of major successes by nonofficial mediators in such major regional conflicts.

The Community of Sant'Egidio is a voluntary charitable Catholic organization based in Rome, but with 15,000 members worldwide and 300 local groups in Europe, Latin America, and Africa (Bartoli 1999). With an explicit commitment to peace and tolerance, Sant'Egidio has combined charitable work and political activities in numerous conflict-torn countries around the world. The Community started working in Mozambique in the late 1970s, forging important relationships with both the Frelimo government and Renamo over the next decade. Don Jaime Goncalves, the Archbishop of Beira, had also forged strong ties with Sant'Egidio while studying in Rome in 1976, thereby linking the local church in Mozambique with the Community in Rome. In early 1989, while official Track I diplomatic efforts to end the war were stalled, Mozambican church leaders launched a second track for exploring possible contacts (Msabaha 1995; Johnston 1994; Hume 1994).

For nearly a year and a half, church officials acted as

an unofficial communications channel between the two sides, relaying messages, building trust, and offering compromise suggestions. In late 1989, Sant'Egidio, together with Archbishop Goncalves and Mario Raffaelli (an Italian MP), offered to host face-to-face talks between Frelimo and Renamo. The parties agreed to face-to-face talks in July 1990, and eleven rounds and two years of negotiations started. Throughout the talks, Goncalves, Raffaelli, Sant'Egidio's founder Andrea Riccardi, and Don Matteo Zuppi (a Sant'Egidio parish priest), acted as the principal mediators, controlling the agenda for the talks, and offering numerous suggestions (Hume 1994). Along the way, the Vatican, the Italian government, the United States, the United Nations, and several other interested governments provided support, resources, and at times additional diplomatic mediation in the form of incentives to the parties. At all times, however, they resisted the temptation to take over the mediation process and turn it into an official Track I intervention. The mediation resulted in the signing of the Rome Agreement in October 1992 (sometimes called the General Peace Agreement or GPA). Over the following three years and with the aid of a major UN peacekeeping operation and continued international mediation by UN diplomats and concerned countries, the two armies were demobilized and reintegrated into a unified national army, free competitive elections were held, a new constitution was adopted, a program of national reconstruction got under way, and a fragile but sustained peace began to take hold.

Evaluating Nonofficial Diplomacy

Assessing the effectiveness of nonofficial diplomacy is problematic for a number of reasons. In the first case, the actors and activities of nonofficial diplomacy are extremely heterogeneous, involving different objectives (conflict management, conflict resolution, conflict prevention, reconciliation, peacebuilding), different time frames (short term, medium term, long term), different parties (top military and political leaders, community-level leaders, local communities, entire nations), and different social levels (individuals, groups, states). At the same time, there are few, if any, agreed criteria for evaluating the activities of nonofficial actors in conflict; in any case, the challenges involved in assessing the long-term effects of peace education, for example, are almost insurmountable. In addition, the work of nonofficial diplomats often requires a level of confidentiality that makes them invisible to the press or even to the academic community. In other words, there is sometimes little information about nonofficial activities to form the basis of more effective or more formal evaluation. Establishing any kind of causal link between the activities of nonofficial actors and peace in the wider society is therefore extremely difficult and requires a greater understanding of internal conflict resolution processes than we currently possess. Nevertheless, it is possible to make some broad generalizations based on both the theory and the practice of nonofficial diplomacy.

The Strengths of Nonofficial Diplomacy

The strengths of nonofficial diplomacy lie in the relative advantages that nonofficial actors possess over official actors by virtue of their organizational structures and characteristics. In addition, the nature of internal conflicts places limits on official actors that nonofficial actors are often exempt from.

Many contemporary internal conflicts preclude official intervention or mediation because they involve nonstate actors, such as insurgents, ethnic groups, militias, or rebellious army units. Diplomatic doctrine and practice—geared to managing disputes between states—denies nonstate actors any recognized role and does not provide adequate means for dealing with conflicts that involve parties not recognized as states (Hume 1994: 25). This is problematic for several reasons. In the first instance, mediator entry into the conflict is blocked when the government side does not want to confer recognition on the nongovernmental actor(s). In practical terms, it can make the apparently simple act of convening talks almost impossible. This issue prevented direct Israeli-PLO talks for many years and was only overcome by highly secret (and deniable) meetings involving nonofficial diplomats. In this sense, making use of nonofficial diplomats who have no official ties and who can bring the parties together in an informal, officially deniable setting, where the question of recognition and status is not an issue, can be a face-saving way out for governments and can overcome the entry problem faced by official diplomatic mediators. Disputants who refuse to recognize each other officially can meet face-to-face in an unofficial and neutral setting.

During the early phase of mediation—the so-called prenegotiation phase—nonofficial mediators can provide a degree of assurance not always available to official mediators. At the same time, their independence can facilitate the building of trust, which is a minimal prerequisite for starting substantive negotiations. Nonofficial mediators are also more easily dismissed without causing embarrassment, and their unofficial status brings with it a certain freedom from the constraints of protocol or oversensitivity to every nuance of the diplomatic process (Mawlawi 1993). They can move about more freely without the kind of publicity that official diplomats often attract. This means that they can achieve access to areas usually inaccessible to official agents.

Another problem with official Track I diplomacy is that diplomatic mediators are more likely to be biased toward state actors. For example, it is unlikely that a state or intergovernmental mediator would ever contemplate secession as a solution to internal conflict and would more likely try to reinforce the territorial status quo. Diplomacy is rooted in the formation of the state system, yet internal groups may be contesting the very nature of existing states (Lederach 1997: 16). Even actors like the UN, which are supposed to maintain strict neutrality in conflict intervention, retain their primary intergovernmental character. It is questionable whether such official bodies can act, or be perceived to act, as neutral parties in internal conflicts.

Nonofficial mediators, on the other hand, are less threatening to conflicting parties in intrastate conflicts precisely because they do not have any official affiliations. Nor do they have any military or economic capabilities that could be used to coerce the parties. Their neutrality (and lack of power) allows them to suggest unconventional remedies or procedures, and they are often less inhibited than a professional diplomat in raising hypothetical questions (Mawlawi 1993).

> The greatest asset that the non-official intermediary has is the freedom to be flexible, to disregard protocol, to suggest unconventional remedies or procedures, to widen or restrict the agenda or change the order of items, to propose partial solutions or package deals, to press the case for constructive initiatives or magnanimous gestures, to isolate those humanitarian issues where the obligations assumed by the parties are unconditional and do not depend on reciprocity. (Bailey 1985: 211)

Official diplomats face ever-increasing numbers of issue areas in their policy agendas, often at the same time as budgetary retrenchment, and there is an increasing need to outsource some functions (Chataway 1998: 272). The vast and growing networks of NGOs—business, academic, humanitarian, religious—are frequently cited as the most effective avenues for outsourcing, including many conflict resolution activities. In part, NGOs are an attractive alternative to official actors because they work at low cost and can "do more for less money" (Van Tongeren 2001). And unlike states, which must perform many functions, NGOs can focus on a single issue or set of issues.

The traditional diplomatic approach has been to employ various soft or hard forms of mediation predicated on the assumption that if a power-sharing agreement—a kind of "balancing"—can be forged between the faction leaders then the conflict can be terminated (Hampson 1997). This assumes that armed conflict is primarily motivated by some variety of "national interest" and solutions lie within a framework of rational political compromise on these issues, usually within a rather short-term frame of reference. In fact, there is frequently a subjective element to internal conflicts: generationally accumulated misperceptions and stereotypes, deep-rooted hatred, fear, and insecurity. Negotiations over substantive interests and issues, as important as they may be for securing an end to the violence, cannot solve the underlying conflict dynamics on their own. Without a more comprehensive and long-term approach that seeks to transform the underlying system of conflict, violence is likely to reerupt. Official diplomacy commonly suffers from an inability to address the psychological aspects of conflict, largely because diplomats do not have sufficient time to develop the necessary close relationships with the protagonists or the long-term commitment to the peace process needed for genuine conflict transformation (Mawlawi 1993).

Nonofficial diplomacy, especially activities oriented toward societal reconciliation and peacebuilding or interactive problem-solving workshops, seeks to deal with the deeper roots of internal conflicts and is a necessary complement to mediation at the leadership level. The psychological tasks generated by many internal conflicts defy the skills of traditional diplomacy. Studies show that resolving the psychological roots of conflict requires elaborate small-group leadership and large-group or nationwide processes involving the rehumanization of the adversary relationship, recognition of past and present grievances, offers and acceptance of forgiveness, and commitments to new higher moral values (Montville 1991: 261). The peace education and advocacy activities of conflict resolution NGOs also seek to address some of the psychological dimensions of conflict by helping to correct wartime propaganda, reshape popular perceptions of former enemies, publicize and prevent human rights abuses, defend minorities, and build confidence in democratic processes.

Nonofficial actors are far better placed than official actors to achieve these kinds of tasks.

Nonofficial diplomats also tend to place a higher emphasis on achieving a just peace than do most governments, laying the foundation for a more durable settlement by dealing with historical political grievances or the relative deprivation of at-risk social groups. This is critical for conflict prevention and long-term peacebuilding—dealing with the structural conditions that give rise to violent conflicts. Furthermore, nonofficial diplomats can often invest the time needed to establish credibility, gain a deep understanding of the underlying issues and dynamics of the conflict, and form relationships of trust with the parties. Many nonofficial diplomats belong to NGOs that have been working in the conflict-afflicted country for many years and are committed to staying through the long and difficult postconflict reconstruction phase. They bring with them a historical perspective and a developed understanding of the critical issues and are often in a better position than outside official mediators to interpret the motives and political objectives of the various factions. Their presence on the ground in poor and unstable regions also gives them a key role and an advantage in early warning and conflict prevention. And many NGOs will continue working in a conflict-affected country long after the world's media attention and diplomatic concern have moved on to the next humanitarian crisis.

Another important advantage for nonofficial actors in conflict situations lies in their decentralized decision-making structures, their mobility, and their flexibility. The ability and willingness to act with speed and respond pragmatically to immediate needs is a great asset in the tumultuous situations of internal war. NGOs are in fact among the best-equipped actors for responding to the sudden challenges of humanitarian crises (Aall, Miltenberger, and Weiss 2000: 97); not only do they have access to vast resources (a great many NGOs have budgets measured in the hundreds of millions of dollars, and collectively the NGO aid community raises billions of dollars for relief and development), but they have previous experience and institutional expertise in dealing with situations of conflict. Western NGOs and global religious organizations have the added advantage that they can act on different levels, both local and international; importantly, they are linked in to large networks and epistemic communities (local, regional, and global) and are capable of accessing global peace constituencies. They can draw upon public opinion to galvanize political will and claim legitimacy by virtue of popular representation.

There is an increased recognition that religious actors have important advantages over other kinds of actors in many of today's internal conflicts. In societies where traditional leaders—spiritual or cultural—play an important role in shaping the motivations of both individuals and entire communities, mediators operating from an ethical or religious point of view may have an advantage as politically nonpartisan agents who can evoke trust and promote reconciliation (Hackett 2000: 274). Peacemaking on the part of religious leaders is seen as consistent with religious belief, and religious leaders are trusted to speak the truth. In some societies, the church is the only institution having moral authority in the eyes of the populace, and it can mobilize community support to reinforce the peace process in ways that other actors cannot (Johnston 1994: 316–17; Sampson 1997: 275). Religious actors possess important assets that can be mobilized to address situations of armed conflict, such as schools, publishing houses, charities, and convening capacity.

The local church, as a community insider, is also in a strong position to follow through on the implementation of a settlement and to promote peacebuilding. In internal conflicts where antagonists live in close proximity and where atrocities and human rights violations have taken place, it is necessary to move beyond conflict management to reconciliation and healing in order to arrest the cycle of revenge and violence (Sampson 1997: 275–76). It is often easier for religious figures to talk about confession, repentance, forgiveness, and mercy—the processes at the heart of reconciliation—than it is for secular leaders or official diplomats, and to date, reconciliation initiatives have tended to emerge from religious, not secular, contexts. The work of Sant'Egidio in Mozambique and elsewhere is a pertinent example of these processes. Based explicitly on its religious piety and commitment to justice and peace, and drawing on its established record for humanitarian care and concern, Sant'Egidio representatives possess a moral authority and respect that allow them to influence individuals and communities even in places like Kosovo and Algeria where the majority population is Muslim. In chapter 11, we describe the role of religious actors in truth-telling and reconciliation processes, such as Bishop Desmond Tutu's leadership of the Truth and Reconciliation Commission in South Africa.

At a broader level, NGOs play a vital role in strengthening the resiliency of societies. Research has shown that a strong civil society enables a nation to survive the destabilizing effects of structural, political, and cultural tensions, particularly through its mediating function (Hackett 2000: 282). As the South African peace process illustrated, a strong civil society, supported by transnational movements and networks, can mitigate violent conflict through a tumultuous period of social transformation (Marks 2000). More broadly, international NGOs, particularly when they work with partners in developing countries, can strengthen democratic processes and the development of civil society.

In sum, nonofficial actors play vital roles at all stages and levels of conflict: early warning and conflict prevention in the lead-up to outbreaks of violence; peacemaking and mediation during violent phases of the conflict; and reconciliation and peacebuilding in the postconflict phase. They also have roles to play in short-term activities like the provision of relief during a humanitarian crisis, as well as long-term activities like strengthening civil society and constructing cultures of peace. And the local, national, and international networks and epistemic communities they are part of create real possibilities for constructing wider peace constituencies. Moreover, empirical studies have begun to demonstrate the extent to which, in a great many conflict situations, civil groups and institutions such as churches and women's groups are able to bring about real conflict resolution and reconciliation at the community level (Mekenkamp, van Tongeren, and van de Veen 2002).

The Challenges of Nonofficial Diplomacy

The strengths of nonofficial diplomacy can, under different circumstances, turn out to be profound weaknesses. Religious actors, for example, can in some societies fuel ethnocultural and nationalist rivalries; at the very least, they may be perceived as being inherently biased toward one side. This is particularly true in countries where religion has been used to mobilize the population for ethnonationalist causes, such as Northern Ireland, the Balkans, Indonesia, Nigeria, and elsewhere. To date, religiously motivated peacemaking has had its greatest impact in conflicts where religion is not a major factor (Sampson 1997: 274–75). We consider the challenges facing nonofficial diplomacy under two headings: the challenge of theory and the practical limitations of nonofficial actors.

Theoretical Challenges

One of the most serious challenges facing nonofficial diplomacy is its lack of a strong theoretical foundation. Like humanitarian intervention (see chapter 8), there is as yet no theory of nonofficial intervention through which to guide strategies or evaluate outcomes (Anderson 1999;

Voutira and Brown 1995). In the first place, there is no standardized lexicon of terms, and concepts like conflict resolution, peacemaking, conflict management, and conflict transformation—to use a simple illustration of the broad goals of nonofficial diplomacy—are used interchangeably by both scholars and practitioners. At a more fundamental conceptual level, there is still a question over whether Track II is simply an extension of Track I or whether it is a different kind of conflict resolution approach altogether. This in turn raises theoretical (and practical) questions about the proper relationship between the official and nonofficial tracks. In terms of the normative goals of nonofficial diplomacy there are also controversies. The question of the use of leverage by mediators, for example, is still highly controversial in nonofficial conflict resolution circles. While some suggest that it is acceptable "to seek to influence the parties to make concessions by exerting pressure and offering incentives" (Touval 1982: 32–33), others argue that "international mediators are ineffective, if not counter-productive, when they deviate from the logic of mediation and apply undue pressure on the parties" (Nathan 1999: 23; see also Burton 1969).

This problem is itself related to other important ethical considerations: Should nonofficial diplomats remain neutral in the face of human rights violations? Under what circumstances is it acceptable to work with a government or an international organization in a peacemaking effort? Does the goal of ending the violence justify making concessions to war criminals and including them in the peace process? How are the goals of peace and justice reconciled, when securing peace may involve giving amnesty to human rights violators? To date, there is little agreement on the ethical principles that should guide nonofficial diplomacy, and each group tends to follow its own path. More fundamentally, there are ethical issues involved in raising the expectations of people who have suffered conflict for a long time and who may perceive that external agencies will automatically be able to improve their lives (Rouhana 1995: 266–67). There is also a whole range of issues surrounding the imposition of cultural and political values: Western NGOs coming to "train" local people in dispute resolution, for example, when traditional modes of conflict resolution already exist. Last, there is a crucial issue surrounding the relationship between the amelioration of physical violence and the persistence of structural violence; in some cases, conflict resolution at the microlevel may act as an agent of control at the macrolevel—a means of preserving the status quo. Groups reacting violently to the structural violence of global economic and military structures, for example, may be persuaded to lay down their arms so the existing order can be maintained. In other words, the relationship between conflict resolution and structural transformation of those conditions that give rise to violence in the first instance—injustice, relative deprivation—has yet to be fully theorized and articulated (Clements 2002; Ramsbotham, Woodhouse, and Miall 2005).

Another theoretical challenge lies in the relationship between methods and goals. This in turn requires a coherent theory of conflict dynamics and conflict resolution (Rouhana 1995: 259–60). There is in fact little evidence that nonofficial diplomats always have a strong theoretical understanding of the nature of internal conflict or of the ways in which their intervention impacts on conflict dynamics (Anderson 1999). Most operate on general assumptions that breaking down stereotypes, for example, will improve communication and lead to reconciliation. Narrow and intuitive approaches such as this ignore other important factors that sustain conflict, such as the power structures, inequalities, and the political economy of internal wars. An exception to this is the problem-solving workshop approach (see Kelman 1992), which clearly specifies how the design of the workshops promotes societal conflict resolution based on a model of conflict dynamics. For the most part, however, lacking clearly articulated goals and methods, many nonofficial diplomats rely on instinct, intuition, and no small amount of experimentation. In addition, there has been very little empirical evaluation of the field's achievements and failures (Voutira and Brown 1995), and there are few formal systems of accountability. This makes progress toward greater effectiveness and efficiency very difficult.

A consequence of the theoretical vacuum is that nonofficial diplomacy, unlike other areas of conflict resolution or professional activity, is unregulated in terms of professional training and standards. Most nonofficial diplomats are motivated and sustained primarily by goodwill. There is therefore a great need to develop some kind of certification process for nonofficial actors that would signify their competence to operate in conflict zones (Weiss 1998: 48).

Practical Challenges

It is now understood that intervention into a violent conflict can never be entirely neutral or nonpartisan; when external actors attempt to mediate or distribute aid they become a part of the conflict setting—whether they are aware of it or not. The impact of their efforts will worsen or ameliorate the conflict, often in unanticipated ways (Anderson 1999). Due to the nature of their activities, NGOs are particularly vulnerable to unwittingly exacerbating the conflict. In terms of resource transfers, for example, the provision of aid can reinforce and prolong conflict through the looting of aid supplies by the combatants; the negative impact of external aid on local economies and productive capacities; raising intercommunal tensions through distributional inconsistencies; and reinforcing war economies. Similarly, when NGOs hire local bodyguards for protection, it reinforces an implicit ethical message that in a war zone it is legitimate to employ arms and that security comes through the possession of weapons. The main challenge for nonofficial diplomacy lies in constantly evaluating the practical outcomes of intervention actions to ensure that such unforeseen consequences do not exacerbate the conflict.

Many of the strengths of nonofficial diplomacy are simultaneously also weaknesses. The lack of official status, for example, means that nonofficial actors have no economic, political, or military sources of leverage with which to extract concessions from the parties. In cases of impasse or deadlock, it may be necessary for the mediator to use some kind of political or economic pressure to move the parties along toward settlement. Nonofficial diplomats have no such leverage at their disposal and must rely on official support or the less reliable process of applying moral pressure. In addition, problems for nonofficial diplomats may include lack of diplomatic skills and experience, lack of the physical resources for complex negotiations, such as the necessary administrative infrastructure (access to information, communication equipment, translators, clerical assistance, constitutional or military expertise), and the lack of diplomatic immunity and privileges accorded to official representatives (Mawlawi 1993). In the Mozambique peace process, for example, the Sant'Egidio mediators had to rely on the Italian (and later the American) government to provide the material resources and expert knowledge necessary for the talks to continue.

Another key challenge for many NGOs lies in securing the funds necessary for achieving their goals. While some NGOs only accept money from private sources (fearing that government funding will necessitate compromises and a loss of independent decision making), others accept public money but maintain an uneasy relationship with government providers. Without official assistance, in fact, a significant proportion of NGO activity would cease altogether. In the United States, 25 percent of the $9.5 billion raised by humanitarian organizations in 1999 came from official sources (Aall, Miltenberger, and Weiss 2000:

99–100). At the same time, the costs of government patronage can be high. Governments often put economic and political considerations above humanitarian ones and prefer short-term relief to long-term development projects. Sometimes governments give assistance to the victims of officially sanctioned violence while maintaining relations with the offending government, in some cases through continuing arms sales and military ties. The need to secure resources therefore imposes a set of complex ethical choices on many nonofficial actors.

Similarly, the coordination of official and nonofficial diplomacy in peacemaking efforts, such as occurred in Oslo and Mozambique, can be risky for nonofficial actors. There is the possibility that official diplomats will use them to test out ideas (which can then be disclaimed) or set them up as a kind of straw man (Chataway 1998: 274). Being manipulated by officials in this way can be damaging to nonofficial diplomats' reputations and block their future involvement in conflict resolution efforts. In other situations, the presence of nonofficial peacemakers in a conflict can become a pretext for government inaction. In this context, NGO involvement can act as a fig leaf to cover the unwillingness of the international community to deal with a difficult and troublesome situation.

A related problem lies in the media-driven interest in humanitarian crises that funds the work of NGOs. The financial life of these organizations is complicated by the fickle nature of public exposure. When public interest dies down due to reduced media exposure or when "donor fatigue" or "compassion fatigue" sets in, the level of donations frequently plummets, leaving NGOs without the financial resources to complete their projects or retain their skilled staff (Aall, Miltenberger, and Weiss 2000: 100). The importance of publicity for raising funds can also create what looks like an unseemly competition among humanitarian organizations. At the same time, the funding community looks for product, whereas the work of nonofficial diplomacy is often focused on process: "Foundations want time-limited projects with clear objectives and measurable outcomes, but conflict resolution is an open-ended process with impossible-to-measure results" (Diamond and McDonald 1996: 41).

The nature of today's internal conflicts pose serious problems for the neutrality of nonofficial actors and ethical dilemmas for all agencies—NGOs as well as official bodies like the UN—that come in from the outside to help. NGOs that seek to provide relief assistance or promote conflict resolution in internal conflicts always run the risk of being perceived as biased toward the groups they are trying to help (Aall, Miltenberger, and Weiss

2000: 106–7). As we have said, there is no such thing as nonpartisan or neutral intervention, and nonofficial diplomats must be constantly aware of the impact of their actions. Lacking the sophisticated intelligence capabilities of the military or of state governments, external NGOs may also find it difficult to understand who the players are in the conflict. They may inadvertently find themselves bringing aid and support to groups who are in fact perpetuating violence, such as the massive humanitarian operation in eastern Zaire in 1994–96 that sustained the Hutu extremists, allowing them to organize cross-border raids back into Rwanda. This places a heavy moral burden on humanitarian organizations, as neither alternative—providing relief aid, which might indirectly contribute to the long-term continuation of the conflict, or refusing to provide relief aid, which could lead to immediate large-scale human suffering—is an ethically desirable outcome. The consequences of relief may not be immediately obvious, after which time it is difficult to then withdraw aid from suffering people. Relief operations can sometimes give support to counterinsurgency tactics. For example, military forces may be encouraged to maintain the levels of hunger and suffering at critical levels to ensure the continuation of large-scale outside relief or to herd civilians into closed camps where the distribution of aid can be controlled. This has been the situation in Southern Sudan for decades.

Despite the general softening of attitudes toward nonofficial diplomats, a measure of discomfort with their increasing involvement in international affairs remains evident. The U.S. government continues to carefully regulate the unauthorized involvement of its citizens in international affairs; in fact, the Logan Act of 1799 is still on the books. This law makes it illegal for any U.S. citizen without authorization to "directly or indirectly commence or carry on any correspondence or intercourse with any foreign government or any officer or agent thereof, with intent to influence the measures or conduct of any foreign government or of any officer or agent thereof, in relation to any disputes or controversies with the United States" (quoted in Berman and Johnson 1977: 2). Diplomats often doubt the sources of information from nongovernmental actors, distrust their motives, look down on their lack of resources, and retain doubts about their ability to act professionally and competently in the world of diplomacy. Because of an inherent official resistance to change and bureaucratic inertia, nonofficial actors remain unrecognized in many diplomatic efforts to resolve conflicts with few formal avenues for involvement in international organizational or governmental decision making, despite being present on the ground. This creates a related coordination problem, as official and nonofficial tracks mostly work independently of each other. This can lead to duplication, competition or even to the disputing parties playing the mediators against each other. Therefore, a key challenge, in addition to overcoming official reticence, is to define the respective roles and responsibilities of Track I and II so that they can function more smoothly together.

Among nonofficial diplomats themselves there are problems of coordination, fragmentation of effort, diffusion of responsibility, and often a flagrant lack of communication as each group tries to keep control over its own projects and activities at the expense of an overall coordinated program. Partly, this is because nonofficial diplomats do not see themselves as being part of a larger system of conflict resolution. Rather, they tend to be somewhat insular, often believing that their goals and activities are the most important track to conflict resolution (Diamond and McDonald 1996: 142). The result is overlap and competition between groups, gaps in the field, missed opportunities for collaboration and mutual enrichment, bottlenecks of resources and information, and a failure of leadership. It can also send an implicit message to the protagonists that it is unnecessary to cooperate with those one disagrees with, thus creating a further obstacle to genuine conflict resolution. Without stronger networking, the free sharing of skills and information, setting up professional standards, the establishment of structures of mutual support, and the coordination of activities in zones of conflict, nonofficial diplomacy is in danger of dissipating its energy in different directions or even undermining its overall goals.

Conclusion

Nonofficial diplomacy—like the other more recent methods of conflict resolution we have examined so far in this book—possesses tremendous potential for dealing with intractable internal wars. Nonofficial actors have advantages over, and can do things, that diplomats and official actors cannot. In a sense, nonofficial diplomacy has emerged partly to fill the vacuum in the international conflict resolution system and to mitigate its most blatant failures. There exists no other international, reputable, reliable institution for peacemaking in internal wars beyond the UN, which is forbidden by its charter from intervening in the "domestic affairs" of one of its members

(Diamond and McDonald 1996: 3). And as we explained in chapter 5, the UN has other in-built limitations for resolving contemporary internal wars. The founding principle of international relations limits all official actors—states and intergovernmental organizations—from effectively intervening in domestically based conflicts. The rise of nonofficial diplomacy and its increasing acceptance as a method of dealing with internal conflict also reflects the growing acceptance of an alternative conflict resolution paradigm (Diamond and McDonald 1996: 24). Among diplomats, especially in the UN, there is recognition that resolving internal conflicts requires more than diplomatic bargaining or the deployment of a traditional peacekeeping operation. It involves a multidimensional approach that simultaneously tackles the political, economic, social, and psychological roots of the conflict and requires a range of actors—diplomats, peacekeepers, NGOs, and external and internal parties—to coordinate their activities in a long-term peacebuilding program (see Miall, Ramsbotham, and Woodhouse 2002). Nonofficial diplomats, then, are active agents in the articulation and practical outworking of this new paradigm. In reality, nonofficial diplomacy is now a permanent feature of the international conflict resolution system; it is probably here to stay. The real question is not whether such actors should be involved in such activities, but how their ubiquitous involvement can be made more effective and how it can be better coordinated with Track I efforts.

The proliferation of nonofficial diplomacy has brought with it an accompanying confusion over roles and aims, serious problems of coordination and competition, and a general vacuum of theory to underpin practice that threatens its overall credibility and acceptance as an alternative paradigm.

Just as the field receives serious scrutiny from skeptics and at a time when its contribution is most needed, it is in danger of going off in the very direction about which critics have warned from the beginning. It would appear that unofficial third-party intervention is at a critical crossroad: If it heads in one direction, it can become legitimized as an area of study and a beneficial method of intervention in ethnic and international conflict that can supplement existing traditional diplomatic methods. If it heads in the other direction, unofficial intervention—unguided by theory and unchecked by professional standards, accountability, and meticulous ethical considerations—it will risk gaining credibility as a legitimate method of intervention, and scholars and diplomatic practitioners will be less inclined to take it seriously. (Rouhana 1995: 256)

We believe that nonofficial actors have important roles to play at every stage in the resolution of internal conflicts, and it is time to bring them into the mainstream of diplomatic practice. For example, they can play key roles in early warning and conflict prevention through their presence in regions of conflict, they can mediate directly with the protagonists in situations where official actors are denied access, and they can be brought into peacebuilding processes to undertake tasks that official actors cannot do, such as reconciliation and relationship-building. In order to realize this potential, however, official actors will need to put greater efforts into establishing mechanisms and procedures for the coordination of Track I and Track II interventions. There are a growing number of examples of such coordination, such as the Mozambique, Oslo, and Tajik peace processes; they provide valuable lessons and insights into the practicalities of coordinated and holistic efforts.

CHAPTER ELEVEN

Reconciliation and Justice

Reconciliation and justice approaches, most often seen in truth commissions (TC) and human rights trials, have emerged in recent years as one of the most visible strategies for national reconstruction of the moral and political order following civil war or repressive dictatorship. Their aim is to deal decisively with the past, particularly the legacy of massive human rights abuses, and lay the foundations for a peaceful and democratic future. Since World War II, there have been more than thirty national truth commissions, plus twenty-four special commissions of inquiry, as well as three international criminal trials—the international criminal tribunals for the former Yugoslavia (ICTY), Rwanda (ICTR), and Sierra Leone (SCSL)—and more than twenty national trials (see Annan 2004; Balint 1997; Hayner 1994). More than half of these commissions and trials have taken place since 1991. Perhaps the most widely known truth commission (as well as being the best-staffed, most well-funded, and most ambitious truth commission yet), the South African Truth and Reconciliation Commission (TRC), was established in 1995 to investigate human rights abuses during the apartheid era. Due to its unrivaled media attention, it soon became an internationally recognized blueprint for other states emerging from war or dictatorship. Highly visible and charged with symbolism and emotion, reconciliation and justice are now a key part of the international diplomacy of intervention, often receiving widespread material and political support. Indeed, the truth commission model has become so popular that it is in danger of being perceived as some kind of magical panacea for societal reconciliation, rather than as simply one of a range of measures

needed to reconstruct societies that have been torn apart by conflict (Popkin and Roht-Arriaza 1995: 80).

Likewise, justice approaches and the concept of "the rule of law" have also emerged as panaceas, bolstered prominently by the well-publicized work of the ICTY and ICTR in trying high-profile suspects like former head of state Slobodan Milošević. The much-heralded establishment of the International Criminal Court (ICC) on 1 July 2002 and its subsequent ratification by more than ninety countries has reinforced this trend. The tacit promise of stability and "the aphoristic sense that law is a prerequisite for peace have imbued the concept with an enduring appeal as a mechanism for restoring long-term stability as well as short-term order to post-conflict societies" (Mani 1998: 2). Consequently, trials, prosecutions, and special tribunals are now the almost automatic method of choice for nations emerging from war or dictatorship.

Unfortunately, reconciliation and justice are still poorly understood and conceptualized, and there is as yet very little empirical evidence to properly evaluate their effectiveness (Hayner 1994: 598; Pankhurst 1999: 239). Their widespread popularity seems to be based on a priori beliefs about their efficacy and the acceptance of human rights values, rather than on any sound theoretical or empirical foundation. In this chapter we present an overview of how reconciliation and justice approaches work—their rationale, the forms they take, and their roles and functions. We also offer a more realistic assessment of their effectiveness in building peaceful societies. We argue that while reconciliation and justice are important for postconflict peacebuilding, they are in danger of being overemphasized and should be considered only one of many postconflict activities that need to be undertaken. There are in fact many problems and challenges involved in pursuing either reconciliation or justice in the aftermath of mass atrocity and human rights violations, and it is perhaps too early to say how useful these approaches really are with any degree of confidence.

The Internationalization of Justice

Reconciliation and justice approaches have emerged in the context of the profound restructuring of the international system that took place at the end of the 1980s. Two key movements in particular have contributed to the spread of these methodologies of conflict resolution. First, there has been the phenomenon of what may be termed "the internationalization of justice" (Newman 2002: 32). This refers to the spread and strengthening of international human rights law and humanitarian law (seen in a growing number of international conventions and treaties—what some perceive as an emergent human rights regime), the diffusion of universal human rights values and ideals, the establishment of international war crimes tribunals and the ICC, numerous national trials of human rights abuses, the emergence of large numbers of human rights–based NGOs and an increasingly active international civil society, and the establishment of more and more international bodies devoted to the promotion and strengthening of universal human rights.

The second movement grew directly out of the end of the Cold War, when a large number of postcommunist states in eastern Europe faced the problems associated with dealing with the repression of the past and constructing stable democracies. Around the same time, a number of military and civil dictatorships in Latin America, Africa, and Asia (the so-called third wave of democracy) began to make way for more participatory forms of government, while a number of long-running civil wars—El Salvador, South Africa, Ethiopia, Mozambique, Namibia, and Cambodia—negotiated an end to the violence, sometimes including the provision of truth commissions or human rights trials as part of the peace settlement. There was at this time an understandable sense of urgency in the quest to find suitable mechanisms for managing transitions and building stable peace in the aftermath of civil war. Reconciliation and justice approaches were seen as the main vehicle for this. Moreover, the overwhelming publicity given to the South African TRC and the percep-

tion that it was extremely successful reinforced the view that transitions from war or dictatorship were best managed by way of truth commissions.

These two movements amount to a paradigm shift in attitudes; it is now increasingly accepted that some form of accountability and justice—whether through truth commissions or prosecutions—is integral to peace and stability in postconflict societies (Newman 2002: 31). This is an important shift from the normal diplomatic practice of disengagement once a political compromise has been agreed to. There is a growing recognition that intrastate conflicts require postconflict peacebuilding measures to ensure that violence does not reignite.

Conceptualizing Reconciliation and Justice Approaches

There is as yet no generally accepted theory of reconciliation and justice, although there are some recognized writings on the subject of "transitional justice" (or "transitology") and postconflict peacebuilding (see Hayner 1994; Kritz 1995; Lederach 1997). There is broad agreement in the literature that some kind of reconciliation and/or justice is a necessary ingredient in postconflict reconstruction. In other words, the rationale of reconciliation and justice is that the past must be dealt with if a more peaceful future is to be constructed. Unlike situations of traditional interstate war, where groups of people in conflict are separated by borders and distance and may choose to simply avoid contact with each other, in intrastate wars people have to continue living together in close physical and emotional proximity. They are usually bound by an array of intimate and complex relationships—various kinds of political and economic interdependencies, social ties, and historical and cultural commonalities. They have no choice but to deal with the issues dividing them and construct a common vision for the future. This is impossible without confronting the past, especially when it involves serious abuses that can form the basis of renewed hostility. Reconciliation and justice approaches, then, fit into the broad array of measures that are needed for postconflict peacebuilding, conflict transformation, and conflict prevention.

Truth-Telling and Reconciliation

At the heart of the theory of reconciliation rests the notion that those who were divided by enmity must be prepared to imagine a shared future. For this to occur, they are required to forgive the past (but not necessarily to forget the past), forsake the search for vengeance, acknowledge a shared humanity with their enemies, and experience an internal healing of the deep emotional wounds generated by the conflict (see Humphrey 2002: 118–19; Rigby 2001: 12–13). Reconciliation is impossible without forgiveness, which is the ability to let go of the pain of the past; but it is difficult to forgive without knowing exactly what happened or who was responsible (Hartwell 1999). As Newman explains, "The restorative meaning of forgiveness—a concept of reconciliation based upon repairing relations—is undermined when it is faced with recalcitrance, lack of information, and disputes about wrongdoing" (2002: 36). Truth-telling, therefore, is a crucial element in the enactment of forgiveness.

But reconciliation can encompass a wider meaning than this. According to John Paul Lederach, reconciliation is the process and the place where truth, mercy (forgiveness), justice, and peace come together.

> *Truth* is the longing for acknowledgement of wrong and the validation of painful loss and experience, but it is coupled with *Mercy*, which articulates the need for acceptance, letting go, and a new beginning. *Justice* represents the search for individual and group rights, for social restructuring, and for restitution, but is linked with *Peace*, which underscores the need for interdependence, well-being, and security. (1997: 29)

In its practical outworking, reconciliation entails the following core elements: the honest acknowledgment of the harm and injury that each party has inflicted on the other; the expression of sincere regrets and remorse for the injury caused and a readiness to apologize for one's role in it; the willingness of the conflicting parties to let go of the anger and bitterness caused by the conflict; a commitment by the perpetrator not to repeat the injury; sincere efforts to redress past grievances and compensate the victims as far as is possible; and the entering into of a new, mutually enriching relationship (Assefa 2001: 340). Reconciliation refers to the kind of relationship that emerges from these processes, and its essence is the voluntary initiative of the conflicting parties to acknowledge their responsibility.

In short, reconciliation is restorative and future- and relationship-oriented, and the forces for change are primarily internal and voluntary. It is on the individual level that reconciliation really takes place and that the "seeds for societal transformation are planted" (Shea 2000: 7).

Truth and reconciliation commissions—the institutionalized expression of the theory of reconciliation—are designed to facilitate the truth-telling part of this process, in the hope that it will engender forgiveness, a measure of catharsis, the forsaking of vengeance, the humanization of both victims and perpetrators, and the chance to articulate the vision of a common future. For example, the truth-telling part of a commission's work is very important for deconstructing enemy images and allowing each party, both victim and perpetrator, to recognize the ordinary humanity of the Other. Such encounters are vital for breaking down the hostility between groups that sustains civil wars and for enabling social reintegration. Furthermore, it is foreseen that through widespread publicity and the ritualistic and symbolic nature of the hearings and the subsequent commission report, reconciliation will spread beyond individuals to the wider society, thereby producing a kind of national healing.

It is worth noting the way in which truth commissions differ from trials in their conception of healing society.

> While truth commissions focus on the ritual "purification" of the individual, trials focus on the ritual purification of society. Truth commissions, focusing on the suffering of individual victims, employ the language of psychology. The legacy of violence is supposed to be expelled from the individual through the cathartic experience of revealing and sharing it. This ritual process is in turn meant to be socially healing through the public witnessing of the truth about the origins of that suffering. Without a trial, reconciliation is focused on containing the violence potentially arising from the victim's desire for revenge. . . . Trials, on the other hand, seek to achieve social healing by identifying the source of the violence and expelling (imprisoning, executing) those responsible from society as a punishment. Society is "healed" through the prosecution and punishment of the perpetrator, who in turn provides the social benefit of the moral renewal of the national community. (Humphrey 2002: 127)

Transitional Justice

If reconciliation approaches are based on a mental health model, justice approaches are based on a legal paradigm. The theory and rationale behind justice approaches to transitions is that the investigation and punishment of human rights violators is necessary for putting back in place the moral order of society. They achieve this by first of all restoring public confidence in state institutions, which can in turn strengthen fragile democracies. Failing to prosecute may generate feelings of cynicism and distrust toward the political system (Huyse 2001: 325). Second, trials are crucial for reestablishing the rule of law and standards of human rights observance; that is, they inculcate codes of conduct based on the rule of law. Third, prosecutions can play a key role in breaking down the culture of impunity and disrespect for human rights and may act as a future deterrent to abuses. Fourth, prosecutions are important for countering the deceptions and justifications of the security forces responsible for the abuses. Fifth, they are useful for moving fairly recent and still potent events into the more distant category of history, thereby establishing a line between past and present. Sixth, trials are important for creating at least the perception of justice being done for the victims. It is argued that successor governments owe it as a moral obligation to the victims of the repressive system. In any case, unacknowledged wrongs constitute a continuing affront to society and may lead to the reignition of conflict later. Last, prosecutions can act as a sort of ritual cleansing process that paves the way for moral and political renaissance (Huyse 2001: 324). In addition, many would argue that there is now an international legal obligation to punish war crimes and large-scale human rights abuses, as well as a "right to know the truth" about the results of such prosecutions (Hayner 1994: 611; Mendez 1997: 259). The debate in 2004 over the exact form of Saddam Hussein's trial for war crimes was notable for its automatic assumption that justice through prosecution was necessary.

Related to this is the idea that at the root of many internal wars and civil conflicts is some form of injustice—social, political, or economic. Therefore, a key element of conflict resolution is the achievement of justice, as without it the underlying causes of conflict remain, waiting to reerupt at a later time. The prosecution of human rights violators can not only go some way to achieving justice for the victims of specific crimes but can highlight patterns of injustice and ill-treatment that need to be addressed by the wider society. In short, there is a growing recognition that there is an ethical dimension to peace, particularly in the kinds of internal conflicts of the post–Cold War.

Policy Options for Dealing with Past Abuses

The choice of how to deal with past abuses, and the major division of opinion, is often framed as a strict dichotomy between reconciliation and justice (Sriram 2000). Either a country can aim at reconciliation through truth-telling and amnesty, or they can aim at justice through trials and prosecutions. In fact, this is a false bifurcation. There is actually a continuum of options that governments can pursue that ranges from trials and prosecutions of all those suspected of human rights crimes at one end of the scale, to total amnesty and social amnesia at the other. Some of these policies are oriented toward the victims of abuses (truth commissions), while others are oriented toward the offenders (prosecutions or amnesties). Moreover, states can pursue several different options simultaneously, attempting to pursue both reconciliation and justice, and to deal with both victims and offenders.

For example, societies may choose one or several of the following options:

- the attempted prosecution of all human rights violators;
- the selected prosecution of only the worst human rights violators, as the current government in Rwanda is doing;
- lustration, which refers to the practice of barring former agents of the state and collaborators from holding public office for a period of time;
- simply establishing the truth about what happened through some kind of investigatory process;
- truth and reconciliation through offering amnesty in exchange for truth, compensation for victims, and the establishment of permanent reminders of the legacy of the past, such as the South African TRC process;
- truth and reconciliation, plus simultaneous prosecutions of the worst war criminals—as in the current process under way in Sierra Leone;
- partial amnesty for some perpetrators;
- total amnesty for all perpetrators;
- amnesia—the deliberate choice to forget and ignore the past in the interests of social harmony.

Essentially, the choices that societies make about which option to take depend upon the answers to two key questions: whether to remember or forget the abuses—the question of *acknowledgment*; and whether to punish the perpetrators of those abuses—the question of *accountability* (Newman 2002). At a philosophical level at least, how a society answers these questions will determine which path they choose to go down. Politically, however, there are a number of factors that can condition the policy options of transitional regimes.

The Context of Reconciliation and Justice

Reconciliation and justice approaches—truth commissions and trials—are normally conceived in two kinds of situations, namely, when democratic governments have replaced authoritarian regimes and in the context of a negotiated (or decisive) end to a civil war. A great number of variables, both internal and external, can determine the choices that societies make in deciding either to pursue the truth commission model or the justice model and how far to go in either case (Huyse 1995; Newman 2002; Sriram 2000).

The most important *internal factors* conditioning these choices include the balance of power between armed groups who can potentially spoil the transition, civil society, and the new government; the timing of the transition—whether it is a recent or distant past; the nature of the demise of the previous regime or end of the civil war—whether it involved decisive victory or a negotiated compromise; the intensity and duration of the abuses; the degree of complicity by the wider society in those abuses; the presence of cultural factors, such as the propensity to forgive, revenge- and vendetta-based cultural practices or traditional reconciliation rites; and the presence of the necessary financial and human resources for such undertakings.

The most important *external factors* that can affect a society's choice include the involvement of third parties in the transition, such as mediators, peacekeepers, and former Cold War patrons; the international context, including the acceptance of international norms and values; the presence of powerful international actors with the willingness and resources to sponsor either truth commissions or trials; the engagement of international NGOs in highlighting justice issues and supporting local human rights groups; the willingness of other states to cooperate in bringing perpetrators to justice and handing over suspects; and the presence of international tribunals or institutions for pursuing justice against war criminals and former dictators.

═══ ═══ ═══ ═══ ═══ ═══ ═══ ═══

Modalities for Dealing with Past Abuses

Past abuses can be dealt with in a range of ways from truth commissions to prosecutions, or a mix of both. We divide these methods into two broad categories—truth commissions, and trials and prosecutions.

Truth Commissions

Truth commission is the term used generically to describe a wide variety of official or quasi-official bodies set up to investigate a past history of human rights violations in a given country during a specific time period. Every truth commission is unique, the product of a particular set of political and cultural circumstances, and has its own unique methodology, mandate, powers, and goals. They range from elaborate multibody, externally supported, and well-resourced commissions, to one-person commissions with very limited resources. Nonetheless, it is generally agreed that there are four primary constituting elements that define a truth commission (Hayner 1994: 604). First, truth commissions focus on past events rather than ongoing or current events. Second, unlike commissions of inquiry, truth commissions attempt to paint an overall picture of human rights violations over a given historical period. Third, truth commissions are temporary bodies with a predefined life span, usually ceasing to exist once they submit their findings. Finally, truth commissions are always vested with some sort of authority to gather information, interpret historical events, assign responsibility for abuses, grant amnesty, and make recommendations for reform.

Types of Truth Commissions

Beyond the broad characteristics common to every truth commission, there are in fact several types of commission, depending upon the actors sponsoring the process and leading the commission. First, and most commonly, truth commissions are appointed by the executive or parliament on an ad hoc basis, following a political transition, and with the broad agreement of key actors in society. They are normally led by prominent and respected national figures. There are numerous examples of national truth commissions, such as the Argentine National Commission on the Disappeared (1983–84), the Bolivian National Commission of Inquiry into Disappearances (1982–85), the Chad Commission of Inquiry into the Crimes and Misappropriations Committed by Ex-President Habre, His Accomplices and/or Accessories (1990–92), the Chilean National Commission for Truth and Reconciliation (1990–91), the South African Truth and Reconciliation Commission (1995–98), the Sri Lankan Commissions of Inquiry into the Involuntary Removal and Disappearances of Persons (1994–97), and the Ugandan Commission of Inquiry into Violations of Human Rights (1986–94), among many others.

Second, international commissions may be established under the auspices of the United Nations or regional organizations. These are normally led and staffed by nonnationals, initiated and sponsored by international actors like the UN, and externally funded. The Commission on the Truth for El Salvador (1992–93), sponsored by the UN and staffed entirely by nonnationals, is the most famous example of an international truth commission. Similarly, in 1995, the UN Security Council called for the creation of an international commission to investigate the assassination of President Mechior Ndadaye in October 1993 in Burundi, which subsequently resulted in the deaths of 50,000 civilians. The five-man commission, appointed by the UN Secretary-General and staffed by international diplomats, released its findings in a report in August 1996.

The third variation involves NGO-sponsored national or international commissions. These normally take place when the political conditions within the affected country are not conducive to a national commission, and there is simultaneously a lack of interest from international organizations or powerful states. For example, the International Commission of Investigation on Human Rights Violations in Rwanda was established by a coalition of four human rights NGOs: Africa Watch (United States); Centre International des Droits des la Personne et du Développement Démocratique (Canada); Fédération Internationale des Droits de l'Homme (France); and Union Interafricaine des Droits de l'Homme et des Peuples (Burkina Faso). After obtaining permission from the Rwandan government, the commission visited Rwanda for two weeks, producing a report in March 1993 that detailed political killings and human rights violations between October 1990 and March 1993. In Uruguay, dissatisfaction with the 1985 Investigative Commission on the Situation of "Disappeared" People and Its Causes resulted in a nongovernmental project led by national human rights groups that published its own report, *Uruguay: Nunca Mas,* on the abuses of the military regime.

A fourth form involves a mixed hybrid of international and national sponsorship, as well as a mix of national and international commissioners. The Guatemalan Historical Clarification Commission (1994–99), for example, was established as part of the peace agreements signed between the government and the National Guatemalan Revolutionary Unit to investigate human rights violations during the country's thirty-six-year armed conflict. It was partly sponsored by the UN and included both Guatemalan and international commissioners. Similarly, Haiti's National Truth and Justice Commission (1994–96) was composed of four Haitians and three foreigners. Mixed UN-national tribunals have also been established in Sierra Leone, Cambodia, Bosnia and Herzegovina, and Timor-Leste.

A final variation involves more permanent national structures, such as an ombudsman's office or a commissioner for human rights. While not strictly the kind of commission we are examining (which is by definition a temporary arrangement), these offices can sometimes play a similar role to truth commissions. For example, the Honduran government established a Commissioner for the Protection of Human Rights in 1992. Responding to pressure from human rights groups, the commissioner immediately began investigating disappearances that took place between 1980 and 1993, eventually producing a report in 1994 that implicated some high-ranking officials and made recommendations for compensation, apology, and reform of the armed forces.

Sometimes, several mechanisms can be adopted simultaneously to overcome impunity and guarantee human rights, such as in El Salvador following peace negotiations between the government and the FMLN guerrillas. Here the UN-sponsored Salvadoran Truth Commission was one of a range of measures that also included a commission to purge the military of human rights violators (the Ad Hoc Commission), the appointment of a new Human Rights Ombudsman, a new civilian police force to replace the old military security forces, and measures aimed at increasing the independence of the judiciary (Popkin and Roht-Arriaza 1995: 86–89).

The Roles and Functions of Truth Commissions

Depending upon their individual mandates, truth commissions can encompass a wide range of roles and functions. These may include finding out the truth about what, when, and where human rights violations occurred; creating an authoritative and objective account of the past; acknowledgment of the facts of human rights violations, the complicity of the perpetrators, and the suffering of victims; educating the society as well as future generations about the crimes and the necessity of human rights protection; promoting a process of social and individual catharsis through public truth-telling; vindicating, compensating, and rehabilitating victims by providing a platform or forum for them to tell their stories, as well as recommending reparations; providing recommendations for legislative, structural, or other changes to avoid repetition of past abuses; and establishing who was responsible and providing a measure of accountability for perpetrators (Popkin and Roht-Arriaza 1995).

For example, the mandate of the Chilean Commission for Truth and Reconciliation (the Rettig Commission) was to "clarify in a comprehensive manner the truth about the most serious violations committed in recent years," establishing "the most complete picture possible of these grave events, as well as their antecedents and circumstances," and "to gather evidence that may make it possible to identify the victims by name and determine their fate or whereabouts" (*Report of the Chilean National Commission for Truth and Reconciliation,* quoted in Popkin and Roht-Arriaza 1995: 84). Similarly, the Salvadoran Truth Commission's mandate was to investigate "serious acts of violence that occurred since 1980 and whose impact on society urgently demands that the public should know the truth," taking into consideration the "exceptional importance that may be attached to the acts to be investigated, their characteristics and impact, and the social unrest to which they gave rise" (quoted in Popkin and Roht-Arriaza 1995: 87). It was also mandated to recommend legal, political, or administrative measures that would prevent the recurrence of such acts and promote national reconciliation.

The Roles and Functions of Trials and Prosecution

Like truth commissions, trials and tribunals can have a wide variety of roles and functions. These may include prosecuting war criminals and human rights violators; exorcising a possible culture of impunity by holding those who commit human rights crimes accountable; achieving a sense of justice for victims; stopping vigilante retribution and acts of revenge; contributing to a coherent body of international and national law that will prevent similar acts in the future; reconstituting and strengthening institutions; reinforcing the rule of law and general respect for human rights; enhancing the credibility of new governments; symbolically and tangibly giving a foundation for a new domestic criminal and judicial system; and subverting collective blame by clarifying that specific individuals, not entire religious, political, or ethnic groups, are to blame for specific crimes (Huyse 1995).

The Role of Third Parties

Third parties—international organizations, interested states, and NGOs—can play a variety of roles in both truth commissions and prosecutions. They may, for example, provide the necessary motivational and ideational impetus for the establishment of the commission or trial process in the first place. International mediators like the UN may suggest that a truth commission be included in the final agreement between the rebels and the government or that once a transition is completed that notorious war criminals be handed over to international tribunals for trial. Third parties can sometimes take full responsibility for the truth commission or trial process, providing leadership, funds, and personnel. The Salvadoran Truth Commission was sponsored by the UN, and all funds and staff came from outside El Salvador. In some cases, the documents and files of domestic and international human rights groups, such as churches, NGOs, and humanitarian organizations, can be used by investigators to uncover evidence of crimes and information on victims and perpetrators. The Rettig Commission, for example, made extensive use of such sources in investigating the thousands of killings during Chile's military rule, especially as the military and police refused to cooperate with the commission. Finally, third parties can play a vital role in publicizing the work of the commission or tribunal, highlighting important issues on the world stage.

Evaluating Reconciliation and Justice Approaches

There are several challenges in evaluating the success of truth commissions and trials in social reconstruction and peacebuilding. In the first instance, each situation is unique; there is no such thing as a standard truth commission or human rights trial. Because every transition is different it is difficult to evaluate truth commissions or trials in terms other than those of the particular commission or trial itself. And what may be true for one situation may not apply for another. Second, the impact of a truth commission or set of trials on a society, and even its success on its own terms, will most likely depend on the passage of time and the accretion of historical memory (Popkin and Roht-Arriaza 1995: 80). They may be perceived far differently after twenty years than they are at the time, and any significant effects may not be evident for decades or generations. Since most truth commissions have only taken place within the last ten or fifteen years, it may be too soon to make any concrete judgments about their long-term impact.

Third, the political and social conditions that led to the establishment of the truth commission in the first instance—the constraints, opportunities, and compromises made by the key parties, the political will of elites, the degree of support from society, the international context, and the presence of interested third parties—may also dictate the limits of its success. These background effects may be impossible to disentangle from the choices made by the commissions, and a seemingly successful commission may be more a reflection of favorable background conditions than anything the commission itself chose to do. For example, the Guatemalan Truth Commission process involved a refusal by the military and the government to commit to following the recommendations of any truth commission or to permit it to name names or recommend judicial prosecution. This was the necessary price of compromise in ending the civil war, but it ensured that the work of the truth commission had a limited social and political impact.

Finally, reconciliation and justice are themselves highly contested concepts, and there is little agreement on what they mean in practice or how to measure their effects. The lack of a common language, moreover, prevents the emergence of any consensus. How can we objectively measure whether a previously divided society is now reconciled? What is justice? Should justice be retributive or restorative? How much justice is enough, and by what measure do we determine that justice has really been done? In one sense, these are subjective value judgments that are impossible to quantify. However, in spite of these difficulties, we believe that it is possible to make some general observations about the strengths and weaknesses of reconciliation and justice, while keeping in mind the inherent limitations of these judgments.

The Strengths of Truth Commissions

The main strengths of truth commissions—as a method for promoting conflict transformation—are that they can be established almost instantly and at relatively little cost. In addition, they can be designed according to the specific needs of a society (see Schlunck 1998). They can also be more flexible than criminal trials in gathering, hearing and evaluating evidence, as they do not have to follow the rigid rules of legal procedure. Moreover, truth commissions can serve a wider range of purposes than criminal courts. Criminal trials are oriented toward establishing the guilt or innocence of individual acts and cannot normally deal with crimes on a much greater scale, such as systematic and widespread human rights violations. Nor can trials give accounts of the historic, economic, political, or social circumstances that led to the crime or the involvement of internal and external political actors in fostering hatred and violence. Providing such accounts

and therefore contextualizing individual acts, and then offering recommendations to prevent future abuses, is exactly what truth commissions do. More specifically, truth commissions can help to reconstitute the moral order and can provide a measure of justice when trials are not an option.

Truth and the Moral Order

One of the greatest achievements of the truth commissions that have been instigated in recent years has been the presentation of authoritative histories that counter the distorted histories of repressive regimes or groups (Popkin and Roht-Arriaza 1995: 113). The authoritative description and analysis of events prepared by respected national or international figures have in many cases gained widespread acceptance and formed the basis of the historical record. Facing up to these aspects of national history and writing the stories of victims into the history books is an essential element in reconstituting the moral order of post-conflict societies. Related to this, the process of writing the commission reports, which involved listening to victims, validating their stories, and involving broad sectors of society was also important in creating new social and political discourses. Participation in a political process by ordinary people is an important step in creating a more democratic culture and giving society a stake in governmental institutions.

Related to this, the truth-telling process is important for deconstructing the kinds of discourses that lie at the heart of many of today's internal wars—discourses based on identity politics, hatred of the Other, exclusion, revenge, and extremism (Jackson 2004; Pouligny 2002). By exploring the social and political conditions that allowed human rights abuses to occur, rehumanizing victims and perpetrators through symbolic encounters, assigning individual rather than group responsibility for acts of abuse, and introducing a new political language (based on truth, reconciliation, forgiveness, and mercy) into the political and wider social arena, truth commissions can deconstruct the power of old discourses and lay the foundations for new discourses based on the nonviolent resolution of conflict.

Truth commissions can be especially useful for dealing with particular types of human rights violations committed under a repressive regime or during a civil war, namely, disappearances and killings by anonymous death squads. The secrecy and deniability on the part of the perpetrators, the scale of the abuses, and the shadowy nature of the killings instill a climate of fear, suspicion, and social withdrawal (Popkin and Roht-Arriaza 1995: 81–82). Uncovering the truth about these events allows family and friends the possibility of closure and helps to break down the social climate of fear and impunity created by the secrecy and deniability. Related to this, investigatory commissions can shortcut some of the difficulties involved in employing normal channels like the police and the courts, which can pose a serious obstacle when both have been complicit in the human rights violations and neither is capable of independent inquiries.

Moral Justice

Truth commissions can be an attractive alternative to prosecution when the new government's room to maneuver is limited by the presence of powerful actors who can destabilize the transition process. In both pacted transitions and negotiations to end civil conflict, the government may have to forgo the full-scale prosecution of human rights violators or the restructuring of offending institutions because of an unfavorable balance of forces. The army, security forces, or rebel movements may still be in a position to derail the peace process if they are punished too severely or perceive themselves to be under attack. A truth commission therefore can be a useful alternative and a first step to other actions or simply a relatively cost-free means of meeting popular demands for an accounting in the absence of trials (Popkin and Roht-Arriaza 1995: 83).

In terms of justice, while truth commissions cannot provide a criminal or civil sanction, the process of public identification and naming perpetrators can provide a social and moral sanction, having negative effects on the reputation, career, and political prospects of individuals (Popkin and Roht-Arriaza 1995: 105). Naming those responsible for major human rights abuses can also be an essential first step in breaking a tradition of impunity, and the public attention engendered by the truth-telling process of exposing human rights abuses may create a moral and political climate in which prosecutions become more feasible. National commissions have some advantages over internationally sponsored commissions in this regard, such as familiarity with local political nuances and access to insider information.

Related to this, in terms of redress for the victims of abuses, the process of compiling a truth commission report can be as important as the final product, having a powerful therapeutic effect on communities and individuals that have suffered both abuse and then disbelief from government officials. Providing victims with a platform

to tell their stories was a feature of both the Chilean and Salvadoran commissions, among several others.

> To finally have a sympathetic hearing from someone backed by either the government or by an international organization, after years of fruitless petition to skeptical functionaries, had a powerful effect on victims. Moreover, the process of providing data, stories, proof from newly discovered clandestine cemeteries, and the like incorporated larger groups of people (families, local villages) in an active process of coming to terms with the past, not simply a spectator's reaction to a finished product. (Popkin and Roht-Arriaza 1995: 100)

In other words, while truth commissions cannot provide the kind of arduous process of working through trauma that an individual therapist can provide, it can offer "therapeutic moments" for a traumatized society (Minow 1998: 333).

The Role of Third Parties

International commissions fulfill a set of functions slightly different from those of national commissions. Whereas a national commission can be useful for promoting social and political reconciliation, an external authority allows some measure of accountability to take place when internal conditions might not favor such an outcome. An international truth commission has certain other advantages (Popkin and Roht-Arriaza 1995: 94; Rigby 2001: 165–80). These include a certain distance from domestic political squabbles and a claim to greater objectivity and disinterestedness. Its status and the involvement of powerful international actors may also afford a higher degree of protection from reprisals than a national commission would be capable of. A key advantage lies in access to greater resources for setting up and running the commission, which may be beyond the capacity of a country that is emerging from a long period of destructive conflict. An international commission also possesses the ability to publicize its recommendations internationally and the ability to employ sources of international leverage to see that recommendations are implemented. It may also have credibility and a reputation for impartiality that a national commission is not capable of. In the case of UN-sponsored commissions, for example, the status of the UN-sponsored Salvadoran Truth Commission led many people to come forward who had never presented their testimony to national human rights groups. Finally, there may be less timidity in the name of maintaining unity from international commissions, as they have nothing to lose by speaking out.

The Strengths of Justice Approaches

There is widespread agreement that justice is part of the positive contents of peace and that addressing justice-related issues (e.g., through criminal prosecutions of human rights violations) contributes to national reconciliation in the long term (Parlevliet 1999; Mendez 1997). Certainly, the failure to account for past abuses may well lay the foundation for renewed violence by reinforcing a sense of impunity among perpetrators and resentment among victims, allowing for conflicting versions of past events and perpetuating enemy images of different groups.

One of the most important and most immediate advantages of justice approaches is that prompt prosecution circumvents vigilante justice and personal vengeance, which can also be a spark for renewed conflict. The focus on individual responsibility in criminal trials, moreover, subverts any notion of collective blame or guilt by showing that individuals and not entire ethnic or political groups were responsible for the crimes. This can also help to break down group hostility and promote national reconciliation (Mendez 1997: 277). Moreover, the vigorous pursuit of justice can have a powerful and long-term deterrent effect on the behavior of potential transgressors, thereby preventing future conflict in transitional societies.

Another key advantage of national trials and prosecutions is their effect on rebuilding the political order of a country. Quick and effective justice can bolster the legitimacy of a transitional government, reestablish the rule of law, break down any lingering culture of impunity, strengthen governmental institutions, and provide the foundation for a new criminal and judicial system. Moreover, national prosecutions can be more sensitive to the nuances of local culture and political conditions.

The Strengths of International Tribunals

In some cases, international tribunals may have certain advantages over national trials. International tribunals may be better resourced—both in terms of skilled staff and financial and material support—than national trials, particularly if they take place in poor countries or if the justice system has been devastated by civil war. In Rwanda, for example, the justice system was almost entirely destroyed in the 1994 genocide. Not only were there few judges remaining (nearly all of Rwanda's judges had been killed in the genocide or fled from the advancing Rwandan Patriotic Front), but 95 percent of the country's attorneys died, fled, or were imprisoned. On top of this, the judicial system was confronted by damaged courthouses, lack of transport, prison housing shortages, and many other serious shortages of personnel and material. The Arusha tribunal established by the UN therefore seemed like a reasonable alternative at the time.

International tribunals are also more likely to function and be perceived as functioning on the basis of independence and impartiality; they will have greater distance from local political events (Newman 2002: 41). National courts can sometimes be perceived as "victor's justice" or retribution, as was the case with Saddam Hussein's trial in Iraq in 2006, and can be tainted by the use of judges whose political loyalties are suspect because they practiced under the old order.

International tribunals are best positioned to convey a clear message that the international community will not tolerate human rights violations and war crimes. This is partly as a result of greater access to the international media and helps to create a stronger international human rights regime. Related to this, being in the international spotlight can put pressure on a wide range of international actors and states to cooperate in bringing human rights violators to justice; international tribunals have a greater chance than national courts to obtain jurisdiction over senior officials who no longer reside in that country.

One key effect of the internationalization of justice through the holding of international trials has been to allow national governments to prosecute perpetrators of human rights abuses even when their crimes were committed in other countries, thereby universalizing responsibility and undermining the impunity of dictators and war criminals. This is actually based on a little-used element of international law known as "the universality principle" that holds that some crimes are so grave that all countries have an interest in prosecuting them (Annan 2004: 16). In April 2001, Belgium's Crown Court prosecuted a number of Rwandan genocide suspects—the "Butare Four"—in the first trial of its kind. In this case, a jury of ordinary Belgians judged people from another country who were charged with war crimes and human rights violations committed during genocide. The Belgian state carried the expense of bringing some 170 witnesses from Rwanda to testify at the trial.

The Challenges of Transitional Approaches

The single greatest limitation of reconciliation and justice approaches is that they are designed to deal with conflicts that have already been resolved politically; they cannot function effectively in situations of ongoing violent conflict. Nevertheless, there is little doubt that reconciliation and justice are key elements in postconflict transitions and can play a number of important roles in conflict transformation and peacebuilding once a conflict is over. Dealing with the past through either truth commissions or prosecutions is a necessary complement to negotiated pacts. In several cases—El Salvador, South Africa, Chile, and others—such processes are believed to have contributed to peaceful transition and democratic consolidation. These methods are imperfect, however, and there are a number of conceptual, ethical, political, and practical challenges facing the practice of truth commissions and human rights trials.

Fundamentally, the challenges faced by reconciliation and justice revolve around two key questions. First, what kind of approach is best suited to postconflict peacebuilding in the particular country of focus—reconciliation or justice? The answer to this question involves resolving a series of important conceptual and ethical dilemmas. Second, what is the nature of the political situation in the country under transition? What is the balance of forces, what are the terms of the compromise that led to the transition, and which groups support the truth commission or trial approach? The success or failure of either reconciliation or justice will be contingent on such factors and will involve surmounting a number of serious political and practical challenges. In addition, there are a number of unique challenges facing international commissions that we consider separately. Although we deal with these issues under different headings they clearly overlap in a number of ways.

Conceptual Challenges

The conceptual challenges of reconciliation and justice revolve first and foremost around the absence of any coherent or systematic theory of truth commissions or theory of human rights prosecutions. There are important theoretical questions that do not yet have any clear answers. Should peace (in terms of the end of violence) be prioritized over justice when the pursuit of justice might destabilize the peace process? Or, are justice and peace mutually reinforcing, and if so, how much justice is necessary to ensure peace? Is absolute justice desirable or even possible? In addition to these conceptual ambiguities, the time frame for evaluating the success or failure of these endeavors is extremely long and difficult to disentangle from background political conditions. There is, therefore, a lack of empirical evidence from which to deduce theoretical propositions about their role and value

in postconflict transitions. The evidence to date is at best ambiguous; it is not clear that one model—of either truth commissions or trials—is more likely than any other to produce a successful outcome (Hayner 1994: 642). It is not surprising that there are contrasting perspectives on whether countries should aim to adopt reconciliation based on truth-telling, mercy, forgiveness, and healing, or whether justice and prosecutions should be a higher priority. There are clearly important arguments to support both theoretical perspectives. Until this conceptual deficit can be rectified the choices made are likely to be based upon political expediencies and the personal values of those in a position to decide.

Nonetheless, there are some obvious areas of concern within the existing theoretical notions surrounding reconciliation and justice. Apart from the debate over the meaning of terms like *truth* and *justice* there are also serious questions about the implicit psychotherapeutic "healing" value of commissions for either individuals or society at large. In the first instance, there are doubts about whether collective psychotherapy is even possible and whether it is appropriate to try to deal with collective memories and perceptions by applying an individual-level psychological model. After all, societies and nations are not like individuals. In any case, while it may be a current article of faith that self-knowledge is a condition of psychic health, the reality is that "every society, including ours, manages to function with only the most precarious purchase on the truth of its own past" (Ignatieff 1999: 184). Most regimes actually depend for their legitimacy on historical myths that are armored against unpalatable truths.

Second, the mere disclosure of truth—especially the inevitably limited versions produced by national commissions—is not enough on its own to bring closure, even for individuals: "Healing does not come from the recovery of narratives of violence but from the cultural processes of acknowledgement which involve learning to live with loss and death" (Humphrey 2002: 114). Moreover, public processes of truth-telling do not on their own engender either remorse in the perpetrators or the willingness to forgive by victims, as it is not actually possible to force people to feel either remorse or forgiveness; they must come to this voluntarily (Newman 2002). In some instances, truth may heighten anger and the calls for revenge once the full extent of the atrocities are made known or may revictimize the victims as they are forced to repeat their humiliation in public (Humphrey 2002: 123). In the South African TRC, for example, far from evincing signs of unconditional forgiveness some victims were incensed at the prospect of being denied justice through normal legal channels, while a few perpetrators were able to gleefully describe their crimes in detail and then earn immunity from prosecution. Truth commissions, in this sense, can usurp "what belongs to the private ethical space of individuality" for a symbolic collective political process (Holiday 1998: 55).

Other problems with both trials and truth commissions are that they can become obsessed with the past over the present, often at a time when a focus on building a common future is needed. They can degenerate into witch hunts, and the process can further fragment an already divided society—especially if the majority of suspected human rights abusers belong to one particular social group. It is also possible that national court systems can be swamped by a large number of prosecutions as a result of the investigations. This can drain resources needed in other areas and can lead to violations of due process for the accused themselves. There is also the possibility that truth commissions and trials can fall victim to being used as political tools. From a theoretical viewpoint then, reconciliation and justice can sometimes have destabilizing effects on a transitional society, rather than contributing to national reconciliation.

In fact, in contrast to the positive tenor of most theoretical writings on the subject, commissions and trials do not have a strong record of catalyzing major structural change, nor can they engender conflict transformation on their own. One of the biggest criticisms leveled at the South African TRC, for example, was its failure to deal with the country's economic injustice, which was the engine of the apartheid system. Truth commissions and transitional justice are an inherently limited and temporary measure that is best applied once a democratic transition is already under way and there is a general consensus on the need to break with the past (Popkin and Roht-Arriaza 1995: 114–15). It is really only under these specific conditions that they can play useful roles in getting some kind of justice for a few of the victims, rewriting history, contributing to a new political discourse, and allowing for closure.

Ethical Dilemmas

There are a number of competing ethical imperatives inherent in any postconflict or postdictatorship transition, particularly if the end of violence involves the cooperation of powerful groups complicit in human rights violations, such as rebel groups, the security services, or the military. Sometimes it may not be possible to fulfill the imperative of both truth and justice at the same time, such as when security services destroy all their records and refuse to cooperate with investigators for fear of bearing the brunt of prosecutions. In the South African case, the TRC overcame this dilemma by trading truth (frank and full confession of crimes) for justice (amnesty from prosecution). At other times, pursuing justice may endanger the peace process itself, such as when political bargains must be made with powerful and armed groups complicit in massive war crimes. In Sierra Leone and Cambodia the peace process depended initially on forging deals with groups that had committed terrible human rights abuses—the RUF in Sierra Leone was responsible for some of the worst war crimes of the century, while the Khmer Rouge in Cambodia was responsible for one of the worst genocides ever recorded. In both cases, peace was traded for justice in the early postconflict phase in order to prevent a return to full-scale civil war. It was only years later when the danger of a return to full-scale war had largely passed that both countries were able to initiate prosecutions against the most notorious war criminals

There is no clear-cut way of getting around these ethical dilemmas. It is simply part of the tragedy of contemporary internal wars that distasteful choices sometimes have to be made (Newman 2002; Sriram 2000). During postconflict transitions, each society will have to find its own answer to the following kinds of ethical and theoretical questions: Is strengthening peace a more important goal than achieving justice or uncovering truth in the initial stages of the transition? Or, is achieving justice actually an important element in creating the conditions for long-term peace? Is truth and confronting the past more important to the process of national healing than achieving a sense of justice? How important is mercy in promoting reconciliation, and should mercy precede punishment and justice? As yet, the relationship between justice, truth, mercy, reconciliation, and peace is not entirely clear, nor are the ethical priorities for societies in transition.

Perhaps one of the most difficult ethical conundrums for reconciliation and justice relates to questions surrounding collaboration and the gray realms of living under conditions of occupation or civil violence (Huyse 1995; Rigby 2001). Collaboration can of course come in many forms—political, military, social, or economic—and it can be undertaken willingly or reluctantly. In a society under occupation or ruled by a repressive regime, it is almost impossible to avoid some kind of collaboration and compromise with the state. It is particularly difficult to avoid cooperating with the agents of the state when economic or physical survival is at stake, family members are threatened, and one is forced to choose between protecting loved ones and betraying one's wider social group. Related to this, in many contemporary internal wars ordinary people have frequently been forced into participating in human rights violations and therefore tend to occupy roles of victims and perpetrators simultaneously. In the context of widespread complicity and collective guilt, plus the ambiguity of being both victims and perpetrators of human rights violations, there are obviously tremendous moral and ethical dilemmas in assigning blame and determining guilt. There are also questions over whether ignorance and indifference to ongoing human rights violations constitutes complicity and whether it is right to punish people for what they did not do as much as for what they did do. In many cases, such as postwar Europe and post-Mengistu Ethiopia, tens of thousands of ordinary people were harshly punished for collaboration, which itself could be construed as injustice (Huyse 1995: 66–70).

Another aspect of this debate relates to the sometimes competing imperatives between the universal international values attached to human rights and humanitarian law and the local traditions and customs of many developing countries where internal wars have taken place (Mani 1998). There may be conflicting priorities, for example, between societies that wish to deal with human rights violators in their own ways, such as through ritual cleansing rites in Mozambique or village trials in Rwanda, and international human rights activists who would prefer to see perpetrators publicly tried in an international court. In recent years local peacemakers in Uganda have come into conflict with the international community over the issue of prosecuting members of the Lord's Resistance Army (LRA), responsible for decades of horrendous war crimes. While Ugandan mediators want to deal with the atrocities according to local customs, international pressure has been to try the perpetrators in the ICC. The question arises, should universal standards of justice enforced by the international community overrule local cultures, or should each society be allowed to choose its own path? In one sense, the competing values of cosmopolitanism and communitarianism come into play over these issues. In another, there are issues about the nature of international law and whether it supersedes national laws.

Political Constraints

In addition to the conceptual and ethical questions raised by reconciliation and justice there is also a set of more practical political constraints that have to be overcome.

For many truth commissions the most significant limitations are those written into their mandates or terms of reference (Hayner 1994: 636). These determine the extent of their investigatory powers, the limits of their investigative reach, the exact abuses and perpetrators they are allowed to investigate, the time line and geographic scope of the commission's investigation, when and to whom the final report must be submitted, the nature of the recommendations to be included in the report, and whether the commission has the power to name names. To date, most truth commissions have been significantly limited in the work they are allowed to do by the narrow scope of their mandates.

Beyond the limitations imposed by their specific mandates, truth commissions and prosecutions are dependent on both favorable political and social conditions, as well as the choices they make in situ for their success (Hayner 1994; Mani 1998). In particular, they are dependent upon the balance of forces in the society, the nature of the transitional bargain between the opposing sides, the willingness and political support of both the general population and the political elite to support the process, and favorable international conditions, most importantly, the political will of international sponsors. In other words, their success is never guaranteed; it is rather, contingent on a range of factors that may sometimes be outside of an individual state's control. For example, if a society is not ready for the truth-telling process or does not get behind the work of the commission—preferring instead a deliberate amnesia, such as occurred in Spain for many decades after the Franco dictatorship—then no matter how hard it works or what strategies it adopts, it will most likely have no lasting impact (Newman 2002: 46). Similarly, if the government does not fully support the work of a truth commission or a prosecutorial process, because it faces other more pressing priorities, for example, its impact may be curtailed. Reconciliation and justice are, in actual fact, extremely vulnerable politically and inherently fragile methods of postconflict peacebuilding.

In some cases, investigatory commissions or public prosecutions face challenges in establishing their independence from all the actors in a contested history and in asserting their moral authority to examine and judge the acts and motivations of perpetrators (Popkin and Roht-Arriaza 1995: 93–95). The involvement of local individuals can undermine the commission's credibility, especially if members of the old order are included on the commission. For example, the Ad Hoc Commission in El Salvador, staffed solely by Salvadorans, was considered less trustworthy than the UN truth commission, and a number of individuals and organizations chose not to share information with it. The problem can be acute for both internationally sponsored commissions, who might be seen as impinging on national sovereignty, and for national commissions where officials may have ties to suspect political groups. Similarly, trials conducted by successor governments may be seen as "victor's justice."

A growing problem for truth commissions and trials is the inability to meet the expectations of those who give testimony and wider national and international constituencies. For those who give testimony, the process inevitably raises expectations that those responsible will be identified and punished, that victims will be compensated, or that at a minimum the full truth will be disclosed (Popkin and Roht-Arriaza 1995: 100). For international donors and local human rights groups, there are normally high expectations that at the very least a strongly worded report will be produced and a number of reforms will be implemented. As we have seen, however, the political context, the mandate and resources of the commission, or the compromises necessary to establish the commission in the first place may severely limit the commission's ability to deliver on these expectations.

National commissions may have difficulties getting their findings accepted and their recommendations implemented, especially if they lack strong international backing. This can be especially problematic in cases where the commission's findings implicate members of the new government. For example, the South African TRC faced at times intense opposition and legal challenges from the ANC government when it initially presented its report, which was critical of the ANC leadership for not properly owning up to abuses during the liberation struggle. After the publication of the TRC Report, and for narrow political reasons, Thabo Mbeki's government suggested giving blanket amnesties to those who did not apply initially or who were turned down. Archbishop Tutu, the former chair of the TRC, argued that a blanket pardon would undermine the entire commission process.

Ultimately, the success of a truth commission is dependent on the government accepting the commission's findings of fact as its own and in acknowledging the state's responsibility for past acts. While representatives of the international community or staff from national commissions can listen to victims and validate their stories, "if the state does not make the commission's conclusions and recommendations its own or publicly accept responsibility for the harmful acts of its agents, an essential part of the healing may be lost" (Popkin and Roht-Arriaza 1995: 101). Unfortunately, in a number of cases—South Africa,

El Salvador, and Haiti, among others—governments have failed to give the truth commissions their full support.

Practical Obstacles

A perennial practical problem for both truth commissions and prosecutions is the necessarily selective approach they are forced to take (Mendez 1997: 274); it is simply not possible to investigate and prosecute every case of human rights abuse. In some cases the scale of the abuses or the extended time period precludes more than a partial investigation. In El Salvador more than 50,000 people were killed and thousands more disappeared, while in Rwanda up to one million were murdered in little over one hundred days. In Guatemala, thousands were murdered over a thirty-year time span. Clearly, it is untenable to even attempt to investigate fully in such circumstances. In other cases, limits on time, staff, and resources means that only a very selective sample of cases can be investigated. Normally, a selection of representative cases is chosen for investigation; clearly, care must be taken in stressing their representative character lest distortions creep into the report.

The problem of access to information—for both truth commissions and trials—can, in some cases, also be acute. In many instances, the clandestine nature of the abuses, combined with the unwillingness of the security forces to cooperate with investigators, can forgo the possibility of a full accounting. The corporate culture and the need to protect the corporate interests of many armed groups— police, army, security services, and rebel armies—complicates the information-gathering process by commissions and prosecutors who must attempt to overcome a climate of hostility and resistance. In most cases, commissions do not have the means to compel testimony or production of documents, and they lack subpoena powers. For example, in many of the Latin American truth commissions, the inability to call hostile witnesses, preserve or obtain documents, or visit some military or police installations meant that the commissions could do little more than provide descriptions of broad patterns. Related to this, these same groups can put up serious obstacles to legal action recommended by the truth commission.

Another problem is that unless the commission has built-in mechanisms for revisiting progress, recommendations can quickly slip into obscurity as the public debate and international interest wanes. This can be particularly problematic if the truth commission makes overambitious or unrealistic proposals for reform, if significant actors such as the army refuse to implement them, and if the truth commission lacks leverage or ongoing power beyond the life of its mandate. Sometimes, a truth commission can become in effect a substitute, rather than a complement, to justice (Popkin and Roht-Arriaza 1995: 113) and act as an obstacle to the search for justice. In other words, by taking human rights violations out of the sphere of judicial action truth commissions may undermine the process of rebuilding judicial institutions.

Trials and prosecutions, for their part, face a number of difficulties, not least of which may be a conflict between legal systems—past and present (Huyse 1995). Many of the acts being prosecuted in the present may not have been crimes under the old order: this is the problem of ex post facto law (Siegal 1998: 439). There are serious questions over whether it is just or fair to punish people for acts that were not considered crimes at the time or to judge them by only recently accepted standards. As well, there are serious questions over the definitions of responsibility and collaboration in situations of lengthy and pervasive totalitarian systems. In such cases, virtually everyone came to some kind of accommodation with the system as a matter of survival and therefore aided in its perpetuation. There is then a real danger of criminal prosecutions leading to political vengeance and partisan trials. In some contemporary civil wars there are problems with the sheer numbers of prosecutions: it is thought that up to 150,000 Hutus participated directly in acts of killing in Rwanda, and there were around 125,000 in detention awaiting trial in 2001 (Humphrey 2002: 137). Many had been in custody for some years without trial, and a large number were there on the basis of denunciation alone. It is estimated that between 20 and 40 percent of these inmates were innocent.

The Challenges Facing International Commissions and Tribunals

Apart from the fact that external actors cannot ever impose a truth-telling or justice-based process on a society, there are a number of problems peculiar to international commissions. First, there may be a perception that the commission is only capable of giving an outsider's version of history (Newman 2002: 41). For example, the report of the UN-sponsored Salvadoran Truth Commission was seen by many in El Salvador as merely a UN document containing conclusions that could be discounted rather than officially assumed (Popkin and Roht-Arriaza 1995: 94). Because the commission process did not bring together diverse national actors to write a common history, the international commission became a target of attack from quarters dissatisfied with its recommendations and findings. Some argued that Salvadoran sovereignty had been violated and judicial functions usurped. In any case, it is certainly true that foreign staff not immersed in the local context may encounter difficulties in perceiving the relative importance of certain cases and the consequences of their decisions and recommendations.

A second problem is that foreign personnel, lacking insider knowledge and local acceptance, may have difficulties obtaining access to relevant information and gaining access to important figures. Third, the international pressure that can be brought to bear to ensure that recommendations are carried out can in some cases act as a substitute for political will within the country. Fourth, the necessarily short-term engagement of international actors in transition processes may limit their long-term impact. It takes constant monitoring and pressure to ensure the proper follow-up to the work of truth commissions, not simply a short-term spotlight. Finally, there are tremendous tensions involved when an international actor like the UN tries to act as both mediator and truth-teller. The contradictions between the pragmatic imperatives of peacemaking and the principled commitment to truth may become untenable, as happened in Guatemala when the UN was implicated in covering up human rights violations in order to avoid jeopardizing the final peace agreement, while at the same time sponsoring the Commission for Historical Clarification (Wilson 2001).

There are some problems peculiar to trials and prosecutions, one of which is the time required to achieve results. In many cases, particularly in the case of international tribunals, it may take several months to well over a year to set up a tribunal and have it issue its first indictments; the first trials may then take several more months to get under way. For example, the International Criminal Tribunal for Rwanda (ICTR) was established in November 1994 but only started its first prosecution in October 1996; it is still working more than ten years after it started. Furthermore, once they are operating, the rules of the tribunal can make it difficult to promptly issue requests for detention or the transfer of suspects, as orders and warrants for the arrest, detention, surrender, or transfer of suspects cannot be issued until the prosecutor satisfies a tribunal judge that a prima facie case exists. In the case of the ICTR, this allowed many of the principal suspects to flee the refugee camps and disappear.

International tribunals are also limited by, and entirely dependent upon, the resources they are provided with, the mandate and enforcement powers they are granted, and the political will of their underwriters and supporters. The

International Criminal Tribunal for the former Yugoslavia (ICTY) has been criticized on all these grounds. In 1994, the tribunal was given $11 million in UN funds when the Secretariat repeatedly requested a budget of $30 million. As well, the tribunal had great difficulty arresting suspects and minimal authority to punish, due to its weak mandate. Many questioned whether the UN could simultaneously negotiate a peace accord and support its implementation while also promoting the prosecution of war criminals. This is clearly a fundamental dilemma for international tribunals established at the end of civil wars. However, the greatest criticism fell on the sponsors and supporters of the tribunal, including NATO and the United States, who publicly resolved not to aggressively pursue custody of the primary organizers of the Bosnian war crimes—including Ratko Mladić, Radovan Karadžić, and Dario Kordić. Neither IFOR nor SFOR was mandated to seek out those indicted by the tribunal, only to arrest them if they encounter them in the course of their regular duties. Similar problems have hampered the tribunal in Sierra Leone; dependent on voluntary contributions, a serious financial crisis in 2004 threatened to abort the court's work.

Conclusion

Several important conclusions can be drawn from this overview. First, dealing with the past is an inescapable task for a postconflict or postdictatorship society. The past cannot be buried. As Ignatieff notes, "the past continues to torment because it is *not* past. . . . Crimes can never be safely fixed in the historical past; they remain locked in the eternal present, crying out for blood" (Ignatieff 1999: 186). Only when a society can recover the saving distance between past and present and between myth and truth can it awaken from the nightmare of internal war and begin to imagine an alternative future. The process of recovering truth, via commissions or trials, must therefore assume a high priority in the minds of decision makers and influential third parties.

Second, despite the absolute necessity of confronting the past, there are no universal solutions to dealing with the legacy of conflict and repression. There is no one best model, nor is there a set of universal rules or recommendations to guarantee success. In each case, difficult choices will have to be made according to local political realities, and competing ethical imperatives will have to be traded. Ultimately, a process tailored to the specific local circumstances and needs of the affected nation will have to be designed, taking into account the legacy of the past and that society's vision of the future. Nevertheless, Hayner suggests some minimal requirements that are necessary for the effective functioning of both truth commissions and human rights trials: commissions and trials should operate impartially and in good faith, independent from political forces; they should be properly resourced and should have free access to the necessary information for a full investigation; commissions and trials should be implemented as soon after the resolution of the conflict or transition process allows; they should operate for a limited, specified period of time; in the case of truth commissions, they should have the power to make recommendations, and it should be agreed in advance that the recommendations are obligatory; commissions and trials should be well publicized; and truth commission reports should be published immediately and be readily available to the public (Hayner 1994: 652).

Third, and perhaps most important, there are no miracle solutions; reconciliation and justice approaches cannot bring lasting peace on their own. Based on the rhetoric of breaking cleanly with the past, healing social and personal wounds, and promoting genuine social and political reconciliation, there are often unrealistic expectations attached to the work of truth commissions in particular. In spite of the undoubted value that they can bring to a postconflict transition, there are also potential problems.

> The danger is that commissions will be viewed a priori as a substitute for other actions, rather than one of a panoply of initiatives designed to uncover the truth, do justice, and thereby facilitate national reconciliation after a period of dictatorship or repression. Even the best efforts along these lines cannot overcome years or decades of ingrained habits of thought and culture. Far more than a truth commission will be necessary to heal the wounds and create conditions for a just society. (Popkin and Roht-Arriaza 1995: 116)

In fact, neither can legal measures alone accomplish these goals. Changes in political institutions, social and economic structures, culture, public and private discourses, and the everyday relationships between individuals and communities are all required to transform conflict and build cultures of peace. The fact is that truth commissions and trials cannot institute change on their own, nor can they bring about reconciliation. The best they can hope for is to create an environment in which change and peaceful coexistence become possible. As Parlevliet notes:

"The past is here to stay, but truth commissions offer a way for society to process and manage it non-destructively based upon the recognition of human dignity and integrity" (1999). To find reconciliation and justice approaches wanting against the aspirations of truly dealing with past abuses, however, is not to find them worthless as a response to conflict. It is rather to recognize their limitations and avoid unrealistic expectations.

Finally, difficult choices and trade-offs are often unavoidable, and there is usually a crucial challenge in striking a balance between the demands of justice and political prudence. However distasteful such choices may be, there is usually no convincing alternative; this is simply the nature of the beast. In the end, memory is the ultimate form of justice: "a truth-telling operation with full exposure of the crimes of the former regime is the least unsatisfactory solution. The truth is both retribution and deterrence" (Huyse 2001: 327).

CHAPTER TWELVE ⬦═══════════════════════════════

Peacebuilding

═══════════════════════════════⬦

Described officially for the first time in UN Secretary-General Boutros-Ghali's groundbreaking *An Agenda for Peace* (1992), peacebuilding is the most recent addition to the international community's repertoire of conflict resolution methods. In an important sense, it represents the acme of the evolutionary development of international conflict resolution theory and practice; going beyond the more limited objectives of conflict management and conflict settlement, peacebuilding is a holistic concept aimed at no less than the complete transformation of the political, economic, and social structures within a nation that can lead to violent conflict. In order to create the conditions for a durable and lasting peace, peacebuilding utilizes and combines the whole gamut of conflict resolution methods and approaches we have examined in this book—mediation, legal processes, preventive diplomacy, peacekeeping, humanitarian intervention, regional task-sharing, nonofficial diplomacy, and justice and reconciliation approaches—in a comprehensive, multidimensional, and long-term conflict transformation project. As with humanitarian intervention, peacebuilding recasts the third-party intervention role into novel and highly controversial forms, not least because it is an intensely political project that goes to the heart of a nation's political structures and economic arrangements.

While external assistance for postwar reconstruction is nothing new, the current theory and practice of peacebuilding evolved out of the larger, activist normative agenda that was elaborated during the 1990s under the umbrella of a revitalized UN (Tschirgi 2004: 4–5). A series of international conferences on population, sustain-able development, gender, and human rights underlined the importance of multilateral approaches to addressing global problems and reaffirmed the centrality of the UN in global governance. Simultaneously, a consensus began to emerge on a new "human security" agenda among international organizations, governments, and nongovernmental actors; campaigns to ban antipersonnel land mines, to regulate the traffic in small arms and light weapons, and to establish the International Criminal Court (ICC) reflected a growing international commitment to promoting real human security (as opposed to traditional conceptions of national security). Other important developments in the emergence of an international normative consensus during this period included the realization that controlling the destructive effects of the "new wars" necessitated far more comprehensive measures than diplomacy, peacekeeping, or traditional development assistance, and the articulation of a new legal-normative framework for humanitarian intervention—as seen in the publication of the International Commission on Intervention and State Sovereignty Report, *The Responsibility to Protect* (2001).

At the same time, the negotiated end to a number of long-running and highly complex internal wars in Namibia, Angola, El Salvador, Cambodia, and Mozambique created a practical demand for UN oversight and assistance in implementing the resultant peace agreements and postwar reconstruction efforts. Securing and consolidating these settlements entailed international involvement in a greatly expanded range of nation-building tasks such as institution-building, disarmament and demobilization, refugee repatriation, the management of elections, political and economic administration, and community development, among others. Together, these two developments—the emerging normative consensus and the practical demands of overseeing postsettlement transitions—led to the rapid evolution of a "postsettlement peacebuilding" template that began to be applied across a range of UN and regional peace support operations. It is these widely accepted peacebuilding standard operating procedures (SOPs), as well as the overall peacebuilding experiment itself, that we examine in this chapter.

Despite its advances, the theory and practice of peacebuilding is still in its infancy; little over a decade old, it remains an undertheorized and much-contested concept, as well as an underdeveloped and sometimes poorly regulated set of policies and practices. This is not surprising, given its extremely rapid evolution since *An Agenda for Peace* and the frequently piecemeal and underresourced manner in which it has been applied in UN operations. However, it does mean that a degree of conceptual confusion remains about both the theory and practice of peacebuilding and its long-term effects on postconflict societies. For example, there are serious questions about whether a standardized peacebuilding program can or should be applied to each and every conflict regardless of local circumstances; or if the neoliberal political and economic prescriptions at the heart of peacebuilding really engender long-term stability or merely perpetuate the conditions of poverty and global marginalization that contributed to the violence in the first place.

In this chapter, we assess the current state of peacebuilding, cognizant that both its theory and practice are in a state of flux and that it is probably too early to provide more than a tentative evaluation of its real potential. Although peacebuilding may take place in the absence of large-scale international intervention—the South African, Israeli-Palestinian, and Northern Ireland cases are all well-known examples of internally directed postsettlement peacebuilding—we focus primarily on the evolution and challenges of internationally directed peacebuilding missions such as those undertaken by the UN.

The Origins of Peacebuilding

The origins of the theory and practice of peacebuilding primarily lie in three interrelated fields: international peacekeeping; conflict resolution and peace research; and parts of development theory. Each of these areas has left its imprint on the evolving body of knowledge about peacebuilding.

In the first instance, as we have already noted, peacebuilding emerged out of developments in UN peacekeeping and peacemaking. The Organization's experiences in the complex internal wars of the early 1990s taught it: "Peacemaking and peace-keeping operations, to be truly successful, must come to include comprehensive efforts to identify and support structures which will tend to consolidate peace and advance a sense of confidence and well-being among people" (Boutros-Ghali 1992). Conceptually, *An Agenda for Peace* identified a set of tools that could be used for dealing with violent conflict: preventive diplomacy, peacemaking, peacekeeping, and peacebuilding. At the time, these were conceived of as sequential activities: *preventive diplomacy* was seen as a preconflict activity aimed at circumventing the outbreak of violence; *peacemaking* referred to the range of diplomatic activities designed to secure a cease-fire once the conflict had escalated to the level of open warfare; *peacekeeping* bridged the period from cease-fire to conflict settlement through interposition and monitoring; and postconflict *peacebuilding* referred to securing and consolidating peace agreements between warring parties after the fighting had ended. At the time, "postconflict" peacebuilding was distinguished from "preconflict" preventive diplomacy and was primarily conceived of as military demobilization and assistance with the transition to participatory electoral democracy. This dual emphasis remains at the core of the UN peacebuilding template today (Ramsbotham 2000: 171).

Since this initial formulation, however, the UN's conception of peacebuilding has progressively expanded in subsequent documents. For example, in *Supplement to An Agenda for Peace*, it was recognized that peacebuilding required multifunctional peace support operations operating across a range of security, humanitarian, economic, and political areas, and that following an initial military intervention phase, as the situation stabilized, responsibility would be handed over first to civilian agencies and then to local agents (Boutros-Ghali 1995). The Brahimi Report of 2000 recommended the addition of further peacebuilding tools and strategies, including the establishment of a Peacebuilding Unit in the UN, the adoption of quick impact projects (QIPs), and the creation of special funds for disarmament, demobilization, and reintegration (DDR) and electoral assistance programs (United Nations 2000). Secretary-General Kofi Annan attempted to systematize the UN's peacebuilding activities even further by arguing that effective peacebuilding required better coordination and synchronization of effort, carefully conceived strategies, flexibility in implementation, institutional capacity, proper evaluation, and a "lessons learned" process and systemwide guidelines and generic methodologies (Annan 2003). Thus, by 2001 the arbitrary distinction between peacebuilding and conflict prevention had been abandoned and the terms were being used interchangeably: peacebuilding was seen as a form of conflict prevention, and vice versa. In fact, peacebuilding came to be conceived of broadly as any activity that contributed to the construction of durable peace structures, regardless of which phase of the conflict it occurred in. In short, since 1992, the UN moved from a simplistic and linear view of the transition from war to peace to an integrated approach that linked the various concepts—conflict prevention, peacemaking, peacekeeping, and peacebuilding—in a coherent overall program. Thus, the UN came to have a more clearly defined and sophisticated understanding of the requirements of peacebuilding: "It came to view peacebuilding as requiring the full range of its capabilities (military, political, humanitarian, human rights, and socio-economic) at the policy and operational levels. The UN also realized that peacebuilding involved the active engagement of many external actors with multiple mandates and capabilities" (Tschirgi 2004: 4).

A second field of study and activity that has contributed to the development of the peacebuilding concept is conflict resolution and peace research (Ramsbotham, Woodhouse, and Miall 2005; Fetherston 2000). In the 1960s, the pioneer peace researcher Johan Galtung distinguished between three main approaches to achieving peace in conflict-ridden societies: *peacekeeping*, which aimed at reducing the overt violent behavior of conflict through the interposition of military forces; *peacemaking*, which aimed at reconciling the political differences of elites through diplomatic means such as negotiation, mediation, arbitration, and conciliation; and *peacebuilding*, which entailed "the practical implementation of peaceful social change through socioeconomic reconstruction and development" (1975: 282–304). At the same time, Galtung introduced the idea of "structural violence," which refers to the injury and harm—physical and psychological—that results from exploitative or unjust social, political and economic systems and structures (1971). Most often, violence of this kind is the result of the hierarchical ordering of categories of people within society and almost always occurs in the context of establishing, maintaining, extending, or challenging the established social order. This emphasis on the structural causes of violence implied that the more intensive process of peacebuilding—as opposed

to peacemaking and peacemaking—was the best way to deal with the deeper structural causes of conflict (Galtung 1975). Peace research also introduced the concepts of negative and positive peace: *negative peace* refers to the absence of direct physical, verbal, or psychological violence, while *positive peace* is defined as social justice, the removal of all forms of structural and cultural violence, the elimination of social impediments to full human self-realization, ecological balance, and the meeting of basic human needs. In this schema, only a holistic and comprehensive peacebuilding project can construct the conditions necessary for the realization of positive peace; in practice, peacemaking and peacekeeping are limited to ensuring a kind of negative peace.

Other conflict resolution scholars, critical of Galtung's failure to focus on the relational dimensions of intractable conflict, expand the notion of peacebuilding to include changing mutually negative conflict attitudes at the grassroots level (Ryan 1990: 50) and the promotion of conditions that create cooperative relationships (Burton 1990: 3). These elements have since been brought together in John Paul Lederach's conceptualization of peacebuilding as all the efforts employed to transform the underlying structural, relational, and cultural roots of violent conflict: "I am suggesting that 'peacebuilding' be understood as a comprehensive term that encompasses the full array of stages and approaches needed to transform conflict towards sustainable, peaceful relations and outcomes" (1994: 14). In particular, Lederach argues for a shift away from a "concern with the resolution of issues and toward a frame of reference that focuses on the restoration and rebuilding of relationships" and for adopting "the relational aspects of reconciliation as the central component of peacebuilding" (1997: 24). In other words, situated in the context of *reconciliation*, Lederach conceives of peacebuilding as a bottom-up, long-term process aimed at the sustainable transformation of societies in which the techniques of peacebuilding become embedded in the localities in which they are employed (Fetherston 2000: 204–7).

A final important strand in the evolution of the peacebuilding concept lies in development theory, particularly the disaster relief and sustainable development literature. In the early 1990s, the reconstruction and rehabilitation of war-torn societies came to be viewed by development agencies as one stage in the unilinear transition from war to peace; considered as part of the "relief-to-development" continuum, postconflict reconstruction became a subspecialty within the broader development agenda (Tschirgi 2004: 5–7; 2003: 7–9; see also Pugh 1995). This was largely driven by the recognition that societies emerging from conflict posed a unique set of challenges due to the combination of short-term humanitarian needs—such as distributing emergency food, shelter, and medical treatment; assisting refugees; and providing clean water—and long-term reconstruction requirements—such as rebuilding infrastructure, economic stabilization, strategic planning and debt relief. These situations were seen to require special hybrid approaches that were drawn from both the flexible, rapid, and responsive strategies of emergency humanitarian operations and the longer-term approaches of sustainable development assistance. As a senior World Bank official put it, "Post-conflict development is something that defies the exact boundaries of traditional forms of assistance: it is neither sustainable development nor is it humanitarian response" (quoted in Tschirgi 2004: 6).

As a consequence, a great many development agencies created specialized peacebuilding units within their organizations that in turn began to implement new peacebuilding programs, projects, and activities that fell outside of conventional humanitarian or development assistance, such as demining, DDR, electoral assistance, and civilian policing. For example, USAID created the Office of Transition Initiatives (OTI) in 1994, UNDP established its Emergency Response Division (ERD) in 1995, the Netherlands founded a Directorate of Crisis Management and Humanitarian Assistance (DCH) in 1996, the Canadian Peacebuilding Initiative was also launched in 1996 with a special Peacebuilding Fund, and in 1997, the UK Department for International Development (DFID) created the Conflict and Human Affairs Department (CHAD) and the World Bank created its Post-Conflict Unit. Although most of these units were small, understaffed, underresourced, and constrained by competing priorities and inconsistent national policy directions, nonetheless, they added an important set of ideas to the emerging theory and practice of peacebuilding.

In sum, the evolution of the peacebuilding project has been shaped and molded by the concerns, epistemologies, and practical operation of these three contributory fields. For example, the UN's peacekeeping experience reinforced the importance of establishing security and rebuilding political institutions from the top-down to the peacebuilding discourse; conflict resolution theory reaffirmed the necessity of rebuilding intercommunal relations and engendering social and personal reconciliation from the bottom-up; and development theory highlighted the reconstruction of the economy and the promotion of sustainable development as a critical element in building durable structures of peace.

Conceptualizing Peacebuilding

Peacebuilding is an evolving, multidimensional, and fairly elastic notion that encompasses multiple perspectives and agendas—from the UN to development agencies to small NGOs working to promote reconciliation. It is also something of a catchall concept, and a range of similar terms are frequently employed as synonyms: *preventive diplomacy, preventive development, nation-building, peace maintenance, conflict resolution, conflict transformation, postconflict reconstruction,* and even *sustainable development.* For these reasons, it is important to try to conceptualize more precisely what the term means and what its dimensions are. In the following subsections, we set out the definition, principles, aims and tasks, and organization of peacebuilding as it is currently understood and practiced.

Defining Peacebuilding

There is as yet no accepted definition of peacebuilding; at present, every official agency, NGO, and scholar defines it in a unique way. The following definitions therefore are merely representative of the range of approaches in the literature. As we noted at the start of the chapter, the first official definition of peacebuilding came in *An Agenda for Peace,* where it was defined broadly as "action to identify and support structures which tend to strengthen and solidify peace to avoid a relapse into conflict" (Boutros-Ghali 1992: 11). The International Peace Academy provides a slightly more precise definition: peacebuilding is "an attempt to reduce the sources of present and ongoing antagonisms and build local capacities for conflict resolution in divided societies—often in the face of open hostilities and raw trauma" (IPA 2001: 2). The Canadian Peacebuilding Coordinating Committee develops the concept even further by introducing the notion of "human security." They define peacebuilding as "the effort to promote human security in societies marked by conflict. The overarching goal of peacebuilding is to strengthen the capacity of societies to manage conflict without violence, as a means to achieving sustainable human security" (quoted in Last 2000: 80).

The Brahimi Report focuses on the actors involved in peacebuilding, arguing that peacebuilding has a strong civilian element and that it is "a hybrid of political and development activities targeted at the sources of conflict" (United Nations 2000: 8). Similar to this, Necla Tschirgi defines peacebuilding as "non-military interventions by external actors to help war-torn societies not only to avoid a relapse into conflict, but more importantly, to establish the conditions for sustainable peace" (Tschirgi 2004: 2). This approach views peacebuilding as a stage coming after military peacekeeping. In fact, other scholars and practitioners see establishing security and maintaining law and order as one of the central tasks of peacebuilding (discussed later) and would therefore include military activities such as protection and disarmament as a central element in any definition (see Lund 2001).

Somewhat as a contrast to these politically oriented definitions, Michael Pugh locates peacebuilding in the context of development-based approaches to dealing with emergencies, suggesting that it "can be defined as a policy of external international help for developing countries designed to support indigenous social, cultural, and economic development and self-reliance, by aiding recovery from war, and reducing or eliminating resort to future violence" (1995: 328). Pugh's approach raises an important issue, namely, that at one level peacebuilding and development appear to be synonymous. Many activities that on paper are defined as peacebuilding translate operationally into traditional development-like activities such as poverty eradication, rebuilding infrastructure, community development projects, economic stabilization, and the like (Griffin 1999: 9). In fact, some agencies regard peacebuilding merely as development in a postconflict environment, as all these activities attack the root causes of conflict. However, there are two critical differences between development and peacebuilding. First, peacebuilding can be distinguished from humanitarian and development activities by highlighting its overtly *political* aims of reducing the risk of the resumption of conflict and promoting reconciliation and reconstruction through the creation of legitimate political authority (Miall, Ramsbotham, and Woodhouse 1999: 188; Ramsbotham 2000: 172). Ultimately, peacebuilding is about reconstituting the political and social order; it entails reestablishing the social norms of nonviolent conflict resolution. Second, while development activities focus on tangible elements like fostering economic growth, peacebuilding includes an additional metaphysical dimension, namely, the healing of human relations within the affected community.

In short, what these definitions suggest is that peacebuilding entails concerted action by international third parties working in both a military and civilian capacity, employing a hybrid of short-, medium-, and long-term political and development activities that are aimed at recovery from war, preventing a relapse into violent conflict,

strengthening local capacities for peaceful conflict resolution, and creating the conditions for genuine long-term human security. In this sense, peacebuilding is a unique concept that goes beyond the confines of terms like *conflict prevention, conflict resolution, postconflict reconstruction, nation-building,* or *sustainable development.* At the same time, it incorporates all of these approaches into a holistic and comprehensive overall program.

Principles and Assumptions of Peacebuilding

A key assumption at the heart of peacebuilding is that violent social conflict has complex and multiple causes that are rooted in the political, economic, and social structures of society, including intolerable poverty, inequality and relative deprivation, injustice, institutional failure, political grievance, and social divisions, among others. This implies that resolving conflict and creating durable structures of peace requires concerted efforts to deal with these deep structural problems—complex causes require complex solutions. Related to this, peacebuilding assumes that the causes of these kinds of conflict are somewhat generic, and therefore, a universal peacebuilding approach or template can be applied across all cases.

One of the most important and most problematic underlying assumptions of peacebuilding relates to its grounding in Western liberal theory and practice: the current international approach to peacebuilding and conflict prevention is firmly rooted in the "liberal peace" concept (Chandler 1999; Paris 1997, 2001; Pearce 1999; Ramsbotham 2000; Shaw 1996). The liberal peace thesis views economic and political liberalization—specifically, a liberal democratic polity and a market-oriented economy—as the most effective and lasting antidote to violent political conflict; simultaneously, peacebuilding involves an inherently interventionist normative agenda. In practice, this means that international peacebuilding tends to focus primarily on the promotion of civil rights, liberal democracy, multiparty elections, judicial reform, independent media, constitutionalism and the rule of law, property rights, good governance and anticorruption, and the adoption of the neoliberal economic model. In other words, there is an underlying belief that stable and developed liberal democracies preclude the possibility of violent internal conflict.

In addition to these general assumptions, there are a number of specific operational principles that can be said to constitute a general consensus on a peacebuilding paradigm (Tschirgi 2004: 9; see also Kumar 1997; Last

2000; Lederach 2001; Newman and Schnabel 2002; Paffenholz 2001; Schnabel 2002). First, there is general agreement that establishing a sense of security and guaranteeing a minimal level of law and order is a prerequisite for postconflict peacebuilding. That is, there is an acceptance that it is virtually impossible to rebuild political institutions, engage in economic reconstruction, or work toward societal reconciliation in the midst of ongoing violence and insecurity.

Second, it is assumed that given the fragility of societies emerging from war, support from external actors is critical for reconstruction and building long-term peace. However, external intervention needs to include both opportunistic and quick-impact interventions, as well as long-term capacity-building interventions: short-term needs have to be combined with long-term vision (Lederach 2001: 845). At the same time, external intervention needs to be supported by adequate, predictable, and flexible funding, and be subject to proper evaluation and accountability processes—there needs to be a genuine commitment to the "do no harm" principle (Anderson 1999). In short, there is a consensus that within peacebuilding endeavors, "proper mechanisms need to be established to ensure that external and internal actors work within a coherent strategy, establish priorities, and mobilize the necessary resources" (Tschirgi 2004: 9).

A third operational principle is that peacebuilding is a multidimensional process with several key elements. While different actors sometimes focus on separate aspects, there is a growing consensus that peacebuilding has security, political, economic, social, and legal dimensions, and that reconstruction activities need to include appropriate responses at the local, national, regional, and international levels (Lederach 2001: 843). Moreover, peacebuilding entails a combination of top-down and bottom-up processes. In addition, it is widely accepted that even though peacebuilding is a multifaceted, holistic approach, it needs to be guided by a carefully conceived political strategy that defines a clear hierarchy of priorities. These priorities need to be responsive to the specific needs of the situation and flexible enough to adapt to changing political dynamics.

Finally, and perhaps most importantly, it is recognized that peacebuilding cannot succeed without the cooperation and ownership of the people who are being helped. Lasting peace cannot be imposed from the outside; it must be generated from within. This implies that local people must be actively involved in setting the peacebuilding agenda, as well as in leading and participating in the process. Related to this, there must be a commitment to local capacity-building from the earliest stages of the operation; the aim must be to engender self-sustaining processes and institutions. In particular, it is critically important to rebuild and strengthen the indigenous dispute resolution systems that may have been undermined or destroyed by the war (Green and Ahmed 1999: 195). In short, there is a growing recognition that peacebuilding "will only work if ownership of the process of capacity building has been transferred to local actors during the transition period" (Newman and Schnabel 2002: 2).

At one level, the growing consensus on these principles is testament to how far peacebuilding has evolved as a coherent field of theory and practice, although there is clearly still some way to go. In addition, as we will demonstrate, there remains a lag between the theory and actual practice of peacebuilding in the field.

The Aims and Tasks of Peacebuilding

The aims and tasks of peacebuilding can be conceptualized in a number of different ways, each of which provides important insights. For example, Oliver Ramsbotham and his colleagues (2005) conceive of peacebuilding in terms of its positive and negative tasks. They suggest that postsettlement peacebuilding is made up of the *negative task* of preventing a relapse into overt violence and the *positive task* of aiding national recovery and expediting the eventual removal of the underlying causes of violent internal conflict (see also Ramsbotham 2000: 171–72; Miall et al. 1999: 187–88). In other words, they argue that peacebuilding is initially aimed at creating or enforcing negative peace through the negotiation of political compromise or the enforcement of cease-fires, followed by the longer-term aim of constructing positive peace through reconstruction, institution-building, and reconciliation and justice.

Krishna Kumar similarly conceives of peacebuilding as having three interrelated tasks: the *restoration* of essential government functions, basic social services, and a minimal level of physical infrastructure and facilities; the *structural reform* of political, economic, social, and security sectors, which may include creating and/or dismantling organizations, institutions, and administrative structures; and *institution building*, which entails rehabilitating existing political and social institutions (1997: 3).

Other scholars conceive of peacebuilding tasks in terms of the priorities of different stages or time frames. Nicole Ball, for example, argues that peacebuilding takes place in two primary phases: *transition* and *consolidation* (2001: 722–23). During the transition phase, the most urgent tasks involve providing an adequate level of security for civilians, establishing a government with a sufficient degree of legitimacy to operate effectively, assisting the return of refugees and internally displaced persons, and starting the process of political and economic reform. The consolidation phase aims to continue and deepen the reform process, embark on substantive economic and social recovery, and promote societal reconciliation. In a slightly more sophisticated delineation of its temporal dimensions, Ramsbotham and his colleagues conceive of peacebuilding in terms of interim or *short-term* tasks, *medium-term* tasks, and *long-term* tasks across a range of sectors—such as security, political, economic, and social (see table 12; Miall et al. 1999: 203).

Another way of focusing peacebuilding tasks is to concentrate on the social level at which they are aimed. David Chandler, for example, divides peacebuilding priorities into *top-down* processes such as the international regulation of elections, institutional development, and economic management; and *bottom-up* assistance to develop a democratic political culture through strengthening civil society (1999: 110). Lederach has famously extended this notion in his conception of the peace pyramid, in which peacebuilding takes place in three inter-

related and interdependent processes (1997). The first process involves *top-down* peacemaking, where highly visible factional leaders negotiate a compromise. The second involves a *bottom-up* process of forging peace and reconciliation at local levels according to the unique characteristics of those local settings. The third process is a *middle-out* approach by middle-ranking political and community leaders that supports the other two processes through providing vertical linkages (2001: 843). Lederach argues that no single level of leadership is capable of delivering and sustaining a peace process on its own; peacebuilding must be aimed at the involvement of all levels and sectors of society.

Due to its field experiences, the UN has a much more practical understanding of the main peacebuilding tasks. *An Agenda for Peace*, for example, describes the practical aims of peacebuilding.

Disarming the previously warring parties and the restoration of order, the custody and possible destruction of weapons, repatriating refugees, advisory and training support for security personnel, monitoring elections, advancing efforts to protect human rights, reforming or strengthening governmental institutions, and promoting

TABLE 12.   A Framework of Peacebuilding Aims and Tasks

	Interim/Short-Term Measures	Medium-Term Measures	Long-Term Measures
Military/security	Disarmament, demobilization of factions, separation of army/police, maintaining law and order, protecting civilian populations	Consolidation of new national army, integration of national police	Demilitarization of politics, transformation of cultures of violence
Political/ constitutional	Negotiate a political pact, manage problems of transitional government, constitutional reform, institution-building	Overcome the challenges of the second election, deepen the reform process	Establish tradition of good governance including respect for democracy, human rights, rule of law, development of civil society within genuine political community
Economic/ development	Humanitarian relief, essential social services, communication	Rehabilitation of resettled population and demobilized soldiers, progress in rebuilding infrastructure and demining	Stable long-term macro-economic policies and economic management, locally sustainable community development, distributional justice
Social	Overcoming initial distrust, facilitating intercommunal dialogue, consultation with local actors	Managing conflicting priorities of peace and justice	Healing psychological wounds, long-term reconciliation, peace education

Sources: Data adapted from Miall et al. 1999: 203; Last 2000: 86.

formal and informal processes of political participation. (Boutros-Ghali 1992: 32)

Shortly thereafter, in *Supplement to An Agenda for Peace,* the central tasks of peacebuilding were expanded to include "demilitarisation, the control of small arms, institutional reform, improved police and judicial systems, the monitoring of human rights, electoral reform, and social and economic development" (Boutros-Ghali 1995: para. 47). Secretary-General Kofi Annan went on to provide an even more extensive list of peacebuilding tasks: "Peacebuilding may involve the creation or strengthening of national institutions, monitoring elections, promoting human rights, providing for reintegration and rehabilitation programs, and creating conditions for resumed development" (Annan 1998: para. 63).

Other scholars have taken this approach to its logical conclusion and drawn up exhaustive lists of peacebuilding tasks. David Last, for example, describes twenty-four peacebuilding tasks across four main sectors: security, governance, relief and development, and reconciliation (2000: 86). Michael Lund goes even further. He outlines ninety policy tools across seven major functional categories: official diplomacy; nonofficial conflict management; military measures; economic and social measures; political development and governance measures; judicial and legal measures; and communication and education measures (2001: 17–18). In addition, Lund divides peacebuilding tasks into the levels of causes of conflict they are aimed at ameliorating. For example, he outlines specific policy tools for dealing with the systemic or structural causes, the proximate or enabling causes, and the immediate or trigger causes of conflict (2001: 18–19).

A careful reading of the literature reveals a broad consensus on the main peacebuilding tasks. In essence, most authors agree that peacebuilding aims can be summarized under four main headings: (1) *security rehabilitation*—establishing and maintaining security and law and order, and security sector reform; (2) *political rehabilitation*—reconstructing political institutions and legitimate government; (3) *economic rehabilitation*—emergency humanitarian assistance and long-term economic reform and restructuring; and (4) *social rehabilitation*—justice, reconciliation, and local capacity-building (see Green and Ahmed 1999; Kumar 1997; Last 2000; Miall et al. 1999; Peou 2002; Schnabel 2002; Tschirgi 2004). Each of the specific policy goals and tools mentioned by different authors fits into one of these areas. We have summarized the primary aims and tasks of peacebuilding in table 12.

The Organization and Coordination of Peacebuilding

By definition, a peacebuilding project is a highly complex, multidimensional undertaking that involves the coordination of numerous types of actors simultaneously working at different levels and in different areas; no single organization is in a position to undertake all the main peacebuilding tasks. Typically, any single peacebuilding operation will involve literally hundreds of different actors working on the ground: international organizations; national and international relief and development agencies and programs; hundreds of NGOs working in areas such as humanitarian assistance, human rights, health care, peace education, community development, social services, and small business development—among others; and a great many indigenous actors, such as the national government of the country, opposition groups, political parties, trade unions, local associations and NGOs, religious groups, women's groups, communities, and professional associations. The following examples are a small sample of the kinds of organizations involved in peacebuilding.

Actors working in the area of security rehabilitation may include UN and regional peacekeepers or "coalitions of the willing"; Civilian Police (CIVPOL) units; DDR programs, such as those run by the World Bank, by various UN agencies and national governments, and by NGOs such as the Bonn International Center for Conversion (BICC); fact-finding, crisis anticipation, and preventive diplomacy by organizations such as the OSCE; demining programs by NGOs such as the Canadian International Demining Center, the Mines Awareness Group, and the Cambodian Mine Action Centre (CMAC); small arms proliferation control action by groups like the International Action Network on Small Arms (IANSA); civilian protection by NGOs such as Peace Brigades International; and human rights monitoring, such as the work of the UN's Human Rights Field Operation for Rwanda (HRFOR), Human Rights Watch, and Amnesty International.

At the same time, political rehabilitation efforts may include electoral observation and assistance programs by organizations like the UN, EU, OSCE, the Carter Center, the International Foundation for Electoral Systems, and the National Democratic Institute; democracy promotion programs by groups like the OSCE Democratization Programme, the Helsinki Citizen's Assembly (HCA), and Partners for Democratic Change; good governance and transparency promotion by groups like Global Witness; civil society promotion by organizations like the Soros Foundation Network and the FRESTA initiative; human rights promotion by organizations like the International Federation of Human Rights (FIDH) and the Helsinki Committee on Human Rights; and independent media support programs by groups like Internews Europe, the Panos Institute, and Press Now.

Economic rehabilitation efforts typically involve international financial institutions such as the World Bank, IMF, and regional development banks like the Inter-American Development Bank (IDB); intergovernmental development agencies such as the UN Development Programme (UNDP), UNICEF, the World Food Programme (WFP), and the Food and Agriculture Organization (FAO); national development agencies such as USAID, the Canadian International Development Agency (CIDA), and the UK's DFID; and a vast number of relief and development NGOs such as CARE International, Oxfam, Catholic Relief Services (CRS), World Vision, Save the Children Fund, Médecins sans Frontières, and the International Committee of the Red Cross (ICRC), among hundreds of others.

The task of social rehabilitation may include the United Nations High Commissioner for Refugees (UNHCR) working to assist the return and rehabilitation of refugees and IDPs; peace education programs by NGOs such as Search for Common Ground, the Transnational Foundation for Peace and Future Research (TFF), and UNESCO's Culture of Peace Program (CPP); conflict resolution initiatives by NGOs like Sant'Egidio, International Alert, International Crisis Group, the Conflict Resolution Training Committee of the University of Bradford (Britain), Quaker Peace, and the International Peace Research Institute, Oslo (PRIO); truth and justice initiatives such as the international criminal tribunals for the former Yugoslavia (ICTY) and Rwanda (ICTR), the Commission on the Truth for El Salvador, and the International Criminal Court (ICC); and reconciliation and trauma-healing programs by NGOs such as Agenda for Reconciliation, the International Fellowship of Reconciliation, the European Community Task Force (ECTF) Psycho-Social Unit, and Pax Christi.

In addition to this vast multiplicity of organizations, all these external actors will often work in partnership with a great many national and local actors. In this sense, peacebuilding is a form of multitrack diplomacy, since it involves a mix of official and nonofficial agencies and international, national, and local actors. Clearly, peacebuilding requires a great deal of careful coordination in order to ensure all the main tasks are adequately addressed and that overlap and duplication is avoided. There is a consensus that at present, the UN is the most capable and most legitimate organization for organizing and coordinating peacebuilding operations, given its long experience in managing complex peace support operations.

An Overview of Peacebuilding in Practice

There are a number of problems with attempting to provide an overview of peacebuilding practice. First, as we noted earlier, peacebuilding is an evolving body of theory and practice that grew out of UN peacekeeping, conflict resolution, and development. This raises a perplexing evaluative question: at what stage did second- and third-generation peacekeeping become comprehensive peacebuilding? Which cases can we include as examples of fully formed peacebuilding projects? Second, there is the valid argument that all postconflict reconstruction processes involve the attempt to create a durable peace, even if the participants in the process are not consciously working to a peacebuilding template. In this sense, the period following the end of every civil war has been a case of peacebuilding—at least in a descriptive sense. Third, should we evaluate peacebuilding solely in terms of coherent and purposeful overall programs, or do we also consider individual peacebuilding activities that are part of a broader development or relief agenda but not necessarily incorporated into a specific peacebuilding project?

In short, there is no general agreement on which cases to include as examples of peacebuilding in practice. Some authors choose to take a broad view and do include all cases of post–civil war transitions to peace. These are usually large-n quantitative studies, such as the seminal study by Michael Doyle and Nicholas Sambanis, which examined peacebuilding in 124 civil wars in the postwar period (2000). Similarly, Stephen Stedman reviews sixteen cases since the Zimbabwe peace settlement in 1980 (2001). Other authors adopt a narrower focus and concentrate solely on UN peace support missions. They include the second- and third-generation peacekeeping operations in Namibia, Angola, El Salvador, Cambodia, Mozambique, and Bosnia as examples of postsettlement peacebuilding—despite the fact that all of these missions except the Bosnian case were conceived before the UN first articulated the notion of peacebuilding (Miall et al. 1999: 194–98; Paris 2001). In an even stricter interpretation, David Chandler argues that the first fully developed peacebuilding operations began when the UN took over civil administration of Bosnia in 1995, followed by the civil administration mandates in Kosovo and then East Timor in 1999 (Chandler 2001: 12–13).

We can resolve this issue by suggesting that peacebuilding practice takes place in three main forms: (1) fully formed, comprehensive UN-directed peacebuilding operations; (2) peacekeeping operations with significant peacebuilding dimensions and postconflict transitions; and (3) a plethora of peacebuilding policies, projects, and programs within the wider activities of a large number of international, national, and nongovernmental development agencies. There is not the space to examine all the peacebuilding projects or policies of the world's development agencies; instead, we focus on the first two categories.

In the first category—large, comprehensive UN peacebuilding operations—we include UNTAG in Namibia; UNAVEM II, UNAVEM III, and MONUA in Angola; ONUSAL in El Salvador; UNTAC in Cambodia; ONUMOZ in Mozambique; UNMIBH in Bosnia; UNMIK in Kosovo; UNAMSIL in Sierra Leone; UNTAET in East Timor; UNMIL in Liberia; UNOCI in Ivory Coast; MINUSTAH in Haiti; and ONUB in Burundi (see table 8, chapter 8). In each of these cases, the operation incorporated most of the core peacebuilding aims and tasks (security, political, economic, and social rehabilitation) and took a holistic, multidimensional approach—even if they were not always adequately resourced or were sometimes prematurely terminated. For example, UNTAG in Namibia was tasked with separation and demobilization of military forces; the demilitarization of the South West Africa Police (SWAPOL); supervision of the interim government and repeal of discriminatory laws; refugee return and resettlement; and electoral registration and election monitoring. Similarly, Cambodia involved one of the most extensive peacebuilding operations ever undertaken. The UN Transition Authority in Cambodia was set the following tasks: verification of the withdrawal of foreign forces; monitoring cease-fire violations; organizing cantonment and disarmament of factions; mine clearance; supervision of local civilian police training; human rights monitoring, education, and training; temporary civil administration of foreign affairs, national defense, finance, public security, and information; electoral registration, education, supervision, and verification; refugee repatriation; restoration of social services and emergency relief; the reconstruction of basic infrastructure; and economic development (see Miall, Ramsbotham, and Woodhouse 1999: 197).

In the second category—peacekeeping operations with significant peacebuilding dimensions and postconflict transitions—we include UNPROFOR in the former Yugoslavia; UNOSOM I and II in Somalia; UNMIH in Haiti; UNAMIR in Rwanda; IFOR and SFOR in Bosnia; the post-Oslo Israel-Palestine peace process; the South African transition; the Northern Ireland peace process; the Tajik peace process; and MONUC in the Democratic Republic of Congo (DRC)—among others. In every case, important peacebuilding components were present, although they were not necessarily part of a comprehensive and deliberate peacebuilding template. For example, the South African transition included a major effort to promote truth and social reconciliation through the Truth and Reconciliation Commission (TRC), as well as the repeal of discriminatory laws, new constitutional arrangements, land resettlement, and a DDR program for former ANC guerrillas, among many other measures. Similarly, the Northern Ireland peace process has involved concerted efforts to build peace at all three levels of society: top-down high-level negotiations between factional leaders and government officials; bottom-up community-level reconciliation and conflict resolution processes; and middle-out vertical linkage building by recognized community leaders. In UN operations such as MONUC in DRC, peacebuilding activities like demobilization, humanitarian assistance, and human rights promotion have also been included.

In terms of the success of peacebuilding as a method of conflict resolution, there are some unique problems with confidently assessing the outcome of such external interventions, not least of which is the relatively short space of time that has elapsed since these peacebuilding measures were enacted. Most of these operations or transitions are little more than ten years old; some are even more recent than this. It may be another decade or so before we can confidently assume that peacebuilding has really taken place. Nonetheless, most studies agree that peacebuilding thus far shows mixed results.

A review of several major statistical studies, for example, found that although peacebuilding has had a number of clear successes, as many have been failures, and others—such as Cambodia—have only been partially successful (Tschirgi 2004: 11–12). Stedman argues that out of sixteen cases of peacebuilding, six can be considered successes (Zimbabwe, Namibia, Nicaragua, Mozambique, El Salvador, and Guatemala), four have been partial successes (Lebanon, Liberia, Cambodia, and Bosnia), and six have been failures (Sri Lanka, Angola I, Somalia, Rwanda, Angola II, and Sierra Leone) (2001: 743). Of course, even this evaluation is highly contestable; recent events suggest that durable structures of peace are still a long way off in Zimbabwe and Lebanon, and Angola and Sierra Leone appear to be well on the way to consolidating peace. In other words, assessing peacebuilding in terms of its negative task of preventing a return to violence reveals a number of genuine successes; countries like Namibia, Mozambique, El Salvador, Guatemala, Kosovo, Bosnia, South Africa, Northern Ireland, and Sierra Leone have thus far avoided a return to serious political violence. On the other hand, peacebuilding has also resulted in some abysmal failures: Somalia, Rwanda, Haiti, Israel-Palestine, and Burundi, for example, all continue to suffer appalling violence, despite past and present peacebuilding efforts.

However, it is in terms of the positive task of building the conditions for long-term human security that the real controversy lies. For example, while some observers include Bosnia as an example of successful peacebuilding, and while it is true that there has not been a return to large-scale violence, others point out that the Dayton Accords reaffirmed the de facto ethnic divisions that existed during the civil war, and the 1996 elections allowed extreme nationalists to consolidate their power (Ball 2001: 722–23; Chandler 1999; Paris 2001: 768–69). These critics argue that many of the divisions and issues that led to war in the first place remain deeply embedded in Bosnian society, despite over a decade of international peacebuilding efforts. Similar arguments are made with regard to Kosovo. In both cases, there is real concern that when international peacekeeping forces eventually withdraw, violence could erupt once again. Cambodia, another case held up as a success by some, is equally problematic: electoral manipulation and a coup in 1997 allowed Hun Sen to consolidate power, real democratic consolidation has still to take place, and the political situation remains unstable (Paris 2001: 769–70). A similarly unstable situation characterizes Timor-Leste, which has seen a military rebellion, social disorder, and an attempted presidential assassination in recent years.

Critics argue that in the operations in El Salvador, Nicaragua, and Guatemala, the imposition of economic liberalization and structural adjustment policies as part of the peacebuilding project produced a great many destabilizing side effects, such as higher levels of economic inequality, increased criminal violence, and mounting social tensions (Pearce 1999; Ramsbotham 2000). In El Salvador, by the late 1990s, urban poverty had risen significantly, the human development index had fallen sharply, and annual violent deaths had risen to levels higher than those experienced during the civil war years (Paris 2001: 770; see also Pearce 1999). A similar deterioration in living standards in Nicaragua and Guatemala appears to have fueled an increase in criminal and gang-related violence and widespread social unrest. Thus, Roland Paris argues that even though the warring parties in these countries have not resumed fighting, if the main goal of peacebuilding is to address the underlying sources of conflict then "these operations lose some of their sheen, because economic liberalization and structural adjustment policies have exacerbated the very conditions that have historically precipitated social unrest and revolutionary violence in Central America: namely, economic hardship and distributional inequalities" (Paris 2001: 771).

In sum, the practice of peacebuilding reveals an ambiguous record. In terms of preventing a return to violence, the peacebuilding record shows a mix of clear successes, a number of obvious failures, and some partial successes. In the longer-term view of constructing durable structures of peace, the evidence is both unclear and highly contested. To some degree, the difficulty of establishing a clear picture resides in the complex issues surrounding the evaluation of such a complex, long-term, multifarious process.

Evaluating Peacebuilding

In trying to evaluate peacebuilding as a method of conflict resolution, we face a number of difficult obstacles. We have already mentioned how peacebuilding is ultimately a long-term process and that it may yet be too soon to determine its effects. We have also discussed how different researchers adopt either a minimalist approach in evaluating peacebuilding—defining it as the avoidance of a return to violence, for example—or a maximalist approach—searching for signs of deeper transformation of conflict-inducing structures. There is in fact no common framework for systematically assessing peacebuilding operations or policies (Tschirgi 2004: 11). We must also add that peacebuilding does not lend itself to causal analysis, as in any single country there are a host of internal and external variables that may have an independent effect on the overall long-term peacebuilding process. For example, Stephen Stedman's study suggests that the construction of durable structures of peace depends less on external peacebuilding policies than on the effects of certain key variables such as the number of warring parties; the presence of a signed peace accord between all the main factions before intervention; collapsed state institutions; disposable natural resources; large numbers of soldiers; the existence of spoilers; hostile neighboring states and the regional environment; and the desire for secession among sectors of the society (2001). In other words, it is possible that peace has held in countries like Namibia, El Salvador, and Mozambique not because of international actions, but due to other factors in the internal or external environment, such as supportive neighboring states or war weariness among the population. In effect, it may be that some countries and conflicts are more amenable to peacebuilding than others. Related to this, there is the question of whether durable peace could have been achieved in these cases without such outside intervention. This is a counterfactual question that can never be finally determined one way or the other (Miall et al. 1999: 200).

In the end, we must avoid either setting such high standards of success that we are left with a record of undifferentiated failure or such low standards that we cannot accept the very real policy failures in ongoing peacebuilding projects (Stedman 2001: 740). It is our belief that peacebuilding has both real strengths and real weaknesses. Intuitively, and at a theoretical level, peacebuilding has the potential for achieving genuine conflict transformation in complex internal wars. There is no question that dealing with intractable violent conflict requires a holistic, multidimensional, long-term solution that seeks to transform the underlying political, economic, and social structures that engender conflict. The general theory and aims of peacebuilding, therefore, are unquestionable. In addition, there is little doubt that major peacebuilding operations in countries like Namibia and Mozambique, as well as more limited peacebuilding activities in other contexts, have positively increased the chances of long-term peace and stability. The lives of millions of people living with the effects of political violence have been greatly improved through external and internal peacebuilding activities in the last decade or so. At the same time, however, we suggest that peacebuilding faces a number of key challenges and obstacles to its effective implementation.

The Challenges of Peacebuilding

When one considers the enormity of the task of postconflict reconstruction, it is not surprising that the peacebuilding record is less than an unqualified success. Typically, countries coming out of war face massive immediate humanitarian needs—for food, water, shelter, medical care—on par with major natural disasters; a shattered and distorted economy; damaged or destroyed physical infrastructure; a lack of political legitimacy; weak or collapsed institutions; widespread lawlessness and insecurity; extensive psychosocial trauma; large numbers of refugees, IDPs and unemployed soldiers; and an abundance of weapons in private hands, among many other equally complex challenges. Peacebuilding is a daunting task at the best of times. As with other multifaceted conflict interventions, such as humanitarian intervention, peacebuilding faces a series of conceptual, normative, political, and practical challenges. Obviously, there is not the space here to examine all the potential problems and pitfalls of peacebuilding; we focus on a number of key issues raised in the literature.

Conceptual and Theoretical Challenges

At a conceptual and theoretical level, peacebuilding remains relatively underdeveloped. Apart from lacking an accepted definition or clear set of evaluative criteria, a more serious problem is that peacebuilding lacks a coherent body of theory that spells out what the deeper causes of conflict are and how specifically targeted peacebuilding strategies can be designed to remove those causes. That is, it lacks a "well-defined framework for political reform and reconstruction that informs its interventions" (Kumar 1997: 4; see also Tschirgi 2003: 9). Related to this, there is still a dearth of data and empirical research on the peacebuilding–reconstruction continuum (Tschirgi 2004: 1). In large part, this is because peacebuilding practice is rooted primarily in the discourses of emergency relief and development and does not draw sufficiently on conflict resolution theory (Green and Ahmed 1999: 190). Consequently, most studies of peacebuilding focus on providing practical advice for implementing peacebuilding projects (see IPA 2001; Reychler and Paffenholz 2001) and evaluating the current practice of peacebuilding as it occurs in UN peace support operations (Chandler 2001; Kumar 1997; Pearce 1999; Ramsbotham 2000; Tschirgi 2004). With only rare exceptions (see Lederach 1997; Miall et al. 1999), there are few attempts to systematize a theory of peacebuilding. In order to improve its effectiveness, this theory-practice deficit will need to be addressed.

A related issue is that current approaches to peacebuilding assume that both the causes and solutions to intractable conflict are generic. Thus, in practice there is a standardized peacebuilding template that tends to be applied in every situation, regardless of the specific local conditions (Green and Ahmed 1999: 200). The problem with this is that it is not clear that every conflict can or should be treated in the same way. It may actually be that approaches that have been effective in one postconflict environment are ineffective or even counterproductive in another (Ball 2001: 728). Roland Paris, for example, argues that the automatic imposition of multiparty elections and neoliberal economic structures can, depending on the circumstances, sometimes lead to greater instability and conflict in the short term (Paris 2001). He suggests that in some cases, elections should be delayed for several years, and the negative side effects of neoliberal restructuring should be mitigated through welfare policies. Rather than adopting a one-size-fits-all approach, several scholars argue that it would be more effective to tailor each peacebuilding mission to the unique conditions of a given case (Fetherston 2000: 194).

Normative Challenges

Apart from the paradox of whether military elements can or should be employed to build peace (see chapter 8 for a discussion on this issue), one of the most serious challenges to peacebuilding comes from what we might call the radical critique. A great many observers suggest that the current practice of peacebuilding, with its neoliberal origins and assumptions, actually ends up reinforcing and perpetuating the conditions of poverty and exclusion that frequently lie at the root of intractable conflict (Duffield 2001; Green and Ahmed 1999; Miall et al. 1999; Paris 1997, 2001; Pearce 1999; Ramsbotham 2000; Shaw 1996; Tschirgi 2004). They suggest that in the context of a global economic system that marginalizes and disadvantages poor developing nations, the imposition of neoliberal economic restructuring can actually lead to greater poverty, exploitation, exclusion, and social tensions. Moreover, they point to the experiences of countries like Cambodia, El Salvador, Nicaragua, Guatemala, Mozambique, Bosnia, and Timor-Leste where UN-directed peacebuilding has resulted in exactly such side effects. In other words, there are fundamental questions surrounding the role of international economic structures in creating the structures of poverty and relative deprivation that lead to violent conflict in the first place: Can durable structures of peace ever be built in countries that lie on the periphery of an international economic order that seems to perpetuate their marginal status? To what extent does durable peace depend on removing the global obstacles to achieving genuine human security? Is it possible to build equitable market economies in developing regions in the absence of

global reform? A study by Jenny Pearce demonstrates that even when microlevel peacebuilding initiatives are successful, they are often undone by external macrolevel economic conditions that impact negatively on local economies (1999). Other studies by the International Peace Academy show that neoliberal economic reforms can sometimes actually perpetuate the war-based shadow economies that had developed during the conflict, such as those based on the illegal trade in diamonds in West Africa (IPA 2003).

Consequently, some of these authors argue that the neoliberal assumptions of peacebuilding need to be reconsidered, and a more radical, antihegemonic peacebuilding agenda—one that challenges rather than reifies existing global power relations—needs to be adopted (Fetherston 2000). Alternately, it is suggested that the imposition of neoliberal economic and political prescriptions needs to be delayed in postconflict cases until a more stable environment has emerged and local institutions have been strengthened to be able to cope with the side effects of economic restructuring (Paris 2001; IPA 2003). In any case, it seems obvious that in contrast to neoliberal orthodoxy, improving state capacity and legitimacy and restoring livelihoods and social capital in the aftermath of war require radically increased government spending on health, education, water, transport, communications, and public service wages (Green and Ahmed 1999: 198–99). Some critics express the same issue from the perspective of the so-called culture question: should the Westernized liberal internationalist model be imposed on the non-Western countries that are the usual targets of peacebuilding? Is peacebuilding an inherently Eurocentric political project?

In addition to these larger normative-analytical questions, there is also the problem of competing moral imperatives inherent in the implementation of peacebuilding tasks. For example, there may be tensions between the short-term aim of stabilizing the security environment and the long-term goal of promoting societal reconciliation and justice, particularly if this entails uncomfortable trade-offs and compromises with armed groups who have been responsible for human rights abuses in order to prevent them returning to war (Miall, Ramsbotham, and Woodhouse 1999: 207–8). In the previous chapter, we discussed the dilemmas that sometimes occur between the demands of justice and truth and reconciliation. Similarly, there may be a tension between encouraging democratic participation, supporting local actors, and involving civil society in political decision making and the rebuilding of trust and social reconciliation; immediately after the war in Bosnia, for example, civil society was dominated by extreme nationalist groups, and democratic participation resulted in the institutionalization of ethnic fragmentation and suspicion (Chandler 1999). In a sense, community reconciliation, peace education, and the transformation of social attitudes needed to take place first before liberal democratic processes were enacted. Alternately, a less adversarial kind of electoral system than multiparty democracy needed to be tried in order to avoid simply reinforcing existing cleavages.

A final normative challenge relates to the fact that peacebuilding principles sometimes come into conflict in practice, in particular, the principle of indigenous ownership of the process. While this should obviously be a priority in any peacebuilding project it may sometimes be extremely difficult to accommodate, especially when external forces are needed to ensure security or when local extremists need to be forcibly excluded from controlling the media or taking over leadership roles. In these cases, peacebuilding actions may have the effect of institutionalizing an international protectorate rather than fostering the emergence of a self-governing democracy (Chandler 2001: 13). At the lower end of the scale, there is the danger that reliance on external actors and support may create a dependency syndrome, as some argue has occurred in Bosnia (Chandler 1999: 111). On the other hand, there is also a risk that indiscriminately supporting indigenous processes may result in the perpetuation of local systems of oppression, exclusion, and exploitation (Miall, Ramsbotham, and Woodhouse 1999: 210). In short, it is frequently very difficult to determine which course of action adheres to the "do no harm" principle.

Political Challenges

One of the greatest challenges to effective peacebuilding is that it requires a significant commitment in terms of resources, political will, and time. Rehabilitating a country devastated by war can take decades and literally billions of dollars in investment; it requires exactly the kind of open-ended commitment that many UN members are desperate to avoid. The problem is that global governance structures tend to be crisis-driven, underfunded, and oriented toward short-term solutions (Lederach 2001: 845; IPA 2001). Frequently, the will to stay and work in a country for the necessary amount of time or to pledge the massive financial resources required is simply not there. This is why even the most ambitious UN peacebuilding operations are usually given no more than two to three years to complete their tasks and are reviewed by

the Security Council every six months. For example, UNTAC in Cambodia was expected to demobilize and disarm more than 200,000 soldiers in 650 locations; begin clearing 6 to 10 million land mines; supervise the workings of government, including the 50,000-strong police force; repatriate more than 360,000 refugees; register 4.7 million voters; oversee the elections at some 1,400 polling stations; instill civic values and respect for human rights; and engage in national reconstruction and rehabilitation—all within an eighteen-month period (Miall, Ramsbotham, and Woodhouse 1999: 192–93). Added to this, donor funding of peacebuilding tends to be of a short-term nature and oriented toward individual projects (Green and Ahmed 1999: 193). Projects oriented toward societal reconciliation, for example, which can be open-ended and problematic to evaluate, have difficulty attracting donor support. The short-term focus of the international community is compounded by the fickle nature of media attention; once the international media has moved on to another crisis it can become difficult for peacebuilding practitioners in the field to attract the ongoing support they need for their activities. In contrast to most UN operations, some conflict resolution theorists have suggested that between two and five years are needed to stabilize the military and political situation, five to ten years are needed to rebuild infrastructures and regenerate the economy, and a whole generation is required to reconcile formerly warring parties and communities (Ramsbotham 2000: 179).

There is a growing awareness that international events since the September 11, 2001, terrorist attacks have had a negative impact on the peacebuilding agenda and now pose serious challenges to its continuation. In particular, the post–Cold War normative consensus from which peacebuilding emerged has largely dissipated in the wake of the "war on terror" (Tschirgi 2003: 2004). In its stead, we have witnessed a rapid return by numerous countries, most importantly the United States, to narrow state-centric conceptions of security and a retreat from hard-gained commitments to human rights, good governance, and rule of law. One consequence of this has been to divert scarce resources from long-term investments in peacebuilding to increased military expenditures and to allocate international resources to Afghanistan and Iraq at the expense of unmet needs and emergencies in other parts of the world like Africa. In many ways, we are witnessing a return to the distorted priorities of the Cold War era, where military assistance to strategic allies outranks both peace and security and socioeconomic development needs. Another consequence has been to weaken the multilateral consensus that was gaining ground at the UN on the limits of military force: in both Afghanistan and Iraq, military responses have crowded out effective peacebuilding strategies. In part, this is also related to the geopolitical fallout from the Iraq War, namely, the deep political divisions that have emerged within the international community since the Gulf War and the relegation of the UN to a secondary role in the security area. Ultimately, this could further weaken the UN's already limited institutional and financial resources and capabilities for peacebuilding.

However, an even more serious problem lies in the way the peacebuilding discourse since September 11 has been conflated with a new discourse of "nation-building," "regime change," and "stabilization and reconstruction," which in turn is predicated on the necessity of the international community employing overwhelming force to secure the stability of weak or failing states (Tschirgi 2004: 17). Not only does such a formulation undermine the peacebuilding principle that constructing durable structures of peace requires patient and responsive partnership with indigenous actors, but it also risks the securitization of development assistance. From one perspective, there is a real danger that peacebuilding segues into a kind of counterinsurgency strategy that employs reconstruction tools (Orr 2004: 7). Such a development would dilute and confuse the central normative purpose of peacebuilding.

Practical Challenges

Peacebuilding poses an enormous coordination challenge: hundreds of international and local actors working in multiple sectors and across all levels of society. Not only this, but different actors may have quite serious conflicts of interest—between radically oriented NGOs and IFIs, for example, or between different states and external and internal actors. It is not surprising, therefore, that peacebuilding operations have been criticized for the way they have sometimes failed to properly manage and coordinate the activities of all the participating actors (Ball 2001: 730; Schnabel 2002: 20). Areas of particular challenge have been in tactical and operational coordination, military and civilian coordination, in cohering and coordinating the activities of intergovernmental agencies and NGOs, and in effectively linking the work of external and local actors. Another key area where coordination has failed has been in maintaining linkages between economic policies and the peace process (Pearce 1999: 57; see also IPA 2003: 7). In particular, macroeconomic sta-

bilization policies by IFIs have frequently been applied without any thought to their impact on peacebuilding or without any real effort at harmonization with UN agencies or NGOs.

Another area of practical challenge lies in the gap between the range of skills needed to support peacebuilding and the skills embodied in typical international missions (Last 2000: 85; IPA 2001: 6). In part, this is due to poor planning, poor infrastructure, and the lack of institutional capacity and logistics for large-scale peacebuilding within organizations like the UN, a situation that is only slowly being rectified through reform (Tschirgi 2004: 8; see also chapter 8). It is also related to the inherent limitation of international organizations (see chapter 5).

Finally, there are a great many criticisms of how peacebuilding operations are worked out in practice. Clearly, there is not the space here to discuss the failings of each and every peacebuilding operation. The main criticisms of UN peacebuilding in particular include the tendency to adopt a state-centric, top-down approach that neglects smaller NGOs, local agents, and indigenous resources (Miall, Ramsbotham, and Woodhouse 1999: 198; Newman and Schnabel 2002). In practice, this means that often there is a tendency to focus on security and political dimensions to the detriment of economic and particularly psychosocial aspects of peacebuilding. Activities such as societal reconciliation, peace education, conflict resolution training, and local capacity-building are frequently accorded low priority in the overall program. It also means that many UN operations fail to work fully with local partners, particularly those elements of civil society committed to building peace (Ramsbotham 2000: 178; Tschirgi 2003: 10). Finally, some peacebuilding operations have seen appalling behavior by UN military and civilian personnel, such as involvement in prostitution in Cambodia and Bosnia and sexual abuse of refugees in DRC. Obviously, such actions by individuals seriously undermine the credibility and purpose of the peacebuilding mission when they happen.

Conclusion

There is little question that peacebuilding is here to stay: the persistence of internal conflict and the need to rehabilitate countries following years of devastation means that international peacebuilding assistance will be required for decades to come, despite both its internal shortcomings and the inhospitable post–September 11 international environment. As both an approach and a set of practices, it has now been institutionalized across a range of agencies, organizations, and programs, including the UN, and there is a growing body of knowledge about its basic principles and operational requirements. The peacebuilding literature has grown exponentially, and a degree of institutional learning has taken place: the international community is now much more aware of the needs of countries emerging from conflict and how to go about meeting those needs.

At the same time, however, peacebuilding is still very much in its infancy, and many of the problems that plagued the very first peacebuilding operations remain in evidence more than a decade later. The central issues facing peacebuilding in the new century lie in two key areas. In the first place, there is an ongoing need for further theory development, the empirical analysis of field operations, and more systematic evaluation procedures. At the moment, there is a lag between the development of cogent theories of peacebuilding and their practical application in the field. In short, much more research is needed to refine and improve the theory and practice of peacebuilding. The second and much more difficult task is the perennial need to mobilize international will and resources: without greater commitment to long-term engagement in affected countries and investment in the institutional arrangements to back these interventions up, it seems likely that peacebuilding missions will continue to be ad hoc, exit-driven, piecemeal affairs. This places an unfortunate limit on what is probably the best method we have at the present time for building durable and lasting structures of peace.

Conclusion

Conflict resolution, which we have taken to mean a range of activities, both formal and informal, designed to limit, reduce, or control the level of violence and to lay the foundation for a sustained effort to address the underlying issues in conflict, is clearly not static. Many changes have taken place in the way conflicts are managed and resolved in international politics over the past century. We believe many of these changes actually constitute progress in conflict resolution. Violence is no longer inevitable, even in the most intractable cases, and a peaceful path can be charted by many parties in conflict. In the current international system, conflict affects us all, and therefore its resolution belongs to us all. Conflict resolution is in a sense the last democratic response of a globalized world where aspects of justice and legitimacy now matter as much as power and order.

In this book, we have in part tried to trace this evolution by reviewing and examining a range of methods and processes used by international actors to manage, resolve, and prevent conflict. Though it is by no means an exhaustive survey, we have nonetheless analyzed what we believe to be some of the most important methods of international conflict resolution. The approaches described here are the means that states, groups, nations, and other actors in international politics use to resolve their conflicts. Several important conclusions follow from our study.

We have seen that there have, in essence, been two different systems of conflict resolution in international relations. There is the system of official interactions between states and their representatives, where they engage in negotiations, mediation, arbitration, bargaining in international organizations, and other diplomatic relations. This is the system that is predicated on the primacy of the state, sovereignty, diplomacy, and the importance of official behavior. Then there are newer and less traditional ways of resolving other, newer forms of conflict. This system of activities embraces actors other than states, relying on NGOs, Track II diplomacy, individuals and other concerned citizens, and a plethora of informal structures and processes.

We suggest that parallel and overlapping international conflict resolution systems exist. The first system focuses on the management of interstate conflicts. We refer to it as a *system* because it involves a set of conditioned responses—conflict management and resolution efforts—to a set of specific behaviors—wars and crises. These systemic responses have a legal and normative basis in the UN Charter and customary international law, and they revolve around a set of specifically tasked institutions—the UN, the ICJ, regional organizations—who have institutionalized routines, mechanisms, and instruments for the management and resolution of conflicts between states. In addition to the formal mechanisms for conflict management, a range of informal and semiformal processes also exist—negotiation, mediation, and peacekeeping. Collectively, this pattern of behavior displays characteristics similar to an industrial dispute resolution system, which, for example, also contains a legal and normative basis, as well as a set of formal and informal processes and mechanisms. Like the international conflict management system, industrial relations systems sometimes fail to resolve the underlying dispute and unregulated conflict behavior, such as violent strikes or lockouts, takes place. The international system of states may be described as "anarchic," but it is not without its norms, patterns of conflict management, and expectations regarding what is permissible and what is not.

The interstate conflict management system is less regulated and institutionalized than similar systems at other levels. It also has a weaker legal and normative basis than domestic conflict management systems and relies more on informal, flexible processes. It is predicated on such elements as voluntarism, optional exits, and freedom to abide by any stipulations of an agreement the parties may reach. It is a system nonetheless, even if it is at a more rudimentary stage of development. In addition, if one takes into account all the formal bodies and processes we have examined, as well as the informal mechanisms, the rules and norms, and the organizational structures of international politics, then it is a far more orderly system than is at first apparent. There is therefore seeming order at the level of the state, even if there is no systemic order (Bull 1977).

With its origins in the practices of the early European state system, the interstate conflict resolution system is by now well developed, with a long list of established procedures and processes. As our study has demonstrated, it offers states a diverse menu of choices for peaceful conflict settlement. Furthermore, the system is, we believe, proving to be relatively effective. Most interstate conflicts—and there are literally hundreds of these each year—are dealt with peacefully through diplomatic negotiations or mediation, in international organizations like the UN or the WTO, or through legal processes like the arbitration courts of numerous international bodies. Rarely are they allowed to escalate to the point of violence, and since 1945 the number of violent interstate conflicts has declined dramatically, in spite of the ever-increasing number of states (see Byman and Van Evera 1999; Wallensteen 2007). While the decrease in instances of interstate war may in part be the result of changes in the international security environment and increasing globalization, we believe it must also be attributed to the effective institutionalization of the conflict management system. Our study, therefore, demonstrates that interstate conflict can be managed peacefully, and that a fairly effective system, in fact, is in place.

Furthermore, the traditional methods of conflict management that make up the state-based system—negotiation, mediation, international organization, peacekeeping, and international law—are generally well-suited to the primary actors of international politics, sovereign states, and to the conditions under which they operate, namely, international anarchy. They provide flexibility, room to maneuver, and, most importantly, high levels of process and outcome control for parties concerned about their sovereignty. No state would entertain entering into a process of conflict management, or indeed any other process, unless it could have choices, freedom to act, and protection of sovereignty. The traditional methods of international conflict management have served states fairly well for many years.

On the other hand, we must accept that the inadequacies of these methods lie in both the nature of states and the accompanying structures of the international system, as well as internal limitations. Negotiations and mediation will only really work if the conflicting states are genuinely committed to the process and are not using it as some kind of a charade. International organizations, similarly, are limited by their members—states—who use them as arenas for the pursuit of foreign policy objectives and national interests. Similarly, international law is limited in the extent to which parties are prepared to opt in or out of certain clauses, and the extent to which it can enforce its precepts. Each method therefore has a set of unique functions, advantages, and disadvantages. Together, they form what has become a relatively durable and fairly effective safety net for states. When a dispute reaches a certain threshold of concern, the state-based system then swings into action. Diplomats are dispatched, the issues are put on the agenda of international organizations, offers and counteroffers are made, and a range of processes are soon under way.

The second conflict resolution system, parallel to but overlapping with the state-based system, takes as its focus the growing problem of intrastate conflicts, or internal wars. Unlike the state-based system, however, the intrastate system is embryonic. Its methods are not fully developed, its conceptual and legal-normative bases have not been fully articulated, its procedures are still improvised, its goals are ill-defined, and its overall approach remains insufficiently coordinated. For example, there is no standard international response to intrastate conflicts that have passed the threshold of concern—that is, when widespread and serious violence takes place. Often, the international response consists of a series of uncoordinated half-measures, or in extreme cases, complete indifference and inaction. While some would argue that the inconsistent international response to intractable internal wars is simply a reflection of great power indifference to the peripheral countries in which they normally take place, it also reflects the failures of a traditional way of dealing with conflicts, a way that is designed to suit the interests of sovereign states, not parties who wish to mobilize themselves in the interests of an ideology, identity, or group.

The emergence of the intrastate conflict resolution system was precipitated largely by the failure of the state-based system to deal effectively with the vicious and intractable internal wars of the immediate post–Cold War period, particularly the wars in Somalia, Bosnia, Sudan, and Rwanda. In each case, traditional methods of diplomatic negotiations, mediation, and traditional peacekeeping proved inadequate to the challenges of the new wars. The new security environment of the post–Cold War interregnum required a new set of conflict resolution methods—preventive diplomacy, humanitarian intervention, task-sharing, the use of NGOs, and reconciliation and justice–based approaches in postconflict peacebuilding. These are now the new lexicon of approaches for dealing with intractable internal wars, born out of necessity rather than design, but with considerable potential nonetheless. We have thus moved from managing conflicts on a sequential, step-by-step approach that suits the interests of states, to a more complete, embracing, and comprehensive approach that seeks to address root causes as well as their manifestations in conflict. The bar in conflict resolution has certainly been raised.

Current approaches to conflict resolution are predicated on the participation of large sectors of a society in the peacemaking process. The process is no longer the exclusive domain of soldiers, diplomats, and the political elite. Conflict resolution in the twenty-first century is truly a nonexclusive process, and it involves Track II practitioners, nongovernmental organizations, civil society groups, and individuals with a stake in the process. Nontraditional approaches to conflict resolution allow many more voices to be heard, many more issues and concerns to be aired, and many different actors affected by a conflict to be represented. Wider participation in conflict resolution is more likely to bring about a lasting settlement and a sustainable peace. The new approaches to conflict resolution are more focused on human security than on state sovereignty. We should not assume that such approaches will immediately supplant traditional approaches.

The greatest obstacle to the development and establishment of a new and nontraditional set of procedures for the resolution of intrastate conflict lies in the challenges they pose to the state-based system. As our study has shown, improving preventive diplomacy, reconciliation, humanitarian intervention, and peacebuilding will necessarily involve increasing the autonomy of regional and international organizations, as well as NGOs and nonofficial actors, giving them the ability to respond quickly to emerging conflicts. States are now far less important as conflict managers than they used to be. Dealing effectively with intrastate conflicts involves a multidimensional, coordinated approach that brings NGOs and reconciliation processes into the mainstream of diplomatic practice. By necessity, this implies a reduction in the power of states and a ceding of control over aspects of the conflict resolution process and outcome. For example, our discussion of humanitarian intervention highlighted the problems of establishing general principles for intervention, coordinating control over operations in which national contingents seek to promote narrow sectional interests, and improving UN capabilities through increased autonomy.

A second challenge to the establishment of an effective intrastate system lies in the necessity for conceptual reorientation. A new paradigm of conflict and conflict resolution will have to replace traditional thinking about issues of international security. The challenges of intrastate conflicts are qualitatively different from interstate disputes, and entirely new approaches will be required that can effectively diagnose the causes of internal conflicts and recommend appropriate remedial actions. In brief, theoretical innovation must proceed alongside institutional innovation. It is not enough to prescribe preventive diplomacy, humanitarian intervention, task-sharing, or postconflict reconstruction without an understanding of exactly what these methods are attempting to achieve. The intellectual and empirical foundations of each method will also have to be established, as, collectively and individually, they challenge notions of state sovereignty, human rights, and the role of nonstate actors. Sovereignty can no longer mean an absolute and complete impermeability of borders irrespective of what happens within. The responsibility to protect human lives, lives that are so much at risk in any intrastate conflict, must be accorded as much importance as the traditional notion of sovereignty. The conditions for intervention—either in preventive diplomacy or humanitarian operations—will have to be clarified and mechanisms established to facilitate timely responses. In turn, this will require establishing measurable thresholds of concern where early warning processes automatically trigger sustained international action.

The interface between the two systems of conflict resolution lies in large part in the coordination challenge. There is clearly a role for traditional methods in intrastate conflict management. At times, power mediation may be required to end hostilities and enforce cease-fires. International legal processes may be needed for settling boundary disputes, prosecuting war criminals, establishing the legal basis for humanitarian intervention, and giving legal status or protection to nonstate actors. International organizations will be required to mobilize and organize forces for peacekeeping and peacebuilding. Diplomatic talks between opposing parties may require third-party facilitation. However, traditional diplomatic approaches will need to be coordinated within an overall multidimensional effort and carefully managed alongside the work of NGOs, peacekeepers, nonofficial diplomats, and broader social reconciliation processes. In the end, the current practice of marginalizing nondiplomatic efforts in favor of traditional Track I diplomacy will have to give way to a more inclusive, cooperative, and coordinated approach. These problems are serious, and they require considerable attention from diplomats, scholars, conflict resolution practitioners, NGOs, and others.

Adding to this growing complexity are the international changes that have occurred in the wake of the terrorist attacks on America in 2001. The subsequent "war on terror" has raised international awareness of the myriad conflicts occurring around the world that involve the persistent use of terrorist violence against civilians by nonstate groups and individuals, as well as by some states such as Zimbabwe and Sudan, and the challenges involved in managing and resolving these types of conflict. The new focus on terrorism has highlighted a significant gap in the theory and practices of international conflict resolution, namely, how to deal with asymmetric conflicts where terrorism is widely employed and with groups that have adopted it as a tactic. Filling this gap will require a great deal of conceptual and empirical work by scholars over the coming years. Moreover, given the nature of terrorism, the effects of the global "war on terror," and the cumulative impact of both on human rights and security, there are very few more pressing issues for our time.

We believe that the field of conflict resolution can offer a number of important insights, principles, and signposts for both scholars and policymakers concerned with the problem of terrorism. Although more systematic and rigorous research will need to confirm it, and we intend to pursue this in future work, we believe that many of the methods and approaches we have discussed in this book could provide effective tools for dealing with terrorism. Importantly, we believe that they could provide nonviolent, peaceful alternatives to some of the force-based responses many states have adopted in the current "war on terror," many of which have so far only succeeded in intensifying conflicts and undermining human security.

However, before we discuss how different conflict resolution methods could work to reduce terrorism, it is important to clarify that terrorism is neither an ideology nor a discrete form of conflict; it is rather, a strategy or *tactic* of political violence employed by actors in a wider context of conflict to achieve political goals, similar to how guerrilla warfare is a tactic of revolution (Jackson 2008a). Nor is it a kind of moral contamination or irredeemable condition, despite popular rhetoric about the "evil" of terrorism. Committing a terrorist act does not make a person or group nonhuman or preclude them from social life (Booth 2008; Toros 2008). In fact, there are a great many former terrorists who have left terrorism behind and gone on to become respected political leaders; some former terrorists have even won the Nobel Peace Prize, such as Nelson Mandela, Menachim Begin, Yassir Arafat, and Sean McBride. In other words, because it is a political tactic, not an ideology, there is always the possibility that individuals and groups can pragmatically choose or be persuaded to abandon the use of terrorism as a tactic. This is what makes this form of conflict so difficult to manage, yet so important to understand.

Similarly, it is important to note that terrorism, in the vast majority of cases, occurs in the wider context of ongoing political conflict and historical struggle, usually over claims to autonomy, statehood, or independence, or other collectively held concerns. In many cases, it emerges as a strategy of choice in conflict situations after other normal forms of political struggle have been perceived to have failed. That a group employs an illegitimate form of violent struggle—terrorism—to advance its cause does not mean that its grievances or broader political program are necessarily illegitimate. Nor does it mean that the groups and individuals involved in the wider struggle who do not employ terrorism are responsible for or even agree with those that do. In short, there is always a history, a context, and a wider set of deeper struggles that form the backdrop to the use of terrorism.

These points suggest that there are some important conflict resolution principles that could be applied to today's terrorism-related conflicts. First, terrorism should be treated as a symptom and not the sole cause of any conflict. By focusing exclusively on acts of terrorism, there is a real danger that the deeper roots of the conflict will be ignored, and more important processes will be neglected. Related to this, terrorism must be dealt with both holistically as part of a broader set of issues, actors, and behaviors, and comprehensively within a wide range of remedial action and activities (Gunning 2009). Terrorism never arises in a vacuum and should never be treated as an isolated problem requiring a single solution; rather, it is almost always part of a long history of conflict and grievance that requires long-term structural, political, and cultural solutions. Critical to these processes is international cooperation between states, international organizations, NGOs, and other actors concerned with conflict resolution. Like war and intrastate conflict, the solution to terrorism lies beyond the capabilities of any single actor and must be addressed collectively.

A second principle in dealing with terrorism lies in recognizing the legitimate political grievances that most terrorist groups and their supporters are seeking to address. This does not necessarily mean legitimating those groups who employ terrorism or legitimating any acts of terror; it is possible to accept a set of valid aspirations while condemning any illegitimate means employed to achieve them. The importance of such recognition lies in the political space it opens up for pursuing peaceful and nonviolent alternatives to violent contention, and the way in which it can halt escalatory cycles of violence and counterviolence. The failure to recognize the genuine grievances of groups struggling for rights or justice, on the other hand, can mean that violence is often viewed as the only remaining option for affecting change. Similarly, responding to acts of terrorism with force alone can often provoke an escalating cycle of terror in which civilians bear the brunt of terrorist group and state counterterrorist actions. There are several cases, including Quebec and India, where the government's acceptance of the legitimacy of the group's grievances and its stated willingness to explore ways of addressing these grievances obviated the need for violent struggle and ultimately delegitimated those groups and individuals who wanted to persist with terrorist violence.

A third principle is the necessity of building relationships of trust as an alternative to continuing cycles of violence and as a means of engaging in constructive dialogue. This is as true for conflicts involving terrorism as it is for other forms of conflict like interstate and intrastate war. Not only does the vast majority of terrorism take place in situations where people and groups have to live with one another side by side, but community policing, demonstrably the most effective means of deterring and apprehending terrorists, requires a relationship of genuine trust between communities and the security forces (Breen Smyth 2008). In addition, trust—the willingness to take risks and make genuine concessions in the context of an ongoing relationship—is a crucial element in advancing the kind of dialogue and negotiation that is required to move beyond violent contention and into a lasting political relationship where all actors respect the rules of the game.

Last, and related to the previous point, a key principle of conflict resolution is that local ownership of the peace process is critical for long-term success; solutions can never be imposed from the outside, even if external actors are sometimes required to act as intermediaries, guarantors, observers, resource providers, or sources of expert advice. In conflicts involving terrorism, this means that the international community cannot expect to resolve conflict solely through outside military intervention; a genuine partnership with local actors and the commitment and involvement of the parties themselves is an essential ingredient. The principle is the same when the authorities attempt to deal with violent radicalization within certain communities; preventing individuals from engaging in terrorism requires partnership with respected individuals and groups and a collective effort by the community to isolate and delegitimate those who would advocate terrorist violence (Jackson 2008b). This suggests that current efforts to construct a solution to the Israel-Palestine conflict, for example, will require some kind of partnership with Hamas, as well as other Palestinian groups (Gunning 2004). Similarly, resolving the conflict in Afghanistan will most probably necessitate constructive engagement with the Taliban and other Afghan groups; it seems unlikely that Coalition forces will ever be able to impose peace using force alone or without Afghan involvement. It also suggests that a range of actors—official and nonofficial—have potentially important roles to play in the resolution of terrorism.

In terms of the conflict resolution methods we have examined in this book, there are a number that would seem to be important for dealing with terrorism-related conflicts. In the first instance, conflict prevention and preventive diplomacy have obvious potential for dealing with the conditions that give rise to terrorism in the first place. Early warning can be employed to highlight situations of growing tension and developing conflict, especially where they involve serious human rights abuses, restrictions in democratic expression, state repression, and growing levels of violence from contending groups. Once a dangerous situation has been identified, international and local actors can be mobilized to try to ameliorate the conflict-causing conditions and provide nonviolent alternatives for the settlement of disputes. Clearly, there is still much work to be done to identify precisely which conditions are likely to engender terrorism.

Second, as we have already suggested, the role of dialogue can be crucial in resolving conflicts involving terrorism, as it provides the disputing parties with a clear alternative to violent strategies of contention, helps to build trust, and permits the emergence of creative solutions to underlying issues. Historically, "talking to terrorists" actually has a strong record of success. For example, negotiation and mediation were important in the Good Friday Agreement in Northern Ireland, the Oslo Accords in Israel, the Rome Accord that settled the Mozambique conflict, and in terrorist conflicts in India, South Africa, Quebec, and elsewhere. However, more research needs to be done to determine when, with whom, and how dialogue with terrorist groups can be undertaken, and under what conditions dialogue and diplomacy are likely to be successful. Are secret talks more likely to succeed than public ones? Do nonofficial diplomats provide the best alternative to diplomatic recognition?

Third, it seems clear that justice and reconciliation approaches will be needed following the end of terrorist conflicts, as terrorism by definition involves violence against innocent civilians, which is a crime against humanity under most legal systems, including international law. In this case, truth commissions, human rights trials, and various other reconciliation activities will be vital for dealing with the past, reestablishing the rule of law, and constructing a shared vision of the future, especially where people have to continue living side by side such as in Israel and Northern Ireland. All of these processes are important for ensuring that conflict does not reerupt or terrorism reemerge. It is also crucial that such processes involve both the terrorist groups and the state agencies fighting them, as virtually every counterterrorist campaign to date has involved serious human rights abuses against individuals and groups seen to be associated with the terrorists. Atrocities on both sides provide grievances that can later be mobilized for a return to violence, and they must both be accounted for. Again, however, there is a real need for further research to determine the optimal alternatives in each unique situation.

Finally, terrorism is a strategy of political violence that most often emerges in the context of much broader, and usually entrenched, cultures of violence. In a sense, terrorism shares the same logic that sees war as an effective means of achieving political goals; it shares a fundamental belief in the efficacy of instrumental violence (Burke 2008). In this respect, long-term, holistic peacebuilding can be an effective means of both deconstructing the broader cultures of violence within which terrorism is situated and simultaneously constructing cultures

of peace in which violence of any kind is fundamentally delegitimated. One of the current challenges of contemporary peacebuilding, however, is that powerful states continue to believe in and employ large-scale violence as a means of achieving their goals and pursuing their interests. This inspires a wide range of actors to similarly believe that they can achieve their aims through violence, including terrorism. As before, however, there is a need for further research exploring the precise ways and mechanisms by which peacebuilding activities can reduce terrorist violence.

In the end, and as with the challenge of resolving intrastate war, resolving terrorism per se requires an initial and effective diagnosis of its underlying causes. Under what conditions do states, groups, and individuals decide to use terrorism in pursuit of their goals? Are there preventive measures that can be taken to foreclose the terrorism option or divert groups into other forms of nonviolent political struggle? Can the underlying causal conditions be ameliorated so that terrorism is not used in future? Related to this, there is also a need to explore how terrorism ends—the processes and conditions under which groups and individuals abandon the use of civilian-directed violence. Such research will provide important insights for practitioners seeking to devise policies for dealing with terrorist violence.

Ultimately, however, the resolution of terrorism requires difficult choices and compromises, and the mobilization of significant resources—material, intellectual, and normative—to deal with the underlying roots of the conflict and the behaviors they engender. In some cases, it will necessitate talking to and making compromises with individuals and groups accused of committing horrendous atrocities, in the same way that the resolution of many contemporary civil wars has involved similar unpalatable compromises with groups such as the RUF in Sierra Leone, the warlords in Afghanistan, and Maoist rebels in Nepal. However, such compromises are sometimes necessary to avoid future cycles of bloodshed and human suffering and the entrenchment of intractable cultures of violence. On the other hand, the international community, states, NGOs, and others will also need to invest heavily in efforts to deal with the grievances and conflict situations that give rise to violence and terrorism. In terms of the current global situation, it seems likely that the Israeli-Palestinian conflict, situations of ongoing military occupation, the denial of civil rights, the lack of democratic opportunity, intolerable gaps between rich and poor, the oppression of minorities, the denial of political aspirations, and a host of other forms of physical, structural, and cultural violence across many countries will need to be addressed before a real reduction in global conflict and terrorism begins to occur.

Perhaps the most important point, however, is that terrorism, like war and conflict more generally, is a human activity and a social construction; if people can make war or terrorism, they can also unmake it and address its harmful effects. It only requires committed, intelligent, and creative human agency to do so. This is ultimately the driving force of conflict resolution, and as we have demonstrated in this book, it has already taken us some way toward the goal of a more peaceful world. Nevertheless, conflict resolution is not a static activity. It is more a journey than a destination, and there remains much to be done if we are to make the twenty-first century more peaceful and less violent than the century that preceded it. Here we have taken some small, but we hope not insignificant, steps toward this goal.

References

Aall, Pamela. 1996. "NGOs and Conflict Management." *Responses to International Conflict. Highlights from the Managing Chaos Conference,* available online at http://www.usip.org/pubs/peaceworks/pwks4.html.

Aall, Pamela. 2001. "What Do NGOs Bring to Peacemaking?" In *Turbulent Peace: The Challenges of Managing International Conflict,* ed. Chester Crocker, Fen Osler Hampson, and Pamela Aall, 365–84. Washington, DC: United States Institute of Peace.

Aall, Pamela, Daniel T. Miltenberger, and Thomas G. Weiss. 2000. *Guide to IGOs, NGOs, and the Military in Peace and Relief Operations.* Washington, DC: United States Institute of Peace.

Acharya, Amitav. 1995. "Regional Organizations and UN Peacekeeping." In *A Crisis of Expectations: UN Peacekeeping in the 1990s,* ed. Ramesh Thakur and Carlyle Thayer. Boulder: Westview.

Ackerman, Alice. 2000. *Making Peace Prevail: Preventing Violent Conflict in Macedonia.* New York: Syracuse University Press.

Adibe, Clement E. 1998. "The Liberian Conflict and the ECOWAS-UN Partnership." In *Beyond UN Subcontracting: Task-Sharing with Regional Security Arrangements and Service-Providing NGOs,* ed. Thomas G. Weiss. London: Macmillan.

Aggestam, Karen. 2002. "Quasi-Informal Mediation in the Oslo Channel: Larsen and Holst as Individual Mediators." In *Studies in International Mediation,* ed. Jacob Bercovitch, 57–79. New York: Palgrave Macmillan.

Alagappa, Muthiah. 1995. "Regionalism and Conflict Management: A Framework for Analysis." *Review of International Studies* 21, no. 4: 359–87.

Alagappa, Muthiah. 1998. "Regional Arrangements, the UN, and International Security: A Framework for Analysis." In *Beyond UN Subcontracting: Task-Sharing with Regional Security Arrangements and Service-Providing NGOs,* ed. Thomas G. Weiss. London: Macmillan.

Aly, Abdel Monem Said. 1994. "The Road to Oslo and Beyond: Prospects for an Arab-Israeli Peace." *Security Dialogue* 25, no. 1: 37–51.

Amoo, Samuel, and I. William Zartman. 1992. "Mediation by Regional Organizations: The Organization for African Unity (OAU) in Chad." In *Mediation in International Relations: Multiple Approaches to Conflict Management,* ed. Jacob Bercovitch and Jeffrey Rubin, 131–43. London: Macmillan.

Anderson, Mary. 1999. *Do No Harm: How Aid Can Support Peace—or War.* Boulder: Lynne Rienner.

Annan, Kofi, United Nations Secretary-General. 1998. *The Causes of Conflict and the Promotion of Durable Peace and Sustainable Development in Africa.* Report of the Secretary-General to the Security Council, 16 April, http://www.un.org/ecosocdev/geninfo/afrec/sgreport/report.htm.

Annan, Kofi, United Nations Secretary-General. 2003. *Review of Technical Cooperation in the United Nations (Report of the Secretary-General),* 19 September, UN Doc A/58/382.

Annan, Kofi, United Nations Secretary-General. 2004. *The Rule of Law and Transitional Justice in Conflict and Post-Conflict Societies,* Report of the Secretary-General, S/2004/616, available online at http://www.reliefweb.int/library/documents/2004/unsc-justice-03aug.pdf.

Arquilla, John, and David Ronfeldt. 1993. "Cyberwar Is Coming." *Comparative Strategy* 12, no. 2: 141–66.

Arquilla, John, and David Ronfeldt. 1997. "Cyberwar Is Coming." In *In Athena's Camp: Preparing for Conflict in the Information Age,* ed. John Arquilla and David Ronfeldt, 23–60. California: Rand Corporation.

Art, Robert, and Patrick M. Cronin. 2007. "Coercive Diplomacy." In *Leashing the Dogs of War: Conflict Management in a Divided World,* ed. Chester Crocker, Fen Hampson, and Pamela Aall. Washington, DC: United States Institute of Peace.

Assefa, Hizkias. 1990. "Conflict Resolution Perspectives on Civil Wars in the Horn of Africa." *Negotiation Journal* 6, no. 2: 173–84.

Assefa, Hizkias. 2001. "Reconciliation." In *Peacebuilding: A Field Guide*, ed. Luc Reychler and Thania Paffenholz, 336–42. Boulder: Lynne Rienner.

Azar, Edward. 1986. "Management of Protracted Social Conflict in the Third World." Paper prepared for the Fourth ICES Annual Lecture at Columbia University, New York, 10 June.

Azar, Edward. 1990. *The Management of Protracted Social Conflict*. Hampshire, UK: Dartmouth Publishing.

Azar, Edward. 1991. "The Analysis and Management of Protracted Conflict." In *The Psychodynamics of International Relationships*, vol. 2, *Unofficial Diplomacy at Work*, ed. Vamik D. Volkan, Joseph V. Montville, and Demetrios A. Julius, 95–140. Lexington, MA: Lexington Books.

Azar, Edward, and John Burton, eds. 1986. *International Conflict Resolution: Theory and Practice*. Sussex: Wheatsheaf Books.

Bailey, Sydney. 1985. "Non-Official Mediation in Disputes: Reflections on Quaker Experience." *International Affairs* 61, no. 2: 205–22.

Bakwesegha, Chris. 1997. "Conflict Resolution in Africa—A New Role for the Organization of African Unity?" In *Out of Conflict: From War to Peace in Africa*, ed. Gunnar M. Sorbo and Peter Vale. Uppsala: Nordiska Afrikainstitutet.

Balint, Jennifer. 1997. "An Empirical Study on Conflicts (of an International and Non-International Character, Civil Conflicts, and Tyrannical Regime Victimization) and Their Outcomes since WWI." Reports on the United States Meeting of Experts on Reigning in Impunity for International Crimes and Serious Violations of Human Rights, 13 April, Washington, DC, International Human Rights Law Institute; DePaul University College of Law, Chicago.

Ball, Nicole. 2001. "The Challenge of Rebuilding War-Torn Societies." In *Turbulent Peace: The Challenges of Managing International Conflict*, ed. Chester Crocker, Fen Osler Hampson, and Pamela Aall, 719–36. Washington, DC: United States Institute of Peace.

Bartanek, Jean, Alan Benton, and Christopher Keys. 1975. "Third Party Intervention and the Bargaining Behavior of Group Representatives." *Journal of Conflict Resolution* 19, no. 3: 532–57.

Bartoli, Andrea. 1999. "Mediating Peace in Mozambique: The Role of the Community of Sant'Egidio." In *Herding Cats: Multiparty Mediation in a Complex World*, ed. Chester A. Crocker, Fen Osler Hampson, and Pamela Aall, 245–74. Washington, DC: United States Institute of Peace.

BBC News. 2004. "Shell Admits Fuelling Corruption." Available from http://www.bbc.co.uk/1/hi/business/3796375.stm.

Bederman, David J. 1992. "The Glorious Past and Uncertain Future of International Claims Tribunals." In *International Courts for the Twenty-First Century*, ed. Mark W. Janis, 161–94. Netherlands: Kluwer Academic Publishers.

Bellamy, Alex, and Paul Williams. 2005. "Who's Keeping the Peace? Regionalization and Contemporary Peace Operations." *International Security* 29, no. 4: 157–95.

Ben-Dor, Gabriel, and David Dewitt, eds. 1994. *Confidence Building Measures in the Middle East*. Boulder: Westview Press.

Bennett, A. LeRoy. 1988. *International Organizations: Principles and Issues*. 4th ed. Englewood Cliffs, NJ: Prentice-Hall.

Benton, Alan, and Daniel Druckman. 1974. "Constituent's Bargaining Orientation and Intergroup Negotiations." *Journal of Applied Social Psychology* 4, no. 2: 141–50.

Bercovitch, Jacob. 1980. "Conflict, Peace, and Peace Research." *International Problems* 19:31–39.

Bercovitch, Jacob. 1984. *Social Conflicts and Third Parties: Strategies of Conflict Resolution*. Boulder: Westview.

Bercovitch, Jacob. 1985a. "International Mediation: Incidence and Outcomes." Mimeo. Department of Political Science, University of Canterbury, Christchurch, New Zealand.

Bercovitch, Jacob. 1985b. "Third Parties in Conflict Management." *International Journal* 40:736–52.

Bercovitch, Jacob. 1986. "International Mediation: A Study of Incidence, Strategies, and Conditions of Successful Outcomes." *Cooperation and Conflict* 21, no. 3: 155–68.

Bercovitch, Jacob. 1989. "International Dispute Mediation." In *Mediation Research: The Process and Effectiveness of Third-Party Intervention*, ed. Kenneth Kressel and Dean G. Pruitt. San Francisco: Jossey-Bass.

Bercovitch, Jacob. 1992. "The Structure and Diversity of Mediation in International Relations." In *Mediation in International Relations: Multiple Approaches to Conflict Management*, ed. Jacob Bercovitch and Jeffery Rubin. New York: St. Martin's Press.

Bercovitch, Jacob. 1996a. "Understanding Mediation's Role in Preventive Diplomacy." *Negotiation Journal* 12, no. 3: 241–59.

Bercovitch, Jacob. 1996b. "The United Nations and the Mediation of International Disputes." In Ramesh Thakur, ed., *The United Nations at Fifty: Retrospect and Prospect*. Dunedin, New Zealand: University of Otago Press.

Bercovitch, Jacob. 1997. "Mediation in International Conflict: An Overview of Theory, A Review of Practice." In *Peacemaking in International Conflict: Methods and Techniques*, ed. I. William Zartman and J. Lewis Rasmussen, 125–54. Washington, DC: United States Institute of Peace.

Bercovitch, Jacob, and Judith Fretter. 2004. *Regional Guide to International Conflict and Management from 1945–2003*. Washington, DC: Congressional Quarterly Press.

Bercovitch, Jacob, and Scott Gartner. 2006. "Is There Method in the Madness of Mediation? Some Lessons for Mediators from Quantitative Studies of Mediation." *International Interactions* 32, no. 4: 329–54.

Bercovitch, Jacob, and Scott S. Gartner, eds. 2008. *International Conflict Mediation: New Approaches and Findings*. London: Routledge.

Bercovitch, Jacob, and Allison Houston. 1993. "Influence of Mediator Characteristics and Behavior on the Success of Mediation in International Relations." *International Journal of Conflict Management* 4, no. 3: 297–321.

Bercovitch, Jacob, and Allison Houston. 1996. "The Study of International Mediation: Theoretical Issues and Emperical Evidence." In *Resolving International Conflicts*, ed. Jacob Bercovitch, 11–35. Boulder: Lynne Reinner.

Bercovitch, Jacob, and Allison Houston. 2000. "Why Do They Do It Like This? An Analysis of the Factors Influencing Mediation Behavior in International Conflicts." *Journal of Conflict Resolution* 44, no. 2: 170–202.

Bercovitch, Jacob, and Richard Jackson. 1997. *International*

Conflict: A Chronological Encyclopedia of Conflicts and Their Management, 1945–1995. Washington, DC: Congressional Quarterly Press.

Bercovitch, Jacob, and Richard Jackson. 2001. "Negotiation or Mediation? An Exploration of Factors Affecting the Choice of Conflict Management in International Conflict." *Negotiation Journal* 17, no. 4: 59–77.

Bercovitch, Jacob, and Jeffrey Langley. 1993. "The Nature of the Dispute and the Effectiveness of International Mediation." *Journal of Conflict Resolution* 37, no. 4: 670–91.

Bercovitch, Jacob, and Jeffrey Z. Rubin. 1992. *Mediation in International Relations.* New York: St. Martin's Press.

Berdal, Matts, and David Keen. 1997. "Violence and Economic Agendas in Civil Wars: Some Policy Implications." *Millennium: Journal of International Studies* 26, no. 3: 795–818.

Berman, Eric, and Katie Sams. 2000. *Peacekeeping in Africa: Capabilities and Culpabilities.* Geneva: United Nations Institute for Disarmament Research.

Berman, Maureen, and Joseph Johnson. 1977. "The Growing Role of Unofficial Diplomacy." In *Unofficial Diplomats,* ed. Maureen Berman and Joseph Johnson, 1–34. New York: Columbia University Press.

Bertram, Eva. 1995. "Reinventing Governments: The Promise and Perils of United Nations Peace Building." *Journal of Conflict Resolution* 39, no. 3: 387–418.

Bilder, Richard B. 1997. "Adjudication: International Arbitral Tribunals and Courts." In *Peacemaking in International Conflict: Methods and Techniques,* ed. I. William Zartman and J. Lewis Rasmussen, 155–90. Washington, DC: United States Institute of Peace.

Bingham, Gail. 1985. *Resolving Environmental Disputes.* Washington, DC: Conservation Foundation.

Bjorkdahl, Annika. 2000. "Developing a Toolbox for Conflict Prevention." In *Preventing Violent Conflict: The Search for Political Will, Strategies, and Effective Tools.* Report of the Krusenberg Seminar, organized by the Swedish Ministry of Foreign Affairs, 19–20 June, 17–22. Stockholm: Stockholm International Institute of International Affairs.

Blake, Robert, and Jane Mouton. 1985. *Solving Costly Organizational Conflicts.* San Francisco: Jossey-Bass.

Blanton, Robert, David Manson, and Brian Athow. 2001. "Colonial Style and Post-Colonial Conflict in Africa." *Journal of Peace Research* 38, no. 4: 473–91.

Booth, Ken. 2008. "The Human Faces of Terror: Reflections in a Cracked Looking Glass." *Critical Studies on Terrorism* 1, no. 1: 65–80.

Boulding, Kenneth. 1982. "Irreducible Uncertainties." *Transaction/Society* 10, no. 1: 11–17.

Boutros-Ghali, Boutros. 1992. *An Agenda for Peace.* A/47/277-S2411, available from http://www.un.org/Docs/SG/agpeace.html.

Boutros-Ghali, Boutros. 1995. *Supplement to An Agenda for Peace.* A/50/60-S/1995/1, available from http://www.un.org/Docs/SG/agsupp.html.

Breen Smyth, Marie. 2008. "Lessons Learned in Counterterrorism in Northern Ireland. An Interview with Peter Sheridan." *Critical Studies on Terrorism* 1, no. 1: 111–24.

Broad, Sophie. 2000. "Examining UN Task-Sharing: Lessons from East Timor." Paper presented to the Third Annual Conference of the New Zealand Army Military Studies Institute and Massey University Defence and Strategic Studies Program, Massey University, Palmerston North, New Zealand.

Brockner, Joel. 1982. "Factors Affecting Entrapment in Escalating Conflicts: The Importance of Timing." *Journal of Research in Personality* 16, no. 2: 247–66.

Broms, Bengt. 1987. "The Role of the United Nations in the Peaceful Settlement of Disputes." In United Nations Institute for Training and Research, *The United Nations and the Maintenance of International Peace and Security.* Dordrecht: Martinus Nijhoff.

Brookmire, David, and Frank Sistrunk. 1980. "The Effects of Perceived Ability and Impartiality of Mediators and Time Pressure on Negotiation." *Journal of Conflict Resolution* 24, no. 2: 311–27.

Brown, Michael, ed. 1993. *Ethnic Conflict and International Security.* Princeton: Princeton University Press.

Brown, Michael, ed. 1997. *International Dimensions of Internal Conflict.* Cambridge: MIT Press.

Bull, Hedley. 1977. *The Anarchical Society: A Study of Order in World Politics.* London: Macmillan.

Burke, Anthony. 2008. "The End of Terrorism Studies." *Critical Studies on Terrorism* 1, no. 1: 37–50.

Burton, John. 1968. *Systems, States, Diplomacy, and Rules.* London and New York: Cambridge University Press.

Burton, John. 1969. *Conflict and Communication: The Use of Controlled Communications in International Relations.* London: Macmillan.

Burton, John. 1972. "The Resolution of Conflict." *International Studies Quarterly* 16, no. 1: 5–29.

Burton, John. 1979. *Deviance, Terrorism, and War: The Process of Solving Unsolved Social and Political Problems.* New York: St. Martin's Press.

Burton, John. 1984. *Global Conflict.* Brighton, Sussex: Wheatsheaf Books.

Burton, John. 1987. *Resolving Deep-Rooted Conflict: A Handbook.* Lanham, MD: University Press of America.

Burton, John. 1990. *Conflict Resolution and Prevention.* London: Macmillan.

Butler, William E. 1992. "The Hague Permanent Court of Arbitration." In *International Courts for the Twenty-First Century,* ed. Mark W. Janis, 43–54. Netherlands: Kluwer Academic Publishers.

Butterworth, Robert L. 1976. *Managing Interstate Disputes, 1945–1974.* Pittsburgh: University of Pittsburgh Press.

Byman, Daniel, and Stephen Van Evera. 1999. "Why They Fight: Hypothesis on the Causes of Contemporary Deadly Conflict." *Security Studies* 7, no. 3: 1–50.

Cairns, Edmund. 1997. *A Safer Future: Reducing the Human Cost of War.* Oxford: Oxfam Publications.

CIIAN (Canadian International Institute of Applied Negotiation). 2006. *Preventing Political Violence.* Ottawa: Canadian Institute of Applied Negotiation.

Carl, Andy. 2000. *Reflecting on Peace Practice Project: A Case Study.* Cambridge, MA: Collaborative.

Carment, David. 2004. "Preventing State Failure." In *When States Fail: Causes and Consequences,* ed. Robert I. Rotberg, 135–50. Princeton: Princeton University Press.

Carment, David, and Albrecht Schnabel. 2003. "Introduction—

Conflict Prevention: A Concept in Search of a Policy." In *Conflict Prevention: Path to Peace or Grand Illusion?* ed. David Carment and Albrecht Schnabel. Tokyo: UN University Press.

Carnegie Commission on Preventing Deadly Conflict. 1997. *Preventing Deadly Conflict: Final Report.* New York: Carnegie Corporation of New York.

Carnevale, Peter. 1986. "Strategic Choice in Mediation." *Negotiation Journal* 2, no. 1: 41–56.

Carnevale, Peter, and Richard Pegnetter. 1985. "The Selection of Mediation Tactics in Public Sector Disputes: A Contingency Analysis." *Journal of Social Issues* 41, no. 2: 65–81.

Chandler, David. 1999. "The Limits of Peacebuilding: International Regulation and Civil Society Development in Bosnia." *International Peacekeeping* 6, no. 1: 109–25.

Chandler, David. 2001. "The People-Centred Approach to Peace Operations: The New UN Agenda." *International Peacekeeping* 8, no. 1: 1–19.

Chataway, Cynthia. 1998. "Track II Diplomacy: From a Track I Perspective." *Negotiation Journal* 14, no. 3: 269–87.

Chopra, Jarat. 1998. "Introducing Peace-Maintenance." In *The Politics of Peace-Maintenance,* ed. Jarat Chopra, 1–18. Boulder: Lynne Rienner.

Chufrin, Gennady, and Harold Saunders. 1993. "A Public Peace Process." *Negotiation Journal* 9, no. 3: 155–77.

Claude, Inis. 1964. *Swords into Ploughshares: The Problem and Progress of International Organization.* London: University of London Press.

Clements, Kevin. 2002. "The State of the Art of Conflict Transformation." In *Searching for Peace in Europe and Eurasia: An Overview of Conflict Prevention and Peacebuilding Activities,* ed. Paul Van Tongeren, Hans van de Veen, and Juliette Verhoeven, 77–90. Boulder: Lynne Rienner.

Coddington, Alan. 1968. *Theories of the Bargaining Process.* Chicago: Aldine.

Cohen, Raymond. 1991. *Negotiating Across Cultures: Communication Obstacles in International Diplomacy.* Washington, DC: United States Institute of Peace Press.

Collier, Paul. 2001. "Economic Causes of Civil Conflict and Their Implications for Policy." In *Turbulent Peace: The Challenges of Managing International Conflict,* ed. Chester Crocker, Fen Osler Hampson, and Pamela Aall, 143–62. Washington, DC: United States Institute of Peace.

Collier, Paul, V. L. Elliott, Havard Hegre, Marta Reynal-Querol, and Nicholas Sambanis. 2003. *Breaking the Conflict Trap.* Washington, DC: Oxford University Press.

Conteh-Morgan, Earl. 1993. "Conflict and Militarization in Africa: Past Trends and Future Scenarios." *Conflict Quarterly* 13, no. 1: 27–47.

Corbin, Jane. 1994. *The Norway Channel: The Secret Talks That Led to the Middle East Peace Accords.* New York: Atlantic Monthly Press.

Cordovez, Diego. 1987. "Strengthening United Nations Diplomacy for Peace: The Role of the Secretary General." In United Nations Institute for Training and Research (UNITAR), *The United Nations and the Maintenance of International Peace and Security.* Dordrecht: Martinus Nijhoff.

Coy, Patrick. 1997. "Cooperative Accompaniment and Peace Brigades International in Sri Lanka." In *Transnational Social Movements and Global Politics: Solidarity Beyond the State,* ed. Jackie Smith, Charles Chatfield, and Ron Pagnucco, 81–100. Syracuse, NY: Syracuse University Press.

Crocker, Chester A. 1996. "The Varieties of Intervention: Conditions for Success." In *Managing Global Chaos: Sources of and Responses to International Conflict,* ed. Chester A. Crocker, Fen Osler Hampson, and Pamela Aall, 193–215. Washington, DC: United States Institute of Peace.

Crocker, Chester A., Fen Osler Hampson, and Pamela Aall, eds. 1996. *Managing Global Chaos: Sources of and Responses to International Conflict.* Washington, DC: United States Institute of Peace.

Crocker, Chester, Fen Osler Hampson, and Pamela Aall. 2004. *Taming Intractable Conflicts: Mediation in the Hardest Cases.* Washington, DC: United States Institute of Peace.

Cross, John. 1969. *The Economics of Bargaining.* New York: Basic Books.

Dedring, Juergen. 1976. *Recent Advances in Peace and Conflict Research: A Critical Survey.* London: Sage.

De Jonge, Chantal. 2001. "Economic Sanctions and International Peace and Security." In *Turbulent Peace: The Challenges of Managing International Conflict,* ed. Chester Crocker, Fen Osler Hampson, and Pamela Aall. Washington, DC: United States Institute of Peace.

De Jonge Oudraat, Chantal. 2007. "Sanctions in Support of International Peace and Security." In *Leashing the Dogs of War: Conflict Management in a Divided World,* eds. Chester Crocker, Fen Osler Hampson, and Pamela Aall, 335–54. Washington, DC: United States Institute of Peace.

Delbruck, Jost. 1987. "Peace through Emerging International Law." In *The Quest for Peace: Transcending Collective Violence and War among Societies, Cultures, and States,* ed. Raimo Vayrynen. London: Sage.

Denning, Dorothy. 2001. "Activism, Hacktivism, and Cyberterrorism: The Internet as a Tool for Influencing Foreign Policy." In *Networks and Netwars: The Future of Terror, Crime, and Militancy,* ed. John Arquilla and David Ronfeldt, 239–88. Santa Monica, CA: RAND Corporation.

Department of Peace and Conflict Research. 2008. "Sierra Leone." Available online from http://www.pcr.uu.se/database/conflictSummary.php?bcID=94.

D'Estree, Tamra, Larissa Fast, Joshua Weiss, and Monica Jakobsen. 2001. "Changing the Debate about 'Success' in Conflict Resolution Efforts." *Negotiation Journal* 17, no. 2: 101–13.

Deutsch, Morton. 1973. *The Resolution of Conflict: Constructive and Destructive Processes.* New Haven: Yale University Press.

Deutsch, Morton. 1978. *The Analysis of International Relations.* 2d ed. Englewood Cliffs, NJ: Prentice-Hall.

Deutsch, Morton. 1993. *The Resolution of Conflict.* New Haven: Yale University Press.

Diamond, Louise. 1999. "Multi-Track Diplomacy in the 21st Century." In *People Building Peace: Thirty-five Inspiring Stories from Around the World.* European Centre for Conflict Prevention, http://www.oneworld.org/euconflict/pbp/index.html.

Diamond, Louise, and John McDonald. 1996. *Multi-Track Diplomacy: A Systems Approach to Peace.* West Hartford, CT: Kumarian Press.

Diehl, Paul. 1985. "Contiguity and Military Escalation in Major Power Rivalries." *Journal of Politics* 47, no. 4: 1203–11.

Diehl, Paul. 1992. "What Are They Fighting For? The Importance of Issues in International Conflict Research." *Journal of Peace Research* 29, no. 3: 333–44.

Diehl, Paul. 1993a. "Institutional Alternatives to Traditional U.N. Peacekeeping: An Assessment of Regional and Multinational Options." *Armed Forces and Society* 19, no. 2: 209–30.

Diehl, Paul. 1993b. *International Peacekeeping*. London: Johns Hopkins University Press.

Dixon, William. 1996. "Third-Party Techniques for Preventing Conflict Escalation and Promoting Peaceful Settlement." *International Organization* 50, no. 4: 653–81.

Doob, Leonard. 1970. *Resolving Conflicts in Africa: The Fermeda Workshop*. New Haven: Yale University Press.

Doob, Leonard. 1971. *Resolving Conflict in Africa*. New Haven: Yale University Press.

Doob, Leonard. 1974. "A Cyprus Workshop: An Exercise in Intervention Methodology." *Journal of Social Psychology* 94, no. 2: 161–78.

Doob, Leonard, and William Foltz. 1973. "The Belfast Workshop: An Application of Group Techniques to a Destructive Conflict." *Journal of Conflict Resolution* 17, no. 3: 489–512.

Doob, Leonard, and William Foltz. 1974. "The Impact of a Workshop upon Grass-Roots Leaders in Belfast." *Journal of Conflict Resolution* 18, no. 2: 237–56.

Dorn, A. Walter. 1996. "Keeping Tabs on a Troubled World: UN Information-Gathering to Preserve Peace." *Security Dialogue* 27, no. 3: 263–76.

Douglas, Ann. 1957. "The Peaceful Settlement of Industrial and Intergroup Disputes." *Journal of Conflict Resolution* 1, no. 1: 69–81.

Downey, Gary, and Juan Lucena. 2005. "National Identities in Multinational Worlds: Engineers and 'Engineering Cultures.'" *International Journal of Continuing Engineering Education and Life-Long Learning* 15, no. 3: 252–60.

Doyle, Michael, and Nicholas Sambanis. 2000. "International Peacebuilding: A Theoretical and Quantitative Analysis." *American Political Science Review* 94, no. 4: 779–801.

Druckman, Daniel. 1971. "The Influence of Situation in Interparty Conflict." *Journal of Conflict Resolution* 15, no. 4: 523–54.

Druckman, Daniel. 1973. *Human Factors in International Negotiations: Social-Psychological Aspects of International Conflict*. Beverly Hills: Sage.

Druckman, Daniel. 1977. *Negotiations: Social-Psychological Perspectives*. California: Sage.

Duffield, Mark. 2001. *Global Governance and the New Wars: The Merging of Development and Security*. London: Zed Books.

Duffield, Mark, Joanna Macrae, and Anthony Zwi. 1994. "Conclusion." In *War and Hunger: Rethinking International Responses to Complex Emergencies*, ed. Joanna Macrae and Anthony Zwi, 220–31. London: Zed Books.

Dwan, Renata. 2000. "Consensus: A Challenge for Conflict Prevention?" In *Preventing Violent Conflict: The Search for Political Will, Strategies, and Effective Tools*. Report of the Krusenberg Seminar, organized by the Swedish Ministry of Foreign Affairs, 19–20 June 2000, 9–16. Stockholm: Stockholm International Institute of International Affairs.

Dzelilovic, Vesna Bojicic. 2000. "From Humanitarianism to Reconstruction: Towards an Alternative Approach to Economic and Social Recovery from War." In *Global Insecurity: Restructuring the Global Military Sector*, vol. 3, ed. Mary Kaldor, 95–120. London: Pinter.

Edmead, Frank. 1971. *Analysis and Prediction in International Mediation*. New York: UNITAR Study.

Ehrlich, Paul, and Jianguo Liu. 2002. "Some Roots of Terrorism." *Population and Environment* 24, no. 2: 183–92.

Elaraby, Nabil. 1987. "The Office of the Secretary-General and the Maintenance of International Peace and Security." In United Nations Institute for Training and Research (UNITAR), *The United Nations and the Maintenance of International Peace and Security*. Dordrecht: Martinus Nijhoff.

Elias, Olawale T. 1979. *New Horizons in International Law*. New York: Sijthoff and Noordhoff.

Fawcett, James. 1971. *The Law of Nations*. Harmondsworth: Penguin.

Fetherston, Betts. 1994a. "Putting the Peace Back into Peacekeeping: Theory Must Inform Practice." *International Peacekeeping* 1, no. 1: 3–29.

Fetherston, Betts. 1994b. *Towards a Theory of United Nations Peacekeeping*. New York: Macmillan.

Fetherston, Betts. 2000. "Peacekeeping, Conflict Resolution, and Peacebuilding: A Reconsideration of Theoretical Frameworks." *International Peacekeeping* 17, no. 1: 190–218.

Findlay, Trevor. 1996. *Challenges for the New Peacekeepers*. SIPRI Research Report No. 12. Oxford: Oxford University Press.

Fink, Carole, Philipp Gassert, and Detlef Junker, eds. 1968. *The World Transformed*. Cambridge: Cambridge University Press.

Fisher, Roger. 1980. "A Third Party Consultation Workshop on the India-Pakistan Conflict." *Journal of Social Psychology* 112:191–206.

Fisher, Roger. 1992. *Peacebuilding for Cyprus: Report on a Conflict Analysis Workshop*. Ottawa: Canadian Institute for Peace.

Fisher, Roger. 2001. "Social-Psychological Processes in Interactive Conflict Analysis and Reconciliation." In *Reconciliation, Justice, and Coexistence: Theory and Practice*, ed. Mohammed Abu-Nimer. Lanham, MD: Lexington Books.

Fisher, Roger, and William Ury. 1981. *Getting to Yes*. Boston: Houghton Mifflin.

Fisher, Ronald J. 1983. "Third-Party Consultation as a Method of Intergroup Conflict Resolution." *Journal of Conflict Resolution* 27, no. 2: 301–44.

Folberg, Jay, and Alison Taylor. 1984. *Mediation*. San Francisco: Jossey-Bass.

Franck, Thomas. 1988. "The Good Offices Function of the UN Secretary-General." In *United Nations, Divided World: The UN's Roles in International Relations*, ed. Adam Roberts and Benedict Kingsbury. Oxford: Clarendon Press.

Franck, Thomas, and Georg Nolte. 1993. "The Good Offices Function of the UN Secretary-General." In *United Nations, Divided World: The UN's Roles in International Relations*, ed. Adam Roberts and Benedict Kingsbury, 143–82. 2d ed. Oxford: Clarendon Press.

Frey, Robert, and Stacy Adams. 1972. "The Negotiator's Dilemma: Simultaneous Ingroup and Outgroup Conflict." *Journal of Experimental Social Psychology* 8, no. 1: 331–46.

Fukuyama, Francis. 1992. *The End of History and the Last Man.* Toronto: Maxwell Macmillan International.

Funken, Katja. 2006. "The Pros and Cons of Getting to Yes: Shortcomings and Limitations of Principled Bargaining in Negotiation and Mediation." *Zeitschrift fur Konfliktmanagement,* available from: http://ssrn.com/abstract=293381.

Galtung, Johan. 1971. "A Structural Theory of Imperialism." *Journal of Peace Research* 8, no. 2: 81–117.

Galtung, Johan. 1975. "Three Approaches to Peace: Peacekeeping, Peacemaking, and Peacebuilding." In *Peace, War, and Defence—Essays in Peace Research,* vol. 2, ed. Johan Galtung, 282–304. Copenhagen: Christian Ejlers.

Gardner, Anne Marie. 2002. "Diagnosing Conflict: What Do We Know?" In *From Reaction to Conflict Prevention: Opportunities for the UN System,* ed. Fen Osler Hampson and David M. Malone, 15–40. Boulder: Lynne Rienner.

Gartner, Scott, and Jacob Bercovitch. 2006. "Overcoming Obstacles to Peace: The Contribution of Mediation to Short-Lived Conflict Settlements." *International Studies Quarterly* 50, no. 4: 819–40.

George, Alexander. 1999. "Strategies for Preventive Diplomacy and Conflict Resolution." *Cooperation and Conflict* 34, no. 1: 9–19.

George, Alexander. 2000. "Strategies for Preventive Diplomacy and Conflict Resolution: Scholarship for Policymaking." *Political Science and Politics* 33, no. 1: 15–19.

George, Alexander, and Jane Holl. 1997. *The Warning Response Problem and Missed Opportunities in Preventive Diplomacy.* New York: Carnegie Corporation of New York.

Gochman, Charles. 1993. "The Evolution of Disputes." *International Interactions* 19, no. 1: 49–76.

Gochman, Charles, and Zeev Maoz. 1984. "Militarized Interstate Disputes, 1816–1976: Procedures, Patterns, and Insights." *Journal of Conflict Resolution* 18, no. 4: 586–615.

Goertz, Gary, and Paul F. Diehl. 1992. "The Empirical Importance of Enduring Rivalries." *International Interactions* 18, no. 1: 1–11.

Goertz, Gary, and Paul F. Diehl. 1993. "Enduring Rivalries, Theoretical Constructs, and Empirical Patterns." *International Studies Quarterly* 37, no. 2: 147–71.

Goertz, Gary, and Paul F. Diehl. 1995. "The Initiation and Termination of Enduring Rivalries: The Impact of Political Shocks." *American Journal of Political Science* 39, no. 1: 30–52.

Goodhand, Jonathan, and Nick Lewer. 1999. "Sri Lanka: NGOs and Peace-Building in Complex Political Emergencies." *Third World Quarterly* 20, no. 1: 69–87.

Goodpaster, Andrew J. 1996. *When Diplomacy Is Not Enough: Managing Multinational Military Interventions; A Report to the Carnegie Commission on Preventing Deadly Conflict.* New York: Carnegie Corporation.

Goulding, Marrack. 1993. "The Evolution of United Nations Peacekeeping." *International Affairs* 69, no. 3: 451–64.

Gowa, Joanne. 1989. "Rational Hegemons, Excludable Goods,

and Small Groups: An Epitaph for Hegemonic Stability Theory?" *World Politics* 41, no. 3: 307–24.

Graeger, Nina. 2000. "Human Rights and Multi-functional Peace Operations." In *Universal Human Rights?* ed. Robert Patman, 175–90. Basingstoke, UK: Macmillan.

Gray, Christine, and Benedict Kingsbury. 1992. "Inter-state Arbitration since 1945: Overview and Evaluation." In *International Courts for the Twenty-first Century,* ed. Mark Janice, 55–83. Netherlands: Kluwer Academic Publishers.

Green, Reginald, and Ismail Ahmed. 1999. "Rehabilitation, Sustainable Peace, and Development: Towards Reconceptualisation." *Third World Quarterly* 20, no. 1: 189–206.

Greenaway, Sean. 2000. "Post-Modern Conflict and Humanitarian Action: Questioning the Paradigm." *Journal of Humanitarian Affairs,* available from http://www.jha.ac/articles/a053.htm.

Greenstein, Fred. 1967. "The Impact of Personality on Politics." *American Political Science Review* 61, no. 3: 629–41.

Greenstein, Fred. 1969. *Personality and Politics: Problems of Evidence, Inference, and Conceptualization.* Chicago: Markham Publishers.

Gregory, Raymond A. 1994. "Democracies, Disputes, and Third Party Intermediaries." *Journal of Conflict Resolution* 38, no. 1: 28–42.

Griffin, Michele. 1999. "Retrenchment, Reform, and Regionalization: Trends in UN Peace Support Operations." *International Peacekeeping* 6, no. 1: 1–31.

Gulliver, P. H. 1979. *Disputes and Negotiations: Cross-Cultural Perspectives.* New York: Academic Press.

Gunning, Jeroen. 2004. "Peace with Hamas? The Transforming Potential of Political Participation." *International Affairs* 80, no. 2: 233–55.

Gunning, Jeroen. 2009. "Social Movement Theory and the Study of Terrorism." In *Critical Terrorism Studies: A New Research Agenda,* ed. Richard Jackson, Marie Breen Smyth, and Jeroen Gunning. Abingdon, UK: Routledge.

Gurr, Ted. 1970. *Why Men Rebel.* Princeton: Princeton University Press.

Gutlove, Paula, and Gordon Thompson. 1995. "The Potential for Cooperation by the OSCE and Non-Governmental Actors on Conflict Management." *Helsinki Monitor* 6, no. 3: 52–64.

Haas, Ernst B. 1983. "Regime Decay: Conflict Management and International Organizations, 1945–1981." *International Organization* 37, no. 2: 189–256.

Haas, Ernst B. 1987. "The Collective Management of International Conflict, 1945–1984." In United Nations Institute for Training and Research (UNITAR), *The United Nations and the Maintenance of International Peace and Security.* Dordrecht: Martinus Nijhoff.

Haas, Ernst B. 1989. "Conflict Management and International Organizations, 1945–1981." In *The Politics of International Organizations: Patterns and Insights,* ed. Paul Diehl. Chicago: Dorsey Press.

Haas, Richard N. 1990. *Conflicts Unending.* New Haven: Yale University Press.

Hackett, Kenneth. 2000. "International NGOs in Preventing Conflict." In *Preventive Diplomacy: Stopping Wars before They Start,* ed. Kevin M. Cahill, 273–86. New York: Routledge.

Hague Permanent Court of Arbitration. 2008. Web site, http://www.pca-cpa.org.

Hampson, Fen Osler. 1997. "Third-Party Roles in the Termination of Intercommunal Conflict." *Millennium: Journal of International Studies* 26, no. 3: 727–50.

Hampson, Fen Osler. 2002. "Preventive Diplomacy at the United Nations and Beyond." In *From Reaction to Conflict Prevention: Opportunities for the UN System,* ed. Fen Osler Hampson and David M. Malone, 139–57. Boulder: Lynne Rienner.

Hartwell, Marcia. 1999. "The Role of Forgiveness in Reconstructing Society after Conflict." *Journal of Humanitarian Assistance,* available from: http://www.jha.ac/articles/a048.htm.

Hartzell, Caroline, Matthew Hoddie, and Donald Rothchild. 2001. "Stabilizing the Peace after Civil War: An Investigation of Some Key Variables." *International Organization* 55, no. 1: 183–208.

Hattotuwa, Sanjana. 2002. "The Internet and Conflict Transformation in Sri Lanka." Paper presented at Oneworld Regional Conference for South Asian Partners, Delhi, 18–19 March.

Haufler, Virginia. 2001. "Is There a Role for Business in Conflict Management?" In *Turbulent Peace: The Challenges of Managing International Conflict,* ed. Chester Crocker, Fen Osler Hampson, and Pamela Aall, 659–76. Washington, DC: United States Institute of Peace.

Hayner, Priscilla B. 1994. "Fifteen Truth Commissions, 1974 to 1994: A Comparative Study." *Human Rights Quarterly* 16, no. 4: 597–655.

HD Centre (Centre for Humanitarian Dialogue). 2002. Web site, http://www.hdcentre.org.

Henrikson, Alan K. 1995. "The Growth of Regional Organizations and the Role of the United Nations." In *Regionalism in World Politics: Regional Organization and International Order,* ed. Louise Fawcett and Andrew Hurrell, 122–68. Oxford: Oxford University Press.

Hermann, Margaret. 1980. "Explaining Foreign Policy Behavior Using the Personal Characteristics of Political Leaders." *International Studies Quarterly* 24, no. 4: 7–46.

Hermann, Margaret, and N. Kogan. 1977. "Effects of Negotiators' Personalities on Negotiation Behavior." In *Negotiations: Social Psychological Perspectives,* ed. Daniel Druckman, 247–74. Beverly Hills: Sage.

Hess, Patrick. 2002. *Cyberterrorism and Information War.* New Delhi: Anmol Publications.

Higgins, Rosalyn. 1994. *Problems and Process: International Law and How We Use It.* Oxford: Clarendon Press.

Hiltrop, Jean M. 1985. "Mediator Behaviour and the Settlement of Collective Disputes in Britain." *Journal of Social Issues* 41, no. 2: 83–100.

Hiltrop, Jean M. 1989. "Factors Affected with Successful Labor Mediation." In *Mediation Research: The Process and Effectiveness of Third-Party Intervention,* ed. Kenneth Kressel and Dean G. Pruitt, 241–62. San Francisco: Jossey-Bass.

Himes, Joseph. 1966. "The Functions of Racial Conflict." *Social Forces* 45, no. 1: 1–10.

Himes, Joseph. 1980. *Conflict and Conflict Management.* Athens: University of Georgia Press.

Hoffman, Evan. 2008. *A Model for a Whole-of-Problem Approach to Preventing Violent Conflict.* Forthcoming.

Holbrooke, Richard. 1999. "The Road to Sarajevo." In *Herding Cats: Multiparty Mediation in a Complex World,* ed. Chester Crocker, Fen Osler Hampson, and Pamela Aall, 325–44. Washington, DC: United States Institute of Peace.

Holiday, Anthony. 1998. "Forgiving and Forgetting: The Truth and Reconciliation Commission." In *Negotiating the Past: The Making of Memory in South Africa,* ed. Sarah Nuttall and Carli Coetzee, 43–56. Cape Town, South Africa: Oxford University Press.

Holsti, Kalevi. 1983. *International Politics: A Framework for Analysis.* 4th ed. Englewood Cliffs, NJ: Prentice-Hall.

Holtzman, Steven, Ann Elwan, and Colin Scott. 1998. *Post-Conflict Reconstruction: The Role of the World Bank.* Washington, DC: World Bank.

Horowitz, Irving. 1962. "Consensus, Conflict, and Cooperation: A Sociological Inventory." *Social Forces* 41, no. 2: 177–88.

Horowitz, Sara. 2007. "Mediation." In *Handbook of Peace and Conflict Studies,* ed. Charles Webel and Johan Galtung, 51–63. New York: Routledge.

Howard, Michael. 1993. "The Historical Development of the UN's Role in International Security." In *United Nations, Divided World: The UN's Roles in International Relations,* ed. Adam Roberts and Benedict Kingsbury, 166–93. 2d ed. Oxford: Clarendon Press.

Human Security Centre. 2005. *Human Security Report, 2005: War and Peace in the Twenty-first Century.* New York: Oxford University Press.

Hume, Cameron. 1994. *Ending Mozambique's War: The Role of Mediation and Good Offices.* Washington, DC: United States Institute of Peace.

Humphrey, Michael. 2002. *The Politics of Atrocity and Reconciliation: From Terror to Trauma.* London: Routledge.

Humphreys, Macartan. 2005. "Natural Resources and Armed Conflicts: Issues and Options." In *Profiting from Peace: Managing the Resource Dimensions of Civil War,* ed. Karen Ballentine and Heiko Nitzschke, 25–46. Boulder: Lynne Rienner.

Hurrell, Andrew, and Louise Fawcett. 1995. "Conclusion: Regionalism and International Order?" In *Regionalism in World Politics: Regional Organization and International Order,* ed. Louise Fawcett and Andrew Hurrell, 309–28. Oxford: Oxford University Press.

Hutchful, E. 1999. "The ECOMOG Experience with Peacekeeping in West Africa." In *Whither Peacekeeping in Africa?* ed. Mark Malan. ISS Monograph No. 36, South Africa.

Huyse, Luc. 1995. "Justice after Transitions: On the Choices Elites Make in Dealing with the Past." *Law and Social Inquiry* 20, no. 1: 51–78.

Huyse, Luc. 2001. "Amnesty, Truth, or Prosecution?" In *Peacebuilding: A Field Guide,* ed. Luc Reychler and Thania Paffenholz. Boulder: Lynne Rienner.

Ignatieff, Michael. 1999. *The Warrior's Honor: Ethnic War and the Modern Conscience.* London: Vintage.

ICISS (International Commission on Intervention and State Sovereignty). 2001. *The Responsibility to Protect.* Ottawa: International Development Research Centre.

ICJ (International Court of Justice). 2008. International Court of Justice Web site, http://www.icj-cij.org/homepage/index.php?p1=0.

Ikle, Fred. 1964. *How Nations Negotiate*. New York: Harper & Row.

Inkson, John, Derek Pugh, and David Hickson. 1970. "Organization Context and Structure: An Abbreviated Replication." *Administrative Science Quarterly* 15, no. 1: 318–29.

IPA (International Peace Academy). 1996. *IPA Seminar on Peacemaking and Peacekeeping, New York*. Pocantico Conference Center, Tarrytown, New York, 3–8 September, 1996. Available online at http://www.ipacadamy.org/nysr.htm.

IPA (International Peace Academy). 2001. *Towards Comprehensive Peacebuilding*. New York Seminar, 7–10 May, available online at http://www.ipacademy.org.

IPA (International Peace Academy). 2003. *Transforming War Economies: Challenges for Peacemaking and Peacebuilding*. Report of the 725th Wilton Park Conference, Wiston House, Sussex, 27–29 October, available online at http://www.ipacademy.org.

Jabri, Vivienne. 1990. *Mediating Conflict: Decision Making and Western Intervention in Namibia*. Manchester: Manchester University Press.

Jackson, Elmore. 1952. *Meeting of Minds: A Way to Peace Through Mediation*. London: McGraw-Hill.

Jackson, Richard. 2000. "The Dangers of Regionalising International Conflict Management: The African Experience." *Political Science* 52, no. 1: 41–60.

Jackson, Richard. 2001. "The Role of Mediation in the Coordinated Management of Complex Emergencies." In *Rethinking Humanitarianism: Conference Proceedings*, 24–26 September, ed. Bronwyn Evans-Kent and Roland Bleiker, 332–33. University of Queensland, Brisbane, Australia.

Jackson, Richard. 2004. "The Social Construction of Internal War." In *(Re)Constructing Cultures of Violence and Peace*, ed. Richard Jackson, 1–13. Amsterdam and New York: Rodopi.

Jackson, Richard. 2005. "Internal War, International Mediation, and Non-Official Diplomacy: Lessons from Mozambique." *Journal of Conflict Studies* 15, no. 1: 153–76.

Jackson, Richard. 2008a. "An Argument for Terrorisim." *Perspectives on Terrorism* 2, no. 2: 25–32.

Jackson, Richard. 2008b. "Counter-terrorism and Communities: An Interview with Robert Lambert." *Critical Studies on Terrorism* 1, no. 2: 293–308.

Jackson, Richard, and Helen Dexter. Forthcoming. *What Causes Intra-State War? A Framework for Understanding Organized Civil Violence*. Manchester: Manchester University Press.

Jacob, Philip, and Alexine Atherton. 1965. *The Dynamics of International Organization: The Making of World Order*. Homewood, IL: Dorsey Press.

Janis, Mark W. 1992. "The International Court." In *International Courts for the Twenty-first Century*, ed. Mark W. Janis, 13–41. Netherlands: Kluwer Academic Publishers.

Jeong, Ho-Won. 2000. *Peace and Conflict Studies: An Introduction*. Aldershot: Ashgate.

Johnston, Douglas. 1994. "Looking Ahead: Toward a New Paradigm." In *Religion, The Missing Dimension of Statecraft*, ed. Douglas Johnston and Cynthia Sampson, 316–38. New York: Oxford University Press.

Jones, Bruce. 2004. *Evolving Models of Peacekeeping: Policy Implications and Responses*. Department of Peacekeeping Operations Best Practices Unit External Study, available online at http://pbpu.unlb.org/pbpu/library/Bruce%20Jones%20paper%20with%20logo.pdf.

Joyner, Christopher. 1992. "The Reality and Relevance of International Law." In *The Global Agenda*, ed. Charles Kegley and Eugene Wittkopf, 202–15. 3rd ed. New York: McGraw-Hill.

Kaldor, Mary. 1999. *New and Old Wars: Organized Violence in a Global Era*. Cambridge: Polity.

Kaldor, Mary. 2000. "Introduction." In *Global Insecurity: Restructuring the Global Military Sector*, vol. 3, ed. Mary Kaldor, 1–23. London: Pinter.

Karim, Abdoul, and Richard Pegnetter. 1983. "Mediator Strategies, Qualities, and Mediation Effectiveness." *Industrial Relations* 22, no. 1: 105–14.

Karns, Margaret, and Karen Mingst. 1994. "Maintaining International Peace and Security: UN Peacekeeping and Peacemaking." In *World Security: Challenges for a New Century*, ed. Michael Klare and Daniel Thomas, 188–215. 2d ed. New York: St. Martin's Press.

Kaufman, Stuart J. 2001. *Modern Hatreds: The Symbolic Politics of Ethnic War*. Ithaca: Cornell University Press.

Kay, Kira. 2003. *The "New Humanitarianism": The Henry Dunant Center and the Aceh Peace Negotiations*. Available from http://www.princeton.edu/research/cases.xml.

Keen, David. 1998. "The Economic Functions of Violence in Civil Wars." *Adelphi Paper 320*. Oxford: Oxford University Press.

Keen, David. 2003. "Greedy Elites, Dwindling Resources, Alienated Youths: The Anatomy of Protracted Violence in Sierra Leone." *International Politics and Society* 2:67–94.

Kegley, Charles, and Eugene Wittkopf. 1992. *World Politics: Trend and Transformation*. New York: St. Martins Press.

Kelman, Herbert. 1979. "An Interactional Approach to Conflict Resolution and Its Application to Israeli-Palestinian Relations." *International Interactions* 6, no. 2: 99–122.

Kelman, Herbert. 1991. "Interactive Problem Solving: The Uses and Limits of a Therapeutic Model for the Resolution of International Conflicts." In *The Psychodynamics of International Relationships*, vol. 2, *Unofficial Diplomacy at Work*, ed. Vamik Volkan, Demetrios Julius, and Joseph de Montville, 145–60. Lexington, MA: Lexington Books.

Kelman, Herbert. 1992. "Informal Mediation by the Scholar/Practitioner." In *Mediation in International Relations*, ed. Jacob Bercovitch and Jeffrey Rubin. New York: St. Martin's Press.

Kelman, Herbert. 1996. "Negotiation as Interactive Problem Solving." *International Negotiation: A Journal of Theory and Practice* 1, no. 1: 99–123.

Kelman, Herbert. 1997. "Nationalism, Patriotism, and National Identity: Social-Psychological Dimensions." In *Patriotism in the Lives of Individuals and Nations*, ed. Daniel Bar-Tar and Ervin Staub, 165–89. Chicago: Nelson-Hall.

Kelman, Herbert. 1998. "Interactive Problem Solving: An Approach to Conflict Resolution and Its Application in the Middle East." *Political Science and Politics* 31, no. 2: 190–98.

Kelman, Herbert, and Seth Cohen. 1974. "The Problem-Solving Workshop: A Social-Psychological Contribution to the Resolution of International Conflicts." *Journal of Peace Research* 13, no. 2: 79–90.

Khadiagala, Gilbert M. 2000. "Mediating Civil Conflicts in Eastern Africa." Paper presented to the African Studies Association of the United Kingdom (ASAUK) Conference, 11–13 September, Trinity College, Cambridge.

Knight, W. Andy. 1998. "Establishing Political Authority in Peace-Maintenance." In *The Politics of Peace-Maintenance*, ed. Jarat Chopra, 19–40. Boulder: Lynne Rienner.

Kochan, Thomas, and Todd Jick. 1978. "A Theory of Public Sector Mediation Process." *Journal of Conflict Resolution* 22, no. 2: 209–40.

Kolb, Deborah. 1983. *The Mediators*. Cambridge: MIT Press.

Kolb, Deborah, and Jeffrey Z. Rubin. 1991. "Mediation through a Disciplinary Prism." *Research on Negotiation in Organizations* 3, no. 1: 231–57.

Krasner, Stephen. 1983. "Structural Causes and Regime Consequences: Regimes as Intervening Variables." In *International Regimes*, ed. Stephen Krasner, 1–22. London: Cornell University Press.

Kraybill, Ron. 1994. "Zimbabwe: The Role of Religious Actors." In *Religion, The Missing Dimension of Statecraft*, ed. Douglas Johnson and Cynthia Sampson, 208–57. New York: Oxford University Press.

Kressel, Kenneth. 1972. *Labor Mediation: An Exploratory Survey*. New York: Association of Labor Mediation Agencies.

Kressel, Kenneth. 1998. *Constructive Conflicts: From Escalation to Resolution*. New York: Rowman and Littlefield.

Kressel, Kenneth, and Dean G. Pruitt, eds. 1989. *Mediation Research: The Process and Effectiveness of Third-Party Intervention*. San Francisco: Jossey-Bass.

Kriesberg, Louis. 1982. *Social Conflicts*. 2d ed. Englewood Cliffs, NJ: Prentice-Hall.

Kriesberg, Louis. 1998a. *Constructive Conflicts: From Escalation to Resolution*. Lanham, MD: Rowman & Littlefield.

Kriesberg, Louis. 1998b. "The Phases of Constructive Conflicts: Communal Conflicts and Proactive Solutions." In *Peace in the Midst of War*, ed. David Carment and Patrick James, 33–62. Pittsburgh: University of Pittsburgh Press.

Kriesberg, Louis. 2001. "Nature, Dynamics, and Phases of Intractability." In *Turbulent Peace: The Challenges of Managing International Conflict*, ed. Chester Crocker, Fen Osler Hampson, and Pamela Aall. Washington, DC: United States Institute of Peace.

Kritz, Neil, ed. 1995. *Transitional Justice: How Emerging Democracies Reckon with Former Regimes*. Washington, DC: United States Institute of Peace.

Kumar, Krishna. 1997. "The Nature and Focus of International Assistance for Rebuilding War-Torn Societies." In *Rebuilding Societies after Civil War: Critical Roles for International Assistance*, ed. Krishna Kumar, 1–38. Boulder: Lynne Rienner.

Lake, Donald, and David Rothchild. 1996. "Containing Fear: The Origins and Management of Ethnic Conflict." *International Security* 21, no. 2: 41–75.

Lall, Arthur. 1966. *Modern International Negotiation*. New York: Columbia University Press.

Landsberger, Henry. 1960. "The Behavior and Personality of the Labor Mediator." *Personnel Psychology* 13, no. 2: 329–48.

Laqueur, Walter. 2003. *No End To War: Terrorism in the Twenty-First Century*. New York: Continuum.

Last, David. 2000. "Organizing for Effective Peacebuilding." *International Peacekeeping* 7, no. 1: 80–96.

Lauren, Paul Gordon. 1983. "Crisis Prevention in Nineteenth-Century Diplomacy." In *Managing U.S.-Soviet Rivalry: Problems of Crisis Prevention*, ed. Alexander L. George, 31–64. Boulder: Westview.

Lederach, John Paul. 1994. *Building Peace: Sustainable Reconciliation in Divided Societies*. Tokyo: United Nations University Press.

Lederach, John Paul. 1997. *Building Peace: Sustainable Reconciliation in Divided Societies*. Washington, DC: United States Institute of Peace.

Lederach, John Paul. 2001. "Civil Society and Reconciliation." In *Turbulent Peace: The Challenges of Managing International Conflict*, ed. Chester Crocker, Fen Osler Hampson, and Pamela Aall, 841–54. Washington, DC: United States Institute of Peace.

Lederach, John Paul, and Paul Wehr. 1991. "Mediating Conflict in Central America." *Journal of Peace Research* 28, no. 1: 85–98.

Leurdijk, Dick. 1998. "Before and After Dayton: The UN and NATO in the Former Yugoslavia." In *Beyond UN Subcontracting: Task-Sharing with Regional Security Arrangements and Service-Providing NGOs*, ed. Thomas G. Weiss, 49–66. London: Macmillan.

Levi, Werner. 1976. *Law and Politics in the International Society*. London: Sage.

Licklider, Roy. 1995. "The Consequences of Negotiated Settlements in Civil Wars, 1945–1993." *American Political Science Review* 89, no. 3: 681–90.

Lieberfeld, Daniel. 1995. "Small Is Credible: Norway's Niche in International Dispute Settlement." *Negotiation Journal* 11, no. 3: 201–7.

Louis, Meryl. 1977. "How Individuals Conceptualize Conflict." *Human Relations* 30, no. 5: 451–67.

Luard, Evan. 1988. *Conflict and Peace in the Modern International System: A Study of the Principles of International Order*. 2d ed. London: Macmillan.

Luck, Edward. 2002. "Prevention: Theory and Practice." In *From Reaction to Conflict Prevention: Opportunities for the UN System*, ed. Fen Osler Hampson and David M. Malone, 251–71. Boulder: Lynne Rienner.

Lund, Michael. 1996. *Preventive Violent Conflict: A Strategy for Preventive Diplomacy*. Washington, DC: United States Institute of Peace.

Lund, Michael. 2000. "Creeping Institutionalization of the Culture of Prevention?" In *Preventing Violent Conflict: The Search for Political Will, Strategies, and Effective Tools*. Report of the Krusenberg Seminar, organized by the Swedish Ministry of Foreign Affairs, 19–20 June, 23–30. Stockholm: Stockholm International Institute of International Affairs.

Lund, Michael. 2001. "A Toolbox for Responding to Conflicts and Building Peace." In *Peacebuilding: A Field Guide*, ed. Luc Reychler and Thania Paffenholz, 16–20. Boulder: Lynne Rienner.

Lund, Michael. 2002. "From Lessons to Action." In *From*

Reaction to Conflict Prevention: Opportunities for the UN System, ed. Fen Osler Hampson and David M. Malone, 159–83. Boulder: Lynne Rienner.

Lund, Michael. 2003. *What Kind of Peace Is Being Built?* Ottawa: International Development Research Centre.

Lund, Michael. 2004. "Operationalizing Lessons from Recent Experiences in Field Level Conflict Prevention Strategies." In *Facing Ethnic Conflicts: Toward a New Realism,* ed. Andrew Wimmer, Richard J. Goldstone, Donald Horowitz, and Ulrike Joras. Lanham, MD: Rowman and Littlefield.

MacFarlane, Neil. 1998. "On the Front Lines in the Near Abroad: The CIS and the OSCE in Georgia's Civil Wars." In *Beyond UN Subcontracting: Task-Sharing with Regional Security Arrangements and Service-Providing NGOs,* ed. Thomas G. Weiss, 115–38. London: Macmillan.

MacFarlane, Neil, and Thomas G. Weiss. 1994. "The United Nations, Regional Organizations, and Human Security: Building Theory in Central America." In The Academic Council on the United Nations System, Chairman's Report and Background Papers, *Regional Responsibilities and the United Nations System,* ACUNS Reports and Papers No. 1994-2. San Jose, Costa Rica, January 12–14.

Mack, Andrew. 2001. "Successes and Challenges in Conflict Management." In *Turbulent Peace: The Challenges of Managing International Conflict,* ed. Chester Crocker, Fen Osler Hampson, and Pamela Aall. Washington, DC: United States Institute of Peace.

Mack, Raymond, and Richard Snyder. 1957. "The Analysis of Social Conflict: Towards an Overview and Synthesis." *Journal of Conflict Resolution* 1, no. 2: 212–48.

Mackinlay, John. 1995. "Military Responses to Complex Emergencies." In *The United Nations and Civil Wars,* ed. Thomas G. Weiss, 51–68. Boulder: Lynne Rienner.

Mackinlay, John, and Jarat Chopra. 1997. "Second Generation Multinational Operations." In *The Politics of Global Governance: International Organizations in an Interdependent World,* ed. Paul Diehl, 175–97. Boulder: Lynne Rienner.

MacQueen, Norrie. 1999. *The United Nations since 1945: Peacekeeping and the Cold War.* London: Longman.

Malan, Mark. 1997. "A Concise Conceptual History of UN Peace Operations." *African Security Review* 6, no. 1, available from http://www.iss.co.za/ASR/6No1/ Malan.html.

Malan, Mark. 1998. "Peacekeeping in the New Millennium: Towards 'Fourth Generation' Peacekeeping Operations?" *African Security Review* 7, no. 3, available from http://www.iss.co.za/ASR/7No3/Malan.html.

Malone, David. 1997. "The UN Security Council in the Post-Cold War World, 1987–97." *Security Dialogue* 28, no. 1: 393–408.

Mani, Rama. 1998. "Conflict Resolution, Justice, and the Law: Rebuilding the Rule of Law in the Aftermath of Complex Political Emergencies." *International Peacekeeping* 5, no. 3: 1–25.

Maoz, Zeev. 1982. *Paths to Conflict: International Dispute Initiation.* Boulder: Westview.

Marks, Susan. 2000. *Watching the Wind: Conflict Resolution during South Africa's Transition to Democracy.* Washington, DC: United States Institute of Peace.

Mawlawi, Farouk. 1993. "New Conflicts, New Challenges: The Evolving Role for Non-Governmental Actors." *Journal of International Affairs* 46, no. 2: 391–413.

McDonald, John. 2003. "The Impact of NGO's on Policy Makers." *Occasional Paper Number 11.* Washington, DC: Institute for Multi-track Diplomacy.

McGrath, Joseph. 1966. "A Social Psychological Approach to the Study of Negotiation." In *Studies on Behaviour in Organisations,* ed. R. V. Bowers, 101–34. Athens: University of Georgia Press.

McLean, Denis. 1996. "Peace Operations and Common Sense." In *Managing Global Chaos: Sources of and Responses to International Conflict,* ed. Chester A. Crocker, Fen Osler Hampson, and Pamela Aall. Washington, DC: United States Institute of Peace.

Mekenkamp, Monique, Paul van Tongeren, and Hans van de Veen, eds. 1999. *Searching for Peace in Africa: An Overview of Conflict Prevention and Management Activities.* Utrecht, The Netherlands: European Platform for Conflict Prevention and Transformation.

Mekenkamp, Monique, Paul van Tongeren, and Hans van de Veen, eds. 2002. *Searching for Peace in Central and South Asia: An Overview of Conflict Prevention and Peacebuilding Activities.* Boulder: Lynne Rienner.

Mendez, Juan E. 1997. "Accountability for Past Abuses." *Human Rights Quarterly* 19, no. 2: 255–82.

Merrills, John. 1998. *International Dispute Settlement.* 2d ed. Cambridge: Cambridge University Press.

Meyer, Arthur. 1960. "Functions of the Mediator in Collective Bargaining." *Industrial and Labour Relations Review* 13, no. 2: 159–65.

Miall, Hugh, Oliver Ramsbotham, and Tom Woodhouse. 1999. *Contemporary Conflict Resolution.* Cambridge, UK: Policy Press.

Miall, Hugh, Oliver Ramsbotham, and Tom Woodhouse. 2002. "Calling for a Broad Approach to Conflict Resolution." In *Searching for Peace in Central and South Asia: An Overview of Conflict Prevention and Peacebuilding Activities,* ed. Monique Mekenkamp, Paul van Tongeren, and Hans van de Veen, 29–34. Boulder: Lynne Rienner.

Minear, Larry. 1995. "The Evolving Humanitarian Enterprise." In *The United Nations and Civil Wars,* ed. Thomas Weiss, 89–106. Boulder: Lynne Rienner.

Minow, Martha. 1998. "Between Vengeance and Forgiveness: South Africa's Truth and Reconciliation Commission." *Negotiation Journal* 14, no. 4: 319–55.

Mitchell, Christopher R. 1981. *The Structure of International Conflict.* London: Macmillan.

Mitchell, Christopher R. 2006. "The Right Moment: Notes on Four Models of Ripeness." In *Conflict Resolution,* vol. 2, ed. Daniel Druckman and Paul Diehl. London: Sage.

Modelski, George. 1964. "International Settlement of Internal Wars." In *International Aspects of Civil Strife,* ed. James Rosenau, 45–63. Princeton: Princeton University Press.

Montville, Joseph. 1987. "The Arrow and the Olive Branch: A Case for Track Two Diplomacy." In *Conflict Resolution: Track Two Diplomacy,* ed. John W. McDonald and D. Bendahmane, 5–20. Washington, DC: U.S. Government Printing Office.

Montville, Joseph. 1991. "Transnationalism and the Role of

Track-Two Diplomacy." In *Approaches to Peace: An Intellectual Map,* ed. Scott Thompson and Kenneth Johnson with Richard Smith and Kimber Schraub, 253–69. Washington, DC: United States Institute of Peace.

Moore, Christopher W. 1986. *The Mediation Process: Practical Strategies for Resolving Conflict.* San Francisco: Jossey-Bass.

Mor, Ben D., and Zeev Maoz. 1996. "Learning, Preference Change, and the Evolution of Enduring Rivalries." In *The Dynamics of Enduring Rivalries,* ed. Paul Diehl. Urbana: University of Illinois Press.

Morley, Ian, and Geoffrey Stephenson. 1977. *The Social Psychology of Bargaining.* London: Allen and Unwin.

Morris, Madeline. 1996. "By Force of Arms: Rape, War, and Military Culture." *Duke Law Journal* 45, no. 4: 652–92.

Msabaha, Ibrahim. 1995. "Negotiating an End to Mozambique's Murderous Rebellion." In *Elusive Peace: Negotiating an End to Civil Wars,* ed. William Zartman, 204–30. Washington, DC: Brookings Institution.

Mueller, John. 2004. *The Remnants of War.* Ithaca: Cornell University Press.

Murphy, John F. 1983. *The United Nations and the Control of International Violence: A Legal and Political Analysis.* Manchester, UK: Manchester University Press.

Nathan, Laurie. 1999. "'When Push Comes to Shove': The Failure of International Mediation in African Civil Wars." *Track Two* 8, no. 2: 1–27.

Nesi, Giuseppe, ed. 2006. *International Cooperation in Counter-terrorism: The United Nations and Regional Organizations in the Fight Against Terrorism.* Aldershot: Ashgate.

Newman, Edward. 2002. "'Transitional Justice': The Impact of Transnational Norms and the UN." *International Peacekeeping* 9, no. 2: 31–50.

Newman, Edward, and Albrecht Schnabel. 2002. "Introduction: Recovering from Civil Conflict." *International Peacekeeping* 9, no. 2: 1–6.

Nichols, Bruce. 1994. "Religious Conciliation between the Sandinistas and the East Coast Indians of Nicaragua." In *Religion, The Missing Dimension of Statecraft,* ed. Douglas Johnson and Cynthia Sampson, 64–87. New York: Oxford University Press.

Nicolson, Sir Harold. 1950. *Diplomacy.* London: Oxford University Press.

Northedge, Frederick, and Michael Donelan. 1971. *International Disputes: The Political Aspects.* London: Europa.

Oellers-Frahm, Karin. 1992. "The Mandatory Component in the CSCE Dispute Settlement System." In *International Courts for the Twenty-first Century,* ed. Mark Janis, 195–212. Netherlands: Kluwer Academic Publishers.

Orr, Robert. 2004. *Winning the Peace: An American Strategy for Post-Conflict Reconstruction.* Washington, DC: Center for Strategic International Studies.

Ott, Mervin C. 1972. "Mediation as a Method of Conflict Resolution." *International Organization* 26, no. 4: 595–618.

Otunnu, Olara A. 1995. "Peacekeeping: From a Crossroads to the Future." Africa News Online Article, available from http://www.africanews.org/usaf/stories/otunnu.hml.

Oudraat, Chantel de Jonge. 2000. "Humanitarian Intervention: The Lessons Learned." *Current History* 99, no. 641: 419–29.

Paffenholz, Thania. 2001. "Peacebuilding: A Comprehensive Learning Process." In *Peacebuilding: A Field Guide,* ed. Luc Reychler and Thania Paffenholz, 535–44. Boulder: Lynne Rienner.

Pankhurst, Donna. 1999. "Issues of Justice and Reconciliation in Complex Political Emergencies: Conceptualizing Reconciliation, Justice, and Peace." *Third World Quarterly* 20, no. 1: 239–56.

Paris, Roland. 1997. "Peacebuilding and the Limits of Liberal Internationalism." *International Security* 22, no. 2: 54–89.

Paris, Roland. 2001. "Wilson's Ghost: The Faulty Assumptions of Postconflict Peacebuilding." In *Turbulent Peace: The Challenges of Managing International Conflict,* ed. Chester Crocker, Fen Osler Hampson, and Pamela Aall, 765–84. Washington, DC: United States Institute of Peace.

Paris, Roland. 2004. *At War's End: Building Peace after Civil Conflict.* Cambridge: Cambridge University Press.

Parlevliet, Michelle. 1999. "Telling the Truth in the Wake of Mass Violence." In *People Building Peace: Thirty-five Inspiring Stories from Around the World.* A publication of the European Centre for Conflict Prevention in cooperation with IFOR and the Coexistence Initiative of the State of the World Forum. URL: http://www.oneworld.org/euconflict/pbp/part1/3_tellin.htm.

Patman, Robert. 1996. "Disarmament in a Failed State: The Experience of the UN in Somalia." Working Paper 162. Peace Research Center, Australian National University, Canberra.

Pearce, Jenny. 1999. "Peace-building in the Periphery: Lessons from Central America." *Third World Quarterly* 20, no. 1: 51–68.

Peck, Connie. 1996. *The United Nations as a Dispute Settlement System.* Boston: Kluwer Law International.

Peck, Connie. 1999. "A More Strategic Partnership for Preventing and Resolving Conflict." In *Searching for Peace in Africa: An Overview of Conflict Prevention and Management Activities,* ed. Monique Mekenkamp, Paul van Tongeren, and Hans van de Veen, 39–45. Utrecht, The Netherlands: European Platform for Conflict Prevention and Transformation.

Peou, Sorpong. 2002. "The UN, Peacekeeping, and Collective Human Security: From *An Agenda for Peace* to the Brahimi Report." *International Peacekeeping* 9, no. 2: 51–68.

Permanent Court of Arbitration. 2008. Permanent Court of Arbitration Web site, available at http://www.pca-cpa.org/showpage.asp?pag_id=363.

Pieterse, Jan Nederveen. 1998. "Humanitarian Intervention and Beyond: Introduction." In *World Orders in the Making: Humanitarian Intervention and Beyond,* ed. Jan Nederveen Pieterse, 1–23. New York: St. Martin's Press.

Pinto, M. C. W. 1990. "The Prospects for International Arbitration: Inter-State Disputes." In *International Arbitration: Past and Prospects,* ed. A. H. A. Soons, 63–100. The Hague: Martinus Nijhoff.

Pondi, Jean-Emmanuel. 2000. "Compensating for Weak Symmetry in the Mali–Burkina Faso Conflict, 1985–1986." In *Power and Negotiation,* ed. I. William Zartman and Jeffrey Rubin, 203–24. Ann Arbor: University of Michigan Press.

Popkin, Margaret, and Naomi Roht-Arriaza. 1995. "Truth as Justice: Investigatory Commissions in Latin America." *Law and Social Inquiry* 20, no. 1: 79–116.

Posen, Barry. 1993. "The Security Dilemma and Ethnic Conflict." *Survival* 35, no. 1: 27–47.

Pouligny, Beatrice. 2002. "Building Peace after Mass Crimes." *International Peacekeeping* 9, no. 2: 202–21.

Princen, Thomas. 1987. "International Mediation—The View from the Vatican: Lessons from Mediating the Beagle Channel Dispute." *Negotiation Journal* 3, no. 4: 347–66.

Princen, Thomas. 1991. "Camp David: Problem-Solving or Power Politics as Usual?" *Journal of Peace Research* 28, no. 1: 57–69.

Princen, Thomas. 1992a. *Intermediaries in International Conflict*. Princeton: Princeton University Press.

Princen, Thomas. 1992b. "Mediation by a Trans-National Organization: The Case of the Vatican." In *Mediation in International Relations: Multiple Approaches to Conflict Management*, ed. Jacob Bercovitch and Jeffrey Rubin, 149–75. Great Britain: Macmillan.

Pruitt, Dean, and Peter Carnevale. 1993. *Negotiation in Social Conflict*. Buckingham: Open University Press.

Pugh, Derek, David Hickson, and Christopher Hinings. 1969. "An Empirical Taxonomy of Structures of Work Organizations." *Administrative Science Quarterly* 14, no. 1: 115–26.

Pugh, Michael. 1995. "Peacebuilding as Developmentalism: Concepts from Disaster Research." *Contemporary Security Policy* 16, no. 3: 320–46.

Pugh, Michael. 1997. "Peacekeeping and Humanitarian Intervention." In *Issues in World Politics*, ed. Brian White, Richard Little, and Michael Smith, 134–56. New York: St. Martin's Press.

Quinn, David, Jonathan Wilkenfeld, Kathleen Smarick, and Victor Asal. 2006. "Power Play: Mediation in Symmetric and Asymmetric International Crises." *International Interactions* 32, no. 4: 441–70.

Raiffa, Howard. 1982. *The Art and Science of Negotiation*. Cambridge: Harvard University Press.

Ramsbotham, Oliver. 2000. "Reflections on UN Post-Settlement Peacebuilding." *International Peacekeeping* 7, no. 1: 169–89.

Ramsbotham, Oliver, Tom Woodhouse, and Hugh Miall. 2d ed. 2005. *Contemporary Conflict Resolution: The Prevention, Management, and Transformation of Deadly Conflicts*. Cambridge, UK: Polity Press.

Randle, Robert. 1973. *The Origins of Peace*. New York: Free Press.

Report of the International Commission on Intervention and State Sovereignty. 2001. *The Responsibility to Protect*, available online at http://www.iciss.ca/.

Reychler, Luc, and Thania Paffenholz, eds. 2001. *Peacebuilding: A Field Guide*. Boulder: Lynne Rienner.

Richmond, Oliver. 2000. *'Post Westphalian' Peace-Building: The Role of NGOs*. Available online at http://www.class.uidaho.edu/martin_archives/conflict_journal/ngo.htm.

Richmond, Oliver. 2002. *Maintaining Order, Making Peace*. New York: Palgrave.

Richmond, Oliver. 2003. "Realising Hegemony? New Wars, New Terrorism, and the Roots of Conflict." *Terrorism and Conflict Studies* 24, no. 4: 295–313.

Rigby, Andrew. 2001. *Justice and Reconciliation: After the Violence*. Boulder: Lynne Rienner.

Roberts, Adam. 1996. "The Crisis in UN Peacekeeping." In *Managing Global Chaos: Sources of and Responses to International Conflict*, ed. Chester A. Crocker, Fen Osler Hampson, and Pamela Aall, 297–319. Washington, DC: United States Institute of Peace.

Roberts, Adam, and Benedict Kingsbury. 1993. "Introduction: The UN's Roles in International Society since 1945." In *United Nations, Divided World: The UN's Roles in International Relations*, ed. Adam Roberts and Benedict Kingsbury, 1–62. 2d ed. Oxford: Clarendon Press.

Rose, William. 2001. "The Security Dilemma and Ethnic Conflict: Some New Hypotheses." *Security Studies* 10, no. 2: 198–223.

Rosenne, Shabtai. 1995. *The World Court, What It Is and How It Works*. 5th ed. The Hague: Martinus Nijhoff.

Rothman, J. 1992. *From Confrontation to Cooperation: Resolving Ethnic and Regional Conflict*. Newbury Park, CA: Sage.

Rouhana, Nadim. 1995. "Unofficial Third-Party Intervention in International Conflict: Between Legitimacy and Disarray." *Negotiation Journal* 11, no. 3: 255–70.

Rouhana, Nadim, and Herbert Kelman. 1994. "Promoting Joint Thinking in International Conflicts: An Israeli-Palestinian Continuing Workshop." *Journal of Social Issues* 50, no. 1: 157–78.

Rubin, Jeffrey. 1980. "Experimental Research on Third-Party Intervention in Conflict." *Psychological Bulletin* 87, no. 2: 379–91.

Rubin, Jeffrey, ed. 1981. *Dynamics of Third-Party Intervention: Kissinger in the Middle East*. New York: Praeger.

Rubin, Jeffrey. 1992. "International Mediation in Context." In *Mediation in International Relations*, ed. Jacob Bercovitch and Jeffrey Z. Rubin. New York: St. Martin's Press.

Rubin, Jeffrey, and Bert Brown. 1975. *The Social Psychology of Bargaining and Negotiations*. New York: Academic Press.

Rupesinghe, Kumar. 1998. *Civil Wars, Civil Peace: An Introduction to Conflict Resolution*. London: Pluto Press.

Ryan, Stephen. 1990. *Ethnic Conflict and International Relations*. Aldershot: Dartmouth.

Sadowski, Yahya. 1998. "Ethnic Conflict." *Foreign Policy* 111:12–23.

Sambanis, Nicholas. 2001. "Do Ethnic and NonEthnic Civil Wars Have the Same Causes? A Theoretical and Empirical Enquiry." *Journal of Conflict Resolution* 45, no. 3: 259–82.

Sambanis, Nicholas, and Michael Doyle. 2000. "International Peacebuilding: A Theoretical and Quantitative Analysis." *American Political Science Review* 94, no. 4: 779–802.

Sampson, Cynthia. 1994. "'To Make Real the Bond Between Us All': Quaker Conciliation during the Nigerian Civil War." In *Religion, The Missing Dimension of Statecraft*, ed. Douglas Johnson and Cynthia Sampson, 88–118. New York: Oxford University Press.

Sampson, Cynthia. 1997. "Religion and Peacebuilding." In *Peacemaking in International Conflict: Methods and Techniques*, ed. William Zartman and Lewis Rasmussen, 273–316. Washington, DC: United States Institute of Peace.

Saunders, Harold. 1987. "When Citizens Talk: Nonofficial Dialogue in Relations between Nations." In *Conflict Resolution: Track Two Diplomacy*, ed. John McDonald and Diane Bendahmane, 49–55. Washington, DC: U.S. Government Printing Office.

Saunders, Harold. 1991. "Officials and Citizens in International Relationships: The Dartmouth Conference." In *The Psychodynamics of International Relationships: vol. 2, Unofficial Diplomacy at Work*, ed. Vamik Volkan, Joseph Montville, and Demetrios Julius, 104–29. Lexington, MA: Lexington Books.

Saunders, Harold. 1999. *A Public Peace Process: Sustained Dialogue to Transform Racial and Ethnic Conflicts*. New York: St. Martin's Press.

Savun, Burcu. 2008. "Information, Bias, and Mediation Success." *International Studies Quarterly* 52, no. 1: 25–47.

Sawyer, Jack, and Harold Guetzkow. 1965. "Bargaining and Negotiation in International Relations." In *International Behavior: A Social-psychological Approach*, ed. Herbert Kelman, 464–520. New York: Rinehart & Winston.

Schelling, Thomas. 1960. *The Strategy of Conflict*. Cambridge: Harvard University Press.

Scheman, Ronald, and John Ford. 1985. "The Organization of American States as Mediator." In *International Mediation in Theory and Practice*, ed. Saadia Touval and William Zartman, 197–232. Boulder: Westview.

Schlunck, Angelika. 1998. "Truth and Reconciliation Commissions." *ILSA Journal of International and Comparative Law* 4, no. 2.

Schmidt, Stuart, and Thomas Kochan. 1972. "Conflict: Toward Conceptual Clarity." *Administrative Science Quartlery* 17, no. 3: 359–70.

Schnabel, Albrecht. 2002. "Post-Conflict Peacebuilding and Second-Generation Preventive Action." *International Peacekeeping* 9, no. 2: 7–30.

Schuman, Frederick. 1969. *International Politics: Anarchy and Order in the World Society*. 7th ed. New York: McGraw-Hill.

Semb, Anne Julie. 2000. "The New Practice of UN-Authorized Interventions: A Slippery Slope of Forcible Interference?" *Journal of Peace Research* 37, no. 4: 469–88.

Sesay, Amadu. 1998. "Regional and Sub-Regional Conflict Management Efforts." In *Africa in the Post–Cold War International System*, ed. Sola Akinrinade and Amadu Sesay, 29–39. London: Pinter.

Sfeir-Younis, Alfredo. 2000. "The Role of International Financial Institutions." In *Preventing Violent Conflict: The Search for Political Will, Strategies, and Effective Tools*. Report of the Krusenberg Seminar, organized by the Swedish Ministry of Foreign Affairs, 19–20 June, 45–50. Stockholm: Stockholm International Institute of International Affairs.

Shaw, Timothy. 1996. "Beyond Post-Conflict Peacebuilding: What Links to Sustainable Development and Human Security?" *International Peacekeeping* 3, no. 2: 36–48.

Shea, Dorothy. 2000. *The South African Truth Commission: The Politics of Reconciliation*. Washington, DC: United States Institute of Peace.

Shea, Gregory. 1980. "The Study of Bargaining and Conflict Behavior: Broadening the Conceptual Arena." *Journal of Conflict Resolution* 24, no. 4: 706–41.

Siegal, Richard Lewis. 1998. "Transitional Justice: A Decade of Debate and Experience." *Human Rights Quarterly* 20, no. 2: 431–54.

Siegel, Sidney, and Lawrence Fouraker. 1960. *Bargaining and Group Decision Making*. New York: McGraw-Hill.

Simkin, William E. 1971. *Mediation and the Dynamics of Collective Bargaining*. Washington, DC: Bureau of National Affairs.

Singer, Linda. 1990. *Settling Disputes: Conflict Resolution in Business, Families, and the Legal System*. Boulder: Westview.

Siniver, Asaf. 2006. "Power, Impartiality, and Timing: Three Hypotheses on Third Party Mediation in the Middle East." *Political Studies* 54, no. 4: 806–26.

Skjelsbaek, Kjell. 1986. "Peaceful Settlement of Disputes by the United Nations and Other Intergovernmental Bodies." *Cooperation and Conflict* 21, no. 3: 139–54.

Skjelsbaek, Kjell, and Gunnar Fermann. 1996. "The UN Secretary-General and the Mediation of International Disputes." In *Resolving International Conflicts: The Theory and Practice of Mediation*, ed. Jacob Bercovitch, 75–106. Boulder: Lynne Rienner.

Slim, Hugo. 1995. "Military Humanitarianism and the New Peacekeeping: An Agenda for Peace?" *Journal of Humanitarian Assistance*, available from http://www-jha.sps.cam.ac.uk/a/a015.htm.

Slim, Hugo. 1998. "International Humanitarianism's Engagement with Civil War in the 1990s: A Glance at Evolving Practice and Theory." *Journal of Humanitarian Assistance*. Available from http://www-jha.sps.cam.ac.uk/a/a565.htm.

Slim, Randa. 1992. "Small-State Mediation in International Relations: The Algerian Mediation of the Iranian Hostage Crisis." In *Mediation in International Relations*, ed. Jacob Bercovitch and Jeffrey Z. Rubin, 206–31. New York: St. Martin's Press.

Smith, Edwin M., and Thomas G. Weiss. 1998. "UN Task-Sharing: Towards or Away from Global Governance?" In *Beyond UN Subcontracting: Task-Sharing with Regional Security Arrangements and Service-Providing NGOs*, ed. Thomas G. Weiss, 227–58. London: Macmillan.

Snidal, Duncan. 1985. "The Limits of Hegemonic Stability Theory." *International Organization* 39, no. 4: 579–614.

Spencer, Doyle, and Huang Yang. 1992. "Lessons from the Field of Intra-National Conflict Resolution." *Notre Dame Law Review* 67, no. 5:1495–1512.

Sriram, Chandra Lekha. 2000. "Truth Commissions and the Quest for Justice: Stability and Accountability after Internal Strife." *International Peacekeeping* 7, no. 4: 91–106.

Starr, Harvey. 1997. *Anarchy, Order, and Integration: How to Manage Interdependence*. Ann Arbor: University of Michigan Press.

Stedman, Stephen. 2001. "International Implementation of Peace Agreements in Civil Wars: Findings from a Study of Sixteen Cases." In *Turbulent Peace: The Challenges of Managing International Conflict*, ed. Chester Crocker, Fen Osler Hampson, and Pamela Aall, 737–52. Washington, DC: United States Institute of Peace.

Stein, Janice. 1985. "Structure, Strategies, and Tactics of Mediation." *Negotiation Journal* 1, no. 4: 331–47.

Stern, Jessica. 2003. "The Protean Enemy." *Foreign Affairs* 82, no. 4:27–40.

Stern, Paul, and Daniel Druckman. 2000a. "Evaluating Interventions in History: The Case of International Conflict Resolution." *International Studies Association* 2, no. 1: 33–64.

Stern, Paul, and Daniel Druckman, eds.. 2000b. *International Conflict Resolution after the Cold War*. Washington, DC: National Academy Press.

Stevens, Carl. 1963. *Strategy and Collective Bargaining Negotiations*. New York: McGraw-Hill.

Stewart, Frances. 2002. "Horizontal Inequalities as a Source of Conflict." In *From Reaction to Conflict Prevention: Opportunities for the UN System*, ed. Fen Osler Hampson and David Malone, 105–38. Boulder: Lynne Rienner.

Strobel, Warren. 1997. *Late-Breaking Foreign Policy: The News Media's Influence on Peace Operations*. Washington D.C.: United States Institute of Peace Press.

Stulberg, Joseph. 1981. "The Theory and Practice of Mediation: A Reply to Professor Susskind." *Vermont Law Review* 6:85–117.

Stulberg, Joseph. 1987. *Taking Charge/Managing Conflict*. Lexington, MA: D. C. Heath.

Stuyt, Alexander, ed. 1990. *Survey of International Arbitrations, 1794–1989*. The Hague: Martinus Nijhoff.

Sullivan, Earl. 1999. "The United Nations: Dealing with Threats to the Peace in the Post–Cold War Era." In *Multilateral Diplomacy and the United Nations Today*, ed. James Muldoon Jr., Joan Aviel, Richard Reitano, and Earl Sullivan, 44–53. Boulder: Westview.

Susskind, Lawrence, and Jeffrey Cruikshank. 1987. *Breaking the Impasses: Consensual Approaches to Resolving Public Disputes*. New York: Basic Books.

Tascan, Joaquin. 1998. "Searching for OAS/UN Task-Sharing Opportunities in Central America and Haiti." In *Beyond UN Subcontracting: Task-Sharing with Regional Security Arrangements and Service-Providing NGOs*, ed. Thomas G. Weiss, 91–114. London: Macmillan.

Terris, Lesley, and Zeev Maoz. 2005. "Rational Mediation: A Theory and a Test." *Journal of Peace Research* 42, no. 5: 563–83.

Thakur, Ramesh. 1993. "The United Nations in a Changing World." *Security Dialogue* 24, no. 1: 7–20.

Thakur, Ramesh. 1995. "UN Peacekeeping in the New World Disorder." In *A Crisis of Expectations: UN Peacekeeping in the 1990s*, ed. Ramesh Thakur and Chandra Thayer, 3–22. Boulder: Westview.

Tharoor, Shashi. 1995–96. "Should UN Peacekeeping Go 'Back to Basics'?" *Survival* 37, no. 4: 52–64.

Thornberry, Cedric. 1995. "Peacekeepers, Humanitarian Aid, and Civil Conflicts." *Journal of Humanitarian Affairs*, available from http://www-jha.sps.cam.ac.uk/a/a017.htm.

Thornton, Thomas. 1991. "Regional Organizations in Conflict Management." *Annals of the American Academy of Political and Social Science* 518, no. 1: 132–42.

Tiruchelvam, Neelan. 1996. "Sri Lanka's Ethnic Conflict and Preventive Action: The Role of NGOs." In *Vigilance and Vengeance: NGOs Preventing Ethnic Conflict in Divided Societies*, ed. Robert Rotberg, 147–66. Washington, DC: Brookings Institution Press.

Toros, Harmonie. 2008. "Terrorists, Scholars and Ordinary People: Confronting Terrorism Studies with Field Experiences." *Critical Studies on Terrorism* 1, no. 2: 293–308.

Touval, Saadia. 1982. *The Peace Brokers: Mediators in the Arab-Israeli Conflict, 1948–1979*. Princeton: Princeton University Press.

Touval, Saadia. 1992a. "The Superpowers as Mediators." In *Mediation in International Relations*, ed. Jacob Bercovitch and Jeffrey Z. Rubin, 232–48. New York: St. Martin's Press.

Touval, Saadia. 1992b. "Gaining Entry to Mediation in Communal Strife." In *The Internationalization of Communal Strife*, ed. Manus I. Midlarsky, 255–72. London: Routledge.

Touval, Saadia. 1994. "Why the UN Fails." *Foreign Affairs* 73, no. 5: 44–57.

Touval, Saadia. 1995. "Mediator's Flexibility and the U.N. Security Council." *Annals of the American Academy of Political and Social Science* 542, no. 1: 202–12.

Touval, Saadia, and I. William Zartman. 1985. "Mediation in Theory." In *International Mediation in Theory and Practice*, ed. Saadia Touval and I. William Zartman, 7–20. Boulder: Westview.

Touval, Saadia, and I. William Zartman. 2001. "International Mediation in the Post–Cold War Era." In *Turbulent Peace: The Challenges of Managing International Conflict*, ed. Chester Crocker, Fen Osler Hampson, and Pamela Aall, 427–43. Washington, DC: United States Institute of Peace.

Tschirgi, Necla. 2003. *Peacebuilding as the Link between Security and Development: Is the Window of Opportunity Closing?* New York: International Peace Academy Studies in Security and Development, available online at http://www.ipacademy.org.

Tschirgi, Necla. 2004. *Post-Conflict Peacebuilding Revisited: Achievements, Limitations, Challenges*. Paper prepared for the WSP International/IPA Peacebuilding Forum Conference, 7 October, New York, available online at http://www.ipacademy.org.

Turner, M. 1990. "Report on Northern Ireland: A Psychological Perspective." *Mind and Human Interaction* 1:2–4. Details.

United Nations. 1990. *The Blue Helmets: A Review of United Nations Peacekeeping*. 2d ed. New York: UN Department of Public Information.

United Nations. 2000. *Report of the Panel on United Nations Peace Operations*, A/55/305-S/2000/809, available from http://www.un.org/peace/reports/peace_operations/.

United Nations. 2001. Web site. Available from http://www.un.org/english/.

United Nations. 2006. "Progress Report on the Prevention of Armed Conflicts." Report of the Secretary-General.

United Nations. 2008. United Nations Peacekeeping Web site, available from: http://www.un.org/Depts/dpko/dpko/index.asp.

Van der Donckt, Charles. 1995. *Looking Forward by Looking Back: A Pragmatic Look at Conflict and the Regional Option*. Policy staff paper for the Canadian Department of Foreign Affairs, September.

Van Tongeren, Paul. 2001. "Exploring the Local Capacity for Peace: The Role of NGOs." In *Prevention and Management of Violent Conflicts: An International Directory*, 21–26. Utrecht: European Platform for Conflict Prevention and Transformation.

Van Tongeren, Paul, Hans van de Veen, and Juliette Verhoeven, eds. 2002. *Searching for Peace in Europe and Eurasia: An Overview of Conflict Prevention and Peacebuilding Activities*. Boulder: Lynne Rienner. Available from http://www.oneworld.org/euconflict/guides/themes/pp3a.htm.

Van Tuijl, Peter. 1999. "NGOs and Human Rights: Sources of Justice and Democracy." *Journal of International Affairs* 52, no. 2: 493–504.

Van Walraven, Klass. 1999. *Dreams of Power: The Role of the Organization of African Unity in the Politics of Africa, 1963–1993*. Aldershot: Ashgate.

Vogal, Tobias. 1996. "The Politics of Humanitarian Intervention." *Journal of Humanitarian Assistance* Article posted 3 September 1996, Feinstein International Center, available online at http://www.jha.ac/author/tobias_vogal/.

Volkan, Vamik. 1988. "'Working' Conclusions." In *The Psychodynamics of International Relationships*, ed. Vamik Volkan, Joseph Montville, and Demetrios Julius, 223–26. Lexington, MA: Lexington Books.

Voutira, Eftihia, and Shaun Brown. 1995. "Conflict Resolution: A Review of Some Non-Governmental Practices—'A Cautionary Tale.'" In *Studies on Emergencies and Disaster Relief No. 4*, Refugees Studies Programme, University of Oxford, Nordiska Afrikainstitutet.

Wall, James. 1981. "Mediation: An Analysis, Review, and Proposed Research." *Journal of Conflict Resolution* 25, no. 1: 157–80.

Wall, James, and Ann Lynn. 1993. "Mediation: A Current Review." *Journal of Conflict Resolution* 37, no. 1: 160–94.

Wall, James, John Stark, and Rhetta Standifer. 2001. "Mediation: A Current Review and Theory Development." *Journal of Conflict Resolution* 45, no. 3: 370–91.

Wallace-Bruce, Nii Lante. 1998. *The Settlement of International Disputes: The Contribution of Australia and New Zealand*. The Hague: Martinus Nijhoff.

Wallensteen, Peter. 2007. *Understanding Conflict Resolution*. London: Sage.

Wallensteen, Peter, and Karin Axell. 1993. "Armed Conflict at the End of the Cold War, 1989–1992." *Journal of Peace Research* 30, no. 3: 331–46.

Wallensteen, Peter, and Margareta Sollenberg. 1995. "After the Cold War: Emerging Patterns of Armed Conflict, 1989–1994." *Journal of Peace Research* 32, no. 3: 345–60.

Wallensteen, Peter, and Margareta Sollenberg. 1996. "The End of International War? Armed Conflict, 1989–1995." *Journal of Peace Research* 33, no. 3: 353–70.

Wallensteen, Peter, and Margareta Sollenberg. 2000. "Armed Conflict, 1989–1999." *Journal of Peace Research* 37, no. 4: 634–49.

Walton, Richard. 1969. *Interpersonal Peacemaking: Confrontations and Third-Party Consultation*. Reading, MA: Addison-Wesley.

Walton, Richard, and Robert McKersie. 1965. *A Behavioral Theory of labor Negotiation*. New York: McGraw-Hill.

Watkins, Michael, and Kirsten Lundberg. 1998. "Getting to the Table in Oslo: Driving Forces and Channel Factors." *Negotiation Journal* 14, no. 2: 115–35.

Watkins, Michael, and Susan Rosegrant. 2001. *Breakthrough International Negotiation: How Great Negotiations Transformed the World's Toughest Post–Cold War Conflicts*. San Francisco: Jossey-Bass.

Wehr, Paul. 1979. *Conflict Regulation*. Boulder: Westview.

Weiss, Thomas. 1995. "Introduction." In *The United Nations and Civil Wars*, ed. Thomas Weiss, 1–12. Boulder: Lynne Rienner.

Weiss, Thomas. 1998. "Humanitarian Action in War Zones: Recent Experience and Future Research." In *World Orders in the Making: Humanitarian Intervention and Beyond*, ed. Jan Nederveen Pieterse, 24–79. New York: St. Martin's Press.

Whitman, Jim. 1995. "A Cautionary Note on Humanitarian Intervention." *Journal of Humanitarian Assistance*, available from http://www.jha.ac/articles/a001.htm.

Wilkenfeld, Jonathan, and Michael Brecher. 1989. "International Crises, 1945–1975: The UN Dimension." In *The Politics of International Organizations: Patterns and Insights*, ed. Paul Diehl, 108–33. Chicago: Dorsey Press.

Wilkenfeld, Jonathan, Kathleen Young, Victor Asal, and David Quinn. 2003. "Mediating International Crises: Cross National and Experimental Perspectives." *Journal of Conflict Resolution* 47, no. 3: 279–301.

Wilson, Richard. 2001. "Violent Truths: The Politics of Memory in Guatemala." In *Negotiating Rights: The Guatemalan Peace Process. Accord, An International Review of Peace Initiatives*, available from http://www.c-r.org/acc_guat/wilson.htm.

Wolfers, Michael. 1985. "The Organization of African Unity as Mediator." In *International Mediation in Theory and Practice*, ed. Saadia Touval and William Zartman, 175–96. Boulder: Westview.

Woocher, Lawrence. 2001. "Deconstructing Political Will: Explaining the Failure to Prevent Deadly Conflicts." *Journal of Public and International Affairs* 12:179–206.

World Bank. 1998. *Post-Conflict Reconstruction: The Role of the World Bank*, Washington, DC: World Bank.

Yarrow, Mike. 1977. "Quaker Efforts toward Conciliation in the India-Pakistan War of 1965." In *Unofficial Diplomats*, ed. Maureen R. Berman and Joseph E. Johnson, 89–110. New York: Columbia University Press.

Yarrow, Mike. 1978. *Quaker Experiences in International Conciliation*. New Haven: Yale University Press.

Young, Oran. 1967. *The Intermediaries: Third Parties in International Crises*. Princeton: Princeton University Press.

Zacher, Mark. 1979. *International Conflicts and Collective Security, 1946–1977: The United Nations, Organization of American States, Organization of African Unity, and the Arab League*. New York: Praeger.

Zartman, I. William. 1983. "The Strategy of Preventive Diplomacy in Third World Conflicts." In *Managing US-Soviet Rivalry*, ed. Alexander George. Boulder: Westview.

Zartman, I. William. 1985. *Ripe for Resolution: Conflict and Intervention in Africa*. 2d ed. New York: Oxford University Press.

Zartman, I. William. 1999. "Intervening to Prevent State Collapse: The Role of the United Nations." In *Multilateral Diplomacy and the United Nations Today*, ed. James P. Muldoon, 68–77. Boulder: Westview.

Zartman, I. William. 2003. "The Timing of Peace Initiatives: Hurting Stalemates and Ripe Moments." In *Contemporary*

Peacemaking, Conflict, Violence, and Peace Processes, ed. John Darby and Roger MacGinty, 120–43. New York: Palgrave Macmillan.

Zartman, I. William. 2005. *Cowardly Lions: Missed Opportunities to Prevent Deadly Conflict and State Collapse.* Boulder: Lynne Rienner.

Zartman, I. William, and Maureen Berman. 1982. *The Practical Negotiator.* New Haven: Yale University Press.

Zartman, I. William, and Jeffery Rubin, eds. 2000. *Power and Negotiation.* Ann Arbor: University of Michigan Press.

Zartman, I. William, and Saadia Touval. 1985. "International Mediation: Conflict Resolution and Power Politics." *Journal of Social Issues* 41:27–45.

Zartman, I. William, and Saadia Touval. 2007. "International Mediation." In *Leashing the Dogs of War: Conflict Management in a Divided World,* ed. Chester Crocker, Fen Hampson, and Pamela Aall, 437–54. Washington, DC: United States Institute of Peace.

Ziegler, David. 1987. *War, Peace, and International Politics.* 4th ed. New York: Little, Brown.

Index

Note: Page numbers that are italicized indicate figures and tables.

academics, as sources for early warning systems, 93
accountability, for past abuses, 154
Ackerman, Alice, 97
acknowledgment, as option for dealing with past abuses, 154
Action with Respect to Threats to the Peace, Breaches of the Peace, and Acts of Aggression (UN Charter), 77
Act of the Brussels Congress (1890), 49
Act of the Vienna Congress, 49
actor reduction tactics, UN Security Council as example of, 62
actors: in conflict, mediation and, 34–35; coordination of UN regime and multitude of, 62; external, peacebuilding and, 173, 175–76; internal, conflicts involving terrorism and, 188; internal, peacebuilding and, 176, 181; international, preventive diplomacy and, 90, 100; intervening, preventive diplomacy and, 95–96; local, credibility of truth commissions and, 163–64; local, importance and potential of, 16; marginalized, terrorism and, 16; multiple, command and control of, 116; new, in conflict resolution, 11–14; nonstate, conflicts involving, 71; nonstate, nonofficial diplomats and, 143–44; nonstate, regional organizations' bias against, 133–34; outside, regional task-sharing and, 125; political, intervention with internal dynamics by, 91; political will and warning-response gap of, 93–94; previously marginalized, 14; private (*see* nonofficial diplomacy); range of, in humanitarian interventions, 103; regional, advantages of, 130; religiously motivated, roles for, 141; state, built-in bias of diplomatic mediators toward, 144; state, built-in bias of IOs toward, 115; traditional conflict resolution, 184, 185; twenty-first-century conflict resolution, 186; UN as amalgam of, 60–61; unofficial, Track II diplomacy and, 9. *See also* parties
Acts of the Berlin Congress (1875, 1888), 49
ad hoc arbitrations, 52

ad hoc coalitions or operations, 35, 121, 123, 126, 135
Ad Hoc Group on Cooperation in Peacekeeping (NATO), 128
adjudication, international: for conflict resolution, 47; definition and nature of, 53; history and development of, 53–54; lessons learned, 59; limitations of, 57–59; preventive diplomacy and, 89; strengths of, 57
administration, of state business: peacekeeping forces and, 10; temporary, by UN peacekeepers, 77, 106
advisory opinions: average per year, of PCIJ vs. ICJ, 56; of the ICJ, 54–55, 70
Afghanistan: engagement with Taliban and other Afghan groups in, 188; MNF operations in, 128; NATO and UN task-sharing in, 128; peace agreement in, 103; political deals with factions in, 112; regional peacekeeping in, *11, 127;* UN Good Offices Mission in Pakistan and, *80, 82*
Africa: civil wars in, 4; conflicts after Cold War in, 2–3; end of superpower patronage and increased conflicts in, 103, 120; international agenda and peacebuilding in, 181; intertribal differences and arbitrary boundaries of colonial powers in, 4; intrastate conflicts at end of Cold War in, 122; judicial methods for territorial dispute resolution in, 59; lack of hegemonic leadership in post–Cold War period in, 62; NGOs and Great Lakes region conflict in, 138; paralysis of UN with conflicts in, 71; regional task-sharing in, 128; relevance of international law for states of, 58; state-centric conflicts during Cold War in, 6; Sub-Saharan, as conflict-prone region, 3; UN and conflict resolution in, 68
African Union (AU): bias toward state actors, 133; charter clause mandating mediation in regional disputes, 40; mediation by, 32; norm-setting role of, 130; peacemaking by, 40; potential internal conflicts and, 131; regional peacekeeping by, *11;* security issues as major concern for, 125
agenda, UN Security Council, 63

Agenda for Peace, An (Boutros-Ghali): on humanitarian intervention, 104; on multidimensional approach to conflict resolution, 11; on peacebuilding, 168, 169, 171, 174–75; on preventive diplomacy, 12, 88–89; on preventive diplomacy, peacemaking, and postconflict peacebuilding, 40; on regional task-sharing, 124, 126. *See also* Boutros-Ghali, Boutros

Agreement on Military Observers and Collective Peacekeeping (1992), 129

agreements. *See* peace agreements

Aideed, Mohammad Farah, 108

Alabama Claims Arbitration (1872), 50

Alagappa, Muthiah, 133

Albania: MNF peacekeeping in, *128;* non-UN peacekeeping in, *11;* UN authorization of MNF operations in, 128

Algeria, Community Sant'Egidio and peace process in, 139

Algiers Accords (1981), 51

aliens, injuries to, international claims tribunals on, 52

alliance-type (regional) organizations, 120, 121

al Qaeda, as decentralized organization, 6

American Treaty on Pacific Settlement (1948), 125

amnesia, as option for dealing with past abuses, 154, 163

amnesty, as option for dealing with past abuses, 154

anecdotal approach to mediation, 36, 37

Angola: ethnic and religious conflict in, 4; institutional support for UN peacekeeping force in, 83; peace agreement followed by fighting in, 139; peacebuilding in, 168–69, 176, 177, 178; peace process after Cold War in, 2; politicized humanitarian aid operations in, 104; regional peacekeeping by, *127;* superpower patronage during Cold War and, 3; UN humanitarian interventions in, *107*

Annan, Kofi, 11, 99, 169, 175

annual report, of UN secretary-general, 65

antecedent dimension of bargaining and negotiation, 24

Arab Deterrent Force, *126*

Arab-Israeli conflict, 4, 41, 65, 188. *See also* Israel; Palestinian Liberation Organization

Arab League, 32, 40, 119, 126, *126*, 129

Arab Security Force in Kuwait, *126*

Arafat, Yassir, 29

arbitration, international: for conflict resolution, 47; definition and nature of, 50; forms of, 51; history and development of, 50–51; lessons learned, 59; overview of, 52–53; preventive diplomacy and, 89; process of, 51–52; strengths of, 57; traditional conflict resolution and, 184

arbitrators, 52, 66, 87

arms control, UN General Assembly on, 65

Arquilla, John, 15

Asia: central, intrastate conflicts at end of Cold War in, 122; East, UN and conflict resolution in, *68;* end of superpower patronage and increased conflicts in, 120; relevance of international law for states of, 58; Southeast, as conflict-prone region, 3; Southwest, India and Pakistan conflict in, 4; state-centric conflicts during Cold War in, 6. *See also specific countries*

Asia Regional Forum (ARF), 94–95

asylum rights, ICJ judgments on, 56

audiences, absence of, in successful conflict management processes, 25

Australia: leadership of INTERFET by, 131, 135; regional peacekeeping by, *127*

Azar, Edward, 9, 10

back-channel diplomacy, 140

Balkans: ambiguous evidence for genocide in, 110; mediation as partial success in, 139. *See also* Yugoslavia, former

Ball, Nicole, 173–74

"band aid" relief, as substitute for resolving conflicts politically, 115

Bangladesh: India's intervention in, 103; intervention during Cold War in, 111

bargaining. *See* international negotiation

Beagle Channel arbitration (1977 between Argentina and Chile), 52–53

Begin, Menachim, 40

Belgium's Crown Court, prosecution of Rwandan genocide suspects in, 160

Bercovitch, Jacob, 95

Berman, Maureen, 30

best alternatives to a negotiated agreement (BATNA), 30

Bicesse Peace Accord (1991), 73

bilateral negotiations, 25, 64. *See also* international negotiation

Bingham, Gail, 34

bipolarity, post–World War II, 122

Blake, Robert, 33

Blitzkrieg, German, of World War II, 15

Bonn Agreements (2001), 128

Bosnia: failure of UN peacekeeping in, 101–2, 108, 123, 186; genocide in, 4; NATO and UN task-sharing in, 128; peacebuilding in, 176, 177, 178; political deals with factions in, 112; regional peacekeeping in, *11, 127;* third-generation peacekeeping in, 106, 112; UN failure to consistently punish violators of norms in, 71; UN humanitarian intervention in, *107;* UN Protection Force (UNPROFOR) in, *107,* 177; war in, Holbrooke's negotiation with Serbian leaders during, 39

Botswana, regional peacekeeping by, *127*

bottom-up processes, for peacebuilding, 174

boundary disputes: in Africa, judicial methods for resolution of, 59; arbitrary boundaries established by colonial powers and, 4, 23; arbitration cases on, 52, 53; ICJ judgments on, 56; international claims tribunals on, 52; maritime, *Gulf of Maine,* 54; UN member states and, 71

Boutros-Ghali, Boutros: on humanitarian intervention, 104; on multidisciplinary approach to conflict resolution, 11; on preventive diplomacy, 12, 88–89; on preventive diplomacy, peacemaking, and postconflict peacebuilding, 40; regional organizations and, 129; on regional task-sharing, 122, 124. See also *Agenda for Peace*

Brahimi Report (2000): on improving peacekeeping, 73, 82; on peacebuilding and peacekeeping, 113–14, 169, 171; on peacekeepers and peacebuilders, 11; on political compromise to build coalitions, 114; on training for UN humanitarian interventions, 116; on UN's organizational capacity, 117

Brecher, Michael, 67, 73

Brown, Michael, 91, 92

buffer zones, 66, 77, 79

Burma. *See* Myanmar

Burton, John, 9, 10, 38, 44

Burundi: non-UN peacekeeping in, *11*; peacebuilding in, 177, 178; political exploitation of ethnic differences in, 5; regional peacekeeping in, *11*; UN humanitarian intervention in, *107*

Bush doctrine of preemption, 104, 110. *See also* war on terror(ism)

Callières, François de, 89

Cambodia: ethical dilemmas of reconciliation and justice in, 162; International Negotiation Network and, 39; intervention during Cold War in, 111; peacebuilding in, 168–69, 176, 177, 178; peace process after Cold War in, 2; peace settlement and humanitarian intervention in, 104; regional peace agreements in, 103; UN humanitarian intervention in, 101, 106, *107*, 109, 117; Vietnam's intervention in, 103

Camp David accords, 40, 81. *See also* Israel

Canada: government officials and NGO representatives in, 138; *Gulf of Maine* maritime boundary dispute and, 54; peacebuilding unit in foreign ministry of, 137

Canadian Peacebuilding Coordinating Committee, 171

CARE, UN Security Council briefing by, 138

Carment, David, 90

Carnegie Commission on Deadly Conflict, 140

Carnevale, Peter, 27–28, 44

Carter, Jimmy, 40

Carter Center, 39, 137

cease-fires: humanitarian aid without benefit of, 104; monitoring, by League of Nations peacekeepers, 76; monitoring, by UN peacekeepers, 79; peacekeeping operations after, 75; separation of forces and, 77; supervision of, by UN peacekeepers, 66; UN General Assembly on, 65; UN secretary-general on, 66; UN Security Council on, 64

Central African Republic: MNF peacekeeping in, *128*, 135; non-UN peacekeeping in, *11*; regional peacekeeping in, *11*; UN authorization of MNF operations in, 126, 128

Central America: regional peace agreements in, 103; UN Observer Group in, *107*. *See also specific countries*

Central American Court of Justice, 53

Centre for Humanitarian Dialogue (HD Centre), 12, 32

certification process, for nonofficial actors, 147

Chad: failure of OAU peacekeeping in, 126, 133; regional and MNF peacekeeping in, *126*

Chamber on Environmental Matters, of the ICJ, 55

Chandler, David, 174, 176–77

Chilean National Commission for Truth and Reconciliation (1990–91), 159

churches, local, peacebuilding and, 145

citizen-based diplomacy, 140

civilians: internal conflicts and deaths among, 16; killed in post–Cold War era conflicts, 87; mutilation of, in modern warfare, 5. *See also* civil society

civilized nations, general principles of law recognized by, 52, 55. *See also* international law; law and order; rule of law

civil society: affairs of, peacekeeping forces and, 10; peacebuilding and, 173; peace process and, 145–46

civil war(s): absence of, mediation and, 42; ethnic conflict and, 4; humanitarian intervention and, 112–13; post–Cold War

era, 87; reconciliation and justice in negotiated end to, 152; simultaneous, UN resources and, 72; UN peacekeepers and, 83; UN success at resolving, 68

Claims Commissions (PCA arbitration case), 52, 53

CNN effect, as pressure for UN action, 104

coalitions: differences in perceptions and interests of actors in, 114; international law enforcement through interventions by, 58; 1990–2005 interventions by, *11*; for peacebuilding, 175; peacekeeping operations and, 75. *See also* regional task-sharing

code of conduct, joint and explicit declaration of, 94

coercive actions, UN Security Council on, 63–64

coercive diplomacy: for conflict deterrence in Cold War, 6; for preventive diplomacy, 95

Cold War: impartiality and rivalries during, 83; increased authority of UN secretary-general during, 66; international conflict after, 1, 2–5; interventions during, 111; intrastate conflicts at end of, 122; regional task-sharing during, 125–26; return to priorities of, peacebuilding and, 181; traditional conflict resolution during, 6–8; UN peacekeeping during, 106; UN's effectiveness with conflicts during, 68, 71; veto use in UN Security Council during, 65. *See also* post–Cold War era

collaboration, ethical dilemma of reconciliation and justice and, 162–63. *See also* cooperative projects

collective bargaining, 25, 26

collective security concept, as basis of UN conflict resolution, 62–63

colonial powers, arbitrary boundaries established by, 4, 23

command and control. *See* military command system

commission of arbitrators, 51

Commission of Mediation, Conciliation, and Arbitration (OAU), 125, 126

Commonwealth of Independent States (CIS): incumbent regimes and, 134; regional peacekeeping by, *11*, *127*, 129; regional task-sharing by, 128; Russia's role in, 134

Commonwealth of Nations ("the Commonwealth"), 121, 129

communal conflicts: high human costs of, 87–88; information on grievances of groups in, 93

communication: advances, nonofficial diplomacy and, 138–39; cultural influences during negotiations on, 29; increased, agreements on, 94; international organizations as links for, 69; among nonofficial diplomatic groups, 149; official and unofficial channels for, 16; process of, negotiation and, 28. *See also* Internet

Community of Sant'Egidio, 139, 142–43, 145, 147

complementarity, regional task-sharing and, 119, 124

complementary interests, in negotiations, 27

complex emergencies, 103, 104, 113

compromis, procedural arrangements for arbitration in, 51–52

compromise: coalition-building on basis of, 114–15; expectations of those who give testimony for truth commissions and trials and, 164; in resolution of terrorism, 189–90

compromissory clauses, ICJ and, 54

compulsory jurisdiction, of the ICJ, 54

conceptual framework(s): for conflict and conflict resolution, 186; for humanitarian interventions, 102–5, 112–14, 118; for international negotiation, 20–21; for mediation, 33; for nonofficial diplomacy, 140–41; for peacebuilding, 171–76,

conceptual framework(s) (*continued*)
179–80; for preventive diplomacy, 88–89; for reconciliation and justice, 152–55; for regional task-sharing, 120–25, 132–33

concessions, reciprocating, 31

conciliation: advantages of regional organizations in, 130; preventive diplomacy and, 89; by regional organizations during the Cold War, 126; UN General Assembly on, 65; UN peacekeepers and, 66; UN secretary-general on, 66

conciliation commission, for peaceful settlement, 64

concurrent dimension of bargaining and negotiation, 24

Conditions of Admission of a State to Membership in the United Nations, ICJ advisory opinion on, 56

Conference on Security and Cooperation in Europe (CSCE), 128

confidence-building measures, in preventive diplomacy, 90, 94–95

confidentiality: of nonofficial diplomats, 143; of UN secretary-general, 70. *See also* secrecy

conflict(s): armed, traditional peacekeeping to limit, 80–81; armed, UN authority in, 60; causes of, 91–92; changing levels from 1946 to 2005 of, 2, ; definition of, 19–20; disputants and multiple mediators of, 73; early warning and response to, 91; humanitarian interventions as appropriate method for managing and resolving, 117–18; humanitarian operations and exacerbation of, 111; information on history and context of, 93; intensity of, mediation and, 42–43; issues defining logical structure of, 22–23; length and complexity of, mediation and, 37; nature of, mediation and, 42, 43; nature of, nonofficial diplomacy and, 147; negotiation viewed as continuation of, 30; nonofficial diplomacy and resolution of, 141–42; ongoing, reconciliation and justice and, 160–61; phases of, 88; reconfiguration of, resolution after, 30; taking a state to court as escalation of, 58–59; traditional peacekeeping and promoting resolution of, 80–81; traditional resolution of, 14

conflict escalation, 88

conflict formation, 88

conflicting interests, in negotiations, 27

conflict maturation, 88

conflict prevention. *See* preventive diplomacy

conflict resolution: changing paradigm from conflict management to, 8–10, 16; definition of, 20; ICJ's record on, 56; international organization and, 61–63; limitations of legal methods for, 57–59; management systems for interstate conflicts, 184–85; multidimensional approaches to, 10–11; new actors in, 11–14; peacebuilding and, 169, 172; perspectives for post-Westphalian world, 14–16; regional organizations and, 129, 130; as response to conflict, 88; shift in theory and practice of, 2; strengths of legal methods for, 57; traditional, of Cold War Westphalian international system, 6–8; "training" by western NGOs in, 146; through the UN, 61; by UN, basis of, 62–63; UN methods of, 63–68; as UN responsibility, 60. *See also* traditional conflict resolution; twenty-first-century conflict resolution

conflict transformation: changing nature of international conflict and, 2; peacebuilding and, 179; problem-solving workshops and, 9; role of NGOs in, 11; sustainable peace and, 10

Congo, Democratic Republic of: ethnic and religious conflict in, 4; humanitarian operation (1994–96) in, 148; International Negotiation Network and, 39; non-UN peacekeeping in, *11*; ONUC prevention of superpower rivalry in, 81, 106; peacebuilding in, 177; regional peacekeeping in, *11*, *127*, 128; superpower patronage during Cold War and, 3; UN failure to consistently punish violators of norms in, 71; UN humanitarian intervention in, *107*; UN Operation in, 65, *80*, 81

Conolly Amendment, U.S. compulsory jurisdiction of the ICJ and, 54

consensus, for UN decisions on peacekeeping, 83

consent, principle of: adherence to, 84; host states, peacekeeping operations and, 83; humanitarian interventions and, 103, 104, 109, 113; peacekeeping operations and, 75, 77–78; in third-generation peacekeeping, 106, 108. *See also* state sovereignty

consequent dimension of bargaining and negotiation, 24

conservatism: of international legal processes, 57, 58; of IOs, 71

consolidation phase of peacebuilding, 173, 174

constraints, mutual agreement on measures of, 94

Constructivist theory, on international organizations, 62

consultation, in regional task-sharing, 124

context: for bargaining and negotiation, 21, 23; for humanitarian interventions vs. traditional peacekeeping, 103; for mediation, 34, 36, *37*

contingency approach to mediation, 37, *37*

contingency plans, for preventive action of potential conflicts, 93

convergence variables, in conflicts, 91

convocation, for UN Security Council–sponsored mediation, 64

cooperative projects, peacebuilding and development of, 89

coordinated operations: overlapping regional organizations and, 132; regional task-sharing as, 122; for terrorism remediation, 188

coordination challenges: for official and nonofficial diplomacy, 148–49, 186–87; for peacebuilding, 182; for UN humanitarian interventions, 115, 116–17

corrupt governance, conflict due to, 3

cost-effectiveness: of humanitarian interventions, 109; of UN peacekeeping operations, 81

costs of peacekeeping, increases over time, 83

Council of Europe, conflict resolution by, 126

criminal organizations, in post-Westphalian system, 5–6. *See also* international crime; international criminal tribunals

crisis disputes: UN Security Council and, 64; UN's response to vs. anticipation of, 72

crisis of expectations, for peacekeeping, 84

Croatia: UN humanitarian intervention in, *107*; UN Protection Force (UNPROFOR) in, *107*, 177

Crocker, Chester, 11–12

crowdedness: competitive peacemaking by regional organizations and, 132; as disputants turn to multiple mediators, 73

Cruikshank, Jeffrey, 44

cultural barriers to successful negotiation, 29

cultural conflict, 3

cultural values, "training" by western NGOs in conflict resolution and, 146

customary law, international conferences and, 49
customs: international, as source of law for arbitrators, 52; international, as source of law for the ICJ, 55; local, for reconciliation and justice vs. international law, 163
cyberwar, parallels with German Blitzkrieg of World War II, 15
Cyprus: failure of mediation in, state's representatives and, 35; identity issues and conflict in, 97; International Negotiation Network and, 39; peacekeepers and hardening of status quo in, 82; stabilization of issues by UN peacekeepers in, 81–82; UN Peacekeeping Force in, *80*

Darfur: failure to engage forcefully in, 114; UN failure to consistently punish violators of norms in, 71
Dayton Agreement (1995), 112, 178
decision making: cultural influences during negotiations on, 29; decentralized, of nonofficial actors, 145
Declaration of Principles, 1993, of Israel and the PLO, 9
decolonization: UN leadership prior to, 66; UN peacekeepers and conflicts over, 77; UN success at resolving conflicts over, 67, 68
defensive alliances, for conflict deterrence in Cold War, 6
Democratic Republic of Congo. *See* Congo, Democratic Republic of
democratization: after end of Cold War, 1; of global governance, nonofficial diplomacy and, 138–39; moral issues in peacebuilding and, 180–81; peacekeeping forces and, 10
demographic indicators and signs of potential conflict, 92, *93*
Department of Humanitarian Affairs (DHA), UN, 105
Department of Peacekeeping Operations (DPKO), UN: Lessons Learned Unit of, 114; management of humanitarian interventions by, 105; Peacekeeping Best Practices Unit of, 73, 82; peacekeeping operations and, 66; regional task-sharing and, 122; on role for hybrid operations, 133
Department of Political Affairs (DPA), UN, 93, 105
Department of Public Information (DPI), UN, 138
Deutsch, Morton, 43
development theory, peacebuilding and, 169, 170–71
diaspora communities, intrastate conflicts and, 4. *See also* mass expulsion; refugees
diplomacy: failure of, peacekeeping operations and, 75; recognition of nonofficial actors in, 148–49; by regional organizations, 135; traditional conflict resolution and, 184; traditional peacekeeping and, 84. *See also* nonofficial diplomacy; preventive diplomacy; quiet diplomacy
diplomatic arbitration, 50
diplomatic immunity and privileges, nonofficial diplomats and, 147
diplomatic missions: to avoid arbitration or adjudication of disputes, 57; for negotiation, 26
diplomatic processes, legal methods for conflict resolution and, 59
diplomatic relations, ICJ judgments on, 56
diplomatic support, in regional task-sharing, 124
diplomats, retired, nonofficial diplomacy by, 142
disappearances, truth commissions and, 158–59
disarmament, UN General Assembly on, 65
dispute resolution services, Peck on creation of, 98
Dispute Settlement Mechanism, OSCE (1991), 50
dissenting opinions, of the ICJ, 55

distributive interactions, in negotiations, 27
documentation of conflicts, for UN Security Council, 63
domestic affairs: norm of noninterference by UN in, 71, 110–11, 149; third-party influence for violence prevention on, 98; UN investigation into, 72. *See also* internal issues or factors; states; state sovereignty
domestic law, application of, in arbitration, 52
domestic leaders, behavior of, preventive diplomacy and, 96, 97
Dominican Republic: OAS peacekeeping operation in, 119, 126; regional and MNF peacekeeping in, *126*
Donelan, Michael, 36, 42
do no harm principle, peacebuilding and, 173, 181
Doob, Leonard, 9, 38
Doyle, Michael, 176
Druckman, Daniel, 24

early warning and response systems: nonofficial diplomats and, 141, 150; for preventive diplomacy, 90, 91–92; signs and indicators in, 92–94, *93;* terrorism-related conflicts and, 188
East Timor. *See* Timor-Leste
Economic and Monetary Community of Central African States, *11*
Economic and Social Council (ECOSOC), UN, 138
economic collapse of a country, peacemaking efforts and, 89. *See also* failed states; weak governance/states
Economic Community of West African States (ECOWAS): Cease-fire Monitoring Group (ECOMOG), 134; incumbent regimes and, 134; Liberian intervention by, 120, 123; Liberia's preference for peacekeepers from UN vs., 110; mediation by, 32; regional peacekeeping by, *11, 127;* regional task-sharing by, 128; security issues as major concern for, 125
economic costs of conflicts, 13, 162
economic deprivation, 92
economic embargoes, preventive diplomacy and, 90
economic indicators and signs of potential conflict, 92, *93*
economic liberalization, side effects from, 178. *See also* neoliberal economic order
economic power: for conflict deterrence in Cold War, 6; globalization of, after end of Cold War, 1; of transnational corporations vs. traditional states, 16
economic rehabilitation, peacebuilding and, 175, 176, 180
economic rights, ICJ judgments on, 56
ECOWAS. *See* Economic Community of West African States
Edmead, Frank, 42
Egypt, UNEF II and signing of Camp David accords by, 81
election monitoring: in Nicaragua, 136; by UN peacekeepers, 79. *See also* administration
El Salvador: humanitarian intervention in, 101, 106, *107,* 109, 117; peacebuilding in, 168–69, 176, 177, 178; peace settlement and humanitarian intervention in, 104; perception of international truth commission in, 165; reasons for durable peace in, 179; selective investigations/prosecutions in, 164; Soccer War and, 130; Washington Peace Conference (1907) and, 53
emancipatory political structures, for post–Cold War conflict resolution, 8

emotional dimensions of conflict: negotiation and, 21; reconciliation and justice and, 152, 153, 161. *See also* psychological factors

empirical studies: on bargaining and negotiation, 21, 23, 24, 25, 31; for conceptual reorientation of intrastate system, 186; on mediation, 32, 33, 37, 41, 43, 44, 46; on nonofficial diplomacy, 146, 147; on peacebuilding–reconstruction continuum, 179, 183; on reconciliation and justice, 151, 161; on terrorism, 187; on UN conflict resolution, 67; on UN vs. regional organization conflict resolution, 126. *See also* conceptual framework(s)

enforcement actions: collective, cost-effectiveness of UN peacekeeping vs., 81; in humanitarian intervention, 102; peacekeeping operations vs., 113; by UN peacekeepers, 66. *See also* law and order

enforcement of international law, 57–58

England, queen of, arbitration by, 51. *See also* Great Britain; United Kingdom

environmental protection, 65, 71

Eritrea: peace process after Cold War in, 2; secession from Ethiopia, 134; UN Mission in Ethiopia and, 75, 79, *80*, 82

Eritrea-Ethiopia Boundary (PCA arbitration case), 52, 53

ethical dilemmas: nonofficial diplomacy and, 146, 148; reconciliation and justice and, 162–63

Ethiopia: failure of mediation in, state's representatives and, 35; International Negotiation Network and, 39; peace process after Cold War in, 2; post-Mengistu, individuals as victims and perpetrators in, 163; superpower patronage during Cold War and, 3; UN Mission in Eritrea and, 75, 79, *80*, 82

ethnic cleansing, in Rwanda and former Yugoslavian conflicts, 88. *See also* mass expulsion

ethnic conflicts: cultural barriers to successful negotiation during, 29; identity issues and, 4–5; interactional factors and, 96; peacemaking efforts and, 89; proliferation of, 3; UN efforts during Cold War with, 7

ethnic groups: relevance of international law for, 58; tensions among, as key variable in conflicts, 92

ethnicity: attacks motivated by, as early warning sign, 92; information on grievances of groups based on, 93; as motivation by local leaders in conflicts, 92; post–Cold War era conflicts over, 87–88; UN success at resolving conflicts over, 68

Europe: eastern, intrastate conflicts at end of Cold War in, 122; eastern, reconciliation and justice after Cold War in, 152; humanitarian intervention as neoimperialism by, 114; postwar, individuals as victims and perpetrators in, 163; state system in, traditional conflict resolution and, 185

European Centre for Conflict Prevention, 137

European Court of Human Rights (ECHR), 53, 54

European Platform for Conflict Prevention and Transformation, 141

European Union (EU): Boutros-Ghali and, 129; Court of First Instance, 53, 54; Court of Justice, 53, 54; as functionalist enterprise, 61; International Conference on the Former Socialist Federal Republic of Yugoslavia and, 123; peacemaking in Bosnia by, 40; regional peacekeeping by, *11, 127*

exclusion, truth commissions and, 158

external factors, reconciliation and justice approaches and, 155

external indicators of conflict, 93, *93*

extremism, truth commissions and, 158

face-saving: framing a conflict in humanitarian terms and, 12; informal mediation through INN and, 39; legal methods and, 57; nonofficial diplomats and, 143; proceedings in multilateral context and opportunity for, 74; UN secretary-general's quiet diplomacy and, 70

face-to-face diplomacy, 140

fact-finding missions, 64, 66, 95

factions: humanitarian operations and resources for, 111–12; intrastate conflicts and, 3; principle of consent and, 108

failed states: post–Cold War era proliferation of, 88; resuscitation of, for post–Cold War conflict resolution, 8; terrorist groups and, 6, 16. *See also* weak governance/states

fig-leaf theory, 115, 134, 148

Fiji, failure of mediation in, state's representatives and, 35

financing: for disarmament, demobilization, and reintegration and electoral assistance, 169; for nonofficial diplomacy, 147–48; for peacebuilding, 173, 181; for peacekeeping operations, 77, 82–83; for preventive diplomacy, 89; for regional task-sharing, 133. *See also* resources

Finland, peacebuilding unit in foreign ministry of, 137

first-generation peacekeeping, 106. *See also* traditional peacekeeping

Fisher, Roger, 30

flood net, cyberwar technique of forcing Internet network offline, 15

Folberg, Jay, 34

food aid, continuation of a conflict due to, 111

force. *See* military force; nonuse of force

force-level peacekeeping operations, 78

forgiveness, 145, 153, 161–62

formal mediation, 39, 44, 64. *See also* mediation

Forum for Security Cooperation (FSC), of OSCE, 128–29

fourth-generation peacekeeping, 75. *See also* nonofficial diplomacy

France: compulsory jurisdiction of the ICJ withdrawn by, 54; non-UN peacekeeping by, *11; Rainbow Warrior* case and, 53, 66; regional task-sharing by, *126;* Rwanda intervention by, 103, 114

free-rider dilemma, 61

free-trade regimes, free-rider dilemma and, 61

Fukuyama, Francis, 2

functionalism, in international relations, 61

functional (regional) organizations, 120, 121

Galtung, Johan, 9, 10, 170

Gardner, Ann Marie, 91–92

gender, war experience differences and, 14, 16

General Treaty of Friendship, Commerce, and Navigation (1794), 50

genocide: in Cambodia, 162; history of, preventive diplomacy and, 97; ICJ judgments on, 56; legal obligation to humanitarian intervention due to, 110–11; severe conflicts and, 4

Genocide Convention, 110

Georgia: Abkhazia civil conflict with, 126, *127*, 134; regional peacekeeping in, *11,* 129; South Ossetia conflict, regional peacekeeping in, *127;* UN Observer Mission in, *80,* 134

Germany: peacekeepers after World War II in, 76; reunification of, 2

global commons, free-rider dilemma and, 61

globalization: awareness of global inequality of wealth and resources, 5; of information and economic power after end of Cold War, 1

global-regional peacemaking system, 120. *See also* regional task-sharing

Golan Heights, UNDOF and quiet in, 81

Goncalves, Jaime, 142, 143

good offices: committees for peaceful settlement, 64; UN General Assembly on, 65; of UN secretary-general, 66

Goulding, Marrack, 76

government agencies, in post-Westphalian system, 5–6. *See also* administration

governments: acceptance of legitimacy of grievances by, 188; acceptance of truth commission findings by, 164; collapse of, as key variable in conflicts, 92; collapse of, humanitarian interventions and, 103; evaluation of IOs vs., 61; financing nonofficial diplomacy by, 147–48; national, as sources for early warning systems, 93; peacebuilding by, 177; political will and warning-response gap of, 93–94; restoration of functions, peacebuilding and, 173. *See also* states

Great Britain: *Alabama Claims Arbitration* (1872) and, 50; Jay Treaty (1794) and, 50; non-UN peacekeeping by, *11*. *See also* England, queen of; United Kingdom

great powers: abuse of UN sanctions by, 110; conflicts in Africa as issues for, 71; humanitarian intervention and existing system of, 112; institutional memory within the UN of, 73; interests of, intervention strategies and, 114; UN and narrow interests of, 61. *See also* superpowers

grievances: early warning information on, 93; over ethnic differences, 5; humanitarian interventions and, 107; over inequality, 92; media for expression of, 15; nonofficial diplomacy and recognition of, 144, 145; peacebuilding and, 172; preventive diplomacy to address, 97; reconciliation and justice for, 153; of terrorists, 187, 188

Griffiths, Martin, 12

Grotius, Hugo, on right of intervention, 110

groupthink, successful negotiations and, 28, 29

guardianship, ICJ judgments on, 56

Guatemala: Community Sant'Egidio and peace process in, 139; OAS and coup in, 133; peacebuilding in, 178; selective investigations/prosecutions in, 164; UN humanitarian intervention in, *107*; Washington Peace Conference (1907) and, 53

guerilla warfare, 187

Guetzkow, Harold, 24

Guinea-Bissau: regional peacekeeping in, *11, 127*; UN authorization of regional peacekeeping in, 126

Gulf of Maine maritime boundary dispute (1984), 54

Gulf War, First (1991), 72, 87, 108, 123

Gulf War, Second (2003–), 72, 182

Gurr, Ted, 5

Haas, Ernst B., 67, 73, 126

Hague Convention for the Pacific Settlement of International Disputes (1907), 50

Hague Peace Conferences, First (1899) and Second (1907), 50–51

Haiti: liberal democracy enforced in, 114; MNF peacekeeping in, *128*; non-UN peacekeeping in, *11*; OAS and coup in, 133; OAS/UN International Civilian Mission in, 136; peacebuilding in, 177, 178; UN authorization of MNF operations in, 126; UN humanitarian intervention in, 104, *107*, 109; UN–OAS joint civilian operation in, 123

Hamas, resolving conflict with Israel, 188

Hammarskjöld, Dag, 76, 79

hard-line, in negotiations, 30

Hattotuwa, Sanjana, 15

Haufler, Virginia, 16

Hayner, Priscilla B., 166

heads of state: foreign, arbitration by, 51; mediation by, 41; summit diplomacy and, 25

healing: collective, truth commissions and, 161–62; peace-building and, 172; religiously motivated actors on, 145; truth commissions vs. trials and, 153

hegemonic leadership: foreign policy goals of one UN member and, 72; in international relations, 62; political will of IOs' membership and, 71; regional, self-interested objectives of, 134

Helsinki Final Act (1975), 13

Helsinki model of confidence-building, 94

Helsinki Summit (1992), 129

High Commissioner for National Minorities (HCNM), of OSCE, 131

Hirschfeld, Yair, 39

Holbrooke, Richard, 39

Honduras: Soccer War and, 130; UN humanitarian intervention in, *107*; Washington Peace Conference (1907) and, 53

hostage-taking, ICJ judgments on, 56

hostile perceptions, as cause of conflict, 91, 92

humanitarian assistance: humanitarian intervention vs., 103; NGO response to need for, 145

humanitarian interventions, 101–18; abandonment of neutrality by, 78; assessing, 108; autonomy of actors in, 186; basis of, 77, 103–5; challenges of, 110–17; conceptual challenges to, 112–14; conceptualizing, 102–5; defining, 102–3; definition of, 75; key principles of orthodox peacekeeping and, 77; legal issues regarding, 110–11; lessons learned, 117–18; method of operation, 104–5; normative questions regarding, 111–12; operational challenges for, 115–17; overview of, 101–2; overview since 1989, 105–6, *107*, 108; peacekeeping operations differences from, 84; political problems with, 114–15; strengths of, 109–10; by transnational organizations, 40–41; by UN peacekeepers, 66

humanitarian mediation, framing conflict dialogue in terms of, 12

humanitarian NGOs, nonofficial diplomacy by, 142

human rights: law on, prosecution by ICC of, 59; norm of noninterference in states' domestic affairs and, 71; peacekeeping forces and, 10; promotion of, for post–Cold War conflict resolution, 8; terrorism and, 187; UN General Assembly on, 65; universal, evolving consensus on, 104, 112, 152. *See also* human sovereignty

human rights abuses: humanitarian interventions and, 103, 104, 111; individuals as victims and perpetrators of, 163;

human rights abuses (*continued*)
  as key variable in conflicts, 92; neutrality of nonofficial
    diplomacy and, 146; past, policy options for dealing with,
    154–55; peacemaking efforts and, 89; trials on, 151.
    See also truth and reconciliation commissions; truth
    commissions
human rights commissioners, 156
human security, peacebuilding as, 171
human sovereignty, Annan on responsibility to protect, 99. *See
    also* human rights
Hun Sen, 178
hurting stalemate, ripe moment for mediation and, 42
Hussein, Saddam, war crimes trial of, 154, 160
hybrid operations, regional task-sharing as, 122

identity: ethnic and religious conflicts and, 4–5; internal
    conflicts over, 68; truth commissions and politics of, 158.
    See also ethnic groups; religious conflict
ideology: humanitarian intervention and, 113, 114; mediation
    and, 42; as motivation by local leaders in conflicts, 92
Ignatieff, Michael, 166
Ikle, Fred, 20
impartiality: adherence to, 84; Cold War rivalries and, 83;
    delivering aid through military force and, 112; humani-
    tarian interventions and, 103, 113; of international courts,
    58; of mediators, 36; peacekeeping operations and, 75;
    principle of, peacekeeping operations and, 78, 81; regional
    task-sharing and, 133–34; by UN peacekeeping operations,
    66; UN's reputation for, 110
impeding factors, in social-psychological approach to negotia-
    tion, 24
India: Bangladesh intervention by, 103; conflict with Pakistan,
    4, 41, 52, 79
indicators, for early warning of conflict, 92
individuals: as intervening actors in preventive diplomacy, 96;
    peacebuilding and appalling behavior of, 182; reconcilia-
    tion among, 153; Responsibility to Protect, 90; role in
    world politics of, 9; twenty-first-century conflict resolution
    and, 184, 186; unofficial, as mediators, 40. *See also* actors
inequality: as cause of conflict, 91; global, 5; as key variable in
    conflicts, 92
informal arbitrations, 52
informal diplomacy, 126. *See also* nonofficial diplomacy; quiet
    diplomacy
informal mediation, 38–39, 44, 64
information: access for reconciliation and justice to, 164;
    agreements on exchange of, 94; globalization of, after end
    of Cold War, 1; for international commissions and tri-
    bunals, 165; requirements, for early warnings of conflicts,
    93. *See also* communication; Internet
insecurity, as cause of conflict, 91
inspections, confidence-building through, 94
Institute for Multi-Track Diplomacy, 141
institutional barriers to successful negotiation, 29
institutional limitations, of UN humanitarian interventions,
    115, 116
institutional memory, of great power within the UN, 73
institutions: capacity-building for, peacebuilding and, 173;
    mediation by, 40–41

integrated operations, regional task-sharing as, 122
integrated strategy, for early warnings of conflicts, 91
integrative interactions: in mediation, 43; in negotiations, 27
interactional factors: mediation and, 43; in preventive diplo-
    macy, 96–97; in social-psychological approach to negotia-
    tion, 24, 27–28
interactive conflict resolution, 140
Inter-African Force, *126*
Inter-African Mission to Monitor the Bangui Accords
    (MISAB), *128*, 133, 135
Inter-American Committee on Peaceful Settlement (1970), 125
Inter-American Court of Human Rights, 53, 54
Inter-American Peace Committee, 126
Inter-American Peace Force, *126*
intergovernmental organizations: evolution of role of, 10–11;
    regional task-sharing by, 121
internal conflicts: in developing countries, UN Security Council
    on intervention in, 123; ethnic conflict and, 42; intensity
    and significance after Cold War of, 1–2; nonofficial diplo-
    macy and, 149, 150; regional organizations and, 131;
    regional task-sharing and, 135; subjective element of,
    nonofficial diplomacy and, 144; understanding the nature
    of, 113, 147. *See also* humanitarian interventions;
    intractable conflicts; new wars
internal issues or factors: humanitarian interventions with, 79;
    post–Cold War era conflicts due to, 87; reconciliation and
    justice approaches and, 155; reluctance of political actors to
    act due to, 91; UN peacekeepers and, 83; UN success at
    resolving conflicts over, 68. *See also* domestic affairs; state
    sovereignty
international claims tribunals: arbitration by, 51, 52; campaign
    for permanent international criminal court after, 13; politi-
    cal questions and judicial scope of, 58
International Commission on Intervention and State Sover-
    eignty, 104
International Committee of the Red Cross (ICRC), 112
International Conference on the Former Socialist Federal
    Republic of Yugoslavia, 123
international conflict: changing paradigm from conflict man-
    agement to conflict resolution, 8–10, 16; after end of Cold
    War, 1, 2–5; intra- and interstate, 1946–2005, *3*; new war,
    postmodern war, beyond war, 5–6; regional distribution of,
    1946–2005, *3*; traditional approaches to conflict, 6–8
international conventions: as source of law for arbitrators, 52;
    as source of law for the ICJ, 55
International Court of Justice (ICJ): composition of, 55; con-
    flict regulation and prevention and, 57; establishment of,
    53–54; on financing peacekeeping operations, 82–83;
    functions of, 56; jurisdiction of, 54–55; procedures of, 55;
    UN secretary-general's access to, 70; UN Security Council
    referral to, 64; work of, 56
international crime, blurred distinctions between warring par-
    ties and, 3. *See also* criminal organizations; international
    criminal tribunals
International Criminal Court (ICC): adjudication by, 53; estab-
    lishment of, 13, 54, 152; law as prerequisite for peace and,
    151; prosecution of human rights law by, 59
international criminal tribunals, 151, 152, 160. *See also* crimi-
    nal organizations; international crime

international customs: as source of law for arbitrators, 52; as source of law for the ICJ, 55

international financial institutions (IFIs): conflict resolution and postconflict reconstruction departments of, 13–14; coordination of peacebuilding and, 182

International Force in East Timor (INTERFET), *128*, 131, 135

International Labor Organization (ILO), 53, 56

international law: application of, in arbitration, 52; arbitration, adjudication and, 47–48; conflict resolution methods based on, 49–56; development of, 49; enforcement issues with, 57–58; functions of, 48–49; inflexibility of, 58; lessons learned, 59; limitations of, 57–59; local customs for reconciliation and justice vs., 163; nature of, 48; norm creation as source of, 69; strengths of, 57; theory of humanitarian intervention and, 112; universality principle under, 160. *See also* civilized nations; law and order; rule of law

International Law Commission, Model Rules of Arbitral Procedure adopted by, 51

International Monetary Fund (IMF), 53

international negotiation, 19–31; approaches to study of bargaining and, 23–25; characteristics of bargaining and, 21; conceptual framework for, 20–21; elements of bargaining and, 21–23; factors influencing bargaining and, 25–29; lessons learned, 30–31; nature of conflict and conflict resolution, 19–20; overview of, 19; strategies for bargaining and, 29–30; traditional conflict resolution and, 184. *See also* negotiations

International Negotiation Network (INN), 39. *See also* Carter Center

international organizations (IOs), 5–6; built-in bias toward state actors of, 115; coordination of peacebuilding and, 182; evaluation of governments vs., 61; functions of, 69; as intervening actors in preventive diplomacy, 96; limits of, 71–72; mediation by, 40; multilateral approaches to conflicts by, 11; peacebuilding units in, 137–38, 171, 177; promotion of universal human rights by, 152; relevance of international law for, 58; role of international regimes vs., 62; role of NGOs in support of, 139; timing of preventive diplomacy by, 98. *See also* regional organizations; United Nations

International Peace Academy, 171, 180

International Tribunal for the Law of the Sea, 53, 54

international truth commissions, 155–56, 159. *See also* truth commissions

Internet, positive and negative uses of, 15. *See also* technology

interpersonal bargaining, 25

interpersonal orientation in negotiation, 26, 31

interposition: by UNEF I in Suez, 79; of UN peacekeepers between conflicting armies, 77

interstate conflict(s): legal methods for resolution of, 59; persistence of, 4; role of regional arrangements in, 135; terrorism and, 189; traditional peacekeeping and, 79; UN role in, 135–36. *See also* traditional conflict resolution

Inter-Tajik Dialogue (1994), 137

intervenor fatigue, preventive diplomacy and, 98

intractable conflicts: in communities with history of hostility, 5; humanitarian interventions for, 117; interactional factors and, 96; nonofficial diplomacy and, 149; in Rwanda and former Yugoslavia, 88. *See also* internal conflicts; new wars; twenty-first-century conflict resolution

intraparty friction, 22

intrastate conflicts: as challenges for UN's peacekeeping capabilities, 108; at end of Cold War, 122; most current wars as, 3–4; from 1946 to 2005, *3*; UN difficulties in resolving, 68, *68*. *See also* intractable conflicts; new wars; twenty-first-century conflict resolution

investigatory commissions, moral order and, 159

Iran: UN Iran-Iraq Military Observer Group in, *80*, 82; U.S. Claims Tribunal, 51, 53

Iraq: MNF operations in, 128; third-generation peacekeeping in, 106; UN Iran-Iraq Military Observer Group in, *80*, 82; UN Iraq-Kuwait Observation Mission in, *80*, 82. *See also* Gulf War, First; Gulf War, Second

Irian Jaya, UN peacekeeping during Cold War in, 106

Islamic Conference, mediation by, 32

Israel: Declaration of Principles, 1993, of the PLO and, 9; informal mediation with PLO and, 39; nonofficial diplomats and talks with PLO by, 143; Oslo peace process and, 29, 137; peacebuilding in, 178; resolving conflict with Palestinians, 188, 189–90; UNEF II and signing of Camp David accords by, 81; UN secretary-general and, 66

issue areas: nonofficial diplomacy and, 139; official diplomat outsourcing to nonofficial diplomats of, 144

issues: in bargaining and negotiation, 21–23; in dispute for mediation, 35, 43; recommended approaches to, 31; in social-psychological approach to negotiation, 26

Italy: Mozambique peace process and, 143; non-UN peacekeeping by, *11*; regional task-sharing by, *126*

Ivory Coast: negotiating Mali–Burkina Faso cease-fire and, 22; non-UN peacekeeping in, *11*; peacebuilding in, 177; regional peacekeeping in, *11*, *127*, 128; UN humanitarian intervention in, *107*

Jackson, Elmore, 35, 36, 42–43

Jay Treaty (1794), 50, 51, 52

Jick, Todd, 44

joint operations, in regional task-sharing, 124

joint requests for mediation, as indication of motivation, 40

journalists, nonofficial diplomacy by, 142

Joyner, Christopher, 48

judgments, average per year, of PCIJ vs. ICJ, 56

judicial decisions and legal opinions: precedential nature of, 59; as source of law for arbitrators, 52; as source of law for the ICJ, 55

judicial scope, political questions and, 58

jurisdictional clauses, ICJ and, 54

justice: internationalization of, 152; strengths of, for reconciliation, 160; transitional, 153–54; use of term, 153. *See also* reconciliation and justice

Kampuchea. *See* Cambodia

Kashmir: identity issues and conflict in, 97; League of Nations peacekeepers in, 76; peacekeeping operations in, 66, 79; stabilization of issues by UN peacekeepers in, 81

Kelman, Herbert, 9, 38, 44

key causal variables of conflict, 91–92

killings by anonymous death squads, truth commissions and, 158–59

Kochan, Thomas, 44

Kolb, Deborah, 44

Kosovo: Community Sant'Egidio and peace process in, 139; exaggerations of human rights abuses in, 111; NATO air campaign in (1999), 132; NATO and UN task-sharing in, 128; NATO's intervention in, 103; peacebuilding in, 177, 178; regional peacekeeping in, *11, 127;* third-generation peacekeeping in, 106; UN authorization of regional peacekeeping in, 126; UN humanitarian intervention in, *107*

Kressel, Kenneth, 44

Kriesberg, Louis, 30, 90, 97–98

Kumar, Krishna, 173

Kuwait: Arab League intervention in, 119; regional and MNF peacekeeping in, *126;* UN Iraq-Kuwait Observation Mission, *80, 82*

lack of political will: as obstacle to preventive diplomacy, 99; warning-response gap and, 93–94. *See also* political will

Lall, Arthur, 20, 35

Langley, Jeffrey, 95

LAS. *See* Arab League

Last, David, 175

Latin America, state-centric conflicts during Cold War in, 6. *See also* Central America; *specific countries*

law and order: guarantees by UN peacekeepers, 66, 77, 106; peacebuilding and, 172, 173, 175. *See also* international law; rule of law

Law of the Sea Conference, 49

lawyers, nonofficial diplomacy by, 142

leadership: individual, interstate conflict and, 130; by nonofficial diplomatic groups, 149. *See also* hegemonic leadership

League of Nations: conflict management and, 6; General Act for the Pacific Settlement of International Disputes of, 51; international law development and, 49; peacekeeping operations and, 76; Permanent Court of International Justice and, 53; traditional peacekeeping under, 78–79

Lebanon: failure of mediation in, state's representatives and, 35; peacebuilding in, 178; peace process after Cold War in, 2; regional and MNF peacekeeping in, *126;* UN Interim Force in, *80,* 81; UN Observation Group in, *80;* UN peacekeeping during Cold War in, 106

Lederach, John Paul: on intrastate conflicts, 3–4; on peacebuilding, 170, 174; on reconciliation, 153; on sustainable peace, 10; on trust of NGOs by local conflict parties, 12

legal-normative basis of humanitarian interventions, 104

legitimacy: of conflict resolution by UN, 69; of intervening actors in preventive diplomacy, 96; of regional task-sharing, 133–34; as third party, UN's reputation for, 110

Lesotho, peacekeeping in, *11, 127*

Lessons Learned Unit, of UN's Department of Peacekeeping Operations, 114

liberal capitalism, post–Cold War, 2. *See also* economic liberalization

liberal democracy: in Haiti, 114; peacebuilding and, 181. *See also* neoliberal economic order

liberal peace thesis, peacebuilding and, 172

liberation movements: IOs and dispute resolution with, 71; relevance of international law for, 58

Liberia: acceptance of UN peacekeepers in, 109–10, 134; agreements to end fighting in, 139; ECOWAS intervention in, 120, 123; ethnic and religious conflict in, 4; International Negotiation Network and, 39; peacebuilding in, 177; regional peacekeeping in, *11, 127,* 128; superpower patronage during Cold War and, 3; UN authorization of regional peacekeeping in, 126; UN humanitarian intervention in, *107;* UN Observer Group in, *80,* 133

Libya, Mali–Burkina Faso conflict and, 22, 23

Lithuania, peacekeepers after World War II in, 76

local organizations: nonofficial diplomacy and, 139; as sources for early warning systems, 93

Logan Act (U.S., 1799), 148

logistics: as obstacle to preventive diplomacy, 98–99; for UN peacekeeping operations, 84

Lomé Peace Agreement, 45

long-term tasks, in peacebuilding, 174

loss aversion, successful negotiation and, 28–29

Lund, Michael, 90, 175

lustration, as option for dealing with past abuses, 154

Maastricht Treaty, 122

Macedonia, regional peacekeeping in, *11*

Mali–Burkina Faso conflict (1985–86), 21, 22, 23

Martens, F. F., 50

mass expulsion, history of, preventive diplomacy and, 97. *See also* diaspora communities; ethnic cleansing; refugees

Mauritania, ICJ's advisory opinion on *Western Sahara* case and, 55

Mbeki, Thabo, 164

McGrath, Joseph, 20

Médecins sans Frontières, 138

media: global, accessibility and pervasive presence of, 14–15; in post-Westphalian system, 5–6. *See also* public information guarantees; public interest; public opinion

mediation, 32–46; advantages of regional organizations in, 130; approaches to, 36–37; characteristics of, 34–35; conceptual framework for, 33; for conflict deterrence in Cold War, 6; as conflict resolution tool in Westphalian system, 8; definition of, 33–36; early phases, nonofficial diplomats and, 143–44; elements of, 35–36; evaluating, 45–46; factors influencing, 37–43; failures of, nonofficial diplomats and, 139; humanitarian, 12; lessons learned, 46; media use for informing constituencies during, 15; nonofficial, 140, 141, 147; overview, 32; peacekeeping operations and, 75; for preventive diplomacy, 95; preventive diplomacy and, 89; by regional organizations during the Cold War, 126; success by international actors, 67; terrorist groups and, 189; traditional conflict resolution and, 184; in twenty-first-century international environment, 87; UN General Assembly on, 65; by UN peacekeepers, 66; UN secretary-general as, 66; UN Security Council on, 64; UN success at resolving conflicts through, 67

mediator(s): expected payoffs as motivation for, 38; identity of, 38–39; institutions and organizations as, 40–41; interactional factors and, 43; interaction between protagonists and, 34; nonofficial, 139; personal attributes of, 35–36; questions on use of leverage by, 146; request for peacekeeping by, 77; states as, 39–40; strategies of, 43–45; UN as, 73–74; UN secretary-general as, 70

medium-term tasks, in peacebuilding, 174

mental models, rigid, successful negotiation and, 28

mercy: reconciliation and, 153, 161; religiously motivated actors on, 145

Meyer, Arthur, 33

Middle East: Arab-Israeli conflict in, 4, 188; confidence-building measures in, 95; as conflict-prone region, 3; League of Nations peacekeepers in, 76; regional organizations in, 132; stabilization of issues by UN peacekeepers in, 81; state-centric conflicts during Cold War in, 6; UN and conflict resolution in, *68;* UN Truce Supervision Organizations mission to, 79

middle-out approach to peacebuilding, 174

military command system: MNFs and, 135; for UN humanitarian interventions, 116–17; UN peacekeeping and lack of, 82; for UN peacekeeping operations, 84

military expenditures, as key variable in conflicts, 92

military force (operations): coordinating humanitarian operations with, 116–17; in humanitarian interventions, 103, 105, 110, 111; peacebuilding and, 182; preemptive, self-defense and, 132

military intelligence: as information deficit for UN, 72; non-official diplomacy and lack of, 148; for UN humanitarian interventions, 116

military observer missions, 77

military security alliances, 124

Military Staff Committee, UN, 63

Millennium Report (Annan), 99

Milošović, Slobodan, 151

Mitchell, Chris, 33

mixed national and international truth commissions, 156

mobilizing causes of conflict, understanding, 91

Model Rules of Arbitral Procedure, 51

Moldova, regional peacekeeping in, *11*

Moldova/Trans-Dneister, regional peacekeeping in, *127*

Montenegro, UN Protection Force (UNPROFOR) in, *107,* 177

Montville, Joseph, 9

Moore, Christopher, 33–34

moral authority, of United Nations, 69

moral issues, in democratization and peacebuilding, 180–81. *See also* ethical dilemmas

moral order, truth commissions and, 158–59

Morley, Ian, 20–21

Morocco, ICJ's advisory opinion on *Western Sahara* case and, 55

motivational factors, mediation and, 41–42

Mouton, Jane, 33

Mozambique: Community Sant'Egidio and peace process in, 139; humanitarian intervention in, 101, 106, 109, 117; nonofficial diplomacy in, 142–43; peacebuilding in, 168–69, 176, 177; reasons for durable peace in, 179; reconciliation and justice in, 163; Rome Agreement (1992) and, 137; superpower patronage during Cold War and, 3; UN humanitarian intervention in, *107*

multidimensional approaches to peacemaking, 10–11

multidimensional peacekeeping operations, 78

multilateral negotiations, 25

multinational corporations, 5–6, 58

multinational forces (MNFs): as ad hoc coalitions, 121; advantages of, 131; limits of peacekeeping by, 134–35; peace-keeping operations, 1990–2004, *128;* UN authorization of, 126, 128

Multinational International Force (IFOR), of UN and NATO, 123

multipurpose (regional) organizations, 120, 121

multitrack diplomacy, 140

muscular peacekeeping, 102

Myanmar (Burma): International Negotiation Network and, 39; interstate conflict in, 4

Namibia: humanitarian intervention in, 101, 109, 117; peace-building in, 168–69, 176; peace process after Cold War in, 2; peace settlement and humanitarian intervention in, 104; reasons for durable peace in, 179; regional peacekeeping by, *127;* UN Transitional Assistance Group (UNTAG) in, 106, *107,* 177

nationality, ICJ judgments on, 56

national security: limitations on ICJ compulsory jurisdiction due to, 54; sacrificing international legal order for, 59

national trials, rebuilding the political order and, 160. *See also* trials

national truth commissions, 155, 156, 164. *See also* truth commissions

nation-building, peacebuilding and, 172, 182

negative peace, 170

negative task of peacebuilding, 173, 178

negotiations: for conflict deterrence in Cold War, 6; as conflict resolution tool, 8; media use for informing constituencies during, 15; moral justice through truth commissions after, 159; peacekeeping operations and, 75; for preventive diplomacy, 95; preventive diplomacy and, 89; proximity, UN peacekeepers and, 66; with terrorist groups, 189; traditional peacekeeping and incentive for, 82; in twenty-first-century international environment, 87; UN General Assembly on, 65; UN secretary-general on, 66. *See also* international negotiation

neoliberal economic order: humanitarian intervention and, 112; peacebuilding and, 169, 172, 180. *See also* economic liberalization; liberal capitalism

Netherlands, peacebuilding unit in foreign ministry of, 137

netwar, as cyber-terrorism, 15

neutrality: intervention into violent conflict and, 147; by nonofficial diplomats, ethical dilemmas of, 146, 148; regional task-sharing and, 133–34; strict impartiality in peacekeeping and, 78

Newman, Edward, 153

new wars: nonofficial diplomacy and, 140; political deals with factions in, 112; politicized humanitarian aid operations and, 104; as postmodern or post-Westphalian, 6; security challenges posed by, 118; traditional Clausewitzian and positivist interpretations of, 113. *See also* internal conflicts; intractable conflicts; twenty-first-century conflict resolution

New Zealand: *Rainbow Warrior* case and, 53, 66; regional peacekeeping by, *127*

Nicaragua: peacebuilding in, 178; UN humanitarian intervention in, *107;* UN Observer Mission in, 136

Nicaragua case, 54

Nicolson, Harold, 20

Nigeria: dominance of ECOWAS by, 134; negotiating Mali–Burkina Faso cease-fire and, 22; regional peacekeeping by, *126, 127*

Nobel Peace Prize: former terrorists as winners of, 187; for UN peacekeeping, 104

nongovernmental diplomacy, 140

nongovernmental organizations (NGOs): conflict exacerbation due to, 147; for conflict resolution in war-afflicted countries, 137; coordination of peacebuilding and, 182; as early warning system sources, 93; emerging crises and flexibility of, 140; global, regional, and local, 10; humanitarian mediation by, 13; human rights–based, 152; international, estimated numbers of, 138; as intervening actors in preventive diplomacy, 96; local, Internet links of, 15; mediation success by, 67; multilateral approaches to conflicts by, 11–12; national or international truth commissions sponsored by, 156; official assistance for, 147–48; peacebuilding by, 175, 177; peacemaking by, 40–41; in post-Westphalian system, 5–6; relevance of international law for, 58; strategies for early warning of conflicts by, 91; twenty-first-century conflict resolution and, 184, 186; UN secretary-general and contacts with, 70; UN subcontracting to, 120. *See also* third parties

nonintervention in internal affairs of member states. *See* domestic affairs

nonofficial diplomacy, 137–50; basis of, 140–41; challenges of, 146–49; conceptualizing, 140–41; evaluating, 143–49; international conflict resolution and, 138–40; lessons learned, 149–50; in Mozambique, 142–43; overview of, 141–43; practical challenges for, 147–49; roles and functions of, 141; strengths of, 143–46; terrorism-related conflicts and, 188; theoretical challenges for, 146–47; twenty-first-century conflict resolution and, 184, 186

nonuse of force, principle of: adherence to, 84; harm to peace-keepers due to, 83; humanitarian interventions and, 103, 109; ICJ judgments on, 56; UN peacekeeping and, 78

Normative theory, on international organizations, 62

norm-based behavior standards: conflict resolution and, 69; contradictions among, 71

norms: collective legitimation of, 130; creation of, as source for international law, 69; human sovereignty as, hesitancies regarding, 99; of noninterference by UN in domestic affairs, 71; of nonviolent conflict resolution, 172

North Atlantic Cooperation Council (NACC), 128

North Atlantic Council, 125

North Atlantic Treaty Organization (NATO): Boutros-Ghali and, 129; Chapter VIII of UN Charter and, 131; conflict resolution and security regulation procedures of, 125; conflict with UN over dual key arrangement in Bosnia, 132; on European security, 123; Kosovo intervention by, 103, 111; military structures and peacekeeping by, 133; regional peacekeeping by, *11, 127,* 128; regional task-sharing by, 128; U.S. mediation in Greece–Turkey disputes and, 40

Northedge, Frederick, 36, 42

Northern Ireland peace process, 177, 189

North Korea's nuclear armament, 27

Norway, mediation by, 32, 139. *See also* Oslo Accords

Norwegian Emergency Preparedness System, 138

Norwegian Resource Bank for Democracy and Human Rights, 138

nuclear proliferation, IOs and issues regarding, 71

Nuclear Tests cases, 54

nuclear threat, state balance of power during Cold War and, 7–8

objective criteria, for mediation evaluation, 45, 46

observation: confidence-building through, 94; by UN peace-keeping operations, 66, 77, 78

observer peacekeeping operations, 78

Occupied Palestinian Territory, ICJ advisory opinion on Israeli construction of wall in, 55

officials. *See* senior officials

ombudsman's office, as truth commission, 156

operational procedures for peacekeeping operations, evolution of, 82

operational support, in regional task-sharing, 124

Operations Center (OSCE), 129

opinions, of the ICJ, 55, 56

oral phase, of ICJ proceedings, 55

Organization for African Unity (OAU): ad hoc mediating committee during the Cold War of, 126; Boutros-Ghali and, 129; conflict resolution by, 126, *126;* Liberia's internal conflict and, 120; negotiating Mali–Burkina Faso cease-fire and, 22; on nonstate actors, 133; norms of nonviolent resolution of interstate disputes and, 130; UN Special Representative in cooperation with, 123, 136

Organization for Security and Cooperation in Europe (OSCE): Dispute Settlement Mechanism (1991), 50; NGO and conflict resolution issues of, 138; potential internal conflicts and, 131; regional peacekeeping by, *127,* 128–29

Organization of American States (OAS): Boutros-Ghali and, 129; charter clause mandating mediation in regional disputes, 40; conflict resolution and security regulation procedures of, 125; conflict resolution by, 126; Dominican Republic peacekeeping by, 119, 126; mediation by, 32; Nicaraguan election monitoring by, 136; on nonstate actors, 133; peacemaking in El Salvador by, 40; potential internal conflicts and, 131; regional task-sharing by, 128; Soccer War and, 130; UN civilian operation in Haiti and, 123; U.S. delegation of conflict resolution to, 122

Organization of American States/United Nations International Civilian Mission in Haiti (MICIVIH), 136

Organization of the Islamic Conference (OIC), 121, 129

Organization of West African States, 45

organizations, mediation by, 40–41. *See also* international organizations; local organizations; nongovernmental organizations; regional organizations

orphan conflicts, 69–70, 72

orthodox peacekeeping. *See* traditional peacekeeping

Oslo Accords (1993), 137; combined Track I and II initiatives and, 139; negotiation and mediation in, 189; peacebuilding in Israel and Palestine after, 177; peace process leading to, 29

Other, the: conflict situations and hostile images of, 29; dehumanization of, consciousness of communities and, 97; truth commissions and hatred of, 158; truth-telling and recognition of, 153

Ott, Mervin, 35, 43

outcomes: antecedent factors in international negotiation and, 24–25; of mediation, 37, *37*

overconfidence, successful negotiation and, 28
OXFAM, UN Security Council briefing by, 138

Pacific Island Forum (PIF), *127*
Pacific region, as conflict prone, 3
Pacific Settlement of Disputes, 77
Pact of Bogota (1948), 125
Pakistan: Soviet Union's mediation of India's conflict with, 41; UN Good Offices Mission in Afghanistan and, *80, 82. See also* India
Palestine: peacebuilding in, 178; peacekeeping operations in, 66
Palestinian Liberation Organization (PLO): Declaration of Principles, 1993, of Israel and, 9; informal mediation with Israel and, 39; nonofficial diplomats and talks with Israel by, 143; Oslo Accords (1993) and, 137; UN secretary-general and, 66
Palestinians, resolving conflict with Israelis, 188, 189–90
Papua New Guinea–Bougainville, MNF peacekeeping in, *128*
paradigm. *See* conceptual framework(s)
parallel operations, regional task-sharing as, 122
Paris, Roland, 178, 180
Parlevliet, Michelle, 166–67
parties: in bargaining and negotiation, 21–22; clear identification of, mediation and, 42; in conflict, mediation and, 34, 35; in conflict, mediation and exclusion of previous relationships of, 42, 43; in conflict, motivation for mediation by, 37–38; consent of, UN peacekeeping operations and, 66, 77–78; disputing, request for humanitarian intervention by, 104; evaluation of issues in conflict by, 23; information on status, traits, and objectives of, 93; on membership and composition of arbitral body, 52; motivation and attitudes of, in negotiation, 28; motivations for mediation by, 42; perceptions of negotiation by, 29–30; presenting case to UN Security Council, 63; procedural arrangements for arbitration and, 51; request for peacekeeping by, 77; UN Security Council and conflicts among, 70; worldviews of, culture and, 29. *See also* actors
partisan perception, successful negotiation and, 28, 29
passage, rights of, ICJ judgments on, 56
payoffs, expected, by interacting parties, for mediation, 38
peace: justice and, 161; reconciliation and, 153; research on, peacebuilding and, 169, 170
peace agreements: facilitation by peacekeeping operations of, 81; just, nonofficial diplomats and, 145; phase of, role of humanitarian intervention in, 117
peacebuilding, 168–83; aims and tasks of, 173–75, *174;* autonomy of actors in, 186; challenges of, 179–82; conceptual and theoretical challenges to, 179–80; conceptualizing, 171–76; for conflict resolution, 89; evaluating, 178–79; in humanitarian intervention, 102, 109, 118; lessons learned, 182–83; nonofficial diplomacy in, 141; normative challenges to, 180–81; organization and coordination of, 175–76; origins of, 169–71; overview of, 168–69; political challenges to, 181–82; postconflict, writings on, 152; practical challenges to, 182; practice of, 176–78; principles and assumptions of, 172–73
peaceful settlement, UN Security Council on, 64. *See also* peace agreements

peacekeeping doctrine: evolution of, 82; Galtung on, 170; peacebuilding and, 169
peacekeeping operations, 75–84; basis of, 76–77; for conflict resolution, 89; danger of tribalization of, 132; definition of, 66, 76; development by UN of, 69; distinction between enforcement and, 113; as element in conflict resolution, 72–73; evolution of role of, 10, 11; fatigue from, large states and, 115; in humanitarian intervention, 102; humanitarian intervention compared to, 103; as improvised response, 76; as improvised UN response and mandate for, 72; increased numbers of, 101; lessons learned, 83–84; method of operation, 77–78; MNFs and structures for, 135; NGOs and, 138; non-UN, 1990–2005, *11;* organization and administration by UN secretary-general of, 66; overview of, 75–76; peacebuilding and, 177; post–Cold War era, 87; regionally organized, during the Cold War, 125–26, *126;* traditional, evaluating, 80–83; traditional, overview of, 78–80; of United Nations, 7; UN Security Council on, 64; UN Security Council's initiation and management of, 69. *See also* humanitarian interventions
peacemaking: Boutros-Ghali on, 169; for conflict resolution, 89; Galtung on, 170; in humanitarian intervention, 102, 109; nonofficial efforts at, 139, 141, 142; religious actors and, 145; third parties and spoiling of, 130–31
peace processes: after end of Cold War, 2; institutional barriers to, 29; long-term framework for, 14
peace pyramid, 119, 120, 174. *See also* regional task-sharing
Peace Research Institute, 3
Peace Treaty of 1856, ending Crimean War, 49
Pearce, Jenny, 180
Pearson, Lester, 76, 79
Peck, Connie, 98
perceptions of groups: bias by religiously motivated actors and, 146; as cause of conflicts, 91, 92; differences in coalitions of, 114; on negotiation, 29–30; qualitative assessments of, 93
Perez de Cuellar, José, 70
Permanent Court of Arbitration (PCA), at The Hague, 50–51, 52
Permanent Court of International Justice (PCIJ), at The Hague, 53, 56
permissive conditions, Brown on conflicts and, 92
Persian Gulf War. *See* Gulf War, First
personal factors: mediation and, 38–39; in social-psychological approach to negotiation, 24, 25–26. *See also* mediator(s)
Peru, OAS and coup in, 133
physical components, in social-psychological approach to negotiation, 26
planning, systematic, for UN peacekeeping operations, 84
Poland: PCIJ advisory opinions on, 56; peacekeepers after World War II in, 76
policy-related indicators and signs of potential conflict, 92–93, 93
political basis of humanitarian interventions, 103–4, 108, 114–15
political basis of peacebuilding, 172, 173
political basis of terrorism, 187
political constraints to reconciliation and justice, 163–64
political context for task-sharing, 122–23

political order, prosecutions and rebuilding of, 160

political rehabilitation, peacebuilding and, 175–76

political values, "training" by western NGOs in conflict resolution and, 146

political will: of great powers, conduct of humanitarian operations and, 115; international commissions and tribunals and, 165; for undertaking preventive action, 93–94, 99

pope(s): arbitration by, 51; mediation by, 32; nonofficial diplomacy by, 142

positive peace, 170

positive task of peacebuilding, 173, 178

post–Cold War era: challenges for UN with security environment of, 102; conflict resolution in, 8–9; lack of hegemonic leadership in Africa during, 62; MNF peacekeeping during, 126, 128, 128; nonofficial diplomacy in, 139; political basis of humanitarian interventions and, 103–4; reconciliation and justice in eastern Europe during, 152; regional task-sharing during, 126, 127, 128–29; size and scope of conflicts after, 87–88. See also Cold War

postconflict phases: peacebuilding during, 89; role of humanitarian intervention in, 117. See also reconstruction, postconflict

postmodern (post-Westphalian) war, 6, 14–16. See also new wars

poverty: conflict due to, 3; marginalization and conflict due to, 5

power, cultural assumptions involving, 29

power politics: conflict resolution using, 6; humanitarian intervention and, 114; international law viewed as, 47; in preventive diplomacy, 96

power relationships: balance of, negotiation and, 28; effects on mediation, 42; in negotiation, 20; parity or disparity in, mediation effectiveness and, 43; of parties in negotiation, 22

precedents: with judicial decisions and legal opinions, 59; UN mediation action as setting of, 73–74

preemption, Bush doctrine of, 104, 110. See also war on terror(ism)

preemptive military force, self-defense and, 132

prescriptive guidelines, for mediation, 36–37

preventive diplomacy, 87–100; actions, 94–95; assessing success of, 99; autonomy of actors in, 186; Boutros-Ghali on, 12, 40, 169; conceptual framework for, 88–89; confidence-building in, 94–95; diplomatic tools for, 95; early warning and response systems for, 91–92; early warning signs and indicators, 92–94; effective, components of regime for, 90–94; factors influencing success of, 95–98; Hammar-skjöld on, 76; humanitarian intervention as extension of, 101; interactional factors in, 96–97; intervening actors in, 95–96; lessons learned, 99–100; narrow and wide definitions of, 89–90; nonofficial diplomacy and, 141; obstacles to, 98–99; overview of, 87–88; peacebuilding and, 172; structural factors and, 97; terrorism-related conflicts and, 188; timing of, 97–98

principled negotiation, definition of, 30

private armies, intrastate conflicts and, 3

private incentives, as cause of conflict, 91, 92

problem solving: in negotiation, 30; nonofficial diplomats and, 140, 144–45; as opposed to concentrating on personalities, 31; workshops, 8, 9, 147

process of mediation, 37, 37

process-related interests, in social-psychological approach to negotiation, 25, 27

Program on Negotiation, Harvard University, 36–37

prosecutions: practical obstacles for, 165; rebuilding the political order and, 160; role in reconciliation and justice, 154; roles and functions of, 157; truth commissions as alternative to, 159. See also reconciliation and justice; trials

protests, increased numbers of, as early warning sign, 92

protracted conflicts, 5. See also intractable conflicts

proximate causes of conflict, Brown on, 91, 92

Pruitt, Dean, 27–28

psychological factors: as barriers to successful negotiation, 28–29; of legal methods of conflict resolution and, 57; nonofficial diplomacy, conflict resolution and, 140–41, 144–45; preventive diplomacy and, 97. See also emotional dimensions of conflict

public information guarantees, by UN peacekeepers, 106

public interest: donor fatigue and, 148; in peacebuilding, 181; truth commission recommendations and, 164–65

public opinion: as indicator of potential conflict, 93; Track II diplomacy and, 9. See also social factors

Pugh, Michael, 172

Pundak, Ron, 39

qualitative assessments, of perceptions, 93

quantitative assessments: of early warning indicators, 93; of peacebuilding, 176

quick impact projects (QIPs), of the UN, 169–70, 173

quiet diplomacy, 64, 66, 69, 70. See also informal diplomacy

racial discrimination, UN General Assembly on, 65

radical critique of peacebuilding, 180

Raffaelli, Mario, 143

Rainbow Warrior arbitration (1986 between France and New Zealand), 53, 66

Ramsbotham, Oliver, 173, 174

Randle, Robert, 35

Rann of Kutch arbitration (1968 between India and Pakistan), 52

rape, mass, in modern warfare, 5

rebel groups, IOs and dispute resolution with, 71

reconciliation and justice, 151–83; autonomy of actors in, 186; challenges for international commissions and tribunals, 165–66; challenges of transitional approaches, 160–66; conceptual challenges, 161–62; conceptualizing, 152–55; context of, 154–55; after end of terrorist conflicts, 189; ethical dilemmas, 162–63; evaluating approaches for, 157–66; internationalization of justice, 152; lessons learned, 166–67; local and national, humanitarian interventions and, 118; nonofficial diplomacy and promotion of, 140, 144–45, 150; overview, 151–52; peacebuilding and, 170; policy options for dealing with past abuses, 154–55; political constraints, 163–64; practical obstacles, 164–65; strengths of justice approaches, 160; strengths of truth commissions, 158–59; transitional justice, 153–54; truth commissions as method for, 155–57; truth-telling in, 152–53

reconnaissance, by UN peacekeepers, 66

reconstruction, postconflict: nonofficial diplomats and, 145;

peacebuilding and, 172, 176, 179; World Bank's support for, 13–14. *See also* postconflict phases

referral of conflicts: formal, UN success in resolving, 67; to regional organizations, 64, 65; to UN General Assembly, 65; to UN Security Council, 63

refugees: displacement by post–Cold War era conflicts, 87; as key variable in conflicts, 92; from Rwanda and former Yugoslavian conflicts, 88; UN estimates of, 139–40. *See also* diaspora communities; mass expulsion

regimes: international, definition of, 62; international law and, 49; terrorist attacks and discourse on change in, 182

region, definition of, 120

regional arrangements, UN Charter on, 131

regionalism: evaluating, 129–35; use of term, 120

regional organizations: advantages of, 129–31; as economic cooperation organizations, 134; as intervening actors in preventive diplomacy, 96; mediation by, 40; mediation success by, 67; peacekeeping and interventions, 1990–2005, 11; peacekeeping operations and, 75; in post-Westphalian system, 5–6; regionalism and, 120–21; as sources for early warning systems, 93; strategies for early warning of conflicts by, 91; timing of preventive diplomacy by, 98; UN Charter recognition of, 123; UN General Assembly referral to, 65; UN Security Council referral to, 64. *See also* regional task-sharing

regional task-sharing, 119–36; challenges of, 131–35; during the Cold War, 125–26, 126; conceptual challenges to, 132–33; conceptualizing, 120–25; evaluating, 129–35; lessons learned, 135–36; overview of, 125–26, 128–29; for peacebuilding, 175; political context for, 133–34; during post–Cold War era, 127, 128–29, 128; practical and operational problems, 133; strengths of, 129–31; with UN in humanitarian interventions, 118

relative deprivation, Gurr's theory of, 5

relief aid, continuation of a conflict due to, 111–12

religion: attacks motivated by, as early warning sign, 92; post–Cold War era conflicts over, 87

religious and spiritually oriented NGOs, nonofficial diplomacy by, 142

religious conflict: cultural barriers to successful negotiation during, 29; fundamentalist movements and, 4; identity issues and, 4–5; interactional factors and, 96; intrastate conflict and, 3

religiously motivated actors: perceptions of bias by, 146; roles for, 141, 145

Report of the Panel on United Nations Peace Operations, 113. *See also* Brahimi Report

resolutions: on conflicts, by UN General Assembly, 64; on conflicts, by UN Security Council, 63; large number of UN actors and effectiveness of, 71

resources: conflicts driven by, 3; for international tribunals, 165–66; for nonofficial diplomacy, 147–48; for preventive diplomacy, 89, 98; for regional task-sharing, 133; for UN humanitarian interventions, 115, 116. *See also* financing

respect, for conflict resolution by UN, 69

Responsibility to Protect, The (International Commission on Intervention and State Sovereignty), 104, 110, 114, 168

Responsibility to Protect, trade-off between state sovereignty and individuals under, 90

revenge, truth commissions and, 158

revolution, guerilla warfare and, 187

Revolutionary United Front (RUF), Sierra Leone, 45

Riccardi, Andrea, 143

Richmond, Oliver, 6, 9, 12–13

ripeness of mediation, 42

Roed-Larsen, Terje, 39

role factors: mediation by states, institutions, and organizations and, 39–41; in social-psychological approach to negotiation, 24, 26

Rome Accords/Agreement (1992), 137, 139, 143, 189

Ronfeldt, David, 15

root causes of conflict, peacebuilding and identification of, 89

Rosegrant, Susan, 26, 27, 28–29

Rubin, Jeffrey, 22, 44

rule of law: reconciliation and justice and, 151; strengths of, 57; successful judicial settlements and, 59; trials and reestablishment of, 154. *See also* civilized nations; law and order

Russia: regional peacekeeping by, 127; role in CIS peacekeeping operations of, 134

Rwanda: ethnic identities and preventive efforts in, 97; failure of UN peacekeeping in, 101–2, 108, 123, 186; France's intervention in, 103, 114; genocide in (1994), 4, 111, 139; "hate radio" use in, 14; international criminal tribunals for, 13, 151, 160; limited use of UN force in, 109; NGO response to genocide in, 140; peacekeeping and peacebuilding in, 177, 178; political exploitation of ethnic differences in, 5; prosecution of worst human rights violators in, 154; reconciliation and justice in, 163; selective investigations/prosecutions in, 164; UN authorization of MNF operations in, 126; UN failure to consistently punish violators of norms in, 71; UN humanitarian interventions in, 107; UN Mission Uganda and, 80, 82

Saar region, Germany, League of Nations peacekeepers in, 76, 79

Sadat, Anwar, 40

SADC (Southern African Development Community), 11, 125, 127, 134

safety net role, of regional organizations, 130

Sahara, Western: case of, ICJ's advisory opinion on, 55; UN Mission for the Referendum in, 107

Sahnoun, Mohammed, 123, 136

Salvadoran Truth Commission, 159, 165

Sambanis, Nicholas, 176

sanctions, UN, 48, 70, 90, 110

Sant'Egidio, Community of, 139, 142–43, 145, 147

Saudi Arabia, regional task-sharing by, 126

Saunders, Harold, 9

Savimbi, Jonas, 139

Sawyer, Jack, 24

Schelling, Thomas, 33

Schnabel, Albrecht, 90

scholarly studies, of mediation, 36, 37

secessionist movements, post–Cold War era conflicts over, 87

second-generation peacekeeping, 75, 106, 117, 176. *See also* humanitarian interventions

secrecy, in successful conflict management processes, 25. *See also* confidentiality secretary-general, UN: on conflict prevention rhetoric and reality, 98; conflict resolution role of, 65–66, 70; limitations of role in conflict resolution by, 72; management of humanitarian interventions by, 105; post–Cold War demands on ad hoc military organization of, 108; referral of conflicts to UN Security Council by, 63; regional organizations and, 129; request for humanitarian intervention by, 104; request for peacekeeping by, 77. See also United Nations

security, international: free-rider dilemma and, 61; terrorism and, 187

security regionalism, 119, 120. See also regional task-sharing

security rehabilitation, peacebuilding and, 175, 180

self-defense, regional task-sharing and, 124, 131–32

self-interests: cooperation among states and, 62; of great powers, UN and, 61

senior officials: bilateral or multilateral negotiations and, 25; mediation by, 39, 41; motivation for mediation and, 40

separation of forces, by UN peacekeepers, 77

sequential operations, regional task-sharing as, 122

Serbia: UN humanitarian intervention in, 107; UN Protection Force (UNPROFOR) in, 107, 177

settlement, terms of: carefully negotiated, successful UN humanitarian operations and, 108; monitoring, by UN peacekeepers, 66; set by UN Security Council, 63–64; UN secretary-general on, 66

shared interests, in negotiations, 27

Shell Oil, conflict in Nigeria and practices of, 16

short-term tasks, in peacebuilding, 174

Sierra Leone: civil war in, 4; ethical dilemmas of reconciliation and justice in, 162; humanitarian intervention in, 109; international criminal tribunals for, 151; mediation of violent conflict in, 45; non-UN peacekeeping in, 11; peacebuilding in, 177, 178; regional peacekeeping in, 11, 127; third-generation peacekeeping in, 108; UN authorization of regional peacekeeping in, 126; UN humanitarian intervention in, 107

signs, for early warnings of conflict, 92

Simkin, William, 33

Singer, Linda, 34

situational factors, in social-psychological approach to negotiation, 24, 26–27

small arms trade, regulation of, UN General Assembly on, 65

Soccer War, in El Salvador and Honduras, 130

social components, in social-psychological approach to negotiation, 26. See also civil society

social constituencies, Track II diplomacy and, 9

social factors: as indicators and signs of potential conflict, 93, 93; of terrorism, 190

social influence strategies, in social-psychological approach to negotiation, 28

social norms. See norms

social-psychological approach to bargaining and negotiation, 24–25; heuristic and prescriptive value of, 31. See also international negotiation

social rehabilitation, peacebuilding and, 175, 176

Solomon Islands, peacekeeping in, 11, 127

Somalia: failure of UN peacekeeping in, 101–2, 108, 123, 186; famine relief in, 109; MNF peacekeeping in, 128; peacekeeping and peacebuilding in, 177, 178; Sudan's need for peacekeepers vs., 114; superpower patronage during Cold War and, 3; UN authorization of MNF operations in, 126; UN humanitarian intervention in, 107; UN/U.S. peace effort in, 139; U.S. domestic concerns and UN failure in, 73

Somali Syndrome, 73

South Africa: civil society and peace process in, 145–46; dominance of SADC by, 134; non-UN peacekeeping by, 11; peacebuilding and transition in, 177; regional peacekeeping by, 127; Truth and Reconciliation Commission, 151, 152, 161–62, 164, 177

Southern African Development Community (SADC), 11, 125, 127, 134

sovereignty. See human sovereignty; state sovereignty

Soviet Union: collapse of, humanitarian interventions and, 103; collapse of, regional task-sharing and, 120; dominance of Warsaw Pact during Cold War by, 125; former, joint UN–OSCE observer and mediation missions to, 129; mediation of India–Pakistan conflict by, 41

special chambers, of the ICJ, 55

Special Committee on Peacekeeping Operations, UN, 65, 76

Spencer, Doyle, 34

spheres of influence, regional organizations and, 132

Sri Lanka, Norway and mediation in, 139

Stabilization Force (SFOR), of UN and NATO, 123

standards, for nonofficial diplomacy, 147

Standifer, Rhetta, 38

Stark, John, 38

states: as building blocks of UN and international order, 61; as defined by colonial powers, 23; failure of (see failed states); foreign, arbitration by, 51; ICJ and disputes between, 54, 56; independence in UN peacekeeping operations of, 82; as intervening actors in preventive diplomacy, 96; legal methods for conflict resolution between, 48, 59; mediation success by, 67; noninterference in internal affairs of, humanitarian intervention and, 110–11; noninterference in internal affairs of, ICJ and, 56; nuclear threat and balance of power during Cold War and, 7–8; perceived advantage of submitting conflicts to UN by, 72; post–Cold War conflicts over formation of, 87; powerful, ad hoc international law enforcement and, 58; power of, humanitarian intervention and, 114; referral of conflicts to UN Security Council by, 63; regional task-sharing by, 121–22; representatives of, mediation and, 35, 44; role in world politics of, 9; single, dominance of MNF operations by, 135; single, mediation by, 32; single, peacekeeping and interventions, 1990–2005, 11; small or large, mediation by, 39–40; sovereign, international law and society of, 49; strategies for early warning of conflicts by, 91; traditional peacekeeping as ideal for conflict resolution among, 81; twenty-first-century conflict resolution and, 186; UN secretary-general and contacts with, 70. See also coalitions; domestic affairs; governments; great powers; heads of state; interstate conflict(s); intrastate conflicts; senior officials; state sovereignty; traditional conflict resolution

state sovereignty: dilemma on right of intervention on humanitarian grounds and, 12–13; as obstacle to preventive diplomacy, 98; preventive diplomacy as challenge to, 90; UN interventions and, 16; Westphalian system and, 2, 6. See also consent, principle of; territorial sovereignty

"Status of Forces Agreement," between conflicting parties and the UN, 78

Stedman, Stephen, 176, 177, 178–79

Stein, Janice, 44

Stephenson, Geoffrey, 20–21

Stern, Jessica, 6

Stevens, Carl, 33

Stockholm model of confidence-building, 94

strategic or structural barriers to successful negotiation, 28

structural causes of conflict: Brown on, 92; conflict prevention and, 90; conflict resolution and, 145–46; understanding, 91

structural changes, peacebuilding and development of, 89, 173

structural factors: for complex negotiations by nonofficial diplomats, 147; mediation and, 42–43; preventive diplomacy and, 97

structural violence, 170

Stulberg, Joseph, 34, 44

Stuyt, Alexander, 52

subcontracting, 119, 120, 128. See also regional task-sharing

subjective criteria, for mediation evaluation, 45–46

subregional organizations, 121

subsidiarity, 120. See also regional task-sharing

substance-related interests, in social-psychological approach to negotiation, 25, 27

substantive orders, average per year, of PCIJ vs. ICJ, 56

Sudan: failure of mediation in, state's representatives and, 35; failure of UN peacekeeping in, 186; International Negotiation Network and, 39; Norway and mediation in, 139; politicized humanitarian aid operations in, 104; regional peacekeeping in, 11; relief organizations and military forces in, 148; Somalia's need for peacekeepers vs., 114

Suez Crisis (1956), 65, 66, 76, 79, 89. See also Israel; Middle East

summit diplomacy, 25

superpowers: breakdown of cooperation after 1945 among, 79; competition during Cold War among, 65; end of Cold War competition among, 103, 120; as intervening actors in preventive diplomacy, 96; regional organizations during Cold War and, 125; UN peacekeeping operations and rivalries among, 81; UN success at resolving conflicts among, 68. See also great powers

supervised devolution, 120. See also regional task-sharing

Supplement to An Agenda for Peace (Boutros-Ghali), 124, 132, 169, 175

supranational organizations, hope of IOs such as the UN as, 61

Susskind, Lawrence, 44

sustainable development, peacebuilding and, 172

sustainable peace, as conflict transformation, 10

Sweden, peacebuilding unit in foreign ministry of, 137

Switzerland, peacebuilding unit in foreign ministry of, 137

Symbolic Arab Security Force, 126

symbolization process, culture and, 29

Taba Boundary arbitration (1988 between Egypt and Israel), 53

Tajikistan: peace process and peacebuilding in, 177; regional peacekeeping in, 11, 127, 129; UN authorization of regional peacekeeping in, 126; UN military observers in, 133

Taliban, in Afghanistan, 112

talks. See negotiations

Tanzania, Uganda intervention by, 103

task-sharing: definitions, types, 121–22; origins and basis of, 122; perceived advantages of, 125; use of term, 120. See also regional task-sharing

Taylor, Alison, 34

Taylor, Charles, 109–10, 134, 139

technology: information and communications, positive and negative uses of, 15; terrorist groups and, 6. See also Internet

terms of reference, for arbitration, 52

territorial boundaries, violation by UN member states of, 71. See also boundary disputes

territorial sovereignty: ICJ judgments on, 56; international claims tribunals on, 52. See also state sovereignty

terrorism: in America in 2001, 122, 128; international law and challenges of, 59; methods for resolving conflicts using, 188–90; netwar as cyber form of, 15; peacebuilding and, 181–82; postmodern (post-Westphalian) war and, 6; principles for resolving conflicts using, 187–88; revised conception of warfare as, 16; UN and challenges of, 74. See also war on terror(ism)

terrorist groups: attacks by, as peace process spoilers, 29; building relationships of trust with, 188; changing nature of international conflict and, 2; harboring, justified intervention and, 104; IOs and dispute resolution with, 71; relevance of international law for, 58

theoretical basis for humanitarian interventions, 104, 112–14

theoretical basis for nonofficial diplomacy, 146–47

theoretical basis for peacebuilding, 179–80

theoretical basis for reconciliation and justice, 161

theoretical interpretations, empirical evidence and, 25

third-generation peacekeeping: definition of, 75; infancy of, 117; peacebuilding and, 176; problems and failures of, 108; scope of, 106. See also humanitarian interventions

third parties: accepting assistance from, 31; in bargaining and negotiation, 22; humanitarian interventions by, 102; influence on domestic politics for violence prevention by, 98; international truth commissions with, 159; as intervening actors in preventive diplomacy, 95–96; legitimate, UN's reputation as, 110; mediation by, 32, 34; mediation for preventive diplomacy by, 95; regional organizations and support by, 130–31; request for humanitarian intervention by, 104; request for peacekeeping by, 77; roles and functions in truth commissions and prosecutions of, 157. See also nongovernmental organizations

threats, use of, 31

time pressure, absence of, in successful conflict management processes, 25

timing: of mediation, 42, 43; for setting up international tribunals, 165

Timor-Leste: genocide in, 4; humanitarian intervention in, 109, 117; MNF peacekeeping in, 128, 131, 135; non-UN peacekeeping in, 11; peacebuilding in, 177, 178; third-generation peacekeeping in, 106; UN authorization of MNF operations in, 128; UN humanitarian intervention in, 107

top-down processes, for peacebuilding, 174

torture, in modern warfare, 5

Touval, Saadia, 36, 44, 73, 74

Track I diplomacy: coordination with Track II diplomacy, 138, 149, 150; by official, diplomatic, and governmental actors, 137; questions of Track II diplomacy and, 146. *See also* traditional conflict resolution

Track II diplomacy: combination of Track I diplomacy and, 139; Declaration of Principles (1993) of Israel and the PLO and, 9; intractable conflicts using Track I diplomacy and, 23; as nonofficial diplomacy, 137, 140; for post–Cold War conflict resolution, 8; regional organizations and, 136. *See also* twenty-first-century conflict resolution

trade structure fairness, UN General Assembly on, 65

traditional conflict resolution: arbitration, adjudication, and international law, 47–59; during the Cold War, 6–8; international negotiation, 19–31; international organizations (UN), 60–74; lessons learned, 184–85; mediation, 32–46; peacekeeping, 75–84. *See also* twenty-first-century conflict resolution

traditional peacekeeping: challenges and weaknesses of, 82–83; evaluating, 80–81; humanitarian intervention compared to, 103; overview of, 1956–88, 78–80; principles of, 77–78; strengths of, 81–82; UN operations, 1956–2007, 80; use of, 75–76. *See also* peacekeeping operations

training challenges: for nonofficial diplomacy, 147; for UN humanitarian interventions, 115, 116

transitional justice (transitology), 152, 153–54. *See also* reconciliation and justice

transition phase of peacebuilding, 173–74

transnational corporations (TNCs), traditional state power vs. power and influence of, 15–16

transnational organizations, mediation by, 40–41. *See also* nongovernmental organizations

transparency: international regimes and, 62; promotion by international organizations, 69; of UN vs. states in mediation, 73

transportation advances, nonofficial diplomacy and, 139

treaties: agreement to settle disputes by arbitration in, 51; ICJ and jurisdictional clauses of, 54

treaty law, international conferences and, 49

Treaty of Westphalia (1648), 6

trials: moral justice through truth commissions with absence of, 159; national, for reconciliation and justice, 151; national, of human rights abuses, 152; for past abuses, context of, 154–55; practical obstacles for, 165; problems with, 162; reestablishing rule of law through, 154; roles and functions of, 157; truth commissions vs., 153. *See also* International Criminal Court; international criminal tribunals; reconciliation and justice

trigger causes of conflict, Brown on, 91

truces, local, UN peacekeepers and, 66

trust: addressing terrorism by building relationships of, 188; nonofficial diplomats and building of, 144; preventive diplomacy and, 94–95

truth: disclosure of, healing and, 161–62; moral order and, 158–59; reconciliation and, 153

truth and reconciliation commissions, 153; context of, 154–55; as option for dealing with past abuses, 154; for post–Cold War conflict resolution, 8; South Africa's, 151, 152

truth commissions (TCs), 151; for dealing with past abuses, 155; moral justice and, 159; political constraints on, 163; roles and functions of, 156–57; strengths of, 158–59; types of, 155–56. *See also* reconciliation and justice

Tschirgi, Necla, 171–72

Tutu, Desmond, 164

twenty-first-century conflict resolution: frightening international environment for, 87; humanitarian intervention, 101–18; lessons learned, 185–87; nonofficial diplomacy, 137–50; peacebuilding, 168–83; preventive diplomacy, 87–100; reconciliation and justice, 151–67; regional task-sharing, 119–36. *See also* traditional conflict resolution

Uganda: intervention during Cold War in, 111; reconciliation and justice in, 163; Tanzania's intervention in, 103; United Nations Mission in Rwanda and, 80, 82

uncertainty, strategic barriers to successful negotiation and, 28

Union of International Associations, 138

UNITA (Uniño Nacional para a Independência Total de Angola), 83, 139

United Kingdom, peacebuilding unit in foreign ministry of, 137. *See also* England, queen of; Great Britain

United Nations (UN): challenges facing conflict resolution by, 70–74; conflict management and, 6–7; conflicts with NATO and U.S. over regional task-sharing, 132; cooperation with regional organizations by, 129; domestic conflict of member states and, 12–13, 16; evaluating conflict resolution by, 68–74; financing peacekeeping operations under, 82–83; General Act for the Pacific Settlement of International Disputes of, 51; as international actor, peacekeeping role in, 81; International Conference on the Former Socialist Federal Republic of Yugoslavia and, 123; international law development and, 49; interstate conflict role of, 135–36; lessons learned, 74; limits of conflict resolution by, 72–73; mechanisms for preserving peace of, 62–63; mediation by, 32, 40; mediation success by, 67; as mediator, 73–74; Mozambique peace process and, 143; NGOs and, 138; overview of conflict resolution since 1945, 67–68; peacebuilding by, 177, 181, 182; Peacebuilding Unit, 169; peacekeeping in Liberia and, 134; peacekeeping operations, 7, 75; Peck on creation of dispute resolution services for members of, 98; regional task-sharing and, 119–20, 128; secretary-general as Chief Administrative Officer of, 65; as source for early warning systems, 93; staff capacity to implement negotiated settlements of, 108; strategies for early warning of conflicts by, 91; strengths of conflict resolution by, 69–70. *See also* international organizations; secretary-general; United Nations Charter; United Nations General Assembly; United Nations Security Council

United Nations Angola Verification Mission I (UNAVEM I), 80, 82

United Nations Angola Verification Mission II (UNAVEM II), 107, 177

United Nations Angola Verification Mission III (UNAVEM III), 107, 177

United Nations Assistance Mission for Rwanda (UNAMIR), 107, 177

United Nations Charter: as basis for regional task-sharing, 123–24; basis of peacekeeping under, 76–77; on collective security framework, 62–63; embodied in transnational institutions, 13; on humanitarian intervention, 103, 104; on ICJ power, 56; norm-based behavior standards in, 69; on peacekeeping, 76; on primary purpose to maintain international peace and security, 60; on regional task-sharing, 119, 131–32; on symbolic role of secretary-general, 70

United Nations Disengagement Force (UNDOF), *80, 81*

United Nations Emergency Force (UNEF I), 65, 79, *80*, 83

United Nations Emergency Force II (UNEF II), *80, 81*

United Nations General Assembly: conflict resolution role of, 64–65; delegation of duties to secretary-general by, 65; humanitarian intervention debate in, 110; leadership during Cold War by, 66; referral of conflicts to UN Security Council by, 63; Special Committee on Peacekeeping Operations of, 76. *See also* United Nations Charter

United Nations Good Offices Mission in Afghanistan and Pakistan (UNGOMAP), *80, 82*

United Nations Interim Administration Mission in Kosovo (UNMIK), *107, 177*

United Nations Interim Force in Lebanon (UNIFIL), *80, 81*

United Nations Iran-Iraq Military Observer Group (UNIIMOG), *80, 82*

United Nations Iraq-Kuwait Observation Mission (UNIKOM), *80, 82*

United Nations Mission in Bosnia and Herzegovina (UNMIBH), *107, 177*

United Nations Mission in Ethiopia and Eritrea (UNMEE), 75, 79, *80, 82*

United Nations Mission in Liberia (UNMIL), *107, 177*

United Nations Mission in Sierra Leone (UNAMSIL), *107, 177*

United Nations Observation Mission in Angola (MONUA), *107, 177*

United Nations Observer Group in Liberia (UNOMIL), *80, 133*

United Nations Observer Mission in El Salvador (ONUSAL), *107*

United Nations Observer Mission in Georgia (UNOMIG), *80, 134*

United Nations Observer Mission Uganda-Rwanda (UNO-MUR), *80, 82*

United Nations Operation in Burundi (ONUB), *107, 177*

United Nations Operation in Côte d'Ivoire (UNOCI), *107, 177*

United Nations Operation in Somalia I (UNOSOM)/Unified Task Force (UNITAF), *107, 177*

United Nations Operation in Somalia II (UNOSOM II), *107, 177*

United Nations Operation in the Congo (ONUC, 1960), 65, *80, 81*

United Nations Organization Mission in the Democratic Republic of the Congo (MONUC), *107, 177*

United Nations Protection Force (UNPROFOR), *107, 177*

United Nations Security Council: Cold War and deadlock in, 66; conflict management and, 7; conflict resolution role of, 63–64, 69–70; cooperation for humanitarian interventions within, 101; delegation of duties to secretary-general by, 65; disputes considered by UN General Assembly vs., 64; divergence among permanent members, humanitarian intervention and, 111; dominance of policies and interests of permanent members of, 114; as hegemonic leader for international peace and security, 62; humanitarian interventions and, 104–5; increased conservatism of, 73; on intervention in internal conflicts in developing countries, 123; Liberia's

internal conflict and, 120; limitations on secretary-general's role by, 72; peace preservation authority of, 62–63; post hoc authorization of peacekeeping, 132; regional task-sharing and, 123–24; Resolution 998 on the Middle East, 79; strict impartiality in peacekeeping and, 78. *See also* United Nations Charter

United Nations Stabilization Mission in Haiti (MINUSTAH), *107, 177*

United Nations Transitional Administration in East Timor (UNTAET), *107, 177*

United Nations Transitional Assistance Group (UNTAG), 106, *107, 177*

United Nations Transitional Authority in Cambodia (UNTAC), *107, 177*

United Nations Truce Supervision Organization (UNTSO) mission to the Middle East, 79

United States: *Alabama Claims Arbitration* (1872) and, 50; conflict with UN over post-Saddam Iraq, 132; dominance of OAS during Cold War by, 125; funding of UN peacekeeping by, 116; *Gulf of Maine* maritime boundary dispute and, 54; humanitarian intervention as neoimperialism by, 114; International Criminal Court and, 13; Jay Treaty (1794) and, 50; Liberia's internal conflict and, 120; Logan Act on nonofficial diplomacy of, 148; Mozambique peace process and, 143; Presidential Decision Directive 25 on involvement in UN operations, 115; on regional task-sharing, 122; regional task-sharing by, *126*; State Department dialogue with unofficial diplomats, 138; UN peacekeeping in Angola and, 83; use of UN for First and Second Gulf Wars by, 72. *See also* war on terror(ism)

United States–Iran Claims Tribunal, 51, 53

United States–Iran *Hostages* case (1980), 54

United States–Mexico Claims Commission (1868–76), 52

Uniting for Peace Resolution (1950), 65

universality principle, 160, 163

unofficial actors, 9. *See also* nonofficial diplomacy

unofficial diplomacy, 140. *See also* nonofficial diplomacy

unresolved disputes, UN General Assembly and, 64

unstable peace, 90

Upper Silesia region between Poland and Germany, League of Nations peacekeepers in, 76

Ury, William, 30

values, cultural assumptions involving, 29

Vatican, Mozambique peace process and, 143. *See also* pope(s)

Versailles, Treaty of, 53

veto power: benefits for permanent UN members of, 68; as safety valve for UN great powers, 70; use in UN Security Council during Cold War, 65

victimhood, narratives of, conflict situations and, 29

victor's justice, 160, 164

Vienna Congress (1815), 89

Vietnam, Kampuchea intervention by, 103

violence: conflicts using new forms of, 58; culture of, terrorism and, 189; ongoing factional, humanitarian interventions and, 103; outbreaks of, as early warning sign, 92; preventive diplomacy to reduce potential of, 89; ritualistic, in modern warfare, 5; structural sources of, 10, 170. *See also* terrorism

voluntary mediators, 34–35, 38. *See also* mediator(s)

Wall, James, 38, 43

war criminals: capture and trial of, 106; recognition during political negotiations of, 112

war economies, humanitarian operations and establishment of, 111

warfare, changes in forms of, 5. *See also* new wars

warlords: employment as security guards for relief operations, 111; intrastate conflicts and, 3; principle of consent and, 108; recognition during political negotiations, 112

warning-response gap, 93–94

war on terror(ism): as basis for intervention, 110; international conflict resolution and, 187; international law and, 59; peacebuilding and, 181–82; regional task-sharing and, 122, 135; U.S. expectations of UN role in, 72

Warsaw Pact, 122, 125

Washington Peace Conference (1907), 53

Watkins, Michael, 26, 27, 28–29

weak governance/states, 3, 88, 123. *See also* failed states

Wehr, Paul, 12, 35–36

Weiss, Thomas, 102

Western European Union (WEU), 121, 129

Western liberal theory, peacebuilding and, 172, 180. *See also* liberal democracy; neoliberal economic order

Western Sahara case, ICJ's advisory opinion on, 55

West New Guinea, UN Security Force in, *80*

Westphalian system: conflict resolution after, 14–16; international relations as academic discipline under, 2; traditional approaches to conflict under, 6–8

wider peacekeeping. *See* humanitarian interventions

Wilkenfeld, Jonathan, 67, 73

withdrawal of forces: supervision of, by UN peacekeepers, 79; UN Security Council on, 64; verification of, by UN peacekeepers, 66

women, as previously marginalized actors, 14

World Bank, 13–14, 53

World Court, 58

world government, UN evaluation against prototype of, 61

World War II, international claims tribunals on claims from, 52

written phase, of ICJ proceedings, 55

Yang, Huang, 34

Yemen: South, peace process after Cold War in, 2; UN Observation Mission, *80*

Young, Oran, 33, 35, 36, 42–43

Yugoslavia, former: ethnic identities and preventive efforts in, 97; humanitarian intervention in, 103, 110; international criminal tribunals for, 151, 166; international tribunal for, 13; netwar by Serb hackers of NATO Web sites, 15; nonofficial diplomacy by internal and external religiously motivated groups in, 142; peacekeeping and peacebuilding in, 177; third-generation peacekeeping in, 106; UN authorization of regional peacekeeping in, 126. *See also* Balkans

Zaire. *See* Congo, Democratic Republic of

Zartman, I. William: on conflict prevention, 90; on impartiality of mediators, 36; on mediation, 44; on power relationships and negotiation success, 22; on preventive diplomacy, 98; on resolution after reconfiguration of the conflict, 30

zero-sum: distributive bargaining as, 27; internal conflicts framed in, 68; negotiation viewed as continuation of, 30; UN's effectiveness with, 71

Zimbabwe: peacebuilding in, 178; regional peacekeeping by, *127*

Zuppi, Matteo, 143

About the Authors

Jacob Bercovitch is Professor of International Relations at the University of Canterbury in New Zealand and one of the world's most respected experts on international mediation in violent or protracted conflicts. Dr. Bercovitch is Fellow of the Royal Society of New Zealand and former Vice President of the International Studies Association. He is the author and editor of thirteen books and more than one hundred papers and articles on various aspects of international conflict. His most recent book is *Handbook of Conflict Resolution*, edited with V. Kremenyuk and I. William Zartman (Sage, 2009). He has received fellowships from, and taught at, many prestigious universities, including Harvard, Georgetown, London School of Economics, and the Hebrew University of Jerusalem. He was a Senior Fellow at the United States Institute of Peace in 2002. He has also acted as an adviser to the government of New Zealand on preventive diplomacy and peacekeeping, and was an affiliate at Harvard's Program on Negotiation.

Richard Jackson is Reader in the Department of International Politics, Aberystwyth University, where he is also the Deputy Director of the Centre for the Study of Radicalisation and Contemporary Political Violence. He is the founding editor of the journal *Critical Studies on Terrorism* and the author of *Writing the War on Terrorism: Language, Politics, and Counterterrorism* (Manchester University Press, 2005) and with Jacob Bercovitch, the coauthor of *International Conflict Management: A Chronological Encyclopaedia of Conflicts and Their Management, 1945–1995* (CQ Press, 1997). He is a regular contributor to the media on issues of terrorism, war, and conflict resolution.

DATE DUE

BRODART, CO.

Cat. No. 23-221